12/02

The
CArTooOn music
Book

Edited by **Daniel Goldmark**
and **Yuval Taylor**

WITHDRAWN

 cappella

Library of Congress Cataloging-in-Publication Data
The cartoon music book / edited by Daniel Goldmark and Yuval Taylor.
    p. cm.
    Includes bibliographical references and index.
    Discography: p.
    ISBN 1-55652-473-0 (alk. paper)
    1. Animated film music—History and criticism. I. Goldmark, Daniel.
II. Taylor, Yuval.
    ML2075 .C36 2002
    781.5′4—dc21   2002012873

Cover and interior design: Rattray Design
Cover Illustration: Chris Ware

Published by A Cappella Books
an imprint of Chicago Review Press, Incorporated
814 North Franklin Street
Chicago, Illinois 60610
ISBN 1-55652-473-0
Printed in the United States of America
5 4 3 2 1

N'aies pas peur bébé agrippe-toi CHRACK!

Je suis là CRASH! pour te protéger TCHLACK!

Ferme les yeux CRACK! embrasse-moi SMACK!

SHEBAM! POW! BLOP! WIZZ!

—SERGE GAINSBOURG

Contents

Foreword
by Leonard Maltin • *ix*

Acknowledgments • *xi*

Introduction
by Daniel Goldmark and Yuval Taylor • *xiii*

Main Title

Untitled
by Chris Ware • *3*

Tunes for Toons: A Cartoon Music Primer
by Neil Strauss • *5*

Part I: An Episodic History of Cartoon Music

Animated Cartoons and Slap-Stick Comedy
by Edith Lang and George West • *17*

Make Walt's Music: Music for Disney Animation, 1928–1967
by Ross Care • *21*

An Interview with Carl Stalling
by Mike Barrier • *37*

**Hidey Hidey Hidey Ho . . . Boop-Boop-A Doop!
The Fleischer Studio and Jazz Cartoons**
by Jake Austen • *61*

I Love to Hear a Minstrel Band: Walt Disney's *The Band Concert*
by David Wondrich • *67*

Disney, Stokowski, and the Genius of *Fantasia*
by Charles L. Granata • *73*

Music and the Animated Cartoon
by Chuck Jones • *93*

**Classical Music and Hollywood Cartoons:
A Primer on the Cartoon Canon**
by Daniel Goldmark • *103*

Music in Cartoons
by Scott Bradley • *115*

**Personality on the Sound Track: A Glimpse Behind the
Scenes and Sequences in Filmland**
by Scott Bradley • *121*

***Make Mine Music* and the End of the Swing Era**
by Stuart Nicholson • *125*

Sublime Perversity: The Music of Carl Stalling
by Will Friedwald • *137*

Carl Stalling, Improviser & Bill Lava, Acme Minimalist
by Kevin Whitehead • *141*

Raymond Scott: Accidental Music for Animated Mayhem
by Irwin Chusid • *151*

**Winston Sharples and the "Inner Casper"
(*or* Huey Has Two Mommies)**
by Will Friedwald • *161*

An Interview with Hoyt Curtin
by Barry Hansen and Earl Kress • *169*

Rock 'n' Roll Cartoons
by Jake Austen • *173*

**"Put One Note in Front of the Other": The Music of
Maury Laws**
by Greg Ehrbar • *193*

Part II: Cartoon Music Today

**Merrie Melodies: Cartoon Music's Contemporary
Resurgence**
by Elisabeth Vincentelli • *203*

An Interview with Mark Mothersbaugh

by Daniel Goldmark • *207*

Robots, Romance, and Ronin: Music in Japanese Anime

by Milo Miles • *219*

An Interview with Richard Stone, Steve Bernstein, and Julie Bernstein

by Daniel Goldmark • *225*

An Interview with Alf Clausen

by Daniel Goldmark • *239*

I Kid Because I Love: The Music of *The Simpsons*

by Will Friedwald • *253*

An Interview with John Zorn

by Philip Brophy • *263*

Rhapsody in Spew: Romantic Underscores in *The Ren & Stimpy Show*

by Joseph Lanza • *269*

Untitled

by John Kricfalusi • *275*

End Title

A Very Visual Kind of Music: The Cartoon Soundtrack Beyond the Screen

by John Corbett • *279*

Cartoon Music: A Select Discography

by Greg Ehrbar • *289*

Bibliography

by Daniel Goldmark • *299*

About the Contributors • *307*

Index • *311*

Foreword

by LEONARD MALTIN

WHEN I WAS a kid and first got hooked on animation, I don't know if I was aware of how much the music meant to my enjoyment of those films. And yet, I don't think I could completely separate the music from the cartoons (having "Merrily We Roll Along" and "The Merry-Go-Round Broke Down" embedded in my brain from infancy). I'm certain that I first developed a love of music from hearing classical themes in the cartoons of the 1930s and '40s I was watching on TV.

I don't think I'll ever hear Liszt's second Hungarian Rhapsody, for instance, without thinking of the building of a skyscraper as Friz Freleng used it in his cartoon *Rhapsody in Rivets* (1941). To me the most exciting development in recent years has been the recognition that has finally come to composers, but when you look at both the enormity of their output and the incredible range of music that they embraced, it is formidable indeed. (Only recently have I learned, in addition, that gifted musicians like Mel Powell and André Previn played on some of those MGM recording dates for Scott Bradley.) You had to be a good musician to play some of that complicated music they wrote.

Music wasn't just punctuation for those cartoons; it was their backbone. Music propelled them, commented on the action, underscored the comedy, enhanced the atmosphere, and accelerated the chases. It was a crucial ingredient to their success and I don't think anyone who's grown up on a steady diet of those cartoons has ever lost his affection for the music that was so much a part of them.

When I wrote my book *Of Mice and Magic: A History of American Animated Cartoons,* there was virtually no research yet conducted on Stalling's or Bradley's work, but I discussed its impact and significance.

One of my favorite pastimes, along with some of my "cartoonaholic" friends, is playing "Name That Tune" with Carl Stalling's scores because they're a compendium of musical fragments from both the popular and classical fields.

In one cartoon you can hear everything from a fragment of Beethoven to a Tin Pan Alley tune by Harry Warren and Al Dubin from the latest Busby Berkeley musical. Looking back at them today, they comprise a sort of catalog of contemporary Hollywood music as well as a primer on the most effective and dramatic themes from the great masters.

There's a lot of talk about the animation renaissance in recent years but there's no question that music has played as big a role in this resurgence as it did the first time around. The enormous success of Disney's recent features cannot be spoken of without credit to the songs of Alan Menken and Howard Ashman and Menken's underscoring. Nor can you accurately pinpoint the appeal of *Tiny Toons* without zeroing in on its infectious theme and the fact that it is played by a full orchestra—not a synthesizer or a "typical" TV soundtrack band. Bruce Broughton's music for that series gives it a full-bodied gusto that we haven't heard since the heyday of the Warner Bros. cartoons some thirty to fifty years ago.

In sharp contrast, what John Kricfalusi did on *The Ren & Stimpy Show* was to turn a liability into an asset. Instead of feeling impoverished by having to use stock from the past that might have been heard weeks before on a travelogue or a Listerine commercial, he has turned library music into a joke of its own and deliberately played cliché music for effect and found choice examples of cartoon music of the past, such as the work of Raymond Scott, which so heavily populated Carl Stalling's scores. Listening to the soundtrack of *Ren & Stimpy* is a treat for any cartoon buff for just that reason.

Music and cartoons have gone hand-in-hand since Walt Disney made *Steamboat Willie* in 1928. Music wasn't just an accompaniment for that cartoon, it was what helped sell the movie to the public and to the motion picture industry. There was virtually no dialogue in that cartoon. What attracted people in those primitive days of "talkies" was the idea that cartoon characters (and even inanimate objects) moved in synchronization to a musical beat. That was the charm of *Steamboat Willie* and virtually all the cartoons that followed for several years from Disney and from his followers and rivals.

It's rewarding to see music coming back to the forefront of cartoons after all these years.

Originally appeared as "Cartoons and Music: Perfect Partners" in The Score: The Society of Composers & Lyricists *Volume VIII No. 2 (Summer 1993). © 1993 by Leonard Maltin. Reprinted by permission.*

Acknowledgments

THE EDITORS WOULD like to thank the following individuals for their assistance and encouragement in putting together this collection and in making it into a book: Jake Austen, Mike Barrier, Jerry Beck, Philip Brophy, Irwin Chusid, Ned Comstock, Tim Edwards, Will Friedwald, Greg Ford, Mark Kausler, John Kricfalusi, Elizabeth Lamers, Thomas Little, Jerome Pohlen, Randy Rogel, Will Ryan, Linda Simensky, Michael Stewart and family, Dace Taube, and Chris Ware, as well as all of the interviewees, past and present, who agreed to share their knowledge and experiences with cartoon music.

All photos in this book are courtesy of Cartoon Research, except where otherwise noted.

Introduction

by DANIEL GOLDMARK
and YUVAL TAYLOR

THE POPULARITY OF cartoon music, from Carl Stalling's work for Warner Bros. to Disney soundtracks and *The Simpsons'* song parodies, has never been greater. Not only are cartoons seen more frequently by more people than ever before (thanks to the Cartoon Network, Nickelodeon's cartoons, PBS's children's cartoons, prime time cartoons such as *The Simpsons,* and feature-length animated films from Disney, DreamWorks, and Pixar), but cartoon music is increasingly regarded as an art form in its own right, distinct from other film music, and well worth listening to outside of the context of its images. Even cartoon pop music, which had not had any notable success since the Chipmunks and the Archies, is now scoring major hits with Gorillaz. Bugs Bunny on Broadway has been touring the world for over a decade, playing Carl Stalling scores in sold-out concert halls; perhaps it won't be long before other repertory groups assemble to perform scores and cues by Scott Bradley, Hoyt Curtin, and even such a recent composer as Richard Stone.

What accounts for this surge in popularity? Perhaps the qualities that make cartoon music unique have now come into vogue. Much of the music for Hollywood's live-action films of the 1930s and '40s, led by the examples of such pioneers as Erich Wolfgang Korngold and Max Steiner, tended to rely on a combination of oft-repeated melodic themes (much in the style of Wagner's leitmotifs) and short spells of frenetic, blood-pumping, "dramatic" music for action scenes. Since a cartoon had only a tenth of the time to get its dramatic point across, the music had to adapt; it necessarily needed to be faster in how it punctuated the gags moving by on screen at 24 frames per second. Cartoon music simply had to be more *telling* than music for live-action films.

Take, for example, the term "mickey mousing." Developed in the early 1930s, it describes the exact synchronization of music and image in a film (think of someone skulking down a dark street, pizzicato bass strings marking his every step). No live-action film composer worth his salt would intentionally "mickey mouse," for it is difficult to be expressive about the story and literal about the action at the same time. In a cartoon, on the other hand, such close movement between score and screen helps to add a sense of vitality to the painted cels photographed in rapid succession, cels that never had any life in them in the first place. While an accusation of mickey mousing would insult most feature film composers, it is not something to shun in cartoons; on the contrary, it implies the very thing that composers strive for: a score that effectively (and affectively) tells the story of the visuals.

It is too simplistic to describe cartoon music as creating a musical version of the story, however. Composers like Carl Stalling and Scott Bradley did more than musically narrate each episode they scored; they added speed to downward falls, pain to the anvils on the head, amorous impact to the love stricken, and swing to every last dance sequence that came across their respective desks. Since cartoon characters can, by definition, do things that we can't (or shouldn't) do, the music exaggerates and celebrates that difference. Cartoon music does more than simply add life to cartoons—it makes cartoons *bigger* than life.

Yet cartoon music has not been kind to its composers, most of whom still languish in obscurity. Film historians have always considered music near the bottom of the hierarchy of cinematic import, particularly because film scores are traditionally created in the final stages of the post-production process, long after the film has been shot and edited for continuity. To make matters worse, animation was seen simply as a throw-away form of amusement, filmic fodder to entertain audiences in the opening hour before the feature began (along with newsreels, coming attractions, live-action short subjects, serials, and other "disposable" material). Add to this the fact that one of cartoon music's implicit roles is to add to the overall comedy of a cartoon—it's meant to be "funny music"—making it even more difficult to take "seriously." Thus cartoon music has received practically no critical or scholarly attention through the years.

This book on cartoon music's past and present aims to take a small step toward correcting the negligence that cartoon music has thus far suffered by collecting interviews with and writings by the principal composers, along with contributions from music critics and cartoonists. Some of these items have been published previously, although none are readily available in book form in the United States; others have been commissioned specifically for this volume.

Carl Stalling, who was responsible for scoring the groundbreaking Walt Disney cartoons of the late 1920s and more than twenty years' worth of Warner Bros. cartoons, receives more attention in this collection than any other composer, and with good reason, for he was the person most responsible for changing people's notions of how much could be accomplished in a seven-minute cartoon score. But he wasn't the only cartoon composer in town, and the others each had his own individual style. This book includes two pieces by Scott Bradley, written while he was the composer for the MGM cartoons, in which he explains his affinity for writing in a more modernist style and his aversion to the use of popular songs. The second of Will Friedwald's three contributions looks at the musical stylings of Winston Sharples, who, like Stalling, worked for more than one studio during his life (Van Beuren, Paramount, Harvey, and Famous), and likewise had a lasting effect on the sound of cartoon music as we know it today. Sadly, we could not cover every composer who ever wrote for Hollywood cartoons: missing are Joe De Nat and Eddie Kilfeather (Columbia); Art Turkisher (Iwerks); James Dietrich, Darrell Calker, and Clarence Wheeler (Lantz); Eugene Poddany (MGM); Philip Scheib (Terrytoons); Eugene Rodemich (Van Beuren); Frank Marsales (Lantz and Warner Bros.); and Bernard Brown (Warner Bros.), to name just a few.

The Cartoon Music Book, therefore, does not purport to be the first and last source for all animated music—but it's a start. In addition to addressing the different approaches of major composers, many of these essays focus on the music of specific cartoons, how different studios approached musical genres such as jazz and classical music, how cartoon music has interacted with pop music over the years, and what cartoon music in general has accomplished and should accomplish. Thus, one of the fortunate by-products of this project is the genesis of new criticism and discourse on the subject, much in areas never properly addressed in the past. David Wondrich's close reading of minstrelsy in *The Band Concert* and Joseph Lanza's discussion of stock library cues in *The Ren & Stimpy Show* deal with productions a half-century apart, yet there's an implicit connection between them: both provide insight into how cartoons have played with and illuminated the high and low distinctions of their particular eras. The interviews printed here are meant to illuminate the details of the cartoon composer's daily life—especially his ability to create so much music under typically impossible deadlines—in addition to giving some insight into composers' own attitudes toward the creative process. Additionally, those interviews conducted with contemporary composers show how the compositional process has changed since the days of theatrical cartoons, while reaffirming the impact of Stalling's and Bradley's legacy on the figures of today's animation world. Last, while we had to limit the perspective of this collection to cartoons produced in the United States, we could not ignore completely the influence of international animation industries on Hollywood; Milo Miles's essay thus addresses the culture of the Japanese anime soundtrack and anime's growing presence in the United States.

There are countless other cartoons and composers that have yet to receive their due. If anything, we hope that these essays and interviews might inspire new work in this area. It's about time that the silliest of all musical genres be taken seriously.

Main Title

CHRIS WARE

Tunes for Toons: A Cartoon Music Primer

by NEIL STRAUSS

"IF YOU CAN write for animation," said Hoyt Curtin, composer for classic Hanna-Barbera cartoons from *The Flintstones* to *Scooby-Doo*, "you can write for anything." Cartoon music is among the most engaging and experimental forms of twentieth-century music, exploring the more outrageous extremes of instrumentation, rhythm, and nonmusical sound. It is a genre in which rapid tempo changes, unusual instrumental effects, experimental percussion, post-modern quotation, shock chords, and musical genre-shifting are de rigeur. From the warped takes on Liszt and Rossini that occur when a fly lands on a conductor's nose to the free-jazz solos that certain animated animals play on the heads of other animated animals, the laughs lie in perverting the sounds we've come to expect from concerts and canines. Just try watching a classic *Tom and Jerry* or *Bugs Bunny* cartoon with the sound off, and see how flat the jokes fall.

The history of this music has rarely been told, for the sole reason that it wasn't until recently that cartoon music was even considered a viable genre unto itself. Cartoon music, for the purposes of this primer, is score—orchestral or instrumental accompaniment—as opposed to the circle-of-life songs of Disney films, the pop hits that fill some big-budget film features, and the tongue-in-cheek parodies that populate *The Simpsons*. Born in the 1920s, cartoon music experienced its golden years in the 1940s and '50s, before television studios increased the workload, lowered the budget, and, with the advent of synthesizers, eviscerated the art.

Interestingly, many of the more modern avant-garde musicians who have been drawn to cartoon music, like John Zorn and Sun Ra, have their roots in improvisation. This makes sense, because many of the early composers for cartoons started out as improvisers themselves, playing organ and other instruments to accompany silent movies.

Perhaps one of the most important chance meetings in cartoon music history occurred in the early 1920s at the Isis Theatre in Kansas City, where Carl Stalling, then a film accompanist and conductor, first encountered Walt Disney, who was just beginning his involvement in film. After Disney left for Hollywood and began producing cartoons, the two renewed their bond (originally created over their shared excitement about combining music and film) and Stalling was soon given the first two silent Mickey Mouse shorts to score. The job was a perfect fit for the wildly talented Stalling, and he was quickly hired as the studio's first music director.

In the meantime, Max Fleischer at Fleischer Studios was experimenting on a more in-depth level with adding music to cartoons. The studio's "Song Car-Tune," *Oh Mabel* (1924), introduced the infamous bouncing ball, which landed on the appropriate lyric to a popular song in time to the music (which was played by the theater accompanist) for audiences to sing along to. The "car-tune" received such an enthusiastic response at its first screening that the theater manager rewound the short and showed it again. A few shorts later, Max Fleischer was introduced to Lee de Forest, who had developed Phonofilm, a method of recording sound on the edge of motion picture film. (Incidentally, the instructional film on the use of Phonofilm was animated. Thus cartoons played an integral part in the advent of sound in film). Fleischer fell in love with the idea and produced the first theatrical film of any kind with a synchronized soundtrack, *My Old Kentucky Home*, in 1926. Subsequently, he added sound to his earlier bouncing-ball films, many of which featured Koko the Clown. These were the first theatrical releases of sound films, predating even Warner Bros.' first live-action motion picture with a music track, *Don Juan* (which preceded 1927's more famous *Jazz Singer* by more than a year).

Even Paul Terry's Terrytoons studio beat Disney to sound with its first Aesop's Fables series film, *Dinner Time* (1928). Terrytoons claimed to be the first studio to prescore its cartoons. Working with brilliant Terrytoons composer Philip A. Scheib, the studio's animators drew frames to fit his scores, which were recorded in one take.

The advent of sound solved a problem that plagued composer Paul Hindemith, a *Felix the Cat* fanatic who composed a score for *Felix at the Circus*, which he attempted to premiere at the Baden-Baden festival. Much to his chagrin, the machine selected to synchronize his pianola roll with the film projector malfunctioned and the composition was subsequently lost.

Determined to keep up with the competition, Walt Disney traveled to New York to work on his first actual sound cartoon, *Steamboat Willie*. At Cinephone studios in 1928, the well-known New York film accompanist Carl Edouarde conducted the score. Sound effects, music, and dialogue all had to be recorded on one track, without mistakes. Any missed cue or unwanted sound meant starting over from the beginning. To keep the beat, the orchestra played to visual cues inked onto the cartoon's print. The synchronization process was so long and laborious that Disney was forced to sell his car in order to pay the musicians overtime.

With Stalling at his side, however, Disney eventually streamlined and updated the sound process, creating innovative Silly Symphonies, which were pre-scored animated shorts choreographed to well-known classical works. His first was *The Skeleton Dance* (1929). The close synchronization between music and on-screen movement popularized by this and earlier shorts came to be known as "mickey mousing." Disney's quirky transpositions of classical works would later reach their height with *Fantasia* (1940), which thrilled Disney to no end by making, in his words, "strange bedfellows" of Bach, Beethoven, and Mickey Mouse.

At Disney, Stalling also invented a tick system for synchronizing music to visuals. It was a forerunner to the click track, now the standard process in both live-action and animated features. One of the first click tracks, a reel of unexposed film with holes punched out to make clicks and pops when the film was run on the sound head, was devised by Disney sound effects man Jim Macdonald and used in *The Skeleton Dance*.

To avoid copyright infringements, musical directors at these studios culled their non-original music from either songs in the public domain or songs from their studio's musicals. The cartoon studio at Warner Bros. was actually created as a vehicle for promoting its musicals' songs, with management originally requiring every cartoon produced there to use a popular song from a Warner Bros. feature. Two ex-Disney animators, Hugh Harman and Rudolf Ising (along with producer Leon Schlesinger), convinced Warner Bros. to start a cartoon studio and began directing Looney Tunes in 1930, with Merrie Melodies following a year later. (Even their directorial credit was a musical pun—"Harman-Ising" or *harmonizing*). Frank Marsales was the original musical director for these, followed by Norman Spencer, Bernard Brown, and then, in 1936, Carl Stalling, fresh from Disney and Ub Iwerks cartoon studios. Stalling remained at Warner Bros. for twenty-two years, scoring over 600 cartoons at the rate of one every eight days.

His working process was fascinating, showing the careful attention to music with which each cartoon was drawn. Before animation, he met with a cartoon's director in order to set the time signatures to which the short was to be drawn. Instead of counting in beats per measure or beats per minute, cartoon animators counted in frames per beat. After animation, Stalling received either the animator's exposure sheets or bar sheets, which broke the animation, dialogue, and sound effects into musical bars for Stalling to score from. For his compositions, Stalling employed musical puns by using popular songs whose titles fit on-screen gags, sometimes for no more than four seconds. This came naturally to Stalling who, as John Zorn puts it, "had an Ivesian sense of quotation."

Often, themes from Warner Bros. live-action films would be played for under four seconds before mutating into an original Stalling piece. The average cue (the unedited period between the commencement and end of a single musical take) was at most two minutes, and at the lower end of the spectrum, two seconds. Most of Stalling's scores were a weighty 500 measures comprised of ten sections, all performed by the Warner Bros. fifty-piece orchestra, who were challenged and taxed far more than they were when they performed undemanding scores for some of Warner Bros. feature live-action films. The opening sequence for most Merrie Melodies was a Warner Bros.–owned tune called "Merrily We Roll Along," with an electric guitar providing the initial sound effect as the Warner Bros. logo catapults forward on the screen. (For the Looney Tunes, a jaunty minor hit, "The Merry-Go-Round Broke Down," by the Tin Pan Alley team of Friend and Franklin was used.)

Stalling's work called to mind composers who had a cartoon sensibility and composed with visual images in mind—from Claude Debussy to jazz stylists like Zez Confrey, Red Norvell, Spike Jones, John Kirby, and, especially, Raymond Scott. Stalling relied so heavily on the 1930s music of Scott, particularly the fast and wacky "Powerhouse" theme that accompanied so many conveyor-belt and chase scenes, that Scott is often considered a cartoon composer himself, although he never intended his highly visual and idiosyncratic swing-based pieces to be used as such. In a decade of big bands, of Benny Goodman and "One O'Clock Jump," when the world was not just on the verge of war but Glenn Miller, Scott wasn't afraid to break every existing rule to make pop music. He put together a small swing band that didn't really swing, kept all his music in his head instead of on charts, worked at tempos more mechanical than human, flirted with the avant-garde, and, above all, maintained a deep, profound sense of humor, especially toward so-called serious music. His songs came from the idiosyncratic mind of an idiosyncratic man, with highly suggestive titles like "Dinner Music for a Pack of Hungry Cannibals" and "Confusion Among a Fleet of Taxicabs Upon Meeting with a Fare." "It was so different," explained original Raymond Scott Quintette saxophonist Dave Harris. "That's why it took off so. People, they didn't know what the hell to make of the Quintette. When you told people you were with the Quintette, they'd look at you like 'where the hell did you come from?' They thought we came from another world."

Milt Franklyn replaced Stalling when he retired in 1958, having already worked as Stalling's arranger for years. He was followed by William Lava in the early 1960s. Though Lava's scores were not as polished as Stalling's, he did add other musical influences, such as world music, to the cartoons. Serving as musical copyist and occasional orchestrator during and after the Stalling years was Eugene Poddany, who later directed the music for a number of Ted Geisel (or Dr. Seuss) classics, which were directed by Chuck Jones. Treg Brown was in charge of the sound effects for the cartoons under all of these composers. Sound effects people like Brown became, in many ways, an adjunct to the cartoon composition process, though there were often battles for whether on-screen action would be accompanied by a musical or sound-effect cue. Like Stalling, Brown was an innovator, often using a sound that was entirely incongruous with the on-screen image, forcing the eye and the ear to send comically contradictory information to the brain.

Besides Stalling, the other giant of cartoon music was Scott Bradley, the self-taught composer at MGM's cartoon studios. With the sound turned off, the jokes in an orchestrated sequence of *Tom and Jerry* fall flat; Bradley's harsh dissonances and move-for-move orchestration bring them to life. With a greater passion for modernism than his predecessors, Bradley's musical sources ranged from wild jazz to twelve-tone rows and musical clusters. "I hope Dr. Schoenberg will forgive me for using his system to produce funny music," he once said, "but even the boys in the orchestra laughed when we were recording it."

In MGM's academy award winning *Cat Concerto* (1947), cartoon cat Tom's piano fingerings exactly follow Bradley's notation of a Liszt Rhapsody arranged for, and recorded by, two pianists. Even Tom's finger and wrist movements are modeled after those of the late pianist Vladimir de Pachman—though the feline virtuoso somehow performs music scored for four human hands. "I wish that our contemporary masters would take interest in cartoon work," Bradley said. "For men like Copland, Bernstein, Britten, Walton, Kodaly, Shostakovich, or Prokofiev, it would be a very fruitful experience."

In a post–John Cage world, in which all sound can be considered music, the sonic possibilities are even greater. In UPA's Gerald McBoing Boing series, scored by Gail Kubik and based on the innovative Dr. Suess children's story, Gerald cannot talk; he can only utter sound effects. The score calls for a narrator, a chamber orchestra, and an imaginative array of percussion instruments. In *Gerald McBoing Boing's Symphony* (1953), Gerald fills in for an entire symphony orchestra in their absence.

At Walter Lantz Studios, home of Woody Woodpecker and Andy Panda, Darrell Calker was doing all the innovation. He was well known in jazz circles and often brought in the likes of Nat King Cole and Meade Lux Lewis to play for Lantz's "Swing Symphonies." Other noteworthy musical directors of the era included Winston Sharples, an innovator responsible for the themes and scores of Felix the Cat, Little Lulu, Casper the Friendly Ghost, and more at Van Buren, Famous, and Paramount Studios; Sammy Timberg and Sammy Lerner at Fleischer studios; Gene Rodemich at Van Beuren Studios; Joe De Nat at Columbia/Screen Gems; and Oliver Wallace, Frank Churchill, Leigh Harline, and others at Disney.

The death knell of the golden age of cartoon music came in the late 1950s, when UPA, MGM, and other studios halted cartoon production and a musician's strike forced studios to use library music from past cartoons, starting a bad habit that plagues today's cartoons. In addition, the large-volume demands of television in the late 1950s forced other studios to put out cheap and hurried work.

When Hanna-Barbera opened its studio after the demise of MGM, the founders called Hoyt Curtin, an aspiring film composer whom they had met while working on a beer commercial, to do some musical spots over the phone. Impressed by Curtin's gift for coming up with hummable melodies in minutes, the pair hired him as the studio's chief composer, and soon he was busy recording three times a week. Due to time and budget constraints, and also due to directors' attempts at modernization, Curtin sometimes had to use all synthesizer cues, "which don't swing," as he said. He scored everything from the big-band-style theme songs of *The Jetsons* and *The Flintstones* to more sedate cartoons like *The Smurfs*. His scores for the *Superfriends* shows created the type of hero music that has become standard fare for the robot and action cartoons that began to dominate Saturday mornings in the late 1980s and '90s; while, in *Jonny Quest*, he turned almost sadistic, writing it in "a killer key," as he says, with the hardest fingering positions he could. "Just murder," is how he describes the experience of playing it. According to Curtin, "Every current Saturday morning cartoon has stolen from me musically."

Another musician who didn't conform to television's low standards was Vince Guaraldi, who composed the memorable piano themes to the *Charlie Brown* specials in the 1970s. Similarly, the iconic music from *The Pink Panther*, with its Henry Mancini themes (written for the Blake Edwards movies) and cues composed at times by William Lava, Doug Goodwind, and Walter Greene, gave new life to a waning art form.

Looking at the state of Saturday morning cartoons today, it often seems that the classical style of animated film composing is dead. Studios hire composers to write a theme song and a few hours of synthesized library music, and then bring in a music editor to fit the library music into cartoon sequences. Most composers are willing to accept these commissions for no salary because, says Peter Wetzler, one of the composers for the short-lived space age cartoon, *The Adventures of the Galaxy Rangers*, "for one nationally syndicated half-hour show, in just one season, a composer can receive one million dollars in royalties."

There are always exceptions, however. Mark Mothersbaugh, the former Devo founder who has scored and writen themes for *Clifford, the Big Red Dog, Rugrats*, and more, studied the scores to Rocky and Bullwinkle cartoons and was amazed to discover how talented a composer Fred Steiner was, inserting as many as 165 separate musical cues into a single cartoon. Mothersbaugh explained his conversion from public performing to cartoon scoring: "After being in this band where we're working on twelve little songs for months and months, to all of a sudden where the first thing that came out of you was going to be on TV was kind of exciting. So I got the bug."

Another modern innovator is Glen Daum, who studied under Gyorgy Ligeti at Stanford. When Daum was commissioned to compose for Ralph Bakshi's TV series *Mighty Mouse: The New Adventures*, he was determined to turn in quality work inspired by past masters. "It's not an electronic score and I'm not trying to fake an orchestra with synthesizers," says Daum of his *Mighty Mouse* and *Chip 'n' Dale's Rescue Rangers* scores. "Unfortunately, I'm one of the few people doing that in present-day animation." His work for

Mighty Mouse is evocative of older, jazz-based cartoons, but something more is added. Daum uses tempos that "go all over the place," hilariously paced and compressed musical cues, and sounds from any and all musical genres, including jazz, Muzak, classical, blues, television show themes, and others. The bits, like the images in the cartoon, are often meant to be satirical. For the show's theme, he had his orchestra learn the original *Mighty Mouse* theme and then told them to play it "like they were in high school." The percussionist falls off beat, the saxophone player can't keep the reed in his mouth, and at the end the music trails off like a wind-up music box running down.

"You can be corny or contemporary; you can do anything," Daum says. "At one point, I had four different sections of the orchestra all playing different stuff at the same time. It was like Elliott Carter had scored the episode."

In the 1980s, a generation raised on Saturday morning cartoons came of age. From the frenetic rock of bands like Faith No More to the game theory pieces and speedball improvisations of avant-garde composer-musicians like John Zorn, cartoon music became a significant influence. "My concept of good music," Zorn says, "was based on what I used to listen to when I was a kid. I never really heard jazz until I was around twenty-one. Cartoon music was very important and the concept of the way the music changed really got stuck in my head."

It was only natural, then, that in the next decade, the work of cartoon pioneers finally began to be taken seriously. Producers Hal Willner and Greg Ford uncovered lost Warner Bros. recording sessions during a trip to California, put out a CD of classic Carl Stalling cues in 1990, and soon the Warner Bros. Symphony Orchestra was on tour, scoring Looney Tunes live. Milan records released a Scott Bradley compilation; Rhino Records put together a box set of Hanna-Barbera and Hoyt Curtin music; and Raymond Scott was rediscovered, with more than half a dozen CDs of his music released, along with tribute albums from musicians including the Beau Hunks and Don Byron. Today, nearly every pioneer of cartoon music has passed away—including Stalling, Scott, Curtin, Sharples, Kubik, and Guaraldi—yet their cartoons live on, bending the ears, expanding the minds, and sonically saving a generation raised on bland teenybopper pop.

Elements of this article originally appeared in Ear Magazine *and the* Village Voice. *Sources include the author's interviews with Hoyt Curtin, Dave Harris,*

Raymond Scott, Chuck Jones, Glen Daum, John Zorn, Sun Ra, Hal Willner, Mark Mothersbaugh, and others; various magazine, journal, and unpublished articles, including the interview with Carl Stalling on pages 37–60 of this volume, the speech given by Scott Bradley on pages 115–120, "A Technical and Historical Overview of Soundtrack Production Procedure in American Animated Film" by Arthur Kegerreis, "Notes on Cartoon Music" by Ingolf Dahl from Film Music Notes, *"Cartoon Post-Production in Video" by Bill Koepnick from* Mix *magazine, "Symphonies for the Sillies" by Ross Care from* Funnyworld, *and "A Sound Idea: Music for Animated Films" by Jon Newsom from the* Quarterly Journal of the Library of Congress; *and several books, including* Film Music: A Neglected Art *by Roy M. Prendergast,* Of Mice and Magic: A History of American Animated Cartoons *by Leonard Maltin, and* Experimental Animation: Origins of a New Art *by Robert Russett and Cecile Starr.*

PART I

♫

An Episodic History of Cartoon Music

Animated Cartoons and Slap-Stick Comedy

by EDITH LANG and GEORGE WEST

In the days before sound and image were physically joined on a piece of film, movie houses and theatres had either a pianist, an organist, or a group of musicians available to play music before, during, and after the shows. Film accompanists could acquire dozens of manuals on how to play for pictures, as well as reams of music well-suited to the task. Little specific information exists on how cartoons—such as the Aesop's Fables series, or *Felix the Cat*—might have been accompanied, as features received most of the attention of accompanying manuals.

One book that does mention cartoons—in the larger category of "comedies"—is Edith Lang's and George West's *Musical Accompaniment of Moving Pictures*, first published in 1920. While we cannot take the instructions below as representative of *all* accompanying practices—especially since there is evidence that cartoons might have just as easily been shown without any music whatsoever—Lang's and West's admonitions give us some idea of the duties facing an aspiring accompanist, as well as some perspective on how short comedies of any sort were valued in the larger performance medium.

MANY A PLAYER, WHO is otherwise admirably fitted to give a musical interpretation of moving pictures, falls down on the animated cartoons and burlesque films. This is due to an absence of the all-important sense of humor, or "comedy touch," which is needed in every-day life as much as in this particular branch of the movie entertainment. Sense of humor is a gift of the gods, but they will not withhold it from any one who seriously tries to acquire it. The player should learn to recognize, and be able personally to enjoy, the fun of the comic situations depicted on the screen. Nothing is more calamitous than to see "Mutt and Jeff" disport themselves in their inimitable antics and to have a "Brother Gloom" at the organ who gives vent to his perennial grouch in sadly sentimental or funereal strains. A cheerful aspect of things, the faculty to laugh with and at the world, are indispensable. In no part of the pictures should the attention of the player be riveted more firmly on the screen than here. If the "point" of the joke be missed, if the player lag behind with his effect, all will be lost, and the audience cheated out of its rightful share of joy. Nor does it suffice, as seems to be the idea of certain picture-players, to be armed with one lively tune that must serve all cartoons, comedies and jokes, invariably and indiscriminately. In the cartoons and in the comedies all sorts of other emotions, besides that of plain hilarity, may come into play; there may be sorrow, doubt, horror and even death; only all these emotions lack the quality of truth, and they must be expressed as "mock" sorrow and grief, "mock" doubt and death. This is very different from reality and should therefore be treated differently in the music. Take as a glaring example the funeral march of Chopin, with its sublime note of tragedy and bereavement, and the exquisite "Funeral March for a Marionette" by Gounod, with its suggestion of fine persiflage. This method, applied to the most serious situation, can naturally be adapted to any other emotion that the player may encounter in a legitimate picture drama and that he will have to "caricature" for the picture farce.

Nowhere does success, the "getting across" of a picture, depend so much on special effects as it does here. It may be stated candidly that these effects, and the best among them, are not always purely musical. As will be pointed out in the chapter on "Special Effects," a battery of traps and other accessories are really needed to emphasize in a comic manner the action on screen. It is often noise, more than music, that is wanted, to arouse the hilarity of the audience; and the noise again may be of various kinds. It should always be broadly imitative when accompanying a fall, a hit, a slide, a whirl or flight through the air, a brawl, the whistle of an engine, the chirping of a bird, the mewing of a cat, or the barking of a dog. In the last analysis it takes very little to make a crowd laugh; only the fuse to its magazine of laughter must be ignited with a live spark. Experience, here as in everything else, will prove the best teacher, and the player will soon find out what effects work best and produce the surest results.

This part of the show is admirably adapted to the introduction of all sorts of popular songs and dances. The player should keep in touch with the publications of popular music houses, since it will repay him to establish a reputation which will make the public say: "Let's go to the Star Theatre—you always hear the latest tune there." This will prove a never-failing drawing card for the younger generation of movie-fans, and it will react most decidedly to the advantage of the organist in his relation to the box-office and his own earning power.

It is well also to keep in touch with the monthly announcements of the latest phonograph records issued. As a rule, these numbers have proved assured successes, and people like to hear their favorite tunes, either those they already have at home, or new ones which they might want to add to their collection. The player's repertoire should always be kept alive by the infusion of new and up-to-date material.

One important factor in these pictorial farces is the matter of speed. "Pep" is the key-note to the situation, with the current "jazz" tunes as a medium. When special effects are to be introduced, or certain moods and emotions are to be "italicized" and burlesqued, this may be done at any point of the composition played, the piece instantly to be resumed. Above all, keep things "going," like a juggler who may be handling two or twenty balls, and occasionally drops one, but must never cease in throwing and catching something.[1]

Originally appeared in Musical Accompaniment of Moving Pictures: A Practical Manual for Pianists and Organists (*Boston Music Co., 1920*)

---

[1] Such pieces as "The Bim-Bims" by Adam, "Lydia" by Fomin, "Donkey Trot" by Leducq, "La Gloria" by Densmore, "With Xylophone and Bells" and "The Juggler Comedian" by Huerter, "On the Hike" by Dumas, "Polka Humoristique" by Lacomb, and "Chatterbox" by d'Ambrosio will prove useful material. The player should have at his command the choruses of such well-known topical songs as "I cannot make my eyes behave," "Every little movement has a meaning all its own," "Where did you get that hat?" "Always go while the going is good," "Waiting at the Church," "What's the matter with Father?" "My mind's made up to marry Carolina," etc., etc. The association of such tunes with their particular text phrase will always insure a quick response in the audience, if the tunes are applied to the proper situation.

Make Walt's Music

Music for Disney Animation, 1928–1967

by ROSS CARE

THE STORY OF music in the animated films of Walt Disney, from 1928 until Disney's death in 1967, is an involved scenario with a cast including many leading and supporting players. The saga also coincides with the early history of American sound cinema, from the first talkies of the late 1920s to the wide-screen/stereophonic sound epics of the 1950s and 1960s. Yet in spite of the continuous exploitation that classic Disney music has received over the decades, from the early cartoon and feature songs released on 78 rpm to CDs of music found at the now-global Disney theme parks (which also recycle music from the studio's very earliest eras), precious little is still generally known about the gallery of composers who launched and sustained this durable legacy. These musicians, among many other artists, labored in relative anonymity under the Disney aegis to create an often remarkable body of imaginative Americana that continues to fascinate in this new millennium.

Dawn of the Golden Age

Disney's very first films were a hodgepodge of silent commercials and animated shorts produced during the 1920s, among them the Alice in Cartoonland series, which placed a live actress in an animated setting, and a brief stint with the Oswald the Lucky Rabbit character. Disney, however, did not own the Oswald copyright and soon lost the series, a setback that, happily, led to the creation of Walt's most famous character, Mickey Mouse.

The Oswald/early Mickey era of Disney also saw a key creation in motion picture history: over a period of several years in the late 1920s the sound film was born. Disney's first Mickey Mouse shorts were originally planned as silent films. When Warner Bros.' *The Jazz Singer* proved a hit in 1927, the intuitive

Disney quickly jumped on the aural bandwagon and arranged for what was actually the third Mouse short, *Steamboat Willie* (1928), to feature synchronized music. Disney and a small staff (which included future director Wilfred Jackson) essentially developed the soundtrack themselves, using public domain tunes and sound effects recorded with a crude system of synchronization that Jackson devised through the use of a metronome and markings on film. The score was recorded in New York with a modest orchestra and a theater conductor who was dubious of the whole affair.

Crude as the results seem today, the first sound cartoon created a sensation. Like the Warners, whose prime interest in sound film was *not* that characters could finally speak onscreen, but that "now we can bring a symphony orchestra to every small town in America," Disney's prime concern was also musical. Only a few words of dialogue are included in *Steamboat Willie*, most of the audio track being a fusion of music and cleverly synched sound effects that must have amazed and delighted the first sound audiences. A highlight of the short is the Mouse's rather sadistic utilization of various farm animals to musical ends (including, in a bit of bawdy barnyard humor exorcised from most later prints, a nursing sow).

Key musical themes in *Steamboat Willie* were the title tune "Steamboat Bill" (an old Irish folk tune) and "Turkey in the Straw." This same pastiche style was applied even more heavily to the *Plane Crazy* score (1928), which features a catalog of familiar public domain tunes—"Ruben, Ruben," "Yankee Doodle," "Dixie," "Hail to the Chief"—fragments of which are dizzyingly stitched together by Carl Stalling in almost Ivesian fashion, and sometimes heard in two- and three-part contrapuntal development. Stalling would apply a similar musical approach to another manic early short, *When the Cat's Away*, in 1929. Both shorts also illustrate how the originally rambunctious Mouse—Mickey is even guilty of blatant sexual harassment of Minnie in *Plane Crazy*—quickly softened into the less irascible but still spunky rodent of *Steamboat Willie*.

With the success of the first Mickey films, the Disney studio was definitely on its way to a decade that would witness remarkable strides in both animation and the integration of music with animated narrative and mood. The musical aspects of this amazing decade are framed on one end by the crude vitality of *The Skeleton Dance* (1929) and other early Silly Symphonies of the late 1920s, and on the other by the polished refinement of the early 1940s, in *Fantasia* and *Bambi*. This trajectory also illustrates Disney's growing interest in classical music and serious original underscoring, both of which peaked in these two pivotal features.

The Disney organization's first musical director/composer was Carl Stalling, who is best known today as the musical genius behind the Warner Bros. shorts. Disney had known Stalling in their Kansas City days, during which the musician was musical director for the Isis Theater, where he both played organ and conducted the orchestra. It was in Kansas City that Disney had produced his early films, one of which included a live-musical accompaniment by Stalling. While en route to New York to record *Steamboat Willie,* Disney again met with Stalling and presented him with the first two Mouse cartoons. Stalling scored both *Plane Crazy* and *Gallopin' Gaucho* (1928) in Kansas City, then joined Disney in New York to record them. After making the move to Hollywood, Stalling composed the scores for about fifteen Mickey Mouse and Silly Symphonies shorts for Disney.

In a published interview, Stalling noted that it was he who suggested the concept for Disney's second series, the Silly Symphonies, which were conceived to showcase more self-contained musical scores. (Due to their plot and gag-oriented nature, the "Mickeys" generally subordinated the music to animated action). Further details of Stalling's brief career with Disney may be found in his 1971 *Funnyworld* interview, reprinted in its entirety elsewhere in this volume, but it might also be noted that the designation "Silly Symphonies" accurately sums up Disney's overall attitude toward music. While always appreciating the audience appeal of popular music, during the 1930s Disney was also increasingly drawn, if always somewhat ambivalently, to classical music. (His comments concerning the abstract Bach sequence in *Fantasia* describe images that came to mind while falling asleep in a concert hall, and in the 1935 Silly Symphonies *Music Land*, the queen of the Symphony Land is first seen dozing on her throne while a sedate minuet plays.)

While not a musician himself, Disney did demand a certain element of quality in his musical scores: he wanted class, but nothing *too* classy, and seriousness, but not the type of music to be taken *too* seriously. Ergo: *Silly* Symphonies. Indeed, his musical ambivalence encapsulates the tension between popular and "serious" music that has been a constant of western civilization since the evolution of music as a major artistic pursuit in the Europe of the 1600s. In many ways, however, the dichotomy between the popular and the serious is also a twentieth century phenomenon, and perhaps even a more distinctly American one, as artistically insecure Americans always feel more at home with labels. (In Europe, Mozart operas and Schubert songs and dance pieces *were* the popular music of the day.)

But as classical music evolved during the Romantic era of the late nineteenth century, conventions did become a bit more rigid until, in the early twentieth century, the adoption of the emerging medium of jazz became a mode of rebellion against the stuffiness of the concert music scene for certain European composers such as Weill (who is said to have admired the music of early Disney), Milhaud, and Ravel, and Americans such as Grofé and Gershwin, who pioneered the new hybrid of the concert world, symphonic jazz. (The new 1920s genre, "concert" jazz, really only continued to flourish in ensuing decades in studio era film scoring, and is specifically parodied by Disney and composer Leigh Harline in the aforementioned *Music Land*).

Essentially, given his desire to reach the broadest possible audiences for his films, Disney (like the rest of Hollywood) wanted to have his music *both* ways. With the simultaneous evolution of the Mickey Mouse and Silly Symphonies series in the 1930s he was able to do just that, with the former shorts featuring essentially pop scores, and the latter flirting with and in some instances achieving scores that rank with the best of early twentieth-century concert music. The two series also illustrate the European/American influences that pervaded the early Disney oeuvre (and indeed Hollywood itself in the 1930s), with the "Sillys" representing the former and the "Mickeys" the latter, a duality that continued in the first animated features, all of which, with the exception of *Dumbo* (1941), were derived from European fairy tales and childhood classics.

With Stalling's departure from Disney in early 1930, Bert Lewis composed music for twenty-five shorts between 1930 and 1935. The studio's music department was soon to be more crucially impacted by two other important additions: Frank Churchill in 1931, and Leigh Harline in 1932. Together these two talented musicians, one a jazz pianist, the other a university-trained musician, would help Disney achieve the dream of the pop/classical fusion he so desired in his collective musical/animation output.

Churchill and Harline were unquestionably Disney's major music men during the key period of the 1930s, and together they created what would become the signature Disney sound: music that is primarily melodic, inventively orchestrated, and essentially simple (sometimes deceptively so) and accessible, yet always with that indefinable X-factor that was another characteristic of Disney's work as a whole: popular appeal.

Disney and his composers—left to right, Leigh Harline, Walt Disney, and Frank Churchill. © Disney Enterprises, Inc. Courtesy of Mike Barrier.

Frank Churchill and Snow White and the Seven Dwarfs

Frank Churchill was primarily a gifted pianist/melodist, an intuitive musician with little formal training who received his musical grounding playing piano in dance bands, on radio, and eventually in Hollywood studios, where Disney discovered him at RKO. His gift for catchy, appealing melody can be heard in such early Mickey Mouse shorts as *The Whoopee Party* (1932) and *Camping Out* (1934), but he created a major commercial success for the studio with "Who's Afraid of the Big Bad Wolf," which became a kind of Depression anthem when heard in *The Three Little Pigs* in 1933. His considerable popular success with *Pigs* led to his composing all of the songs for Disney's

Snow White and the Seven Dwarfs (1937). While hailed as the cinematic milestone it certainly is, musically Disney's first feature is more backward-looking than pioneering. Songs *are* fluidly linked to character and incident, yet the mode is still more one of nostalgic operetta than of the American musical comedy that was slowly evolving on Broadway during this same decade. The arrangements, likewise, were scored for a modest theater orchestra sound, slipping in some mildly jazzy Paul Whiteman–esque touches only for some of the up-tempo interludes. The operetta ambiance is reinforced by the twittery coloratura soprano of Snow White herself, playing opposite the stolid baritone of her Prince Charming (with the dwarfs themselves filling in as a self-contained operetta chorus). Indeed the first third of the film verges on opera, with one musical number following another in rapid succession and linked by continuous orchestral underscoring (most notably the Gothic cues for the Magic Mirror/Wicked Queen scenes).

But Disney's fusion of high-tech animation and traditional operetta struck a chord with late 1930s audiences, and the film was a global popular and critical success. Many of Churchill's tunes made the hit parade and won the composer one of the top ASCAP ratings up to that time. *Snow White* also launched the first commercially released original film soundtrack ever, a bestselling 78-rpm album on RCA Victor, and its songs, particularly "Someday My Prince Will Come," one of Churchill's most poignant melodies, continued to be recorded by artists such as Dave Brubeck and Miles Davis in the 1950s and '60s.

Unfortunately, Frank Churchill's musical gifts and popular success were not to lead to a Disneyesque happy ending. Troubled by nervous tension and alcoholism, Churchill committed suicide on his ranch near Newhall, California, on May 14, 1942. The music for *Dumbo* (co-scored with Oliver Wallace) had just won an Oscar for best score, and Churchill's touching song, "Baby Mine," had been nominated for best song. Churchill can be seen in the studio tour sequence in *The Reluctant Dragon* (1941), which he also partially scored. Two of his melodies turn up as late as 1949, in *The Adventures of Ichabod and Mister Toad* (the song "Merrily on Our Way"), and 1953, in *Peter Pan* (the crocodile motif).

Leigh Harline and Pinocchio

In the 1930s, the versatile and prolific Leigh Harline also worked on both the Mickey Mouse and Silly Symphonies shorts, creating some of his most striking work for the latter. A trained musician who graduated from the University of Utah, he received his first professional experience in radio, doubling in various capacities ranging from composer/arranger to singer/announcer. If Churchill was Disney's major pop star of the 1930s, Harline was his concertmaster. (Due to the voluminous output of shorts in the mid-1930s, Harline and Churchill sometimes co-scored shorts, including *Lullaby Land* [1933] and *Funny Little Bunnies* [1934], two of the most profligately melodic shorts in the series.) But while Churchill continued to turn out his appealingly accessible and distinctively American tunes, Harline created sophisticated scores for some of the most narratively and musically ambitious Silly Symphonies shorts, and was most overtly influenced by both European wellsprings and classical music forms. *The Pied Piper* (1933) features a cantata-like score for solo voices, chorus, and orchestra, and the familiar plot line is told entirely in sung dialogue and orchestral underscoring. The same is true of Harline's *The Goddess of Spring* (1933), an operatic mini-feature in which Harline also proved his pop credentials with "Hi-de Hades," a Cotton Club–like jazz number for the scene in which hell becomes a Harlem night club to distract the distraught Persephone.

Besides his elaborate vocal writing, Harline created a number of sophisticated orchestral scores for the "Sillys" as well. *Music Land* is a droll musical spin on Romeo and Juliet in which a prince from the Isle of Jazz falls in love with a princess from the Land of Symphony. After an Ivesian battle between the two kingdoms, in which Harline contrapuntally pits Wagner against his own sprightly jazz passages, the lovers are united and eventually, one assumes, give birth to Symphonic Jazz. In addition, all the "dialogue" is spoken by musical instruments imitating human speech.

The Old Mill (1937) is perhaps both Disney's and Harline's most masterful and sophisticated Silly Symphonies score. Harline's impressionistic symphonic poem, divided into suite-like movements, underscores a plotless, wordless fantasia of mood and atmospheric special effects during a stormy night in an abandoned windmill. While *The Old Mill* was allegedly produced as a test run for the multiplane camera scenes in *Snow White*, the film is also an emphatic precursor of *Fantasia*, though with a totally original score. Indeed, the entire Silly Symphonies series was a training ground for techniques, both visual and musical, employed in the features. With the success of *Snow White*, the "Sillys" were soon phased out of production.

Harline (along with Paul Smith) contributed supplemental scoring for *Snow White*, including the music for the Magic Mirror/Wicked Queen transformation sequences. But Harline's personal Disney masterpiece is his ambitious score for the studio's second feature, the epic *Pinocchio* (1940), a work all the more remarkable in that Harline composed both songs (including the classic "When You Wish Upon a Star") and most of the sophisticated underscoring. *Pinocchio* had a difficult pre-production period, and while Harline composed a number of accessible tunes for the score, the darker nature of the film itself required a musical approach that was different from *Snow White*, a necessity to which Harline responded with an orchestral score that moves from the warm Old World lyricism of the opening sequences to cues that aptly reflect the darkness into which the small hero descends in the course of an often disturbing series of adventures. (Smith, along with Edward Plumb, also contributed very minor scoring to *Pinocchio,* but the major mass of the score is definitely the work of Harline).

Disney perhaps got more than he bargained for musically with Harline's *Pinocchio*, and, ironically, he was reportedly not especially fond of the score that contained what eventually became the Disney signature theme song. When *Pinocchio* won two Oscars, for best song (with lyrics by Ned Washington) and best score, Disney further damned the score with faint praise, saying "Maybe it wasn't so bad, after all." But no matter what Disney's true feelings were, there was little doubt that Harline's double win for his elaborate score and warmly sophisticated song enabled him to move on to a major Hollywood career elsewhere. He was the only Disney staffer ever to do so. Departing Disney in 1941, Harline freelanced at various studios including RKO, Twentieth Century-Fox, and MGM until his death in 1967. Some of his important feature scores include *Isle of the Dead* (RKO, 1945), *Pickup on South Street* (Fox, 1953), *Broken Lance* (Fox, 1954), and *The Seven Faces of Doctor Lao* (MGM, 1964).

Wilfred Jackson, one of Disney's key animation directors of the golden age, worked closely with both Churchill and Harline when scores were worked out in detailed director/composer sessions in what came to be called the studio's Music Rooms. Jackson offered these perceptive comments on the two composers' respective sounds: "Frank Churchill was primarily an accomplished pianist. He seemed to have an endless variety of numbers in his repertoire, and when he really got wound up and going good he seemed to have an equally endless number of his own tunes. Frank's music was melodic and uncomplicated, and you could whistle or hum it easily. I believe Leigh Harline had a much broader musical education than Frank, and his music seemed quite different. Leigh's music was melodic enough, but it depended much more on musical elements other than melody for its effectiveness: his counter-melodies, harmonic structure, things like that which I do not understand about music, all contributed so much more to the final effectiveness of his scores."

Walt and Music

But what, exactly, was Walt Disney's actual role in all this? From most reports, while he was not a musician, Disney's sense of what worked for his films, as well as what appealed to the public *musically,* was as keen as his brilliant story editing skills. Music was thrashed out and discussed in detail during the studio's celebrated story conferences at which, in the early years, a composer was usually in attendance, and all music was emphatically subject to Disney's input and final approval. Jackson also recalled: "Walt was not easily satisfied with either the collectively developed story or musical ideas for his cartoons and had to feel right about the total material for a picture before going ahead with it. This was especially true of his films in the late 1930s and early '40s."

An excerpt from a 1939 story conference for *Pinocchio* would seem to verify Jackson's comment:

WILFRED: Up to the point where they say, "What you do is hoodoo," is it the [musical] feeling you want?

WALT: Yes, but then it begins to get too modern—it may be too much melody in it there—I would see it more à la Raymond Scott.

LEIGH [HARLINE]:   That's even more sophisticated. It's the kind of thing you have to work out with color more than modern licks.

WALT: You can do it with color, and not have so much the modern harmonies back there playing it. [He then describes an unorthodox big band arrangement he had heard and liked on the Edgar Bergen radio show the previous evening.] I think the world is waiting for someone to bust wide open all musical rules—that's what Scott did.

HAL [KING, AN ANIMATOR]:   We had a bazooka in there. Did you like that?

Seven more pages of the conference transcript are devoted to a detailed discussion of a musical episode, an African variation in the Stromboli marionette show sequence, which never appeared in the final film.

Bambi

Though Harline was initially considered as composer for *Bambi* (1942), the music was ultimately the work of Frank Churchill, who had composed the songs prior to his untimely death, with the remainder of the score posthumously developed from his instrumental themes and sketches (and sometimes augmented) by a staff of Disney composer/arrangers. The *Bambi* music crew was headed by Edward Plumb (who also composed some of the score's more modernistic passages), and included composers Paul Smith and Charles Wolcott, conductor Alexander Steinert, and choral director Charles Henderson (who was borrowed from Fox). Plumb, primarily an arranger, also served as musical director—a kind of liaison between the animation departments and conductor Leopold Stokowski—on the classically scored *Fantasia*. He continued to orchestrate at Disney studios through the 1950s. The *Bambi* score, with its hints of Ravel and Stravinsky, emphatically manifests Disney's interest in classical music during this period.

For an in-depth article that explores the development of early Disney's most refined feature score, from the rudimentary preliminary and often simplistic sketches of Churchill through to its final polished symphonic/choral realization, readers are referred to my article in the book *Wonderful Inventions* (Iris Newsom, editor, Library of Congress, 1985).

Oliver Wallace/Paul Smith: Into the 1950s

The second half of the 1930s would see the addition of several other composers to the Disney studio music department. Al Malotte (who, as Albert Hay Malotte, composed the definitive musicalization of "The Lord's Prayer") worked briefly at the studio from 1935 to 1939, mostly on the Silly Symphonies series. Two other new composers, who would remain with the studio for several decades, also joined up at this time. Paul Smith composed the music for seventy shorts between 1936 and 1953. He provided supplemental scoring for Churchill and Harline (on both *Snow White* and *Pinocchio*), as well as scoring other 1940s projects (including many Donald Duck shorts).

But Smith really came into his own in the 1950s with his scores for the True Life Adventure nature documentary series and live-action feature work, including a substantial score for Disney's CinemaScope epic, *20,000 Leagues Under the Sea* (1954). His score for the feature-length *The Living Desert* (1953) also ranks with the best studio music of the decade.

The London-born Oliver Wallace joined Disney in 1936 and remained at the studio until his death in 1963. Originally a theater organist in Seattle, he moved to Hollywood in 1930, doing some work at Universal, which included playing the pipe organ part in Franz Waxman's *The Bride of Frankenstein* score. Eventually he scored over 140 shorts for Disney, including some of the best Donald Ducks. His contributions also included secondary songwriting and arranging/underscoring for a variety of features. A few of Wallace's classic shorts include *The Little Whirlwind* (Mickey Mouse, 1941) and the droll *Tea for Two Hundred* (Donald Duck, 1953), as well as several installments in the CinemaScope People and Places series of the 1950s. His best feature animation underscoring includes the Headless Horseman chase in *Ichabod and Mister Toad*, several original cues in *Alice in Wonderland* (1951), which Wallace amusingly developed from Sammy Fain's song melodies, and the Peter Pan/Tinkerbell music in the opening section of *Peter Pan*. Wallace's theater organ background often manifested itself in his use of the Novachord, an early electronic keyboard that can be heard in his "Pink Elephants on Parade" sequence in *Dumbo*, and in many of the shorts, notably *The Little Whirlwind*, in which the spacey sounding instrument represents the mischievous title character. Wallace scored one Donald Duck short, *Duck Pimples* (1945), a parody of suspense radio, entirely with the Novachord.

Dumbo

The charming, primarily pop score for *Dumbo* was the joint work of Wallace and Frank Churchill. Churchill wrote the music for three of the major songs, including the poignant "Baby Mine," while Wallace composed the two final numbers, "Pink Elephants on Parade" and "When I See an Elephant Fly." Wallace also composed most of the underscoring, including a jauntily lyrical theme for Dumbo himself, the manically explosive circus music, and the series of variations on his own "Pink Elephants" number, which underscores one of the most fantastically animated numbers in early Disney.

After Bambi

One might speculate that all the Disney films after *Fantasia* were a reaction to the initial failure of Disney's most deliberate excursion into high art. While the film's critical lambasting definitely dampened Disney's enthusiasm for culture, it's also true that the tepid reception of *Bambi*, the bitter animators' strike of 1941, and World War II all also contributed to the end of an era for both Disney animation and Disney music. (America's entry into the war also prevented Disney from distributing *Fantasia* with the expensive system of stereophonic sound heard in the original New York reserved-seat engagement.) With Churchill's death and Harline's departure, Wallace, Smith, and Charles Wolcott (who also joined the studio in the late 1930s) were the primary musical holdovers from the earlier era.

The post-*Bambi* features also launched Disney's policy of hiring commercially successful, non-studio songwriters to create the songs for his features. From 1942 on, the Disney studio would have no in-house songwriters under exclusive contract until the Sherman brothers in the 1960s. The difficult post-*Bambi* 1940s were also the era of the "package" feature—films consisting primarily of miscellaneous shorts and sequences strung together on a loose and often musical theme. Oddly enough, these features also seem to align themselves in pairs, and all illustrate Disney's almost aggressive shift to music of a popular commercial mode.

The two Good Neighbor Policy films, *Saludos Amigos* (1943) and *The Three Caballeros* (1945), are scored mainly with Latin American pop tunes ("Brazil," "Baia"), only a few of which were actually written for the films. Charles Wolcott (who eventually worked at MGM during the 1950s) and Paul Smith contributed original underscoring to both. (One of Wolcott's themes, "Llama Serenade" from *Saludos Amigos*, eventually ended up on a 1960s Martin Denny album, *Primitiva*.) *The Three Caballeros* is especially notable for the explosive and colorful orchestrations of Wolcott, Smith, and Ed Plumb.

Fun and Fancy Free (1947) and *The Adventures of Ichabod and Mister Toad* are both films comprised of two major sequences each. Disney's tactic of using commercially established Tin Pan Alley hit songwriters (rather than staff composers) is exemplified by both of these films. (Gene DePaul and Don Raye, known for such 1940s hits as "Cow Cow Boogie" and "Star Eyes," wrote the songs for *Ichabod*.) The same is true of a pair of *Fantasia*-like pop music anthologies, *Make Mine Music* (1946) and *Melody Time* (1948). While all four of these films, especially *Make Mine Music*, are a very mixed bag stylistically, collectively they offered some of the most charming, if still obscure, entries in the Disney pop song catalog, among them "Lazy Countryside" and "My Favorite Dream" from *Fun and Fancy Free*, and "Once Upon a Wintertime" and several other original numbers in the much better *Melody Time* (which also included "Trees" and a final psychedelic Latin American sequence based on another Latin tune, "Blame It on the Samba"). Indeed, the beautifully designed and scored *Melody Time* lays the groundwork for the renaissance of Disney feature animation that commenced with *Cinderella* in 1950.

But Disney's most musical (and now reviled) mid-1940s feature is *Song of the South* (1946), a live/animated period piece woven around the classic Uncle Remus tales, and which is mirrored by another similarly formatted nostalgia opus, *So Dear to My Heart* (1949). Both films feature a compendium of songs by various songwriters and teams, as well as sensitive underscoring. *Song of the South* produced Disney's biggest song hit of the 1940s, "Zip-A-Dee-Doo-Dah" by Allie Wrubel and (lyricist) Ray Gilbert, but Charles Wolcott's bluesy "Sooner or Later" and several other tunes were also popular. (This entire score of songs can still be heard instrumentally if one waits long enough, or often enough, in the line for Splash Mountain in Disneyland.) The sophisticated underscoring was handled by Hollywood composer Daniele Amfitheatrof, who scored the live-action, and Paul Smith, who did an imaginative job with the animated sequences. Smith also underscored the lovely *So Dear to My Heart*. Ken Darby handled the important vocal direction for both films, as he would for *Melody Time*.

The beautifully designed and cohesive "populuxe" style of the 1950s Disney that *Melody Time* ushered in was unified musically by studio veteran Oliver Wallace, who, to varying degrees, arranged and integrated the work of the various Tin Pan Alley songwriters into his own original background scoring. *Cinderella* was the work of three songwriters—Mack David, Jerry Livingston, and Al Hoffman—with Wallace and Smith providing the underscoring, a highlight of which was Wallace's "Midnight/Wild Ride Home" cue. *Alice in Wonderland* was similar to *Song of the South* in its variety of songwriting contributions, including some secondary tunes by Wallace, but the major songs were by Sammy Fain and lyricist Bob Hilliard. While Fain's melodies were used as important motifs in the underscoring, Wallace also managed to include a few original cues, notably the drolly eerie music for the Tulgy Wood episode.

Fain also contributed the major songs to *Peter Pan* (with lyrics by Sammy Cahn). In both *Alice in Wonderland* and *Peter Pan,* Wallace developed a unique style of recitative-like underscoring that managed to musicalize both films' reliance on spoken dialogue. This technique (that both constructs musical phrasing on, and punctuates the rhythm of, the spoken dialogue) may be noted especially in the amusingly schizophrenic Queen of Hearts scenes in *Alice,* and in the first Captain Hook scenes in *Peter Pan.*

The End of the Second Golden Age

After these three classic animated fairy tales of the early 1950s, animation music under Walt's personal supervision somewhat slacked off until the commercially successful Sherman brothers era of the early 1960s. This was, it may also be noted, the period when Disney's creative focus was diverted into live-action film making and, more crucially, the development of the Disneyland theme park. Sonny Burke provided the music, and Peggy Lee the lyrics, for the rather routine *Lady and the Tramp* (1955) songs, so the prime musical interest therein remains Wallace's lovely and profuse Americana underscoring.

George Bruns, a new addition to the Disney music department in the 1950s, adapted Tchaikovsky for Disney's Technirama/stereophonic sound epic *Sleeping Beauty* in 1959, primarily on the strength of his having composed the mega-hit "Ballad of Davy Crockett" for a Disney TV show in the mid-1950s. (In the liner notes for one of his jazz albums on Disneyland Records, Bruns admits he "threw together" the Crockett tune in two hours.) Before joining Disney, Bruns was a jazz-based musician who arranged for Jack Teagarden and played tuba in Turk Murphy's San Francisco Dixieland Band. Bruns had also scored for Disney's 1950s rival, United Productions of America, and Disney's answer to the stylized UPA look—*101 Dalmatians* (1961), scored by Bruns with only one major song, "Cruella De Vil," by Mel Leven— is the least musical of the last features actually supervised by Disney himself.

In 1961, in an unprecedented move for the studio, Disney put two song-writing brothers, Richard and Robert Sherman, under exclusive contract, primarily because of material they had written for ex-Mouseketeer and Disney protégée Annette Funicello. The Shermans would produce a tremendously popular score for Disney's major hit of the 1960s, the live/animated *Mary Poppins* (1962), and they also scored the last Disney-supervised animated features, *The Sword in the Stone* (1963) and *The Jungle Book* (1967), not to mention creating a virtual catalog of TV, live-action, and theme park songs as well. While the Shermans produced many commercially successful numbers, the previously interesting Disney background scores slipped into a kind of sameness, mostly due to the somewhat bland sound of George Bruns, who managed to make even Tchaikovsky sound generic in *Sleeping Beauty*, and who continued to music direct and underscore (often in a rather Mancini-esque mode) the last Disney-supervised animated features.

The Mickey Mouse shorts series also ended with a whimper rather than a bang with *The Simple Things*, scored by Paul Smith in 1953. A number of new musicians gradually replaced the dwindling staff of studio veterans, and also contributed to Disney's burgeoning television output. Joseph S. Dubin, younger bother of lyricist Al Dubin, scored about twenty-five of the last cartoons, among them *Donald's Apple Core* (1952) and the UPA-esque 3-D short, *Melody*, a companion piece to the CinemaScope *Toot, Whistle, Plunk, and Boom* (both 1953.) (Songwriters for such cartoon "specials" as *Melody*, *Toot*, and *Trick or Treat* [1952] remain uncredited on film.) Many composers (including Smith, Bruns, Buddy Baker, William Lava, and head Mouseketeer Jimmie Dodd) collectively co-scored the Mickey Mouse Club and other 1950s TV shows.

Walt Disney's death on December 15, 1966, marked the end of an era for the Disney studio, although Disney's consuming interest in animation had begun to fade in the early 1950s when his creative energy was diverted to the Disneyland theme park, which was to remain the focus of his attention until his death. While *The Jungle Book* was a commercial and critical success, Disney's death and the ensuing absence of strong creative leadership threw the studio, and particularly the animation department, into a creative limbo from which it did not really emerge until the late 1980s.

Commencing with *The Little Mermaid* in 1989, the team of Alan Menken and Howard Ashman, best known for their off-Broadway musical, *The Little Shop of Horrors*, launched a series of Broadway-style musical extravaganzas that revived both the animated feature and Disney's reputation as a force in popular music, as well as winning several more Oscars for best song for the studio. The cycle peaked early with *Beauty and the Beast* (1991), and was curtailed by Ashman's death from AIDS in 1991. *Beauty and the Beast*, along with the score composed by Elton John for the equally popular *The Lion King* in 1994, enabled Disney to successfully enter the live Broadway theater arena with two successful properties that are still running at the dawn of the new millennium. *The Lion King* also marked another phase of Disney music in which successful, if slightly over-the-hill pop stars such as John, Sting, and Phil Collins created scores for the late 1990s and post-millennium animated features (although the corporation had experimented with this approach as early as 1973, when Roger Miller wrote the score to the studio's animated remake of *Robin Hood*, and pop tunesmiths including Barry Manilow and Billy Joel contributed to 1988's *Oliver and Company*). After Disney's death, serious film composers including Max Steiner, Elmer Bernstein, Jerry Goldsmith, Lalo Schifrin, Henry Mancini, John Barry, and many others also contributed underscoring to a variety of the studio's animated and live-action releases.

But it is the unique body of work created under Disney's personal and often demanding supervision by a staff of still often sadly uncredited composers that stands as the most interesting and original phase of the Disney studio's voluminous contributions to film and popular music. Frank Thomas, a key Disney animator and himself a working musician with the studio's famous Firehouse Five Plus Two animator jazz band, succinctly summed up the contributions of the many composers who collectively struggled to please Disney, and in the process created this first and most unique phase of the studio's musical history: "All of these men were tremendously talented and did a memorable job, quietly and earnestly. They deserve much credit."

Further Reading

Barrier, Mike. "An Interview with Carl Stalling." *Funnyworld,* Volume 13 (Spring 1971).

Care, Ross. "Cinesymphony." *Sight and Sound,* Volume 46, No. I (Winter 1976/77).

Care, Ross. "The Film Music of Leigh Harline," *Elmer Bernstein's Filmmusic Notebook,* Volume 3, No. II (1977).

Care, Ross. "Symphonists for the Sillies: The Composers for the Disney Shorts." *Funnyworld,* Volume 18 (Summer 1978).

Care, Ross. "Threads of Melody: The Evolution of a Major Film Score: Walt Disney's *Bambi*." *Wonderful Inventions*, Iris Newsom, Editor. Washington, D.C.: The Library of Congress (1985).

An Interview with Carl Stalling

by MIKE BARRIER

Carl Stalling was the person most responsible for changing people's notions of how much could be accomplished in a seven-minute cartoon score. Stalling was born in Lexington, Missouri, on November 10, 1891. Beginning with the time he spent working with Walt Disney in Kansas City, Missouri, in the mid-1920s, Stalling would have a profound effect on the sound and style of cartoon music throughout the three-decade studio cartoon era. While he did not score *Steamboat Willie* (1928), he wrote the music for the first dozen Mickey Mouse cartoons, while simultaneously inspiring Disney's second series of shorts, the Silly Symphonies, which he also scored for a year. After spending time at Ub Iwerks' studio and doing instrumental and arranging work for Disney, he ended up at Warner Bros., where he worked as musical director for the animation division from 1936 to 1958.

When Disney's attention began shifting away from his shorts to the animated features, Warner Bros. and other studios plowed full-bore into the cartoon world. Stalling's style—already established by his work with Disney and Iwerks—became even more clearly defined in his Warner Bros. scores. He combined a pastiche approach of using melodies from every possible genre (folk, Tin Pan Alley, swing, classical) with short, original instrumental lines to create a ongoing sense of motion, deftly matching the implicit rhythmic pulse inherent in the Warner Bros. shorts. With the nonstop popularity of Bugs, Daffy, Porky, and their compatriots, the Looney Tunes and Merrie Melodies cartoons have been on television for forty years on end, firmly placing Stalling's animated sounds in the ears of every aspiring composer—for animation or otherwise. His death on November 25, 1971, did nothing to increase his practically nonexistent fame as a composer; only with the release of *The Carl Stalling Project*, volumes one and two (1990 and 1995, respectively), did music fans truly begin to appreciate the music that had defined not only hundreds of Warner Bros. shorts, but countless other cartoons produced in the last seventy years. The importance of this interview comes not just from how much Stalling describes how he approached his work—it was also the *only* extensive interview of any kind ever conducted with him, and was published only once, in 1971, years before his popularity would soar to its current heights.

IT'S INSTRUCTIVE TO listen to the soundtrack of a Warner Bros. Cartoon—especially one in pantomime—without watching the pictures. The music and the sound effects are mirrors of the action, so completely integrated into the whole that, for many of us, Carl Stalling's music and Treg Brown's sound effects are the common thread that holds the Warner cartoons together. Stalling's music is always as vigorous, funny and inventive as the animation. He composed the scores for more than six hundred Warner cartoons.

Milton Gray and I recorded an interview with Carl Stalling on June 4, 1969, at his home in the Hollywood Hills. Milt and Bill Spicer recorded a second interview on November 25, 1969, and those interviews have been supplemented with many letters since then. All of this material has been pulled together in the interview that follows.

—MIKE BARRIER

MILTON GRAY: How did you become a composer of music for cartoons?

CARL STALLING: As I recall, I first met Walt Disney in the early twenties. He used to come to the Isis Theater, where I played the organ and had my own orchestra. This was music to accompany silent movies, and I played the whole afternoon and evening. When I wasn't at the organ, I'd be conducting, or playing the piano and conducting. I had a pianist for a number of years, and then I just conducted. Walt was making short commercials at that time, and he'd have us run them for him. We got acquainted, and I had him make several song films. *The End of a Perfect Day,* showing a sunset . . . Victor Herbert's "A Kiss in the Dark." The words would come on one at a time, with the music. This was before sound, of course.

Walt left for Hollywood shortly after that time, and I didn't see him again until 1928. I started writing him when sound pictures came in, and in our correspondence back and forth, we just agreed that there would be a position for a musical director at his studio. He came through Kansas City on his way to New York to record the music for *Steamboat Willie* (1928). I didn't go with him, since he already had that all set up. I had nothing to do with that.[1] Walt took a taxi to my home, and we talked principally of how sound pictures were causing a revolution in Hollywood. He had two silent pictures—*Gallopin' Gaucho* and *Plane Crazy*—already made, and he left those with me. I wrote most of the music for them at home in Kansas City. I met Walt in New York to record that music and we shared the same hotel room; we both washed out our socks in the same bathroom sink. I was with Walt when *Steamboat Willie* was previewed at the Colony Theater, down on Broadway, and we got the audience reaction. The reaction was very good. We sat on almost the last row and heard laughs and snickers all around us.[2]

MIKE BARRIER: I've read that while you were still in Kansas City, Walt wrote you from Hollywood to ask for a loan of two hundred and fifty dollars. Is that correct?

CS: Yes, and after joining him in Hollywood, I loaned him two thousand dollars. He repaid me in full long before 1933, but I don't remember the date.

BILL SPICER: Had you done any composing before your first cartoon work for Walt?

CS: No; I improvised at the theaters, and that's composing, but it's not writing it down.

BS: Could you tell us about the music you did for *The Skeleton Dance* (1929), the first of the Silly Symphonies?

CS: It was mostly original; that was forty years ago, and I can't remember if I used anything else or not. But it wasn't Saint-Saëns' *Danse Macabre*, although some writers have said it was.

MG: I've read that Walt wanted to use that music, but couldn't get copyright clearance, so he asked you to compose something similar.

CS: That's what he usually did when something was copyrighted, but my music wasn't similar at all to the *Danse Macabre*. It was mostly a fox trot, in a minor key.

© Walt Disney Enterprises, Inc.

MB: I've been told that you used some of the music from Grieg's *Peer Gynt Suite* in *The Skeleton Dance*. Do you remember using that music?

CS: No. When we were working out a story, usually for the Silly Symphonies, I would sometimes use a musical number as a pattern, suggesting a certain style or mood. I would play it on the piano for the director, and then write something similar, but original, for recording.[3]

Walt never wanted to pay for music; he wanted me to just make up something. In one picture, he wanted to use the song "School Days," but he would have had to pay for it. So he said, "Carl, can't you write something that sounds like 'School Days' but isn't?"

The Skeleton Dance goes way back to my kid days. When I was eight or ten years old, I saw an ad in *The American Boy* magazine of a dancing skeleton, and I got my dad to give me a quarter so I could send for it. It turned out to be a pasteboard cut-out of a loose-jointed skeleton, slung over a six-foot cord under the arm pits. It would "dance" when kids pulled and jerked at each end of the string.

MG: So the idea for *The Skeleton Dance* was really yours. And the story, too?

CS: If you call it a story. We'd all get together on gags, in what they called a gag meeting.

MG: What did Walt say when you brought up the idea for *The Skeleton Dance*? Did he like it right away?

CS: He was interested right away. After two or three of the Mickeys had been completed and were being run in theaters, Walt talked with me on getting started on the musical series that I had in mind. He thought I meant illustrated songs, but I didn't have that in mind at all. When I told him that I was thinking of inanimate figures, like skeletons, trees, flowers, etc., coming to life and dancing and doing other animated actions fitted to music more or less in a humorous and rhythmic mood, he became very much interested. I gave him the idea of using the four seasons, and he made a cartoon on each one of those. I scored one of them [*Springtime* (1930)] before I left.

For a name or title for the series, I suggested *not* using the word "music" or "musical," as it sounded too commonplace, but to use the word "Symphony" together with a humorous word. At the next gag meeting, I don't know who suggested it, but Walt asked me: "Carl, how would 'Silly Symphony' sound to you?" I said, "Perfect!" Then I suggested the first subject, *The Skeleton Dance,* because ever since I was a kid I had wanted to *see* real skeletons dancing and had always enjoyed seeing skeleton-dancing acts in vaudeville. As kids, we all like spooky pictures and stories, I think.

That's how the Silly Symphonies got started. Of course, everyone knows that if it had not been for Walt Disney, then in all probability there would never have been a Mickey Mouse. This makes me wonder sometimes, would there ever have been a Silly Symphony or who would have suggested *The Skeleton Dance*—if?[4]

BS: What are your recollections of *The Skeleton Dance* preview?

CS: It was a late show at the Vista Theater down on Hillhurst and Sunset in Hollywood, a small theater. Walt was disappointed in it. There were very few people there, no house. We saw *Steamboat Willie* in New York at eight or nine o'clock, with a full house. But here in Hollywood, at eleven o'clock, there were only a few stragglers. There wasn't any reaction, and Walt didn't think it went over at all. He said, "What the hell's the matter with the damned thing?" But they did ship it that night, I think, by Air Express to New York. The next we heard it was running at the Roxy, for two weeks. They liked it so well they ran it for another two weeks, a return engagement.[5]

MG: How was Walt as a boss? Was he demanding, or easy to work for?

CS: Well, he couldn't explain just what he wanted, at times. We'd go crazy trying to figure out what he wanted. But he inspired us that way. We wanted to help him, we wanted to do it, and we all worked together in that respect. That was his genius, I think, inspiring the people who worked for him to come up with new ideas.

MB: Did Walt tell you what he wanted in the way of music?

CS: He had definite ideas sometimes, and sometimes it'd be the other way around.

MG: Did you work in the same room with the animators at Disney's?

CS: Yes; everybody worked in one big room.

MB: Was that room the one called "the music room"?

CS: I only remember one big room, outside of the two business offices.[6]

MB: You invented the "tick" system of recording music for animated cartoons, didn't you? Do you recall the circumstances that led to that?

CS: The "tick" system was not really an invention, since it was not patentable. Perfect synchronization of music for cartoons was a problem, since there were so many quick changes and actions that the music had to match. The thought struck me that if each member of the orchestra had a steady beat in his ear, from a telephone receiver, this would solve the problem. I had exposure sheets for the films, with the picture broken down frame by frame, sort of like a script, and twelve of the film frames went through the projector in a half second. That gave us a beat.

MG: . . . If you chose a twelve-frame beat. You had other beats, too.

CS: Six, eight, ten, etc., depending on the kind of music used. We made recordings of "tick" sounds at different beats—a tick every eight frames, or ten frames, or twelve frames—and played this on a phonograph connected to the recording machine and to earphones. Each member of the orchestra had a single earphone, and listened to the clicks through that. It wasn't necessary for the conductor to give a beat, but I did, because one or two of the musicians didn't like to use the earphones. We had a woman cello player at Warner's, and she didn't like to use the earphones because they hurt her head or something. She was a fine cellist, so we couldn't criticize her too much, and she didn't get off the beat much.

MG: Did you record before the animation was completed, or after?

CS: Both, but usually before. The animators and I all worked from that same exposure sheet, and I just recorded from our beat, without seeing the picture. By the time they had the picture ready, I had the recorded music ready.[7]

MB: Did you pre-score much of your music at the Disney studio—did the animators fit their actions to your music, instead of the other way around? I was reading a Disney book by Bob Thomas called *The Art of Animation* again recently, and I came across this paragraph about how the early Disney cartoons were made: "The musician put the songs and tuneful bits together and handed the score to the animator [Thomas means the director]. The animator timed the music on his yellow exposure sheet and then fashioned the action to fit the music." That seems to contradict your statement that you composed your music after the exposure sheets were prepared, and not before. Is that what happened, or is *The Art of Animation* correct?

CS: Both statements are correct. Sometimes the director made the action fit a certain piece of music, and other times I wrote music to fit certain actions.

Most of the time, the directors and animators were free to do what they thought best to make the action most effective.

MB: Do you mean that not even *The Skeleton Dance* and the other Silly Symphonies were pre-scored?

CS: No. I pre-scored the music only when it wasn't possible to animate without pre-scoring. At Iwerks' and Warner's, I worked almost entirely from exposure sheets.[8]

MB: If you wrote most of your music at the Disney studio after the exposure sheets were prepared, did you confer with Walt about the beats *before* the sheets were prepared?

CS: Yes, usually, to prevent monotony. A change of beat would mean a change of tempo or rhythm, or both.[9]

MG: When was your "tick" system first used?

CS: It must have been in 1929, at Disney's, on *The Skeleton Dance.*

MB: How did you record the music for cartoons before you started using the "tick" system?

CS: I had lines drawn on the prints of the cartoons that I used for recording. The lines would show on the screen so that the whole orchestra could see them, and that's how I got my beat when I was conducting.

When I was composing the music for *Gallopin' Gaucho* and *Plane Crazy,* the two silent pictures, I had the cartoons shown at the theater where I worked, so that I could decide what music would be appropriate. I was having trouble figuring out how to get the music synchronized with the picture, then I hit on the idea of drawing 'half-moon' lines on the film that started on the left side of one frame, then moved to the right across the following frames, and then back toward the left, with the beat occurring when the line returned to the left side of the screen. That way, the beat didn't catch the musicians by surprise when we were recording. We also used these lines when we recorded the music for *The Barn Dance* [1928] in New York.

MB: I've read that Walt drew marks on the print of *Steamboat Willie* that they used for recording in New York, so that the conductor could watch the marks as they flashed on the screen and stay on the beat.

CS: I don't think he did that, because the pictures and the music seemed out of sync at times.[10]

MB: Wilfred Jackson has said that there was another line system that Ub Iwerks worked out, based on your system. He said that Ub animated a horizontal line rising and failing, and that the line was photographed at different speeds so that the complete cycle of rising and falling took eight frames, or twelve frames, or whatever the beat happened to be. He said that these loops of film would then be projected on a screen that the orchestra could watch as they recorded the music.

CS: Yes, we did that for a while. We used the line moving up and down for the fifth and sixth Mickey Mouse cartoons, *The Op'ry House* and *When the Cat's Away* [both 1929], and then we started using the "tick" system on *The Skeleton Dance.*

MG: How long was it that you had to record everything—the voices, the music, the sound effects—in one take?

CS: That was true at Disney's and for part of the time at Iwerks. But it was just two or three years until they had built a recording machine that would record three or four tracks at once onto a master negative. This is called *dubbing.*

MG: When you were at Disney's, you must have arranged and conducted both.

CS: No, I had an arranger, but I conducted.[11]

MG: You've told me that you were the first voice of Mickey Mouse; how many cartoons were made before he spoke?

CS: Not too many. They couldn't decide whether they wanted him to speak or not. I was his voice in only one picture. I don't recall the title [probably

Wild Waves (1930)] but Mickey was a lifeguard at the beach, and saved Minnie's life. She said, "My hero," and Mickey said, "Oh, shucks, that's nothin'," in a falsetto. One of the girls in the inking department did the voice for Minnie. I left not long after that, so I don't know what they did about Mickey's voice after that.[12]

MG: How was it decided that you were to do the voice for Mickey?

CS: Walt probably told me to try it. All the animators were taking a shot at it, those who wanted to. It was just a falsetto voice.

MB: Did you ever do any other cartoon voices?

CS: Yes, I did a walrus voice [also in *Wild Waves*]. I sang "Rocked in the Cradle of the Deep," but instead of using the words of the song I just sang the syllable "wa" to each note of the music. It got a lot of laughs, especially on the last note, a low, low C.

BS: How did you finally decide to leave Walt?

CS: We had different offers, from other studios. Everybody said Walt was a failure, but I realized later that it was just a trick, that they just wanted to break Walt. I went with the "Aesop's Fables Studio," but I soon gave up that contract altogether. Ub Iwerks and I left Disney at about the same time, but we went our own ways. The thing was, I wasn't going to leave unless Ub left. When Ub left I thought something was wrong. When Roy Disney told me that Ub was leaving, I told him, "Well, I guess I'll be leaving, too." It's not very pleasant to think about, because we were all good friends. But we were getting worried. Walt paid only half salary for a year or two, and I had a home and expenses. "Aesop's Fables" offered me about three times as much money.[13]

BS: How long did you stay with "Aesop's Fables"?

CS: A few months. I didn't work on any cartoons; they didn't have anything for me to do, they already had a musical director. It was all just a trick to break Walt. I couldn't live in New York, anyway. So, after freelancing for a year or more I joined Ub's studio on Western Avenue, and was with him when he moved his studio to Beverly Hills.

MB: Was Walt upset when you decided to leave?

CS: Yes, but he wasn't as upset as Roy, his brother. That was pretty hard. We were all very good friends, Walt and Roy and Ub and I. Of course, I owe everything to Walt Disney; he gave me that first break in Hollywood.

As I remember, Walt offered me a third of the Silly Symphonies, long before Ub and I left. I never had any stock in the Disney company, but I was to receive one third of the profits of the Silly Symphonies for as long as I worked at the studio. I accepted, but leaving Walt voided the agreement.

I was with Ub for six months or so, until 1932, when I left. I did some freelance work and some arranging and piano playing for Walt. I worked on *Three Little Pigs* [1933] and about ten other cartoons. I arranged the score and played the piano during the recording on all of them. When you see one little pig playing the piano in *Three Little Pigs,* you're hearing my playing.

That was the last Disney picture I worked on. In the summer of 1933, I rejoined Ub in Beverly Hills and stayed with him until I went to Warner Bros. in 1936.

MB: I've always heard that Walt resented people leaving him—did you see any evidence of that when you worked for him on *Three Little Pigs?*

CS: None at all.

MB: Did you ever see Walt in later years?

CS: Yes, and he was always very courteous. I called him once, after Warner's closed

Carl Stalling during his years with Ub Iwerks' studio in the 1930s. Courtesy of Mike Barrier.

in 1953 for six months, and I asked him if there was any work there, and he said no, and asked me if I had any gray hairs. I said, "Yeah, what's left."

MG: Have you ever had any regrets about leaving Walt?

CS: No, except for pleasant associations. It was all very new and exciting. My leaving turned out better for Walt and it turned out better for me. At Warner Bros., I could use a lot more popular songs; they didn't mind paying for them, as they had their own music publishing firm.

MG: Was there much difference in working for Walt and working for Ub and Warner's?

CS: No, it was about the same, with the advantage of experience.

MG: You were just salaried with Iwerks, weren't you? You weren't given a share of the studio?

CS: Right.

MG: Did you have an assistant at the Iwerks Studio?

CS: No, it was all mine, including the arranging.

MB: How large an orchestra did they use at the Disney and Iwerks studios?

CS: Eight to twelve players. At Warner's we had as many as fifty or so, their main studio orchestra. We had a vocal group, too, once in a while. The chorus director wrote the music for them.

MB: Did you go from Iwerks to Warner after the Iwerks studio closed, or was it still open when you left?

CS: It was closed, but I was idle for only a few weeks before I went to Warner's.

MB: When you first came to Warner's, they had somebody else writing cartoon music, didn't they?

CS: They had a man who had had some trouble with Leon Schlesinger, who was making the cartoons at that time. I was hired to replace him, in 1936. I don't know what the trouble was about, but the inside of the music room desk was all cluttered with empty whiskey bottles.

MB: Schlesinger knew of your work already?

CS: Oh, yes. There was a director and story and gag man working for Schlesinger named Ben Hardaway—they called him "Bugs"—who had been a newspaper cartoonist back in Kansas City, and I knew him there. He was also at Ub's, when I was there, and then he went to Schlesinger's. He was there when my predecessor was laid off, and he recommended me very highly to Schlesinger.

MB: Now, after you went to work for Schlesinger, you were the only composer Warner's had until you retired?

CS: For the cartoons, yes, for twenty-two years. I retired in 1958.

MB: Did your music differ much at Warner's from what it had been at Disney's and Iwerks'?

CS: Yes, because at Warner's, I could use popular music. That opened up a new field so far as the kind of music we could use. At Disney's, we had to go back to the nineteenth century, to classical music, to "My Old Kentucky Home."
    When I came out here, there was no law that cartoon music was copyrightable. That went into effect in the late forties. Then they started paying royalties retroactive from the day I started with Warner Bros. They're still paying, on the television reruns. Royalties are paid to composers whose music I used, and also to me for my original music.

MG: Apart from the increased use of popular songs, did you notice much of a change in your music over the years, as you composed it?

CS: It depended on the picture. When we had a very modern picture, I used as much music in the modern style as I could think up—augmented intervals, and so forth. But other than that, my style didn't change much.

MB: Of your music for cartoons, how much was other composers' music that you reworked and how much was original?

CS: Eighty to ninety per cent was original. It had to be, because you had to match the music to the action, unless it was singing or something like that.

MB: Were you ever ill, so that someone else had to be called in to do some cartoons for you?

CS: Yes, once. I had a brain operation in 1950. I bumped my head and a clot as big as my hand formed in between my skull and my brain. I was ill for four or five weeks. Gene Poddany, Chuck Jones' composer now, and Milt Franklyn filled in for me.

MG: They were making four cartoons every five weeks at Warner's back in the Forties, so you had to turn out almost one complete score every week. How did you turn out so much work?

CS: We had an arranger, of course. I would write the piano part—the basic, skeleton parts, you might say—and jot down all the cues and everything, then send it to the arranger, who worked at home. He arranged the music for orchestra, but whenever I wanted to feature an instrument or instruments in the orchestra, I'd make a notation. It took about a week, maybe eight days for me to prepare each score.

MB: Did you ever get really pressed for time?

CS: No, I had that schedule, and I stayed on time, although I sometimes had to do some homework in the evenings.

MB: Were there ever any cartoons that you had trouble writing music for, where the music didn't seem to suggest itself naturally?

CS: No. You see, I had played in theaters for about twenty years before sound came in. We improvised all the time, on the organ. I'd have to put music out for the orchestra, for features, but for comedies and newsreels we just improvised at the organ. So I really was used to composing for films before I started writing for cartoons. I just imagined myself playing for a cartoon in the theater, improvising, and it came easier.

MB: Did you have certain instruments that you liked to use more than others in your cartoon scores?

CS: The bassoon . . . the trombone, the slides on the trombone . . . the violin, with the glissandos, for comic effects. The viola is very good for mysterious effects.

MG: Did you ever record your music at Warner's before the exposure sheets were completed, so that the cartoon was fitted to the music?

CS: Yes, when there was a song, usually one that Mel Blanc sang. They'd indicate so many frames for each word on the exposure sheets.[14]

BS: Did you write the music for the opening of the Warner cartoons, with the shield and the bullseye?

CS: No, I selected it, but that was a tune already owned by Warner Bros., "Merrily We Roll Along."

BS: How was the opening sound done, that "boinngg"?

CS: That was done with an electric guitar.

BS: Was the sound electronically altered?

CS: No, they just struck a chord and brought it down.

MB: Playing for a cartoon score would be hard for many musicians to get used to, wouldn't it?

CS: The musicians said they enjoyed the cartoons more than anything else. They looked forward to coming down to record the cartoons. It was screwy stuff, you know.

A cartoon score was usually made up of about ten sections. We'd run through a section once or twice—usually just once—and then record it. We had a wonderful orchestra at Warner's. It took about three hours to record a cartoon score.[15]

MG: Did the directors show you the storyboards, and you then decided from that what music would be most suitable?

CS: That's right.

MB: Did the directors tell you what they wanted in the way of music? Did they want a certain kind of music for particular scenes?

CS: As a rule, no. Sometimes they'd just want something with a twelve-beat for one sequence, and then maybe an eight-beat for the next sequence, and so on. Sometimes they'd build a whole picture around a song like "What's Up, Doc," which I wrote, but many popular songs were treated likewise, using the song title as the cartoon title.

I'd say Chuck Jones and Friz Freleng were the easiest directors to work with, because they had something there. Tex Avery was also great, and Bob Clampett was really inspiring, he really had ideas. He was a fascinating guy. I hated to see Bob go.

MB: Were there any cartoon characters that it was especially enjoyable to write scores for, or did it make any difference?

CS: Each character had a different feeling, enjoyable, and, of course, very original, but there weren't any that were especially enjoyable to work with, unless it would be Bugs Bunny. He was the standout.

BS: Did you ever get tired of doing music for cartoons with "funny animals"?

CS: No, there were several directors at Warner's, and when you got through with one there was another one waiting for you. There was plenty of variety.

MG: Many times, you used the music to tell the story. In *Catch as Cats Can* (1947), Sylvester the cat swallowed a bar of soap and was hiccupping bubbles, and the music was "I'm Forever Blowing Bubbles." Did you make up those gags yourself, or did the directors help you with that?

CS: It happened both ways.

MB: You worked closely with the sound effects men, didn't you, to keep the music and sound effects coordinated?

CS: Yes; Treg Brown handled all the sound effects. Treg had thousands of sound effects on short reels, and he would make up a whole soundtrack out of these, as well as adding new ones for each cartoon. He had been there for three or four years when I came to Warner's. His room was next to mine.

MB: Did you ever actually write your music so that a sound effect came out as part of the music?

CS: Yes, and sometimes I'd just lay out altogether and let the sound effect stand alone.

MB: In some of Chuck Jones' Road Runner cartoons, there are long, involved gags for which there's no music; nothing is heard except the sound effects. Was this something Chuck wanted to do, or was this your idea?

CS: I don't remember, but I do remember that if the sound effect called for it, we'd stop the music altogether. And, of course, for a lot of the dialogue we would stop the music or we'd cut it down to just a few strings.

MG: Did you find a cartoon with lots of dialogue harder to compose for?

CS: Yes, because you don't dare drown out the voices. Sometimes on television, or in features, the music is way too loud, and you can't hear what they're saying. One trouble with cartoons today is that they do so much dialogue that the music doesn't mean much.

MB: Was it your idea to use Mendelssohn's "Fingal's Cave" for the Minah Bird's walk in Chuck Jones' Inki cartoons?

CS: Yes, and it went over so well that we had to use it every time.

MB: Did you ever suggest a cartoon idea to a director that would involve a certain kind of music? Did you, say, ever suggest to Chuck Jones that he might make a cartoon using a certain piece of classical music?

CS: It could be, but as a rule, he worked out the ideas first.

MB: Did you ever do any composing for live-action features?

CS: I did one reel of a feature for Jack Benny, *The Horn Blows at Midnight,* and it was just as bad as the picture, which was a big flop. I didn't want to do it, but Leo Forbstein, the orchestra's general musical director—he'd hire all the musicians—and head of the music department, wanted me to. I'd played with him in Kansas City theaters, the Royal and Newman Theaters. So when I came out here, I liked it much better at Warner Bros. than at Disney's, because of that association. We'd known each other and worked together for years. He played violin and I played piano, and sometimes for the morning shows, that's all we'd have for an hour or so, and then I'd go up and play the organ.

MB: When you'd written your music, and had it ready to go, did anybody else have to look at it first and approve it before you recorded it?

CS: No, no one.

MB: Was there ever a time when you'd recorded your music that somebody said something should be different, and wanted to change it?

CS: Yes, once. Ray Heindorf, director of the Warner orchestra now, took Leo Forbstein's place when Leo passed on. He said a certain four bars sounded like the tune "Chicago." I thought I knew that tune, and I couldn't hear any similarity, but he had me change it. They didn't want anything that might cause a lawsuit over copyrighted music.

MG: Before you retired, did you start training other composers to take over your job? I know that some screen credits list you and another composer, Milt Franklyn.

CS: He was my arranger, and then he took over composing after I left. He died, I think in 1962. He was a very fine musician.

MG: What was your schooling before you went to work in the theaters?

CS: I had a private teacher; I started when I was six years old. My dad was a carpenter, and he found a broken toy piano. It was all broken to pieces and had little metal keys, like xylophone keys. One of them was missing, so he had to make one himself. He gave me a little frame box, and put the keys on that, and made some little hammers, and I started picking out tunes on that. That's how they started me studying piano.

MB: So then you started formal study of the piano after that, when you were six, and really learned how to play it.

CS: Yes. I couldn't reach the pedal when I started playing; somebody had to pedal for me. I couldn't do the pedaling on the old church organs, either. I started playing them when I was eight or ten years old.

MB: How old were you when you started playing in theaters?

CS: Seventeen or eighteen. I didn't finish high school; I only went two years. My ear gave me trouble and I couldn't hear the teachers, so I had to quit.

MG: So you couldn't hear too well even while you were composing all that music for Disney and Warner Bros.?

CS: I had trouble there, but the trouble was only in talking with the boys, not with the music.

MG: What was your very first job as a musician?

CS: I played the piano at a theater about a block from former President Truman's home in Independence, Missouri, around 1910. That was my first job in the Kansas City area, but I'd played the piano in 1904 at Lexington, where I was born. Lexington is forty miles east of Independence. In those days, they just wanted a piano going while the operator was changing reels. In the cities, they had two machines, so you didn't have to wait for the next reel, but in little towns like Lexington they hadn't gotten that far yet.

MB: Do you remember when you saw your first movie?

CS: The first movie I ever saw was *The Great Train Robbery*. I saw it in a tent at a street fair in Lexington, around 1903. It made such an impression on me that from then on I had only one desire in life: to be connected with the movies in some way.

Originally appeared in Funnyworld, *Volume 13 (Spring 1971), 21-27. © 1971 by Mike Barrier. Reprinted by permission.*

------

[1] Wilfred Jackson has described the preparation of the *Steamboat Willie* music track this way: "I played the harmonica so that Walt could tell the tempo that he wanted for 'Steamboat Bill' and 'Turkey in the Straw' [two public-domain tunes used in the score for the picture]. I would set the metronome and play 'Steamboat Bill' or 'Turkey' or whatever, and when Walt heard what sounded good for the tune and his action both, then he knew that was the beat he wanted. Walt knew how fast film went, and I knew about the metronome. Putting the two together made it possible to pre-time music to animation when the music would be recorded later, just by simple mathematics.

"Walt made up the exposure sheet for *Willie*. What I worked out was a bar sheet or dope sheet, to indicate measures of music. It wasn't like a score, because it didn't have five bar lines. It had a little square for each beat in each measure, and it had an indication of the tempo; it was in twelve frames, or sixteen frames, or whatever, to the beat. Within that square, the key action and the scene number was indicated, so that the bar sheet showed that each scene began so many frames before a certain measure. That way, we were able to synchronize the scenes, which were shot separately, of course. Each individual scene would be shot from the exposure sheet, but from the bar sheet, you could tell where to lay the scene in against the music track, once you found out where the first beat of the music was. My contributions to sound cartoons were that I knew what a metronome was, and I worked out what was first called a dope sheet and later a bar sheet."

Walt later told Jackson that when he stopped at Kansas City and showed Jackson's "score" to Carl Stalling, Stalling's comment was, "This man's no musician." Jackson says that Walt enjoyed kidding him about that thereafter, and adds, "Carl was right."

[2] According to David Smith of the Disney Archives, a telegram from Walt Disney to his brother Roy, dated October 24, 1928, says: "Carl arrives Friday." That would have been October 26, 1928. *Steamboat Willie* premiered on November 18, 1928 (the September date usually given is wrong).

Walt and Carl returned from New York in December 1928, and Walt mentioned in a letter that he had been there three months and had synchronized four cartoons (*Willie, Gaucho, Plane* and *The Barn Dance*). Carl Stalling recalls that they made at least one other trip to New York, in 1929, to record the music for *The Op'ry House.*

[3] According to David Smith of the Disney Archives, the studio obtained a license to use "The March of the Dwarfs" from Grieg's *Lyric Suite* in *The Skeleton Dance*. The rest of the score was original music by Carl Stalling.

[4] Wilfred Jackson adds his recollection of the start of the Silly Symphonies: "Walt and Carl would time the pictures in Walt's office. Timing them consisted of working out what the music would be and what the action would be." (The director—Walt, in this case—would prepare the exposure sheets after agreement had been reached on the timing. Later, the Disney directors had assistants who would transfer the timing onto the sheets.) "A lot of times Walt would want more time or less time for the action than could fit the musical phrase. So, there would be a pretty good argument going on in there. We'd sit out there, in the next room, and enjoy it. Walt could be pretty stiff when he got in an argument, and we'd be glad we weren't on the other end of it. But, finally, Walt worked out a thing with Carl. He said, 'Look, let's work it out this way. We'll make two series. On the Mickey Mouse pictures you make your music fit my action the very best you can. But we'll make another series, and they'll be musical shorts. And in them music will take precedence and we'll adjust our action the best we can to what you think is the right music.' Those were the Sillys, and that was a way of getting something done and not getting in a dog fight all of the time.

"Both of those people could be pretty obstinate when they felt like it. Carl could stand up to Walt and give him what for and when it came to the music, if you pushed him a little too far he could put up a pretty good argument."

[5] Differing accounts of *The Skeleton Dance* previews have been published in two books. Diane Disney Miller, in *The Story of Walt Disney*, describes two different previews—one in the morning, before a small audience, and another at a large, important theater, with favorable reactions both times. Bob Thomas, in *The Art of Animation,* says, "At the preview, the theater was rocked with laughter." Mrs. Miller describes in considerable detail the tribulations of the cartoon before its successful run at the Roxy, saying that exhibitors refused to accept it at first.

[6] Wilfred Jackson recalls that when Stalling and Walt Disney timed the pictures, they moved the piano into Walt's office, and that became the first "music room"—the room shared by the animation

director and the music director. Later, when production had become more specialized, and there was a story department, the story men would work on their stories to a certain point and then move the story boards into "the music room" (there eventually were several), where the director and the composer would work on them. Jackson says that the "one big room" that Stalling remembers was divided by partitions that were open at the top.

[7] Wilfred Jackson recalls that recording the soundtrack for an early Disney cartoon was usually delayed until the cartoon was complete or production had reached the point where it was reasonably certain that no more changes would be made in it. (Even after the exposure sheets had been prepared, an animator could suggest spreading out or compressing a gag, or making other changes.) This practice continued even after the introduction of the "tick" system. Jackson believes that Stalling is "covering a broad spectrum" and referring to his career at the Warner studio as well as at Disney's.

[8] Bob Clampett has said that the action and music were synchronized for the first Looney Tune, in 1929, this way: Hugh Harman and Rudy Ising decided on a beat with their musician, then timed the cartoon on the sheets of written music, indicating so many frames for each action. The action was coordinated with the bars of music. The timing was transferred from the music sheet to exposure sheets, and then the music was recorded with the tick earphones. Hugh Harman has confirmed the accuracy of this description.

[9] For more on this, see footnote 4.

[10] Diane Disney Miller, in her 1956 biography, *The Story of Walt Disney*, quotes her father as saying, "We drew a mark on our film every twelve frames with India ink. As that mark went through the projector, it made a white flash on the screen and if he watched for that flash and used it as a visual substitute for the tick-tock of an old-fashioned metronome, the man who was conducting our orchestra could stay on the beat."

Bob Clampett has pointed out that black India ink marks wouldn't make white flashes when projected, but rather black flashes, unless they projected the negative, which is of course extremely unlikely.

Wilfred Jackson believes that marks of some kind may have been used during the recording: "That might have been, they had to do a little work with it back in New York due to the fact that they didn't have a score that could be followed." Jackson believes there is nothing wrong with the synchronization.

[11] During his tenure as the Disney studio's musical director, Carl Stalling composed the music for nineteen of the first twenty Disney sound cartoons. They are listed below in order; all are Mickey Mouse cartoons except for the Silly Symphonies, indicated by an (S).

Gallopin' Gaucho
Plane Crazy
The Barn Dance
The Op'ry House
When the Cat's Away

The Skeleton Dance (S)
The Barnyard Battle
The Plow Boy
The Carnival Kid
Mickey's Follies
El Terrible Toreador (S)
Mickey's Choo Choo
Springtime (S)
The Jazz Fool
Hell's Bells (S)
Jungle Rhythm
Merry Dwarfs (S)
The Haunted House
Wild Waves

The second series of Disney cartoons began with two Silly Symphonies, *Summertime* and *Autumn*, that continued Stalling's series based on the seasons, but Stalling doesn't believe that he scored them.

[12] Minnie's voice for most of her career was supplied by Marcellite Garner (now Mrs. Richard Wall, Sr.). However, Mrs. Wall believes she began doing Minnie's voice by singing for the soundtrack of *The Cactus Kid* (1930), which was made after Stalling had left the Disney studio. Wilfred Jackson believes that *The Cactus Kid* was the first cartoon for which the dialogue was recorded in advance, so that the animation could be tailored to the dialogue. Before that, the voices were recorded when the music was recorded, and the dialogue had to be recorded to a beat, to synchronize it with the action.

Walt Disney himself did Mickey Mouse's voice most of the time up until the middle 1930s, when Jim Macdonald, a veteran sound effects man at the studio, began doing it. Macdonald also did the voices for Gus and Jacques in *Cinderella*. On one occasion, while Walt was still doing Mickey's voice, Clarence Nash (better known as the voice of Donald Duck) filled in as Mickey while Walt was in Europe.

Mickey had spoken in cartoons before *Wild Waves*, although his dialogue was limited, and (according to Mark Kausler, who has seen the film recently) in at least one early Mickey cartoon, *The Carnival Kid*, Mickey speaks in a "most un-Mouse like voice."

[13] According to David Smith of the Disney Archives, Iwerks left the Disney studio on January 25, 1930, and Stalling left the same week.

[14] Bob Clampett has said that songs were pre-scored for the Warner cartoons this way: Mel Blanc's singing would be recorded beforehand, but not the accompaniment. Blanc would sing in time with a tick record that he listened to through his earphones. The recording of Blanc's voice would be read off onto exposure sheets by Treg Brown, and given to the director of the cartoon. Stalling then wrote the musical score from the exposure sheets, including the accompaniment for Blanc's song. Stalling agrees with Clampett's account.

[15] Bob Clampett has contributed his own memories of the recording sessions: "Many's the time that Carl, Treg [Brown] and I waited while the fifty-piece Warner Bros. orchestra would finish recording

the score for a Bogart or Bette Davis feature, and then bat out one of my Bugs Bunny or Porky shorts. When Leo Forbstein [the orchestra's director] told them to put our cartoon score on their stands, a wave of relief would spread through the entire orchestra. Suddenly, two violinists would pop up and begin dueling with their bows, or some such horseplay. Others would call out things in jest, and by the time Carl stepped to the podium, raised his baton and they broke into the unnaturally rapid tempo of our Merrie Melodies theme song ('Merrily We Roll Along'), or subtitle, or whatever, they would be in a completely different mood for Bugs than for Bogey."

Hidey Hidey Hidey Ho …
Boop-Boop-a-Doop!

The Fleischer Studio and Jazz Cartoons

by JAKE AUSTEN

WHILE THE MUSIC composed for animation may have drawn on a wider variety of sources than almost any other twentieth-century musical genre, it rarely drew from the powerful, sexually charged, gritty music that emerged from African American pockets of the South and the urban North. This is not surprising, considering that the prevailing aesthetic of cartoons has been one of good, clean fun. But the Fleischer studio was a far cry from this wholesome model. As opposed to its slick competitor (and eventual usurper) Disney, Fleischer was known for raw, dark, instinctual, horny animation that reflected New York's urban landscape. As home of the erotic Betty Boop, the uncouth Popeye, and Koko the naughty inkdrop of a clown, Fleischer was the edgiest of the animation houses. It is only natural that this studio would be the one to merge two of the great American art forms most successfully. For a brief period in the early 1930s, Fleischer would produce a handful of shorts that stand out as the greatest jazz cartoons ever made.

Visionary Max Fleischer, with his brother Dave (who directed the cartoons and came up with many of the frantic, bizarre gags that were a studio signature), pioneered animation not only in an artistic sense, but also scientifically. They patented innovations and experimented with technology that revolutionized American animation. Most significantly, Max developed the Rotoscope, a method of filming live action and then tracing over it frame by frame. Ideas like the Rotograph (which helped combine animation and live action) and multi-layered 3-D moving backgrounds followed. But it was the studio's experiments with sound that led to some of its greatest successes.

Years before Disney broke through with the soundie *Steamboat Willie* (1928), the Fleischers teamed with Dr. Lee DeForest, an inventor whose stubbornness when dealing with the studios stymied the success of his cinematic audio innovations. It is not surprising that the Fleischers were the ones to create the first sound cartoons, because their previous breakthrough had audiences filling movie houses with song during the silent era. While sing-alongs in theaters, led by the organist and lyrics projected, one line at a time, with the use of glass slides, were not uncommon, the Fleischers were the first to perfectly weave the sing-along and the motion picture by making cartoons featuring a bouncing ball that led the audience through the lyrics printed on screen. In the summer of 1924 sound was added to these "Song Car-Tunes," to the delight of audiences.

When sound became an integral part of Fleischer Studios, Lou Fleischer, a musician, joined his brothers and became a valuable asset. Before this, Lou had operated a music school and worked as a professional ukulele arranger. At Fleischer he chose songs, did arrangements, composed background music, and physically bounced the ball in the Follow the Bouncing Ball cartoons (the actual ball wasn't animated, but rather filmed live through an innovative process. Note that the ball was on a stick, so Globetrotter-esque dribbling skills were not required to keep up with the music). Max Fleischer was less invested in featuring original music than Disney. Dave's initial role involved creating soundtracks by choosing to either play copyright-free music or 78-rpm records from the catalog of their distributor, Paramount. When the musician's union put a stop to this practice, they relied more on the house composers Sammy Timberg and Sammy Lerner (who created Betty Boop's endearing short songs; Lerner also wrote the *Popeye* theme) and on the Paramount orchestra, with its conductor, Manny Baer.

Paramount's pull also allowed for a different kind of musical collaboration, leading to the remarkable jazz cartoons that stand out as some of the Fleischers' best work. The Fleischers used Paramount's studios to film live performances by popular musical acts including Cab Calloway, Louis Armstrong, Don Redman, the Royal Samoans, Rudy Valee, the violinist David Rubinoff, Ethel Merman, and the Mills Brothers. Fleischer then produced cartoons in which the artists would be seen briefly performing live at the beginning of the picture, after which their song would be incorporated into animated adventures. In exchange for appearing in the cartoons for a modest fee, Paramount agreed to book the acts in their theater chain, with the cartoons serving as advance work in the weeks preceding their appearances. Calloway reported that this method was very successful, drawing huge crowds to his shows. He also is said to have been extremely delighted by his appearance as an animated ghostly walrus in the *Minnie the Moocher* (1932) cartoon.

The jazz-themed shorts that featured Armstrong and Calloway are some of the most striking cartoons ever released, both for their bizarre visual style and their disturbing racial politics. The Fleischers' New York production house, with its history of producing work with a densely packed, dark, urban, ethnic vibe (contrasting with Disney's West Coast bliss), easily connected with this music. In fact, the Fleischer animators seemed to engage in a form of jazz themselves. While the laborious process of animation can never involve instantaneous improvisation, what the Fleischers presented on the screen almost belied this limitation. The *Betty Boop* cartoons feature every character (and in these films the animals, vegetation, machines, and household objects are likely to be or to become characters at any instant) constantly bouncing and swaying to the rhythm of the soundtrack, ready to riff when their moment to take a solo (with a sight gag) comes around. When Popeye walks down the street, he's scatting a sailor's song or mumbling a free-associated series of one-liners and non-sequitors (provided by the clever Jack Mercer). According to Fleischer biographer Leslie Cabarga, Mercer and May Questel (who played Boop and Olive Oyl) "ad-libbed like crazy," which is why the characters' mouths often don't move when we hear them speaking.

Also adding to this free and loose sensibility was the studio's signature use of surrealism and a near disdain for continuity (why is Betty in the jungle? How come the witch turned into a dragon?). Leonard Maltin, in his history of animation, *Of Mice and Magic,* writes of the Talkartoons (the Song Car-Tunes' successors) that "any semblance of script in them is purely coincidental." This freedom from traditional narrative allows the cartoons to fully delve into the grotesque while also allowing gags and visual absurdities to fly at an exhausting pace. This otherness, however, does not function as escapist fantasy. Through the surrealism, Fleischer's work seems to be addressing adult fears and lusts in a hyperrealistic way. As Max Fleischer's long tradition of mingling live action and animation suggests, these cartoons are always about the real world. When Disney would Rotoscope, you get Snow White's dreamy ballet-like movement. With Fleischer, you get a confrontational clown or a Harlem-shuffling Calloway.

The bizarre, elaborate visual contents of Fleischer's four most powerful jazz cartoons are impossible to describe fully, but they are so important in the histories of animation and filmed African American music that some attempt needs to be made. *Minnie the Moocher*, *Snow White* (1933), and *Old Man of the Mountain* (1933) all feature Cab Calloway and his orchestra. *I'll Be Glad When You're Dead You Rascal You* (1932) features what was long considered some of the earliest surviving footage of Louis Armstrong. While these films contain challenging racial imagery, they also contain amazing, electric energy, and a strange, disturbing synergy between the sound and visual tracks.

All three of the Calloway films involve Betty being pursued by monsters, either in caves or on a mountain. In *Minnie the Moocher,* she leaves the oppressive but safe confines of her ethnic, immigrant home to find the outside world a dark, creepy place filled with African American music, ghosts (spooks?), skeletons, and some of the most ghoulish sight gags ever animated. In Calloway's most bizarre "appearance," his voice and Rotoscoped body movements are enacted by a blubbery ghost walrus. At one point, exposure to this alien, racially charged world actually turns Betty and her boyfriend Bimbo black. In *Snow White* (filmed half a decade before Disney's famed version), Betty stars in a convoluted version of the fairy tale involving an evil witch and a seductively incomprehensible transformation of Koko into a ghost who sings and Rotoscope dances to Cab Calloway's "St. James Infirmary." In *The Old Man of the Mountain* (the cartoon that most conforms to Calloway's song), the disgusting, lecherous Old Man threateningly pursues Betty, until his long phallic nose is tied in a knot, limping flaccidly. Early in the film we are informed of his hypersexuality when a hippo reveals that he fathered her bearded triplets.

The Old Man is distinctly Caucasian. At no point in the Calloway films does a character who appears to be black sing with Cab's voice. While perhaps this was intended to appease conservatives who did not want to see blacks and whites on screen together, it is the contemporary liberal audience who benefits from this. Surely the "jigaboo" character designs the animators might have employed would make these far more difficult to watch today (see the ape-like "Africans" in the Armstrong picture or the Fleischer *Superman* cartoons for reference). However, even as a spectral sort of walrus, when Cab begins to dance, his Rotoscoped moves are unmistakable. If the slinky, sexy spirit of the song was not already conveyed by the raw, soulful animation, this striking black dance performance (with the walrus's tail serving as an unmistakable waggling penis) drives everything home.

Louis Armstrong should have been so lucky as to have been portrayed as a thick-shlonged, racially ambiguous sea creature. In *I'll Be Glad When You're Dead You Rascal You*, nearby Harlem is abandoned for "the Dark Continent," as Betty, Bimbo, and Koko go on safari. (Actually, jungle themes, as well as plantation themes, were prevalent in the Harlem nightclubs where whites would go see jazz performed, so some of this motif may have been inspired by Lou's trips uptown to watch the acts when choosing songs for these movies.) After being wooed by a monkey, Betty and company are captured by natives who look like slightly larger monkeys wearing grass skirts. After Bimbo and Koko escape from the cannibals' cooking pot they are chased by a native who begins to fly and then becomes a giant, detached head (with thick white lips, a monkey nose, and bulging eyes). Then that head morphs into Armstrong's. As Satchmo's mammoth, live-action flying head chases the duo, singing about fried chicken, I imagine the NAACP Image Award may have been slipping away from the filmmakers. The ugliness intensifies when drummer Tubby Hall is visually linked with a cannibal stirring a cooking pot. Once again the Fleischers introduce the idea that to enter a black world (signified equally by jazz and cannibalism) is both a perilous endeavor and a thrilling adventure. More significantly, these scenarios fit right into Betty's world as the not-for-the-kiddies lyrics (with absolutely overt references to hard drugs and sex) seem to match the Fleischers' transgressive visuals perfectly.

Several writers have implied that the Fleischers were unaware of the explicit content of the jazz lyrics, but I find that doubtful. The drug references seem to be embodied by the "psychedelic" surrealism of the piece, and sex was a consistent feature of Betty Boop cartoons. With her thick, gartered thighs, high heels, and cleavage, Betty was (until the Hays Code cleaned things up) always the object of her costars' (and the audience's) desires. She would have her clothes fall off (revealing sexy lingerie), her skirt blown upward, her body revealed by a strong backlight, and she would occasionally "go native," performing a topless hula dance (she even lures Popeye with this ploy). In fact, her irresistibility is one of the redeeming factors of the racial politics in her jazz pictures. Despite all the disturbing elements, the fact that black men (or creatures with the voices of black men) are chasing her is not *The Birth of a Nation* revisited. Betty is routinely chased by every race, species, and inanimate object, from fish to fossils. In fact, race mixing as a concept should not bother Betty and doesn't seem to threaten audiences. Her boyfriend Bimbo is another genus (he's a dog, as was Betty in her initial appearances). If anything, Betty seemed to challenge preconceived notions of white femininity.

Though we now think of cartoons as kiddie fare, in this era cartoon shorts were primarily shown as parts of packages including adult features, and Max Fleischer never made real kiddie cartoons. His work was always aimed squarely at an adult audience, with sex washed down with plenty of alcohol references (when Betty becomes president she repeals Prohibition; a flea in the Old Man of the Mountain's beard delivers a frosty mug of ale from the Old Man's shaggy facial hair to quench his thirst as he chases Betty). Paramount's promotion department called this use of mature subject matter "smartness for the sophisticates." To Max Fleischer, animation was "adult," and not only in the X-rated connotations of the word. Two of the dream projects he worked on were an animated version of the sinking of the Lusitania and a feature-length film (containing only spare animation) explaining Einstein's theory of relativity. An inventory of Fleischer's most popular characters makes it clear that his movies never had the youthful portion of the audience in mind: Betty Boop looks like a hooker and Popeye is a crude, brawling sailor (*Mad* magazine had Popeye offer this depreciating self-analysis: "I gets into silly fights all the time, I talks lousy engclich . . . an' I goes out wit' skinny, ugly broads!"). Even the Fleischers' seemingly wholesome characters have a dark side. Their Superman seems to focus on the dire, violent burden of his great power, and Koko, the mischievous clown who was the studio's star of the silent era, certainly calls to mind the ominous aspects of circus jesters that make them the subject of children's nightmares.

Ultimately, what the Fleischer Studio cartoons may represent is an indulging of the artists. Max Fleischer rose to fame not only as producer, but also as a costar of his early movies: each Koko the Clown "Out of the Inkwell" movie opens with Max's hand dipping a pen into ink to create his star. This is a perfect symbol of how the artistic process, as opposed to the calculated product, may have been what motivated the originality in the strongest Fleischer cartoons. The animators' indulgence of their lusty desires results in shocking, but magnetic, Betty Boop features. Their use of stream-of-consciousness visual imagery (and improvisational dialogue) allowed for nonlinear narrative logic and powerful surrealism. In these ways the artists at Fleischer had more in common with the jazz musicians they worked with than their competitors had. Perhaps there's a clear path from "Hidey Hidey Hidey Ho" to "Boop-Boop-a-Doop," and even from "Boop-Boop-a Doop" to bebop.

I Love to Hear a Minstrel Band

Walt Disney's The Band Concert

by DAVID WONDRICH

WALT DISNEY. ANIMATOR. Entrepreneur. And, by the evidence of his 1935 short, *The Band Concert,* social historian and musicologist.

Quick cut to our text. The cartoon—the first Mickey Mouse short in color, and often cited as Disney's best—opens with Mickey conducting an old-fashioned (even by 1935 standards) small-town brass band: a half-dozen pigs, cows, dogs, and horses, wearing uniforms that don't match and brandishing the standard assortment of brasses (cornet, trombone, tuba), woodwinds (piccolo, clarinet), and percussion. They've just fin-ished what the program card identifies as "Selections from Zampa." Change of cards. Now, it's "Overture—William Tell." Mickey moves everyone through the preliminaries with-out incident, save for a little business with the sleeves of his coat, which are too long. But then, just as they're gearing up for the Lone Ranger riff, a rau-cous voice is heard—"Ice cream, lemonade." It's Don-ald Duck, pushing an ice cream cart. He spots the band, smiles, whips a wooden flute of some kind out of his sailor suit, and hops up on stage.

© Disney Enterprises, Inc.

While the band kicks into the "da-da-dat da-da-dat da-da-dat-da-daaa," the duck bows, sets his foot to stamping and starts play-ing. Only he's playing "Turkey in the Straw"—same beat, it turns out. One by one, the bandsmen fall under his spell until they're all pumping out "Turkey in the Straw." Mickey, furious, stalks over to Donald, glares at him, and then—grinning evilly—snatches the flute and snaps it in two. The duck magically produces a replacement. Repeat with variations, Mickey's fury growing with each iteration. Meanwhile, the other band members stomp away, William Tell forgotten.

Okay. Let's pause here for a minute. This is the standard cartoon struggle between mouse—or pig, or human, or whatever—and duck (why is it that ducks are always such hoodlums?), order and disorder, superego and id, right? Sure. But there's something else going on here. Consider the musical battleground: on the one hand, Rossini; on the other, "Turkey in the Straw." First off, what the hell is a brass band—a *marching* band—doing playing opera? Where's the Sousa?

Oddly enough, Rossini's 1829 *William Tell Overture* was a frequent target of plunder by the brass bands in the decades during which they dominated the American musical landscape: the period from right after the Civil War to around World War I; the period in which the cartoon, where the men wear bowler hats, the horses wear collars, and there's not a car or telephone wire to be seen, is clearly set. (Almost as plundered, for that matter, was Louis-Joseph-Ferdinand Hérold's 1831 *Zampa, the Pirate.*) Sure, the bands did play marches—but consider the program of a show Sousa's Marine Band gave on April 17, 1891: the audience had to sit through Wagner, Weber, Bizet, Rossini (the *William Tell Overture*, of course), Gounod, and a couple of lesser lights in that vein before they got to any actual Sousa, and that was a "symphonic poem" on "Ben Hur's Chariot Race." Serious music, or at least the appearance of it.

And that appearance was important. The America of the band era was an uneasy side-by-side of two worlds. One—let's call it Topworld—was Northern, civilized, and white (there was a black Topworld, too, but the only people who recognized it as such were other blacks). It was overwhelmingly middle class, a world created by self-satisfied shopkeepers and senior clerks, people with fine penmanship and clean collars and a knack with machines; a forward-looking world of skill and professionalism, of taste (according, as always, to prevailing standards) and restraint and deep sublimation. Its music had to be polite, asexual, and serious—but in no way intellectual, mind you (I'm leaving the intellectuals out of this; in American culture, they're Third World). It had to walk that narrow strip between "pure" art and "mere" entertainment. It's hard to keep that from being dull (look at modern jazz, or college rock).

The solution, as always, was to cheat. To graft the gentility and taste of the symphony onto the power and punch of the marching band. In practice, this meant that the bands moved from the parade ground to the concert hall or band shell, and presented a mass of light classics, arranged—or rather, eviscerated—for wind instruments, with plenty of flashy solos and variations spliced into them. (The overall effect must have been not unlike Emerson, Lake, and Palmer.) Bands of that era cultivated an entire repertoire of pretentious dreck with titles like "Carnival in Capri" and "Danse Banale" from which they drew. If they were American in their scale and execution, they were still essentially European in their outlook and their music.

OK; so much for the *William Tell Overture*. The other world—let's call it Underworld—belonged to those whom Thomas Pynchon calls the "preterite," the "*second sheep*, without whom there'd be no elect." The passed over, the left out, the not-catered-to. People with callused hands. People who drank whiskey in the morning and ate pigs' feet with their hands and weren't afraid to swing their partners do-si-do. People who were being replaced by machines. People who couldn't or wouldn't get with the program—and who, it must be pointed out, didn't have the luxury of importing their musical culture from Europe, but had to make their own out of materials at hand. Southern, rural, colored, poor: their music sweated roughness, unease, wrath. And sex, of course. It was dangerous.

But it wasn't boring, and folks on top knew that too. Each world wanted some of what the other had. Underworld craved respect, legitimacy, be-some-bodyship; Topworld craved the freedom to be nobody special, just another human animal with all the needs and desires appertaining thereto and no obligation to maintain one's precious dignity. The border between them was porous—if you were white, anyway—but everyone knew more or less where it was; often it ran right through them. Two worlds grinding up against each other, drawn inescapably together by the force of their mutual attraction.

And what was Underworld's music? There was a bunch of soppy, sentimental stuff not germane to the immediate point (e.g., songs like "The Baggage Coach Up Ahead"—which turns out to contain the crying baby's mother, in a box; like that). Here and there, you might find some of the music from the old country, gone to ground. But to find the Underworld equivalent of the band concert, where the values of the community were put on display through music, you'd have to follow the smell of burning cork.

Vulgar, insolent, cheap, lazy, indecent, insulting—the minstrel show seemed to embody everything that Topworld officially despised about America. Stretching across the stage was a semicircle of musicians, a mook with a tambourine at one end and one with a pair of rib bones at the other. These two endmen, "Mr. Bones" and "Mr. Tambo," as they were invariably known, were always blacked up (even if they were black already, as many were); the musicians between them could go either way. One guy, however, generally eschewed the cork. He stood in the middle and let the endmen bounce jokes off of him. "Mr. Interlocutor," as he was called, was both emcee and straight man. He was Topworld's emissary to the minstrel stage.

Meanwhile, there was music—loud, stompy, ragged-sounding music, with a big beat and a simple, repetitive melody. Music you could play on a fiddle and a banjo, without written notes or formal lessons. Example: "Turkey in the Straw." Originally, back in the 1830s, this Africanized Celtic fiddle tune traveled under the title "Zip Coon." It tells the story of ol' Zip—short for Scipio—Coon, "a larned scholar, for he plays upon de banjo 'cooney in de hollar.'" Ebonics. Sometime in the 1840s, one Daniel Decatur Emmett got ahold of the melody and changed its name to "Turkey in the Straw" (he also wrote minstrel hits such as "Old Dan Tucker" and, of course, "Dixie"—*that* "Dixie"). Eventually, his name for the song prevailed, and the tune, with its primitive syncopation, became one of the backbones of rural American rhythm.

So. Back to *The Band Concert*—but now we can give the characters their proper names. Donald, Mr. Bones—or Mr. Tambo, take your pick—is producing flutes (ducks are always endmen: Donald, Daffy, Howard). Mickey, Mr. Interlocutor, is breaking them. The band's playing "Turkey in the Straw." In fact, they're playing it even when Donald's not—and well, with full arrangement. Clearly, they know the song. They even start throwing in a few most un-dicty whoops.

The thing is, Mickey knows the song, too. Flash back to *Steamboat Willie*, 1928, the third Mickey Mouse cartoon, the first with sound; the cartoon that made him. Mickey, on a steamboat going up a lazy river, teases the big ol' cat piloting the thing and then kicks out the jams on a bunch of improvised instruments—pots and pans, squealing cats, cow's teeth, what have you. The song? Yep. "Turkey in the Straw." And if you plug Mickey into the min-strelometer, it flashes "endman." Black face, white eyes, and snout—what mouse looks like that, anyway? The only thing that does is the standard min-strel-show "coon" (the term of art prevalent in minstrelsy). Walt Disney's audi-ence would've twigged to that immediately.

Disney himself, by the way, must've known his minstrels: he grew up in Kansas City in the aughts and teens, when the town was a hotbed of ragtime and cakewalking and other pre-jazz black popular entertainment, all of which was propagated nationwide through the medium of minstrelsy, both black and white. In any case, Disney was responsible for one of the best minstrel bits on film, the crow scene from *Dumbo* (1941).

Somewhere between 1928 and 1935, Mickey tried to go Topworld, to shuck off his minstrel mask. The white part of his face is now, in *The Band Concert*, faintly pink. Donald's aggression is that of the man who sees his comrade attempt to rise above his station; the disproportionate, destructive wrath with which Mickey retaliates—does he *have* to break the duck's instru-ment, right off the bat?—is a manifestation of Topworld's ever-present fear of backsliding. As Donald is, so was Mickey.

Poor mouse. The thing is, when he climbs up on that bandstand, he doesn't *know* he's Mr. Interlocutor. He thinks he's clean out of the life, free at last from the ragged music and raucous humor. The baggy sleeves of the hand-me-down coat that Disney et al. saw fit to kit him out with should've clued him in, but "dey is none so blin' as dem what will not see" (to use the appropriate argot). The duck makes him see: he's not really Topworld after all, he's just playing it on stage. Joke's on him.

The battle between Donald and Mickey is finally brought to its end when the horse holding down the trombone chair uses his instrument to lasso Don-ald, shake all the fifes out of him, and pitch him away from the stage. Back to the program. Before Donald can properly organize a second attack, he tan-gles with a most bothersome bee; then the musicians launch into the storm scene from *William Tell Overture*, and a tornado blows up and sweeps every-one into the air—but since this whole bit of business is irrelevant to my pur-poses here, I'll cut to the end. The musicians land back on stage, more or less, and finish up their piece. Donald, the sole audience member, claps and pulls out his fife. "Turkey in the Straw." The band throws its storm-battered instruments at him in disgust. From inside the tuba, which has landed on his head, he blows 'em off. The last word, on the screen as in life: by 1935, popular music—from jazz to hillbilly, blues to Broadway—was all "Turkey in the Straw," all imbued with that vulgar American concern with rhythm. And Walt Disney knew it: when Donald gets the band going on "Turkey in the Straw," it sounds *fine*. No joke.

Disney, Stokowski, and the Genius of *Fantasia*

by CHARLES L. GRANATA

"The beauty and inspiration of music must not be restricted to a privileged few, but made available to every man, woman, and child."
—Leopold Stokowski, 1940

"Fantasia is not the final expression of this new union of color and music and action. It is the beginning of a new treatment and technique for the screen, as well as an indication of the greater development of sound recording and reproduction."
—Walt Disney, 1940

Opening Night

November 13, 1940, 7:30 P.M. The Broadway Theater, 1681 Broadway, New York City.

It's a cold, rainy Wednesday. A new motion picture is to be premiered—an unusual one, with an odd name. A Disney production about cartoons and classical music. . . .

The theater is one of the grandest film houses in New York. Heads are turning, people are buzzing. Walt Disney smiles while shaking hands with reporters. And everyone is making a fuss over a distinguished gentleman with white hair: the conductor, Leopold Stokowski.

The house lights dim, the curtain ascends, and the screen is filled with the loveliest indigo hue. Music stands and a podium anchor the scene; musicians, appearing as shadowy, backlit images, file onto the cinematic stage. The players take their customary seats within the orchestra and begin tuning up.

Enter musicologist Deems Taylor. "What you're going to see," he explains in his filmed introduction, "are the designs and pictures and stories that music inspired in the minds and imaginations of a group of artists. In other words, these are not going to be the interpretations of trained musicians, which I think is all to the good. What you will see on the screen is a picture of the various abstract images that might pass through your mind if you sat in a concert hall listening to the music."

The narration concludes, and a conductor, also in silhouette, takes his place before the orchestra. Suddenly, a vaguely familiar symphonic melody begins to swell. As Stokowski signals the entrance of each instrument, a mélange of colors erupt, and more shadows and light spill across the screen. The graceful curve of the stately harp casts a sensuous, foreboding arch across the azure backdrop. One by one, the string, woodwind, and percussion sections appear; the bell of a lone tuba glows in sync with its staccato entrance. The deeply saturated colors fade from pastel green to fiery orange and back again, as the orchestral snapshots melt into a series of flexible, free-form illustrations. From the skies float abstract images of fiddle bows and strings, their dances mimicking the ebb and flow of the music, stretching lazily across the ethereal landscape. As Bach's *Toccata and Fugue in D Minor* unfurls triumphantly, the warm, throaty roar of the music—which began in the front— begins to envelope the audience. Even a live performance has never sounded this rich, transparent, detailed. The brilliant sheen of the strings is like a velvet cushion: a foil for the crisp brass, rumbling kettledrums, and delicate harp.

Later, as Moussorgsky's *Night on Bald Mountain* tumbles onto the screen, the audience becomes immersed in a pool of pleasurable sound, firing from every direction: sixty-eight loudspeakers strong, pushing the instruments at them, pulling away, following the dramatic movement of the unusual images on the screen. It swoops from the front left and back right, creeping up the aisle like subway steam escaping through a sidewalk grate. When church bells toll ominously from behind, the entire audience turns in their seats, staring at the back wall of the theater in disbelief.

The audience members are talking now, excitedly—remarking on the purity of sound. "Could there have been a live orchestra in the pit . . . ?" These few moments of aural and visual bliss have given them a new respect for cartoons and classical music. A privileged few, they have experienced the world premier of the very first stereophonic motion picture—Walt Disney's *Fantasia*—in all of its original "Fantasound" splendor.

Birth of an Art Form

What makes *Fantasia* so special? Why is it revered as a technical and aesthetic milestone?

Though largely ignored by audiences of its day (and scorned by classical music "elitists"), *Fantasia* was the movie with which Walt Disney stepped boldly into the unknown. Taking tremendous financial risks while pushing every talent at his disposal to maximum capacity, he was hoping to create a masterpiece.

"*Fantasia* was made at a time when we had the feeling that we had to open the doors here," Disney once explained. "This medium was something we felt a responsibility for, and we felt we could go beyond the comic strip and do some very exciting, entertaining, and beautiful things with music, and picture, and color. So, we just went ahead and tried it out."

Disney's notion to produce a film marrying animation and classical music was born long before *Fantasia*'s raw footage hit the editing desk. In 1929, Disney and composer Carl Stalling conceived and produced a non-Mickey short in which music usurped the action. This film (*The Skeleton Dance*) included a snippet of Edvard Grieg's "March of the Dwarfs," and became the first in a series called Silly Symphonies. In 1932, a Silly Symphony called *Flowers and Trees*—set to the music of Mendelssohn and Schubert—became the very first 3-strip Technicolor film.

Disney purposefully kept Mickey Mouse out of the Silly Symphonies. But toward the late 1930s, Mickey's character began to sag, sending Walt scurrying to spice up his image. Thinking of the musical shorts, he devised an ingenious plan: Mickey would star in an animated version of *The Sorcerer's Apprentice,* a Goëthe fairy tale set to the music of French composer Paul Dukas.

Soon after, Disney accidentally stumbled into a great fan of his cartoons—famed conductor Leopold Stokowski. "I first met Walt Disney in a restaurant," Stokowski recalled. "I was alone having dinner at a table near him and he called across to me. 'Why don't we sit together?' Then he began to tell me that he was interested in Dukas's *The Sorcerer's Apprentice* as a possible short, and did I like the music. I said I liked it very much, and would be happy to cooperate with him." Stokowski went to work immediately, focusing on the orchestration and recording of Dukas's music. It was a task the musical demigod relished.

As their work intensified, the pair had lengthy discussions about art and music. Eventually, Stokowski began recommending other classical compositions that could lend themselves to similar treatment. Though admittedly not a classical music lover, Disney was intrigued, and quickly decided that instead of a two-reel short, *The Sorcerer's Apprentice* would become part of a full-length film: a series of vignettes based on classical works of contrasting tempo and tone.

Originally, Disney called it *The Concert Feature*. But as production commenced, he realized the new creation needed a catchier name—one befitting its musical form. He found the title in a musical term denoting "compositions unrestricted by formal design," and soon, the seeds planted by Stokowski and *The Sorcerer's Apprentice* were blossoming into the filmmaker's watershed animated feature.

Abstract Conceptions

Disney's concept of marrying classical music and abstract animation reflected his adventurous nature. Classical music is spiritual and descriptive, and few men possessed the sensitivity, skill, or audacity to blend the two art forms as provocatively as he did. "Walt was first and foremost a storyteller," said animation historian and author John Culhane. "But Walt was the storyteller as techno-buff."

The filmmaker laughed when people probed the meaning of *Fantasia*'s illustrative concepts. "It was just a very arbitrary thing on our part—a lot of people tried to figure out," he said. "They thought that we were very profound about this thing [*Fantasia*], and tried to analyze the whole darn thing. We went ahead and made these forms move. It was just a bunch of stuff thrown in there, you know—splashes of color, movements."

One scene, "The Soundtrack," offers a superb example of Disney's abstraction at its best. A single line (representing a sound wave) assumes the personalities of various instruments in the orchestra—dancing and moving to the "vibes" the studio artists perceived those instruments would create. The segment is playful, informative, and stimulating: sparked by the clever illustrations, viewers are compelled to imagine what shape *they* believe each instrument's sound reflects.

Disney immersed himself vigorously in the subject at hand. He held lengthy story meetings and met often with Stokowski, with whom he listened to dozens of works, searching for those offering the varied contrasts and textures he sought.

The selections Disney approved represent some of the most expressive compositions in the literature of classical music: Bach's stately *Toccata and Fugue in D Minor,* Dukas's *The Sorcerer's Apprentice,* Tchaikovsky's beloved *Nutcracker Suite,* Beethoven's *Pastoral Symphony,* Stravinsky's bombastic *The Rite of Spring,* Ponchielli's *The Dance of the Hours,* and Mussorgsky's terrifying *Night on Bald Mountain.* For the conclusion, he chose Schubert's heavenly *Ave Maria.* "This covers four minutes in our picture, and it's going to be four precious minutes when we're through," he told his staff when describing the climactic scene. "The beauty we can get from controlled color and the music and everything we use here will be worth it."

A scene from the "Nutcracker Suite" sequence in *Fantasia.* © Disney Enterprises, Inc.

In one of the daily brainstorming sessions, Disney outlined his ideas for the *Nutcracker Suite* sequence. For this interpretation, Disney wisely chose to forego the traditional overture and march—and the toys and nutcracker as well.

> We'll open on the Sugar Plum Fairy idea, with the fairies decorating the setting, and possibly building to the point that they give life to things. Then, we come down from that, and bring in the mushrooms. The little vamp in the music brings them to life, and they begin to dance this cute little Chinese dance. . . .
>
> From that, we lead into the dance of the flutes, and that will serve as a spot to bring in the flowers and things that will dance to that. Even the mushroom personalities won't be out too strong. It's like something you see with your eyes half closed—you almost imagine them. The leaves begin to look like they're dancing, and the blossoms floating on the water begin to look like ballet girls in little skirts. It will be like if you're out in the night, and a firefly comes along, you can almost think it's a fairy, decorating with dew.
>
> You know how I think this oughta come in? With a ripple—no background at all. And the ripple carries life. The petals fall down on the water. It'll all be a ballet of flower petals on the water. Those little flowers? I see no reason why they can't dance right on the water. If you throw a flower blossom on the water, it floats. They could skim right on the water—it would make a beautiful setup.

This free-flowing style was an artistic departure for the animators on Disney's staff, although some experimentation with unusual forms had begun long before Disney dreamed of *Fantasia*. "The abstractions that were done [for *Fantasia*] were no sudden idea," he explained. "Rather, they were something we had nursed along for several years but never had a chance to try, due to the fact that the pictures being made up to that time didn't allow us to include any of this type of material in them. These abstract designs were an outgrowth of our effects department, which we organized long before we had any contact with Stokowski."

The Maestro

In Leopold Stokowski, Walt Disney found his musical counterpart: an abstract thinker with a distinct flair for showmanship. "I enjoyed working with Walt because of his boundless imagination and simple direct approach to everything," Stokowski explained. "His instinct for perceiving great gifts in young artists reminded me of [Ballet Russe founder] Diaghilev."

Born in London on April 18, 1882, Stokowski studied piano and organ, and at age twelve made his conducting debut in front of a children's orchestra. "That did it," he later said. "That night I didn't sleep a wink. I had but one thought—to become a conductor!"

In 1905, he came to New York, serving as choirmaster and organist at St. Bartholomew's Church. His charismatic persona aided him in securing the post of conductor of the Philadelphia Orchestra in 1912; he remained there until 1940. It was with the Philadelphia that Stokowski carved his reputation, developing extravagant gestures that inspired and delighted musicians and audiences alike. Prior to Stokowski's emergence, few conductors became personalities in their own right; fewer still influenced the masses as strongly as he did. Only Leonard Bernstein, who made his conducting debut with the New York Philharmonic in 1943, enjoyed an equally celebrated presence.

Until the mid-1930s, the conductor's role was largely misunderstood. Composers of the nineteenth century had created works containing far more expressive range than their predecessors, thus compelling the leader to employ musicianship and rhythmic skill to extract the subtle complexities of a score, and aid the orchestra in proper dynamic projection.

Stokowski was a firebrand who altered our perception of the *maestro*, carefully defining his image and function as the interpretive leader of the orchestra. Violinist Yehudi Menuhin once explained why "Stokie" left such a strong impression on us. "Stokowski knew the visual value of the conductor, for the audience as well as the players," he said. "For the first half of the [twentieth] century, Stokowski epitomized for most Americans what the symphony conductor should look like, how he should behave, and in large measure helped to popularize the symphony orchestra in North America."

Moreover, Stokowski was an intuitive collaborator, as passionate about recording technology as he was about the music itself. "In recording, it was always a joy to work with Stokowski," said RCA Victor Red Seal producer Charles O'Connell. "He understands the recording of sound, and conducts his orchestra accordingly." The conductor was so enthusiastic about recording that he once professed, "The recording process will one day produce music better than heard in the concert hall."

Stokowski's interest in sound was exceptional. While many of his contemporaries detested the recording process (the irascible Arturo Toscanini comes to mind), Stokowski embraced it, learning all of its technical intricacies. O'Connell, who spent hundreds of hours in the studio with the maestro, emphasized the conductor's skill at blending the science of recording with the art of performing. "He was always more interested in orchestral tone than any other conductor, and knew more about it: how to produce it, how to employ it, and how to make it register on record. And he decided that, given sympathetic cooperation in the recording room, he could accomplish more by manipulation of the orchestra than by revolving a rheostat. He accomplished his results, therefore, through conducting technique, leaving entirely to me the adjustment of the electronic-mechanical factors."

From his orchestra, Stokowski nurtured a rich, luminous tone known as the "Philadelphia sound." Much of that sound evolved through trial and error, and a good measure of risk taking. In spite of the occasional reproach of fellow conductors who frowned on his offbeat ideas, Stokowski remained accountable to just one individual: himself.

Though Stokowski's positioning of instruments within the orchestra was unconventional, his changes improved the spaciousness and clarity of its overall sound. While other conductors were dictatorial when it came to technique and interpretation, Stokowski allowed unlimited freedom of expression among his players. His string section, for example, was encouraged to "free bow," which meant the players could move their bows up and down as they pleased, thereby producing a *legato*-style sound much smoother than that of the traditional (synchronized) method. All of his players, from bassoonist and trumpeter to contrabassist and percussionist, were encouraged to violate every technical rule of playing—if it ultimately enhanced the beauty of their phrasing, or the sonority of their tone.

Who, other than Stokowski, would dare abandon the coveted symbol of a conductor's power, the mystical baton? *He* did, and despite the absence of a wand, he managed to draw infinite shadings and sweeping musical dynamics from the virtuosi under his command.

Legendary Hollywood violinist Sid Sharp, concertmaster for Stokowski's Hollywood Bowl Orchestra during the 1950s, fondly recalls the master's touch. "Stokowski was inspiring. The way he conducted, the way he looked at you, the way his hands moved . . . you could just feel everything coming out of him. In turn, that unspoken energy transpired, and came into *you*. He did something to an orchestra that brought out the absolute best in them. Stokowski was the greatest painter when it came to coloring the music of the great composers.

"He was feared, but respected. His expectations were very high, and he wanted the best from his players. When he was on the podium, he didn't want anyone lagging behind. He wanted you to give everything you had. He knew that when he put his hand down to give us a downbeat, we would be there. There was something mystical—*indescribable*—about the sound of Stokowski's strings. Sitting there, in the midst of that tremendous swell of strings, was mesmerizing."

The Maestro and the Man Behind the Mouse

The conductor's passion was of tremendous value to Walt Disney and the technical team responsible for the complex recording of *Fantasia*'s music tracks. Disney welcomed his input on all levels, and the maestro's hand in bringing Disney's fanciful vision to life cannot be overemphasized.

By 1937, Stokowski was a familiar face on the silver screen. He'd appeared in *The Big Broadcast of 1937*, and later backed Deanna Durbin in Universal's *100 Men and a Girl*, a soundtrack recorded with a multi-channel recording technique developed by RCA. This process employed nine microphones, spread throughout the orchestra to capture individual instruments. Though the nine tracks were mixed to a single monophonic track, the sound was far less distorted than it was with previous film recording methods.

When it came to imparting a sense of depth and space in their work, Disney and Stokowski were of one mind. "[Walt] had a sense of place, which meant that you walked in and lived in those wonderlands," explained John Culhane. "You needed a sense of depth, and so he got his technicians to develop the multiplane camera, and with the multiplane camera you go *into* those worlds. But when you went into *Snow White and the Seven Dwarfs* [1937], you had a feeling of going into a story such as the best storyteller gave you with their voice. . . . Walt gave it to you with all your senses involved. Except smell! And he was always working on that. . . ."

That *Fantasia* would take full advantage of Technicolor animation was a given. But the fidelity of a standard monophonic motion picture recording couldn't convey the realism the collaborators were after. For *Fantasia,* the traditional method of recording sound for film simply wouldn't do. What Disney and Stokowski envisaged was a soundtrack rivaling the vivid boldness of the film's spectacular color: a panoramic showstopper that would suspend the viewer in a rich, golden bath of sound—as if they were sitting in the center of the orchestra at a live performance.

Against tremendous technical odds—and a full fifty years before 5.1 "surround sound" become *de rigueur* for theatergoers—the pair found the answer in a revolutionary system developed by William Garity and the Walt Disney Studios sound department. They called it "Fantasound."

Sound Ideas

When the Disney Studios embarked on developing the first multi-channel "stereophonic" film recording system in late 1938, the technology of film sound recording was still in its infancy.

The Jazz Singer (1927) heralded the birth of the talking picture, although research and development in the area of film sound reproduction was in full swing much earlier at Thomas Edison's West Orange, New Jersey, labs. Improvements such as electrical and optical film recording (made between 1915 and 1927) foreshadowed the inevitable success of the sound film medium.

By the time Disney assigned his staff the seemingly impossible task, both Bell Labs and RCA had made substantial progress in developing multi-channel recording techniques. The focus, though, was on clarity and not on "dimensional" sound. At MGM, the engineers were recording film sessions on four discrete tracks called "angles." Although the individual channels represented different orchestral and vocal views, they were always mixed to mono for the final soundtrack. Film soundtracks (as encoded on their 35mm projection prints and played in the theater) remained monophonic recordings, played back through a speaker behind the screen.

The difference between mono and stereo is like night and day. Monophonic sound has no spatial depth or directionality: all of the sound comes from the center. It is akin to listening with just one ear. Stereophonic sound allows us to perceive recorded music with distinct depth and separation, approximating what we might hear during a live performance.

Disney's Fantasound system differed from others, as it boasted nine separate music tracks (recorded with widespread microphone placement) that were eventually mixed to three-track "stereo." On playback, Fantasound's dozens of speakers surrounded the viewer with a three-dimensional sea of sound. So impressive was the effect that the Philadelphia *Evening Bulletin* hailed it as the screen's "greatest departure since the introduction of sound."

Stokowski once explained the diffusionary technique used in the system. "In *Fantasia,* we had three separate sound channels [for playback], which put at our disposal several new possibilities. [A] great advantage of three sound channels is that the tone of the various instruments can be blended in the air after the sound has left the speakers. This corresponds somewhat to the blending of colors in *pointillism,* the method of painting in which the colors are not mixed on the canvas, but are blended in the spaces between the canvas and our eyes as we look at the picture."

In the Studio

Technically, it was William Garity (Disney's head sound engineer) and a crew of associates who masterminded Fantasound's design, putting Disney and Stokowski's theoretical concepts to work.

Except for *The Sorcerer's Apprentice* and the vocal portions of *Ave Maria* (which were recorded at RKO/Pathe Studios in Hollywood), the sessions for *Fantasia* were held at the Philadelphia Academy of Music. Ever the eccentric, Stokowski insisted on recording in the wee hours of the morning. "The men drink coffee to keep awake," he confessed. "It makes everybody alert."

Disney director Jim Algar once described the January 9–10, 1938, session. "Stokowski's session for *Sorcerer* [ran from] 12:00 midnight to 3:00 A.M. [With] one rehearsal, Stokowski galvanized eighty-five musicians to a pitch of tenseness that produced, in three short hours, the complete recording of Dukas's music. He then stepped down, soaked with perspiration from head to foot. No mere handkerchief could mop his steaming brow; he was handed two man-sized bath towels." ("I can attest to that," affirms Sid Sharp, commenting on his 1950s performances with the master. "At the end of rehearsal, I had to change my clothes—I was completely wet from sweating. And the same thing would happen in the evening—after the concert performance.")

The stereo sessions for *The Sorcerer's Apprentice* were not without incident. An intricate "shell," designed to isolate sections of the orchestra and absorb unwanted frequencies, failed to work as expected. The recordings were completed, but Disney decided to move the scoring to the Philadelphia's sonically superior Academy of Music. "I remember that in the basement, right underneath the audience, was a big, round brick wall," said Disney associate Dick Huemer. "Across the top of this there were stringers, or beams—very much like the sounding board of an instrument. I guess the architect's idea was that the theater would reverberate like a huge instrument or something, and maybe it does, because those acoustics are famous."

In Philadelphia, a temporary control room was set up in the Academy's basement. Fearing a nitrate fire, administrators allowed the recording team to keep just one spare reel of nitrate recording film per optical recorder in the building; a truck was brought in and served as a mobile storage facility and darkroom. Over a two-month period during the summer of 1939, the technicians recorded and processed more than 400,000 feet of sound negative film.

The Academy's concerns were not unfounded, given nitrate's potential for spontaneous combustion. In the 1940s, the risk of nitrate fires and explosions wasn't limited to film stored in vaults: on occasion, theater projection booths became deadly chambers, as heat from a projector's carbon arc lamp could swiftly ignite the fast-burning material.

To faithfully capture the wide dynamic range of the orchestra, engineers placed up to thirty-three RCA 44 ribbon microphones among the musicians. The mikes were fed to a mixer, and the pre-mixed instrumental sections they represented were separated into six discrete channels as follows: (a) violins; (b) violas; (c) cellos and basses; (d) brass; (e) woodwinds; and (f) timpani. The seventh channel was a direct-feed combination of channels one through six, and the eighth channel recorded an overall, distant take of the entire orchestra (thereby preserving the essential "room tone" of the recording hall.)

Sound mixers monitored the recording levels with oscilloscopes, as overmodulation would create distortion on the optical film track. Signals were recorded onto separate strips of 35mm nitrate optical film, using customized RCA Class A optical recorders.

Introduced by RCA and Western Electric in 1930, optical recording was adopted by the major studios in 1935, and quickly revolutionized the industry. With the optical system, a light beam is projected through a series of lenses, which concentrate and focus the light. The condensed light is then passed through a light valve containing ultra-thin ribbons. As the electrical impulses generated by a microphone hit the light valve, the ribbons modulate (vibrate), and as the light passes through a second set of lenses, it is focused directly onto a very narrow portion of the film, which is coated with light-sensitive photographic emulsion.

The Finishing Touch

After the Philadelphia sessions, the separated music tracks were brought to the Disney Studios, and carefully rerecorded (mixed) to a single, four-channel 35mm strip that became the final music track. The film was recorded optically on custom designed printers that could print four tracks side by side. On this master soundtrack, channels one, two, and three contained the stereophonic music and dialog mix, and channel four contained a special tone that functioned as a synchronizing "control" track, automating the fades and pans on playback.

Stokowski himself supervised the rerecording, as John Hench of Disney Story Development recalled. "Stokowski was fascinated by the mixing board," Hench explained. "He recorded each section separately—strings, winds, horns, etc.—and he mixed them all himself. He said this was 'the ultimate in conducting.' He could dial up the strings, or turn down the others, getting exact mixtures of sounds. With the [mixing] panel he could control the whole orchestra. That little sound board on the Hyperion Avenue's soundstage gave him a great sense of power."

The rerecording phase of production is where *Fantasia*'s surround-sound characteristics came to life. Since they were forging new paths in stereo reproduction, Garity and his men were forced to improvise and invent the electronic means that would allow them to take the separated music stems and manipulate the sound to match the on-screen action.

How did they move the sound back and forth across the screen? What makes a particular instrument "fly" from the back of the room to the front? To create these brand new effects, the technicians designed "pan pots"—rotary dial controls that allowed the sound source to be moved around the aural soundstage. (As testament to their ingenuity, many of their innovations became standard tools in the recording industry, and are still in use today.)

The final mix was impressive, and delighted everyone—especially Stokowski.

"In the thunderstorm part of Beethoven's *Pastoral Symphony* are certain phrases for bassoon, clarinet, and oboe, which have an urgent, agitated expression," he wrote in *Music for All of Us*. "These phrases are almost inaudible in the concert hall, because the rest of the orchestra is playing loud and furiously. In *Fantasia,* we were able to give these important passages their true value by making the melodic lines for bassoon, clarinet, and oboe soar above the rest of the orchestra without emasculating the rushing, stormy music of all the string instruments. Because of the inherent lack of balance in the orchestration, I have never before heard these phrases given their due prominence and tonal importance."

In the Theaters

Presenting *Fantasia* created unique problems.

Scoring a multi-channel motion picture in the early 1940s was one thing; building a practical system to play it back in theaters across the country was an entirely different matter. While most other films contained both picture and soundtrack on the same strip of 35mm film, the Fantasound system called for a separate music track: in a full, Fantasound theater setup, a regular projector would be used for the visuals, and a special four-track "film phonograph" would be employed to play the music track, in synchronization with the picture.

Disney knew that if the public were to appreciate the full impact of the film's glorious stereo soundtrack, he would need specially equipped theaters, suited to flatter Fantasound's virtues. With this in mind, he staged the presentation of his precious experiment decisively.

To add to the prestige, he assembled a "road show" package. As such, the film would be shown twice a day, with reserved seating and advance ticket purchase—similar to a Broadway show or symphonic concert. Handpicked associates were coached by Disney himself and dispatched to theaters as his personal emissaries. They carried with them precise instructions for opening and closing the curtains, setting up the sound and lighting, selling full-size color programs, and ushering patrons to their seats.

The stereophonic soundtrack—the film's greatest attraction—would be presented with Fantasound installations at theaters in major cities. The equipment included eleven amplifier racks, power supplies, two sound film phonographs modified to four-track, two selsyn distributor units, three loudspeaker horns, and dozens of smaller loudspeakers. The amplifiers and power supply racks stretched over thirty feet, and used more than 400 vacuum tubes. "The works" were packed into forty-five cases totaling nearly 15,000 pounds.

The object of celebration itself was three years in the making, and cost the studio in excess of $2.5 million to produce, including a music tab of nearly $400,000. (For reference, if created in 2001, the overall film would cost roughly $31 million, the music $5 million, and the opening night festivities in excess of $1 million.)

Fantasia had arrived.

First up was the New York world premier. No expense was spared in staging the evening's extravaganza at the Broadway Theater. More, perhaps, was spent on this premier than on any other in Hollywood history, to that point. $85,000 alone went to the manufacture and installation of a custom-designed projection and Fantasound playback system; untold thousands were lavished on publicity, travel, and miscellaneous necessities.

In a post-premier interview, Disney was asked about his taste for classical music. "I never liked this stuff," he told a reporter from the New York *World-Telegram.* "Honest, I just couldn't listen to it. But I *can* listen to it now. It seems to mean a little more to me. Maybe it can give other people the same thing. When I heard the music it made pictures in my head. . . .

"Stravinsky saw his *Rite of Spring,* and said that that was what he had in mind all the time. None of that matters, I guess. This isn't a picture for just music lovers. People have to like it. They have to be entertained. We're selling entertainment, and that's the thing I'm hoping *Fantasia* does—entertain. I'm hoping, hoping, hoping."

Reviews poured in. The critics roared. Classical music purists howled. And public attendance waned.

Bosley Crowther of the *New York Times* raved. "Motion picture history was made last night," he wrote. "*Fantasia* dumps conventional formulas overboard and reveals the scope of films for imaginative excursion. . . ."

Peyton Boswell, editor of *Art Digest,* called it "an aesthetic experience never to be forgotten," and *Time,* which featured Leopold Stokowski on its November 18, 1940, cover, gushed over the sound. "As the music sweeps to a climax, it froths over the proscenium arch, boils into the rear of the theater, and all but prances up and down the aisles. . . ."

Not everyone waxed poetic. Classical aficionados, led by influential critics, applauded the sound—but deemed the dilution of the music a sacrilege. (Most routinely objected to the visual interpretation of *any* classical music, prompting one to wonder what they made of the ballet.) Worse, parents stayed away, resenting the stiff road show prices the theaters charged to admit their youngsters.

It was clear that the masses were not ready for a groundbreaking film like *Fantasia.* People just didn't get it.

While *Fantasia* ran for a year at the Broadway in New York, it cost far more to maintain the Fantasound production than the box office was taking in. The increasing financial instability caused by the war didn't help, and in 1941, all but one of the existing Fantasound systems were dismantled and donated to the government for the war effort. Theaters that continued to show the film projected it in monophonic sound, encoded on the single-track strip next to the picture.

Although a sequel had been planned, the failure of the original precluded one.

Post-premier

World War II and the ravages of time contributed to *Fantasia*'s virtual disappearance after its celebrated premier.

In April, 1942, RKO Radio Pictures released an edited version of the film, slashing it from 133 minutes to a paltry 82 minutes—a virtual desecration. Disney was crushed.

By 1955, the original unmixed nitrate sound negatives had deteriorated and were unusable. Fortunately, the studio had a four-track print, which had survived in good condition. From this sole surviving nitrate print, a three-track transfer was made to magnetic film (via telephone lines) from the only existing Fantasound system at Disney Studios in Burbank to the RCA building in Hollywood. A Superscope wide-screen print was rereleased in 1956, to lukewarm reception.

Fantasia's greatest success came during the following decade, upon its rereleases in both 1963 and 1969. It wasn't until the latter—three years after Walt Disney's death—that the film began turning a profit. Would he have been sad to learn that the group most enamored of his cherished creation was psychedelic thrill seekers, tripping on acid?

Another rechanneled version appeared in 1977, and in 1984, the worst atrocity of all was inflicted on the debilitated classic: the original Stokowski soundtrack, now beyond repair, was removed from the film. In its place, a newly recorded digital version, conducted by Irwin Kostal, took its place alongside the original 1940 visual segments. To those who knew and loved the film, *Fantasia* was now beyond salvage.

There is a happy ending, though.

In 1991, the Disney organization revisited *Fantasia*. Audio restoration techniques had improved tremendously and, for the first time in decades, Hollywood studios were taking inventory, addressing the preservation of their valuable film libraries moldering in the vaults.

The nitrate film stock used by Hollywood studios prior to 1951, without properly controlled storage, has a tendency to shrink, destroying the audio and visual information contained on it. With time, the film disintegrates into a mass of dust. Nitrate deterioration—the bane of every film historian's existence—was responsible for the loss of *Fantasia's* glorious, first-generation Stokowski recordings.

Could technology overcome this impediment, and restore the luster of the original 1940 Fantasound soundtrack from the 1955 "phone line" transfer? The assignment went to Terry Porter, a recording engineer at Disney's own Buena Vista Sound. As Porter began to evaluate the elements, he realized that—for the first time since its 1940 release—it might be possible to re-create the sonic experience of the original Fantasound presentation.

Employing a wide array of computerized noise reduction programs, Porter de-noised, filtered, and equalized the damaged soundtrack. Poking around in the archives, he found Stokowski's original score sheets. The pages contained the conductor's handwritten notes, explaining in full detail where the music was to go. The notes became Porter's remixing gospel. "It would say 'Left wall, rear wall, kill the fronts' for a certain passage—it was a complete map to exactly what they did in the auditorium," he explained.

Following Stokowski's guide, Porter converted the original Fantasound configuration to the six-channel, 70mm format. "The original Fantasound was six dimensional: screen left/center/right and auditorium left/rear/right," he explained. "I just used all six channels, full-bandwidth, for the music."

After sixty years, the technology inspired by Walt Disney's folly—multichannel, digital surround sound—had come full circle, making his beloved *Fantasia* whole again.

Coda

It was clear, even in 1940, that Walt Disney never intended *Fantasia* to stand on its own. A studio press release from that year explained his philosophy. "After two and a half years which went into the making of *Fantasia*, Disney and

Stokowski feel that it is not a finished product but an indication of the great possibilities the future may develop in this new entertainment medium. . . ."

What the filmmaker surely foresaw was not just the increased use of his ingenious Fantasound recording system, but a perpetually evolving, ever-changing *Fantasia*, designed to reflect the technical innovations and creative sensibilities of future generations. *Fantasia's* inherent malleability would allow for infinite reshaping, and one of Disney's early ideas was to "update" the feature on a regular basis, retaining certain segments while replacing others.

There are many indications that before the paint had dried on the storyboards, Disney was planning an encore. By October 1940, Disney and Stokowski had begun story meetings, and the filmmaker inked a deal to use several works by Igor Stravinsky, whose controversial *Rite of Spring* was a dramatic highlight of the original film. He also agreed to include Prokofiev's charming *Peter and the Wolf*—a promise he kept by making it part of a 1946 film featuring popular music called *Make Mine Music*.

Though these extensions were never realized, with the original *Fantasia*, Disney succeeded in visually interpreting the infinite subtleties that refined music embodies. The intensity of his creation—musically, sonically, and artistically—has rarely been equaled. Yet, despite the mountains of praise heaped upon his many successes, Disney never considered his craft an art. "Art is never conscious," he said. "Things that have lived were seldom planned that way. If you follow that line, you're on the wrong track. We don't even let the word 'art' be used around the studio. If anyone begins to get arty, we knock them down. What we strive for is entertainment."

Long before Les Paul invented multi-track recording, or magnetic film and tape supplanted optical nitrate and discs as the preferred medium for sound recording, or surround-sound found its way into the mainstream movie houses, there was *Fantasia*, the pioneer of all these innovations, an eminently entertaining film that miraculously turned some far-fetched dreams into reality.

The author kindly acknowledges the generous contributions and assistance of Linda Corona, Michael Feinstein, Scott McQueen, Sid Sharp, Sheila Stafford, and Bob Waldman.

Select Bibliography

Books

Ammer, Christine. *Harper's Dictionary of Music*. New York: Harper & Row, 1987.

Culhane, John. *Walt Disney's Fantasia*. New York: Abradale Press/Harry N. Abrams, Inc., 1983.

Iwerks, Leslie, and Kenworthy, John. *The Hand Behind the Mouse*. New York: Disney Editions, 2001.

O'Connell, Charles. *The Other Side of the Record*. New York: Alfred A. Knopf, 1947.

Stokowski, Leopold. *Music for All of Us*. New York: Simon & Schuster, 1943.

Articles

"Disney Cinesymphony." *Time*, November 18, 1940.

Garity, William E., and Hawkins, J.N.A. "*Fantasia* Sound." *Journal of the Society of Motion Picture Engineers*, August 1941.

Heuring, David, and Turner, George. "Disney's *Fantasia*: Yesterday and Today." *American Cimematographer*, February 1991.

Peck, A.P. "What Makes *Fantasia* Click." *Scientific American*, January 1941.

Plumb, Edward H. "The Future of Fantasound." *Journal of the Society of Motion Picture Engineers*, July 1942.

"Revolution in Film Sound: Two New Methods of Recording Stokowski Spadework." *Newsweek*, December 23, 1941.

Audio Interviews and Sound Bites

Disney, Walt. Undated audio interview on commentary track of *Fantasia*, DVD, 2001.

McQueen, Scott. Telephone interview with the author, December 2001.

Sharp, Sid. Telephone interview with the author, January 2002.

Music and the Animated Cartoon*

by CHUCK JONES

Charles M. "Chuck" Jones (1912–2002) was responsible for directing some of the most well-known cartoons Warner Bros. ever produced, including *What's Opera, Doc?* (1957), *Duck Amuck* (1953), *The Rabbit of Seville* (1950), *The Scarlet Pumpernickel* (1950), and *One Froggy Evening* (1955), as well as for producing a series of Tom & Jerry shorts and several one-shot animated films for MGM, including *Dr. Seuss's How the Grinch Stole Christmas* (1966), *The Dot and the Line* (1965), and many more.

While Jones would state repeatedly that he had no musical background, his legacy in animation centers prominently on his treatment of music, since many of his cartoons either explicitly focus on musical performance (*Long-Haired Hare* [1949], *Baton Bunny* [1959], *Nelly's Folly* [1961]) or rely on the musical underscore to tell the story in lieu of *any* dialogue—witness the Coyote and Roadrunner series. Because of his belief in visual, almost pantomimic humor—letting the character's expressions, however subtle, create comedy—Jones's cartoons usually had the optimum sonic space for the music and effects to interact. In this 1946 article, Jones tries to enlighten the reader to the myriad possibilities in a cartoon soundtrack for the director or composer who wishes to experiment with music, foreshadowing much of his own later work in the medium.

The animated cartoon, in its mature form, can be the most facile and elastic form of graphic art. Since the first Cro-Magnon Picasso hacked etchings on his cave wall every artist has longingly sought the ideal medium—one that

---

*Author's Note: The title of this article may be misleading, as it implies an easy skill and familiarity with both the animated cartoon *and* music. It is rather an animation cartoonist discussing some of the potentialities of his medium with the musician.

would contain within its structure color, light, expanse, and movement. The animated cartoon can supply these needs. It knows no bounds in form or scope. It can approach an absolute in technical realism and it can reach the absolute in abstraction. It can bridge the two without taking a deep breath. The technical problems present in live action, when it tends toward the unreal or fantastic, are simply not present to the animator. The transition of Dr. Jekyll to Mr. Hyde is workaday routine to the animator. He can do it and add three pink elephants to the transition. He can do it while stifling a yawn. In fact, he frequently does. A red ant can grow to a golden elephant under his hand, a flying horse recede to a black pearl. He can create thunderstorms, tidal waves, flying carpets, talking hornets, dancing orchids, all with credibility, all with no technical obstructions.

Yet in spite of these potentialities the animated cartoon has been severely restricted in its growth. Its use as an educational device is a comparatively recent development, stimulated by wartime needs. Culturally, the animated cartoon is in the toddling stage, as it is politically. It has made few profound statements about anything. Like all other motion pictures, it is dependent on a wide and highly diversified audience approval—the thing known in some quarters as "box office," and "box office" in terms of animated cartoons is judged almost wholly by the degree of audible audience reaction. The appreciative chuckle, the pleased cluck, does not add up—in animation circles— to good "box office." This has resulted in a wave of reaction throughout the industry against the type of cartoons known as "Rembrandts"; that is, any type of cartoon except those based on the "boff" or belly laugh. One producer asked his artists to use lots of purple in the backgrounds because, as he put it, "purple is a funny color." Well, I think G-flat is a funny note. I mention these instances, not because I am unsympathetic with the producer's viewpoint or wish to suggest that the imperative pressures of the box office can be disregarded, but because I believe that a deeper understanding of the aesthetic and cultural possibilities of the medium can serve to broaden its usage and increase its popularity. My purpose here is the appraisal of one of these possibilities— the function of music in relation to the cartoon.

All cartoons use music as an integral element in their format. Nearly all cartoons use it badly, confining it as they do to the hackneyed, the time-worn, the proverbial. The average cartoon musician was a theater organist during the silent era and so *William Tell* takes quite a beating in the average cartoon. For some reason, many cartoon musicians are more concerned with exact synchronization or "mickey mousing" than with the originality of their contribution or the variety of their arrangement. To be sure, many of the cartoons as they reach the musician are something less than inspirational, but most of them, even the best, gain less than they should from his contribution. I have seen a good cartoon ruined by a deadly score. If you can visualize *Death and Transfiguration* as a theme to *Peter Rabbit*, you get the idea. Nor is this a diatribe against the practicing musicians in the cartoon field; many are excellent and conscientious artists (among them Carl Stalling, Warner Bros.; Scott Bradley, MGM; Frank Churchill, Paul Smith, Larry Morey, and others for the Disney features and shorts), but many tend to underrate the medium and to disregard its musical potentialities.

Here are two examples of what I believe to be the nearly perfect wedding of music and graphics which occurs when the visual and auditory impacts are simultaneous and almost equal. Both examples are from the picture *Fantasia* (1940); both are bits. One consumed about four seconds in the *Toccata and Fugue* sequence. It pictured simply a ponderous, rocklike, coffinlike mass that waddled into a murky background accompanied by a series of deep bass notes. I should not say "accompanied," because this Thing was the music: to my mind there was no separation; the fusion of the auditory and the visual was perfect. The second of my two instances represents, I believe, the happiest, most perfect single sequence ever done in animated cartoons, perhaps in motion pictures: the little mushroom dance from the *Nutcracker Suite*. Here was an instance of almost pure delight; again, an entrancing blend of the eye and the ear in which I found the music itself personified on the screen. There was a personal quality to these sequences, too, that was generally lacking throughout the rest of the film. It may be that if the makers of future *Fantasias* will be less concerned with the pageantry of their project and will search harder for the humanness of the music, we will have better films *and* better box office; for I believe that the mushroom dance has universal appeal, that it will go well in St. Jo and Walla Walla—as well as it will go in Hollywood or New York.

I am not going to attempt a general survey of the use, or misuse, of music in the cartoon of today. It is rather my purpose to suggest certain potentialities.

These potentialities may be classified in six rough categories: (1) Musical Education, (2) Television, (3) Program or Narrative, (4) Regional and Folklore, (5) Satire, (6) Abstract or Absolute.

1) MUSICAL EDUCATION. This is a wide and exciting field, one in which the cartoonist and musician must band together. Here the simple, strong diagrams of the cartoonist in conjunction with the sound track can do for a classroom of embryo musicians what only individual instruction could do before. I do not mean that we are going to have platoons of Bachs underfoot, but we can have a musically intelligent generation, a thing that has not been particularly feasible heretofore. But we must be guarded in our use of this new medium, because it will be quite possible to teach a thousand children the simultaneous rudiments of the glockenspiel—a result hardly to be desired. Therefore the musician must be there to direct that artist in what to teach and how to teach it; and he may be sure that the artist will do an exciting and interesting job of presentation. It is important at this time to remember that visual education has a head start on other educational methods in that we have a sympathetic audience to start with. The motion picture is widely known and widely appreciated. It is our responsibility to maintain this attitude, and we have learned valuable lessons during the war in so doing. Education can be fun, it can be attractive, but only if we, as teachers, keep it so.

2) TELEVISION. The signature music of today's radio must be bolstered in tomorrow's television by some sort of visual image, something in the nature of MGM's lion, Warners' shield, and so on. Many educational programs will also use the cartoon, as will children's programs, comedy, and musical programs. The opportunities here hardly need elucidation; they are obvious. The points I shall stress in ensuing categories will of course apply to television as well, because the broadcasting of motion pictures will represent an important feature of television.

3) PROGRAM OR NARRATIVE. Here is another wide and tremendously provocative field for the animator and musician to explore together. Here we are free from the prejudice resulting from the visual interpretation of more abstract music.

Peter and the Wolf, Hänsel and Gretel, Don Quixote, among many others, are exciting possibilities. Richard Strauss' ballet, *Schlagobers* (*Whipped Cream*), about the nightmare of a cream-puff addict, seems to me to offer an enormous amount of fun. And consider two titles of Erik Satie's, *The Dreamy Fish* and *Airs to Make One Run*, parts of which, the composer noted, should be played "on yellow velvet," "dry as a cuckoo," "like a nightingale with a toothache." He must have seen us coming. *Rip Van Winkle, The Fire Bird.* The list is endless.

The animated cartoon medium is the logical medium vehicle for these, because, among all media, it lends the greatest credence to fantasy. And in this field the greatest delight is measured in the degree of credibility. The magic of the great juggler, of the trapeze artist, of Charlie McCarthy, of the story-teller, lies in his ability to convince you that the impossible is quite possible—nay, is logical; is, in fact, as the children say, "Reely!" The animated cartoon can match, enhance, make credible the melodic fantasy of the composer. Overlapping here a little bit, I believe that the educational system will one day demand a library for its public schools of just such pointless introduction to classic and semiclassic music.

4) REGIONAL AND FOLKLORE. I believe that the animated cartoon has immense advantage in the exhibition of regional and national dances, songs, and cultures, because here we can combine the folk art with the folk dance. Straight cinematography covers this field to a certain extent, but seeing strange people in unusual costumes, dancing sarabands or tarantellas, gives us little insight into the thought of these people, their dreams, or their desires. But folk art does. It gives us a rich insight into the hopes and needs of a people. The pottery, furniture, and fabrics of any nationality suggest colorful fields for the artist. The bright blues, yellows, and reds used by the Scandinavian artisans in the creation of the jaunty figures which decorate their dish cupboards, ski shirts, and aprons would make a dancing, happy accompaniment to Grieg's *Norwegian Dances* or Stravinsky's *Norwegian Moods*. No live-action color camera could do for the West Indies what Covarrubias has done in painting. I have often thought that the *Habañera*, or even a group of Calypsos, against his silky greens, murky jungle yellows, and luminescently coppery islanders, would be a striking experiment. Javanese, Egyptian carvings can be brought to life to the sounds of their ancient rhythms and instruments.

Mosaics and tapestries have enchanting stories to tell—in fact, will become understandable to most of us only when they become more human. The run-of-the-mill tapestry contains about the same degree of credibility to me as a petrified salamander. I can't believe the salamander ever salamandered, and the tapestry looks about as human as a geological fault. We can do something about it if we will, and there are several reasons why we should—among them a personal one of my own concerning a seventeenth-century bucolic tapestry called "Apollo and the Muses." The things is crowded with variously voluptuous and idiotically unconcerned ladies in déshabille, surrounding a handsome rube, dressed in a shirt, with a twenty-five pound lyre poised lightly in his off hand. His other hand is daintily uplifted, preparatory to a downward strum. He apparently is a past master at his instrument because his head is upturned toward a sort of Stuka angel whose power dive has carried him within about three feet of our hero's face. This little monster is on the point of releasing a very lethal-looking arrow. For three hundred and forty years this scene has remained in a state of suspended animation, and I, for one, would like to unsuspend it—if only to determine whether our friend succeeds in finishing his piece or gets spitted. His girl friends may be unconcerned, but I am not.

5) SATIRE. Satire, as I use it here, is best exemplified in such cartoons as *The Band Concert* (1935) and one we made at Warners called *Rhapsody in Rivets* (1941). I shall consider the latter because I am more familiar with it. Friz Freleng, who made the picture, seems to have a complete disregard—perhaps contempt—for the pomp, ceremony, and sacred concept of music. *Rhapsody in Rivets* took the second *Hungarian Rhapsody* of Franz Liszt and performed a nice job of first-degree premeditated murder. The visual theme was the construction of a building. The job foreman served as orchestra conductor, using the blueprints as a score. The riveting machines served as instruments. As I describe it, this may sound like the usual cornily gagged cartoon; I assure you that it was not. The music was not used as a background, but as the dictating factor in the actions of the characters. Thus, when the musical pace was *allegro* their actions became quick and lively; if the music moved to *prestissimo* they became frantic in their endeavor to keep up with it. It moved from there to *mysterioso, grave,* or *pianissimo*; in any case, the characters were dragged inexorably with it. It didn't take the audience long to appreciate what was happening—I can tell you they laughed. They split their stitches.

In this field of satire one factor constitutes a limitation of sorts: the piece selected should have a certain amount of familiarity, because this adds anticipatory enjoyment for the audience. Other than this the field is limited only by the imagination of the cartoonist and the satiric ability of the musician. They should "hoke" the number to the nicest degree of subtlety, the cartoonist going the composer one point better in his degree of shading, particularly in pace and arrangement. (Friz Freleng, who displays an unusual mastery of this sort of thing, seems to have a preference for Hungarians; because he later directed a take-off on the immortal Three Little Pigs, using as his theme the immortal Brahms *Hungarian Dances*.)

6) ABSTRACT OR ABSOLUTE. Here is the greatest field for controversy because here the composer does not define his intention; he does not tell us

what he means, or what ax he is grinding. So we all form our own ideas, and when some lout comes along and presumes to interpret *his* way, we get all stuffy and hot under the collar, and resentful, and start muttering, ". . . where the devil does *he* get off, the big stuffed shirt." Rightfully, too. He has the right to think or say what he wants to, and ours is the right to disagree as vociferously as we will. Dorothy Thompson found *Fantasia* fascistic; she is entitled to that opinion, even though it was a little startling to the artists who made *Fantasia*.

I believe that the best solution to interpretation of abstract music is to go along with it; that is, to be abstract graphically. Audiences may read into your drawings the thing they've been visualizing all the time. I don't mean that you can throw a blob of ultramarine on the screen and hope thereby that the lady in the third row is going to find her dream prince, while the old gentleman in the right rear is mentally gulping flagons of sparkling mead. But there are some generally accepted symbols in art as in music. Just as the low note of a contrabassoon does not conjure in your mind "hummingbird," a single scarlet line does not, in drawing, say "elephant." These are definite things, yet it is possible to find abstract sounds and abstract images that are sympathetic. Here are two abstract shapes.

And here are two abstract words: "tackety" and "goloomb." The words become sounds when spoken, but they have no specific meanings. Yet it is simple to match the abstract words and sounds to the abstract shapes. The angular shape is obviously "tackety," and the curved one "goloomb."

Or, and now we are approaching music, take these two figures:

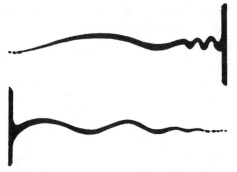

And take two sounds: "ooooooooooomp" and "poooooooooooo-o-."

To go clear into music, which of these is the bassoon, and which is the harp?

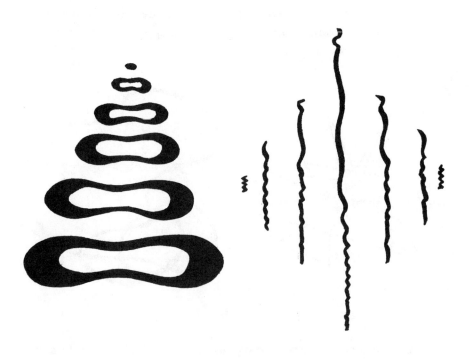

Andante thus becomes:

Abandon:

Crescendo could be thus:

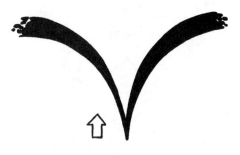

Diminuendo so:

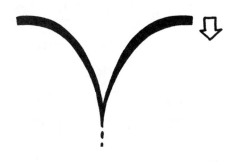

These are static examples of what are mostly static sounds. The art of animation brings them to life, brings them fluidity and power; endows them, in short, with qualities of music. The field of graphic symbols is a great but highly unexplored field. It will, I believe, prove an important one to the musician, and to any audience that is interested in satisfying the visual appetite, side by side with the auditory appetite.

An article of this kind can only be sketchy. We are dealing with a relatively new but immensely versatile and horizonless medium. The ideas suggested in this paper serve merely to suggest, or outline, a few possibilities from *one* viewpoint. Any imaginative person can easily elaborate on it. My sincere hope is that

A lobby card from one of Chuck Jones' later musical (ad)ventures, *High Note*.
© Warner Bros., Inc.

such people in the motion picture industry will see fit to do so. Only one serious danger confronts the animator: an underevaluation of his medium. If the motion picture producer, writer, or musician believes the end purpose of the animated cartoon to be the cartoon short of today, then it must follow that the end purpose of easel painting is the comic strip. The animated cartoon as an artistic, educational, and entertainment medium is in its infancy. Its maturity depends on you.

Originally appeared in Hollywood Quarterly *Vol. I, No. 4 (July 1946), 364-370. © 1946 by The Regents of the University of California. Reprinted by permission.*

Classical Music and Hollywood Cartoons

A Primer on the Cartoon Canon

by DANIEL GOLDMARK

AT THIS VERY moment, people of all ages throughout the United States—in fact, all over the world—are learning the rudiments of "classical music," that all-encompassing genre distinction that includes music not just from the so-called Classical era of the mid- to late eighteenth century, but music from about the 1700s clear through to the turn of the twentieth century as well. But they aren't learning about Beethoven, Chopin, and Liszt in the classroom or the concert hall; no, scads of people are getting their first exposure to such composers from animated cartoons. From *Rhapsody in Rivets* to *Fantasia 2000*, classical music has always been essential to the sound of the Hollywood cartoon, giving directors and writers story ideas while simultaneously providing cartoon composers with familiar—and, therefore, surefire—material for musical underscore.

The integral role of any form of music—classical or otherwise—can be seen in cartoons just by looking at their names: Silly *Symphonies*, *Musical* Miniatures, Color *Rhapsodies*, Merrie *Melodies*, and so on. These cartoons all let you know from the start that music plays a big part in their existence. Classical works found a welcome home in cartoons very early on, especially when directors could use a piece of music as the basis for a short—the original *modus operandum* for Disney's Silly Symphonies. ("Program music," with a ready-to-go plot to explain the music, was especially useful; this includes pieces like Rossini's overture to the opera *William Tell* or Mendelssohn's symphonic overture *The Hebrides*.)

While the list of classical works used in cartoons numbers in the hundreds,[1] a select few appear in short after short. These pieces have, over the years, established themselves as a veritable cartoon canon, a collection of works whose status as animation fodder has been cemented in recent years with their inclusion in such classical CD anthologies as RCA Victor's *Cartoon Classics: Classical Favorites from Classic Cartoons* and Deutsche Grammophon's *Mad About Cartoons*, which sports the tagline "Over 70 Minutes of Digital Madness." While Rossini's *William Tell Overture* tops the list handily, its concurrent life as the theme to *The Lone Ranger* radio and television series helps to explain its popularity. Far less easy to explain, however, is a mid-nineteenth century work for piano, and later, for piano and orchestra: Franz Liszt's second Hungarian Rhapsody, a piece that has become synonymous with cartoon music.

Let's spend a moment with this piece: the Rhapsody shows up as the featured work in more cartoons than any other single piece, including *Bars & Stripes* (Columbia, 1931), *Rhapsody in Rivets* (Warner Bros., 1941), *Rhapsody Rabbit* (Warner Bros., 1946), *The Cat Concerto* (MGM, 1947), *The Magic Fluke* (UPA, 1949), *The Convict Concerto* (Lantz, 1954), and even one of George Pal's Puppetoons, *Dipsy Gypsy* (Paramount, 1941; with violin work by Andre Koestelanetz). Mel Blanc, as Daffy Duck, even performed a vocalese-cum-patter song version of the Rhapsody on one of the singles Capitol Records released featuring the Looney Tunes characters in 1950, titled "Daffy Duck's Rhapsody"; likewise, when Bugs Bunny and Tweety join Doris Day and Jack Carson in a musical dream sequence in *My Dream Is Yours* (1949), their song begins as a spoof of the Rhapsody. No other piece of classical music has been so closely associated with the state of being animated.

Friz Freleng's *Rhapsody in Rivets* gives us as an ideal example of how cartoons can approach an individual piece of classical music, even if the setting is, in this case, less than refined.[2] Instead of taking place in a concert hall or outdoor auditorium, *this* performance of Liszt's Rhapsody transpires at a construction site, where the onlooking audience, peering over the privacy fence, applauds the arrival of the conductor/foreman from his dressing room/office. He is replete with long hair and a cigar—giving the performance's leader at once a touch of refinement and mundanity. With a ruler replacing a baton and the score supplanted by blueprints, the show begins with the rhapsody's familiar strains played on instruments—instruments of mass construction (sledge, jack and ball-peen hammers, cement hoppers, saws, trowels—the works) that emphasize the percussive side of Liszt's bombastic piece.

With a piece this familiar, Freleng could easily rend the rhapsody tune by tune, working out each visual gag mimetically with its matching melody before moving onto the next. As he put it, "[The Rhapsody is] one of my favorite numbers. I know it and I can manipulate it. I can make it stop, like a conductor. Or I can slow it down. That's one thing about the number: You can use a phrase, you can repeat it, and it still works!"[3] The Rhapsody consists of a collection of short, idiosyncratic, and interrelated melodies—making them that much easier to remember—that Liszt repeats or revisits numerous times. The repetitive nature of the piece lends itself well to a cartoon translation. Each reiterated motif allows the director to continue to hammer on a visual gag until it hits home. For example, a series of fast, upward glissandi near the Rhapsody's conclusion becomes an ideal bit of underscoring for a bricklaying octopus; the creature lays four bricks in a row, followed by a troweling of cement, precisely in concert with each phrase of the music. Freleng found such passages of the Rhapsody so visually evocative that he focused on the same moments four years later during Bugs's performance of the piece in *Rhapsody Rabbit*.

A slowly building freneticism beneath the various folklike tunes reveals the other quality of the Rhapsody that suits it to animation: its madcap, near-entropic career into musical chaos. By its conclusion, the music comes so quickly that it's all Freleng and his builders can do to keep up with what Liszt is throwing them—making the cartoon that much funnier. If ever in doubt, speed things up.

Proof that this piece remains *the* archetypal/paradigmatic/stereotypical performance piece for cartoons—and I *do* mean a piece to be performed, not just played—appears in *Who Framed Roger Rabbit?* (1988). When private detective Eddie Valiant ventures to the Ink & Paint Club for a "'Toon Revue—Strictly Humans Only," he is greeted by a four-hand performance of the Rhapsody as played by two cartoon ducks—Daffy *and* Donald—both of whom are attempting to outdo one another in a pianistic duel. (Donald, wearing a tuxedo, plays on a grand piano, while the typically nude Daffy plays a less prestigious upright.) While Valiant looks askance at the performance's explosive finale, Marvin Acme giggles, "Those ducks are funny. They never get to finish the act!" Once again, the Rhapsody is served up as *the* example of cartoon classical music. It's especially appropriate in a venue for "humans only," as we've been led to believe over the years that this is perhaps the only music cartoon characters even know!

Perhaps the greatest irony of the Rhapsody's presence in cartoons is that we cannot consider it as a masterwork of the classical canon—it's not even close. It may have Liszt's parental pedigree, but it is neither serious enough, nor of the proper nationality (that is, Germanic), to fulfill the criteria held by the more austere members of the canon. Symphonies and chamber works don't typically appear in cartoons, usually because their melodies are not as easily excerpted; the theme from Beethoven's Fifth Symphony marks an obvious and important exception (particularly with its instantly identifiable four-note rhythmic/melodic motive). Instead, we find symphonic or operatic overtures and short piano pieces, all with well-known melodies and past histories of use in early film and marching bands, making up the bulk of the cartoon canon.

The overture to Rossini's opera *William Tell* tops the list, of course, but there's also his overtures to *The Thieving Magpie* and *Semiramide*; other composers include Franz von Suppé (*The Light Cavalry*; *Poet and Peasant*; *Morning, Noon, and Night in Vienna*; *Jolly Robbers*, and *Beautiful Galatea*); Felix Mendelssohn (*The Hebrides* and *Ruy Blas*); and Richard Wagner (*Rienzi, The Flying Dutchman,* and *Tannhäuser*). Some of the more obscure or unusual choices include works by Bederich Smetana (*The Bartered Bride*), Mikhail Glinka (*Russlan and Ludmilla*), Friedrich Flotow (*Martha*), and Ferdinand Hérold (*Zampa, the Pirate*).

While Liszt's rhapsody may hold the record for most onscreen performances in a cartoon, Figaro's first aria from Rossini's *The Barber of Seville*, "Largo al Factotum," certainly wins as the opera selection featured most often, either in its entirety (*Barber of Seville* [Lantz, 1944], *Magical Maestro* [MGM, 1952]) or in pieces (*You Ought to Be in Pictures* [Warner Bros., 1940], *Notes to You* and its remake, *Back Alley Oproar* [Warner Bros., 1941 and 1948], *The Whale Who Wanted to Sing at the Met* segment of *Make Mine Music* [Disney, 1946], and *Long-Haired Hare* [Warner Bros., 1949]). Once again, a mixture of the piece's stature as a popular favorite among singers and audiences alike, its easily recognizable melody that can be divided into numerous sections, and its overall quick and playful nature give it an edge over almost all other contenders. It even appears briefly in *Rhapsody Rabbit*; as Bugs reaches the end of one of Liszt's phrases on the piano that resembles the Rossini, he begins singing "Fi-ga-ro! Fi-ga-ro!" For ensemble numbers, the sextet from Donizetti's *Lucia di Lammermoor* appears more often than any other; especially popular gags for this piece have all of a recently deceased cat's nine lives singing the various parts (as in the finales to *Notes to You* and *Back Alley Oproar*).

With such a variety of pieces to choose from, it's no wonder that classical tunes immediately found their way into the earliest sound cartoons, especially since all the pieces listed above were in the public domain, and would cost the typically cash-strapped animation studios nothing to license.[4] For the first decade or so after *Steamboat Willie* (1928) made sound in cartoons a necessity, all the studios used classical music to underscore scenes—western spoofs using the "Lone Ranger"/*William Tell* music, maritime moments referencing the overture to Wagner's *The Flying Dutchman*—or as the inspiration for a story, either symphonic (Harman-Ising's *A Tale of the Vienna Woods* [1934]) or operatic (Lantz's *Chili con Carmen* [1930]). One particularly popular plotline involved the corruption of good (that is, classical) music with its biggest foe and rival, jazz (or swing or boogie woogie or ragtime or crooning). Hollywood features constantly played off the proponents of good and wholesome classical music against the evil forces of lasciviously dancing, morals-breaking, elders-ignoring, swing/jazz-loving kids, seen in films like *100 Men and a Girl* (1937), *Babes in Arms* (1939), and, of course, *The Jazz Singer*. As with anything else happening in Hollywood cinema, Hollywood cartoons followed suit—and then some. Some examples include a literal battle between the lands of classical and jazz in Disney's *Music Land* (1935) and Warner Bros.'s animated adaptation of *The Jazz Singer*, *I Love to Singa* (1936), a heartwarming story about the young Owl Jolson and his desire to sing "about the moon-a and the June-a and the spring-a."[5]

Then, in 1940, *Fantasia* happened. Like everyone else, the Disney studio had approached the classics faithfully and respectfully, throwing in some good-natured interruptions with cartoons like *The Band Concert*.[6] *Fantasia* forever positioned Disney on the side of highbrow music aficionados, not only by giving beautiful visual tales to go along with the musical narratives, but also by showing Disney's allegiance to such cultured personages as Leopold Stokowski and Deems Taylor. While the technological and budgetary excesses of the Fantasound system, combined with the off-putting highbrow bent of the film's overall message, meant that *Fantasia* would not financially break even for decades, the film threw down an ideological gauntlet. Naturally, other studios took up the challenge; references and jokes to Disney, especially when dealing with classical music, appeared continually through the years. The attempt to plant classical music—and by extension, the idiosyncrasies of concert hall culture—safely upon an ivory tower only meant that it had to be violated.

Warner Bros., and in particular Bob Clampett, Friz Freleng, and Chuck Jones, seemed most interested in the attack. The studio's cartoons in this vein include *Rhapsody in Rivets, A Corny Concerto* (1943), *Pigs in a Polka* (1943), *Rhapsody Rabbit, Long-Haired Hare, The Rabbit of Seville* (1950), and *What's Opera, Doc?* (1957). While these cartoons all share commonalities, each director glommed onto singular aspects of *Fantasia*'s worldly image to frustrate. Clampett's interpretations of Johann Strauss's "A Tale of the Vienna Woods" and "The Blue Danube" in *A Corny Concerto* take Disney's balletic Silly Symphonies approach to storytelling and torment it ruthlessly. Elmer Fudd's presence—in place of Deems Taylor—immediately sets the stage. He tries to describe for the audience the "whispering rhythm of the woodwinds," but his starched collar (a brilliant anti-highbrow gag) refuses to cooperate and keeps erupting from his shirt front to hit him in the face—a sign of what's to come. Bugs and Porky perform the prototypical Warner Bros. hunting sketch in "A Tale of the Vienna Woods," but Clampett's sense of humor—from Porky's holding up a sign saying "I'm Hunting That *!?@# Rabbit!" to Bugs pirouetting off at the end in a pink bra and tutu—shows that he saw the music as ripe for a less serious interpretation than Disney might attempt.

Chuck Jones's cartoons concerning classical music—all created with Mike Maltese as writer—are both the most loving and scathingly critical satires of the culture of the concert hall ever created. Of particular interest to Jones and Maltese seem to have been the artificiality of the performance of classical music and the aura of sanctity that clung to it, a cultural shield strengthened by proponents such as Stokowski. It comes as no surprise when, in *Long-Haired Hare*, Bugs makes an appearance as none other than the great man himself, as the terrified instrumentalists gasp "Leopold!" in his wake. In *The Rabbit of Seville*, Bugs likewise sidetracks a performance, with Elmer as an unwilling participant. Sticking to the safety of the overture to *The Barber of Seville* (parodied almost as often as Figaro's "Largo al Factotum"), Jones creates a contrafactum overture, an opera within the opera that has more to do with the perennial Bugs-Elmer chase than with the opera itself. The music may guide the action, but the sequence of gags (Bugs sending a snake-charmed electric razor after Elmer, Elmer getting his bald pate massaged by Bugs the Barber) is about slapstick, not opera.

What's Opera, Doc?, easily one of the most well-known short cartoons ever created, draws on a complex gathering of musical and cultural conventions to construct a generalized view of the Wagnerian universe and the world of opera as a whole. Jones's approach could not have been simpler: he took the most familiar parts of Wagner from the whole of the composer's dramatic oeuvre—including a hodgepodge of famous tunes and a set of stereotypical plot devices for a story—and poured them into the prefab form of his most famous work, *The Ring of the Niebelungen*. This allowed Jones to, as he put it, "take fourteen hours of *The Ring of the Niebelungen* and reduce it to six minutes."[7] His choice of Wagner for his operatic parody makes sense from the perspective of spectacle: Wagner's fantastic worlds of knights, goddesses, and magic made for a far richer visual presentation then the less-than-spectacular comedies of mistaken identity and class conflict associated with Rossini and other comic opera composers. Yet Wagner's vocal writing did not work well as cartoon music; his interminable melodies could not be excerpted easily. *What's Opera, Doc?* thus consists of excerpts of various orchestral portions of Wagner's operas, usually the overtures. This includes pieces of *Rienzi* (Wagner's second opera, nowadays almost totally out of circulation), *Tannhäuser, Der fliegende Holländer, Die Walküre,* and *Siegfried*. Instead of taking the *Ring* and condensing it, Jones appropriated those parts of Wagner's operas that were guaranteed to get an audience reaction. Likewise, the dramatic elements in the story do not

come from any opera in particular, but are rather archetypical operatic situations: an overture, a love duet/dance, a show of magic, a masculine hero/warrior type on display, and a tragic death scene. In the end, Jones and writer Maltese presented their view of Wagner as they knew him, in the hopes that audiences could appreciate it from either level: highbrows could look at it as a witty play on opera with many subtle in-jokes, while non-initiates could jeer at the silly, overwrought singing and acting of *all* operas as parodied by Bugs and Elmer.

Jones's colleague at Warner Bros., Friz Freleng, also had a penchant for tackling classical themes; in Freleng's case, however, the piece itself, not necessarily the performer or the place, was the target. As with Jones, we have a satirical triptych: *Rhapsody in Rivets*, *Rhapsody Rabbit*, and *Pigs in a Polka*. These three cartoons not only have the same director, they share a nationality: Hungary. Both of the *Rhapsody* cartoons focus exclusively on performances of Liszt's second Hungarian Rhapsody, while *Pigs in a Polka,* the musical setting of the Three Little Pigs, uses four of Brahms's Hungarian Dances (numbers 5, 6, 7, and 17). We also cannot forget about *Pizzicato Pussycat* (1955), which turns the Bermuda Triangle of cat, mouse, and piano—held up for all to see in the Tom & Jerry shorts *The Cat Concerto* and *Johann Mouse* (1952)—on its side. Rather than having the cat play on his own or having the mouse lead the performance astray (as in *The Cat Concerto*), here the mouse is the virtuoso (Padermouski, as the cat dubs him), while the feline simply takes advantage of the situation for some quickly gained (and even more quickly lost) fame—alas, no fortune. Perhaps even more shocking is the appearance of a distinctly non-canonic (in any sense of the term) work at the cartoon's climactic performance. At the cat's Carnegie Hall debut—for which, we see on the street poster, Leopold *Stabowski's* performance has been hastily rescheduled—the cat breaks the mouse's spectacles, causing the tiny pianist to play, as Will Friedwald has described, "frightening Cecil Taylor-like thumps which cause press and public alike to reject the miracle cat as a fraud (the squares)."[8]

Other studios, of course, took their own approaches to the classics. Hanna and Barbera approached classical music only three times during their tenure at MGM, although the public seemed quite taken with their ideas; of the seven Academy Awards for animated short subject they won for MGM, two featured classical music: *The Cat Concerto* and *Johann Mouse. The Cat Concerto* is almost identical to *Rhapsody Rabbit* in scope, although the preexisting relationship and antagonism between Tom and Jerry makes their struggle somewhat more believable, while the rodent that interrupts Bugs's performance seems simply an arbitrary mouse in the ointment. *Johann Mouse* places Tom and Jerry in Johann Strauss's Vienna, one of the numerous costume roles the pair would have in the 1950s (such as *Two Mouseketeers* [1952]). There is also *Tom and Jerry in the Hollywood Bowl* (1950), a cartoon that seems to have inspired Chuck Jones's *Baton Bunny* (1959): both involve the star (Tom and Bugs, respectively) leading a performance at the Bowl, only to have it led astray by Jerry in the former, an anonymous fly in the latter.

Walter Lantz's studio created the only series of shorts dedicated exclusively to classical music, the Musical Miniatures. These began in 1946 with *The Poet and Peasant*, followed by *Musical Moments from Chopin*, *Overture to William Tell*, *The Band Master*, *Kiddie Koncert*, and *Pixie Picnic*, all released from 1946 to 1948. The approach to classical music in these films—all of which were directed by Dick Lundy, who came to Lantz as an animator in late 1943 and was made a director a few months later—is to find a gag in every possible nook and cranny and not proceed to the next scene until every idea has been exhausted. Unlike Warner Bros. or Disney, Lantz used the

Jerry in *The Cat Concerto*. ©Turner Entertainment Company

orchestra pit as a place rife with high jinks—and a likely place it seemed to be, as the jokes just kept coming.

By the time television took over, assaults on specific pieces of music—or even on concert hall culture in general—occurred less often, due in part to the slowly waning popularity of high art music in the United States. This does not mean that cartoons don't still take on opera and orchestras: the plot of an early episode of *The Flintstones* ("The Flintstone Flyer") involves Wilma and Betty going to the opera while Barney supposedly cares for an ill Fred. *The Simpsons* regularly includes references or outright jokes about classical music and opera; at a performance of *Carmen* during the first-season episode "Bart the Genius," Lisa tells Homer that a large singer is the bullfighter, causing Bart to retort "No way a bull's gonna miss a target *that* big, man!!!"

To this day, pieces such as the overtures to *William Tell* and *The Barber of Seville*, Liszt's Rhapsody, and even the Valkyrie leitmotif from Wagner's *Die Walküre* (in Elmer Fudd's voice—"Kill the WA-bbit!") cannot be divorced from the images created for them in cartoons. Indeed, I became a musician because I wanted to learn to play a piece I had heard in a Bugs Bunny cartoon. This phenomenon (and it is a phenomenon—other people have told me similar stories over the years) shows that the imaginary world of animation really does fit well with classical music—a point Disney tried to make more than sixty years ago with *Fantasia*. With cartoons like *What's Opera, Doc?* and *Fantasia* as popular as they've ever been, classical music will never die—just like any other cartoon character.

----

[1]While a surfeit of dramatic and chamber works from the classical tradition have found new lives in cartoons, only a handful of traditional "classical" composers ever wrote music for use in cartoons. The few examples include Paul Hindemith, whose player-piano score for *Felix at the Circus* (1927) is presumed lost; Dimitri Shostakovich, whose scores for the animated shorts *The Tale of the Priest and His Servant Balda* (op. 36, 1934) and *The Silly Little Mouse* (op. 56, 1939) were recently recorded (the latter for the first time ever) on *Shostakovich: Film Music* (Citadel CTD 88129); Paul Dessau, the German composer whose semi-improvised scores for several pre-synchronized-sound Disney "Alice Comedies" still exist; and Alfred Schnittke, another Russian composer who wrote music for such cartoons as *Butterfly* and *Glass Harmonica*. There also exists a classical work whose origins in animation have been misstated: Sergey Prokofiev's symphonic fairy tale *Peter and the Wolf*, which figured largely in the Disney musical compilation film *Make Mine Music* (1946), came into this world as a dramatic work for the Moscow Children's Musical Theatre in 1936. Only after its success did it become a candidate for a Disney treatment a decade later.

[2] To read Chuck Jones's comments on this cartoon, see his "Music and the Animated Cartoon" elsewhere in this volume.

[3] Friz Freleng and David Weber, *Animation: The Art of Friz Freleng* (Newport Beach, CA: Donovan Publishing, 1994), 127.

[4] See "Animated Cartoons and Slap-Stick Comedy" by Lang and West elsewhere in this volume for one approach to cartoon music in the days before synchronized sound.

[5] Jazz's role as the chaos-maker in an otherwise stable world continually appears throughout the years. Even within the sanctity of the Liszt *Rhapsody,* jazz rears its ugly head; during both concert performances of the piece in *Rhapsody Rabbit* and *The Cat Concerto,* momentary derailments occur when the errant mouse begins playing a form of boogie-woogie into which the pianist (Bugs and Tom) cannot help but be drawn.

[6] See Dave Wondrich's essay on *The Band Concert* elsewhere in this volume.

[7] Chuck Jones, "'What's Up, Down Under?' Chuck Jones Talks at *The Illusion of Life* Conference," in *The Illusion of Life: Essays on Animation,* edited by Alan Cholodenko (Sydney, Australia: Power Publications, 1991), 39.

[8] Jerry Beck and Will Friedwald, *Looney Tunes and Merrie Melodies: A Complete Illustrated Guide to the Warner Bros. Cartoons* (New York: Henry Holt and Company, 1989), 268-269. Freleng also directed several cartoons in which Romantic music makes up the majority of the soundtrack, such as *Holiday for Shoestrings* (1946) and *Mouse Mazurka* (1949). The latter shows once again Freleng's apparent love for Eastern Europe, as Sylvester chases a mouse around the house with yet more of Brahms's Hungarian Dances (again nos. 7 and 17), Strauss' "Pizzicato Polka" and "One Heart One Mind Mazurka," and "Cosatchoque," a long-forgotten chestnut by Alexander Dargomïzhsky, a Russian composer who was a contemporary of Glinka's and who was most famous for his operas *Rusalka* and *The Stone Guest.*

Music in Cartoons

by SCOTT BRADLEY

Scott Bradley was born the same month *and* year as Carl Stalling—November 1891. The two had vastly different forms of musical training, however, as Bradley indicates in the self-penned autobiography that follows the first of these pieces. His entire career in cartoons—as far as we know—was spent scoring shorts for MGM, from the very first Harman-Ising production in 1934, *The Discontented Canary*, to the last Tom and Jerry short produced and released under Hanna-Barbera's supervision, *Tot Watchers* (1958). During this entire period, he apparently never once met Carl Stalling—probably his most formidable colleague. When not scoring cartoons, Bradley spent a great deal of time espousing the advantages of being a composer for cartoons, particularly to other composers; he felt that the animated medium offered modern composers the greatest opportunity for creative expression.

One can hear the differences between the Stalling and Bradley styles in seconds. Bradley much preferred to write original music at all possible times, taking the less-than-complimentary idea of mickey mousing and developing it into some of the most directly expressive film music ever created. Because the MGM shorts—those featuring Tom and Jerry, in particular—had more action and less dialogue than the Warner Bros. cartoons, Bradley developed a compositional style that went back and forth between two states. For moments of

A publicity photo of Scott Bradley from the late 1920s, before beginning his career as a composer for cartoons. Courtesy of University of Southern California, on behalf of the USC Specialized Libraries and Archival Collections.

comedy or cartoon zaniness, he would use one of a dozen or so songs to set up a gentle rhythm to the scene, moving things along without commenting directly on the action. When a chase or other madcap action emphasized movement, he used tense clusters of harmony ("shock chords," as he called them) and rapid melodic lines to focus the viewer's attention on each distinct movement a character made. Not that he didn't get tired of writing for cat and mouse games all the time: as he once put it, "It's fights, fights, fights for me . . . and how I am getting tired of them. A beautiful, developed tune—alas, that's never the fate of Scott."[1]

The two pieces that follow are written transcripts of talks Bradley gave in the 1940s, and which were later published in a film music and a music educators journal, respectively. Clearly perceptible in both talks is Bradley's overwhelming desire to raise the public's awareness of the new and innovative work by composers appearing in the world of animation.

We shall show you two examples of cartoon scoring, the first one being *Dance of the Weed* [1941]. In this instance, the usual procedure was reversed, and the entire music score was composed and recorded before the story was written. I believe this is the first attempt to give the composer a break, and is, of course, the ideal way from our own selfish viewpoint. You will note that the music in the opening scenes is in the manner of French Impressionism. The ballet of the flowers is a waltz movement in which the themes of the little weed and the wild rose are combined. Later the terrible snapdragons (who menace w. & f.)[2] are represented by bassoons and basses, while strings and woodwinds play a different theme in the high register. I hope you will notice that we use neither saxophones nor trumpets in the orchestra. However, we use three horns and two trombones; of course we use trumpets and saxes when the action calls for it—in fact all music in pictures must be subordinated to the action. We may feel like writing a string quartet, but if the picture demands *Chinese* music, we write *Chinese* music. Let's have the picture, please.

Now, let us see the *standard* way in which music is written to cartoons. The story is first worked out in close detail, after which time we discuss the music, tempo, feeling, etc., and each sequence is laid out in chronological order. A special page of paper is used, upon which the story, action, camera and color instructions are written on the space provided. The lower part is devoted to what some careless people call music—three staves upon which all of the musical atrocities are committed. These are called "Detail Sheets," and are the Encyclopedia Britannica for all departments. Any changes must be recorded there, otherwise music and action would not synchronize; if we miss the $64 question, it's no radio joke. Incidentally, we never see the picture when we are recording, but depend upon ear phones, in which a click track plays a metronome-like beat for each division of the measure. All departments synchronize to this beat, so that when all parts of the crossword puzzle are assembled, they fit perfectly.

In fact my part is the easiest of all! I just have to write "funny music," that's all—just funny music. Did you ever try to write funny music? Maybe you'd better stay *healthy* and *normal*. You see, since humor is obviously the basis of all cartoons, people need them as an escape from the horrors of war, and we must for the present make only funny pictures, occasionally satirizing the war, as in the subject we shall presently see entitled *Bear Raid Warden* [1944]. But what is "funny music?" It may be funny because of funny circumstances surrounding it.

Music may be funny because it distorts a familiar phrase, such as Gracie Allen's "Concerto for Index Finger." You remember how she played the C-major scale, but always missed the top note and played C#?[3] My own method, if you could call it such, is in trying to maintain a continuous melodic line, and follow the action with new harmonization and orchestration of conventional patterns. This sometimes leads to very harsh dissonances, but remember, we are trying to make it funny, and music can't be both funny and beautiful.

Some years ago, when cartoons were new, it was easy to follow a character up the steps with an ascending scale passage and down again when he ran down. But these patterns soon became too obvious, and we had to dress them up in new fashion. Here are a few examples: take the common diminished seventh arpeggio of D-natural above middle C—it sounds rather ordinary, I am sure, but now, add the diminished seventh arpeggio of A-natural, and play them in parallel fourths—rather fast. To me, it is very exciting, and sounds quite modern. Take the simple chromatic scale—an octave apart—and play it up scale. Sounds like the practice hour, doesn't it? But now, take G-C in the right hand, and add B-natural, D# in the left, proceed chromatically up the keyboard—but don't blame me if the neighbors throw a shoe through your window! So much for scales. When they are orchestrated in this manner for strings and woodwind, they create a feeling of surprise and suspense, and we are not conscious of the fact that they are basically just chromatic scales. Now, try this on your Steinway! One of you lay the melody of "Yankee Doodle" in the key of C, treble, and another one play the accompaniment in the key of B-natural, as a duet. But look out for the neighbors—they will probably throw the other shoe at you. By the way, this may be a good way of getting another pair of shoes without the #3 airplane coupon.

I would like to tell you about a problem which I ran into recently in one of our "Tom & Jerry" cartoons. A little mouse was running around with the mask of a dog over his head—you saw only the little fellow's feet carrying this big head, and it looked very grotesque and funny, but I was stuck for a new way of describing the action musically, and for a whole day I worried about a two-measure phrase. Everything I tried seemed weak and common. Finally, I tried the twelve-tone scale, and *there it was*! This scene was repeated five times within the next fifty seconds and I had only to use my scale—played by the piccolo, oboe and bassoon in unison. I hope Dr. Schoenberg will forgive me for using *his system* to produce funny music, but even the boys in the orchestra laughed when we were recording it.

In the next picture you will hear many instances of musical effects produced with the orchestra, and particularly with the woodwinds. The bassoon is the voice of the bear, while the clarinet or oboe describe the little lightning bug, which makes the old bear's life so miserable. Also, the effect of the bug's tail-light heating up is produced by the violins tremolo, piccolo and xylophone. Those of you who happen to play violin will recognize the first Kreutzer etude where the bear jumps out of bed and goes tearing down the hall. But all of this will be clearer to you after we see the cartoon *Bear Raid Warden*.

♫

Well, that's the story, experimentation, trial and error. If it works, use it—if not, throw it out and try again, for we must always progress, and never be satisfied to use the same formula over and over, otherwise we would still be writing diatonic and chromatic scales. You might like to know that the average amount of music in a cartoon, due to its fast tempo, is about 500 measures. But in spite of it all, scoring cartoons is a lot of fun. We get to thinking of those little characters as human beings who believe in "direct action," and the world needs a few laughs in the midst of so much suffering.

As to the future, I believe that this medium offers the serious composer far more possibilities than the live-action pictures. The animated fantasy of the future will, I hope, be adapted to *pre-composed* music. We have only to imagine a Debussy composing "The Afternoon of a Faun" as the basis of such a picture, to visualize the importance of music in cartoons.

Biography of Scott Bradley

Scott Bradley, musical director for the M-G-M Cartoon Studio, has been living in Los Angeles since 1927. He was conductor for Stations KNX and KHJ from 1930 to 1932, and in 1934 started scoring cartoons for Harman-Ising. In 1938, he joined the Metro-Goldwyn-Mayer Cartoon Studio, composing music for the M-G-M cartoons; conducting the M-G-M orchestra, and occasionally scoring for Pete Smith (ex. "Lions on the Loose").

His compositions include three Symphonic Poems for Orchestra, a Cantata for Chorus and Orchestra (which he conducted with the Los Angeles Philharmonic and Oratorio Society in 1934), and a Suite for Orchestra, "Cartoonia," which was played by Pierre Monteux and the San Francisco Symphony Orchestra in 1940. Setting quite a record for an American composer, "Cartoonia" was subsequently played fifty-six times in Southern California as part of the Los Angeles High School Music Education program.

The National Federation of Music Clubs presented Scott Bradley with an award for his score to the Metro-Goldwyn-Mayer cartoon, *The Homeless Flea* [1940].

His ambition is to score a feature-length cartoon, using an original, pre-composed score—the exact opposite of *Fantasia.* The music for the M-G-M cartoon *Dance of the Weed,* which Bradley composed, is a small example of this idea. He is interested in the application of *modern music* to all pictures, and in original as opposed to adapted scores at all times.

At present, Bradley is writing a Suite for Violin and Piano for Louis Kaufman, based upon humorous themes from cartoon scores.

Although not specializing in the field of jive, Scott Bradley will compose some jive music for a couple of "Tom & Jerry" cartoons which Mr. Quimby has on his production schedule for the near future.[4]

Excerpts from a talk given at The Music Forum, October 28, 1944, which originally appeared in Film Music Notes *IV:III (Dec. 1944). Reprinted by permission of the Scott Bradley estate.*

----

[1] Ingolf Dahl. "Notes on Cartoon Music." *Film Music Notes* 8:5 (May-June 1949), 6.

2 *Editor's note:* Weed and flower.

3 *Editor's note:* A performance of this piece can be found in the movie *Two Girls and a Sailor* (1944).

4 *Editor's note:* Fred Quimby was the producer of the animated shorts at MGM.

Personality on the Soundtrack

A Glimpse Behind the Scenes and Sequences in Filmland

BY SCOTT BRADLEY

BEETHOVEN STARTED IT. The great innovator of the orchestra, in his Pastoral Symphony, imitated the birds of the forest with instruments of the orchestra. However, the music of this beautiful symphony suggests rather than imitates the call of various birds. At least, Beethoven's quail sounds are unlike the ones which awaken me in our San Fernando Valley home. California quail simply give out a joyous, rapid "chup-chup-chup," which is indeed great music in the early morning stillness.

Richard Strauss was more realistic. His imitation of the sheep in the Second Variation of *Don Quixote* is clever enough to fool even the wariest sheep. Saint-Saëns (*Carnival of the Animals*) and Respighi (*The Birds*) are among the other famous composers who gave musical personality to the non-speaking animals.

The whole thing may well have stopped there, had it not been for the evolution of the sound film which gave auditory rather than abstract identity to them. Then came the animated cartoon, which added fantasy and, more often, slapstick. Finally, the film composer appeared—last, as always—but equipped with the devices and tone colors of the modern orchestra, and supplied the music which attempts to personalize the various birds and animals as they appear in cartoons and live-action pictures. We shall discuss in this paper examples of both, the first with live animals. The picture is MGM's *Courage of Lassie* [1946], for which I had the pleasure of composing the music for the forest and animal sequences. The musical treatment presents a special problem, since the first twenty-five minutes contains no dialogue, and music must carry the burden of the story by giving to each animal a certain identity and personality.

The picture opens with a lake scene, which dissolves into a series of short cut-backs to various animals and birds. There are two ways of scoring such a sequence: the first, and by far the easier, is to treat it simply as part of an overall scene, creating a general mood of wild life and nature; the second way is to give each a definite character through the medium of orchestration, with short musical phrases, all blending into a unified composition. The latter seemed the better way, so the scene opens with a tranquil melody in the oboe and solo violin, with harp and strings. Soon the scene cuts to three birds on a tree branch; a syncopated figure, first in flute, then oboe, then bassoon, gives identity to each. Now a beaver is seen drying his face with his hands; he draws two clarinets, playing an eccentric figure in minor seconds. Then a timid little rabbit emerges from a tree trunk, and the oboe hesitates right along with him.

The scene cuts to a little quail hobbling along (a string is tied to his leg to keep him from running away), described by a jumpy little theme in the flute. No attempt is made to imitate his call (who am I to try to improve on Beethoven), but the music synchronizes his action. Here now is a nervous little chipmunk on a log; he gets two piccolos and two oboes in high register. A grumpy old porcupine was given the bassoon treatment, accompanied by glissando celli and low clarinets. The sequence is completed with repetition of the rabbit and bird fragments as the camera cuts back to them. All of this happens in just 121 seconds! How simple. Just be ready with the right music at the right time.

You have probably noted in the above analysis that, for the most part, only a few instruments are playing, chiefly woodwinds, which offer endless combinations in tone color. Why should the whole orchestra be playing (er—pardon me, Mr. Petrillo!) when only these naive and simple characters are having their brief moment in the spotlight? We hear too much "full swell, coupled to great" scoring in pictures, and the human ear gratefully accepts a little contrast.

Later in the picture Lassie, who is only a puppy at the time, meets a huge black bear, and they become good friends. Again, the woodwinds come to the rescue, the contra-bassoon playing a clumsy theme for the bear, while the upper clarinets and flutes play a counter theme for the puppy, playfully blending in complete accord to the friendly action, accompanied of course by the rest of the orchestra. Presently, a vicious eagle swoops down on the puppy; the eagle gets three horns, playing in consecutive fifths (pardon me, you purists, this is drama!). Later, as dialogue is now heard, the orchestra reduces to strings alone.

This is lesson number one in scoring pictures: If you want to hear your music, write for string quintet under dialogue or suffer the consequences. Just throw in a few muted trumpets or staccato wood-winds, and your brain child fades out in favor of the spoken word.

With animated cartoons, it is a different story. Here the action is lusty and uninhibited, and music has a fighting chance to be heard above the sound effects. I stoutly maintain that any progress in creative contemporary film music will be made in this medium because endless experiments in modern harmony and orchestration are acceptable. Since it deals in pure (sometimes, alas, not too pure) fantasy, more freedom in composition is allowed. Established rules of orchestration are blandly ignored, since beauty in cartoons is rarely even skin deep, and we must employ "shock chords" which sometimes reach the outer limits of harmonic analysis.

In the cartoon *The Milky Waif* [1946], we find a scene near the beginning in which a basket is placed upon little Jerry Mouse's doorstep. Suddenly it begins to move, although no one knows what the basket contains nor what causes it to move. Here again music must tell the story, since neither Tom nor Jerry ever talk, thank goodness! No one knows what the music is either, for it is based on a modified form of the twelve-tone scale, quasi Schoenberg. Don't listen for tonic or dominant rest points, for the clarinets, muted trumpets, piano and oboe go their own way entirely independent of each other. Luckily for the audience the scene is brief, and soon the music relaxes into conventional diatonic progressions. Later in the cartoon, a scene definitely demands "Shortenin' Bread." Although original music is usually better for all film scoring, we sometimes have to use well-known tunes as cues. Yes, from Schoenberg to Nelson Eddy all in one reel!

Again, in a recent MGM cartoon, *Dr. Jekyll and Mr. Mouse* [1947], we find burlesque mystery melodrama, as Tom mixes the witches' brew while trying to exterminate Jerry Mouse. The music is mock-dramatic, with the horn motive in C-sharp against a four-octave tremolo in C-major in the strings. The dark colors of English horn, bass clarinet and viola add intensity to little Jerry's dilemma, as he unsuspectingly samples the potion. However, the tables are turned on Tom, as the poison, far from exterminating Jerry, makes a raging demon of him. As he stalks relentlessly after Tom, the full orchestra plays an ostinato march, the harmonic structure being based on parallel fourths in altered form, while the timpani and four horns blast out the *Superman* theme. Fun? Loads of it! I'd rather score a cartoon like this than a half-dozen ordinary live-action pictures. No noisy actors shouting at the top of their voices, drowning perfectly good music!

But whatever the situation, be it cartoon or live action, the orchestra is always ready to supply personality on the soundtrack—pointing up the highlights of one scene, emphasizing the intensity of another, and making possible long sequences of silent action which, but for the music, would be unbearable.

Originally appeared in Music Educators Journal *Volume XXXIII, No. 3 (January 1947), 28–29. © 1947 by MENC. Reprinted with permission.*

Make Mine Music and the End of the Swing Era

by STUART NICHOLSON

Make Mine Music (1946) was widely seen as the follow-up to Walt Disney's critically acclaimed animated feature *Fantasia* (1940) and is remembered today not so much for what it was, but for what it was not—another *Fantasia*. With the passage of time it has consequently become both undervalued and overlooked. Although one of Disney's long-held ambitions was to make a sequel to *Fantasia,* it was by no means clear when work began on it in 1942 that it would turn out to be such a modest production as *Make Mine Music*. Even so, it received mostly favorable reviews when exhibited at the first Cannes Film Festival in September and October 1946, although *The Times* in London had earlier noted that "Mr. Walt Disney . . . turns over the medal that was *Fantasia;* Benny Goodman, Dinah Shore, and the Andrews Sisters take the place of Beethoven and Bach and instead of embarking on a voyage on perilous seas . . . for the most part, dabbles about in the swimming pool."[1] In a sense this review sums up the long shadow cast by *Fantasia.*

I wish to explore here the reasons why Disney was forced to turn away from his critically acclaimed use of animation to reflect the programmatic and coloristic aspects of classical music that had produced the enduring classic *Fantasia*, and probe the assumption that because he turned to popular culture in *Make Mine Music,* the latter should be considered a lesser work. Indeed, two frequently ignored episodes for the film, made in collaboration with the immensely popular bandleader Benny Goodman, represent the most successful marriage of jazz and animation yet, and—although no one realized it at the time—perhaps the final great flourish of the swing era.

♫

While *Fantasia* might not have been an instant hit at the box office, it nevertheless drew wide critical acclaim. In particular, three key scenes based on the extradiegetic soundtrack of Bach's *Toccata and Fugue in D Minor*, Stravinsky's *Rite of Spring*, and Moussorgsky's *Night on Bald Mountain* were cited for particular praise. Encouraged, Disney had begun to conceptualize a sequel to *Fantasia* as early as 1942. Eight pieces of classical music were chosen to provide inspiration for the animators, including Claude Debussy's "Clair de Lune," originally cut from the final print of *Fantasia*; John Alden Carpenter's "Adventures in a Perambulator"; Carl Maria von Weber's "Invitation to the Waltz"; and Sergei Prokofiev's *Peter and the Wolf.* However, plans were put on hold because of Disney's wartime commitments to the U.S. Government and military.

These commitments, together with his "violent, vivid efforts at propaganda on behalf of the South American republics,"[2] intermittent labor problems, and the inaccessibility of the European market, seriously affected the studio's profitability. It meant that Disney "finished the war deflated, downhearted, and short-tempered."[3] His brother Roy attempted to stimulate him by reviving the plans for a *Fantasia* sequel, but the cash-strapped studio was unable to contemplate a project of such ambition. Instead, it downscaled the project, using cut-price shorts and popular singers such as Dinah Shore, Nelson Eddy, the Andrews Sisters, and, as a sop to Disney's musical pretensions, Prokofiev's *Peter and the Wolf.* What emerged was *Make Mine Music*, described in its opening shots as "a musical fantasy in ten parts" that gave Disney's Silly Symphonies the impossible task of matching the gravitas of the classical canon. It is only when *Make Mine Music* is viewed in the context of the earlier *Saludos Amigos* (1943) and *The Three Caballeros* (1945) (which also combined separate animated sequences, the latter also using live sequences) and the later *Melody Time* (1948) that its more modest aspirations become clear.

♫

In late May 1944, *Hollywood Review* announced that Disney had resumed production on the previously shelved musical feature, now provisionally titled *Swing Street*, describing it as a "saga of music from modern classic to boogie woogie." But even the *Swing Street* concept was thought too elitist for a studio that desperately needed to generate a quick return at the box office, so it soon gave way to a more populist approach renamed *Make Mine Music. Fantasia*, it must be remembered, was not a box office hit when it was first released in 1940, and it was not until decades later that the original cost of the film was recouped. *Make Mine Music* had ten unrelated musical segments and was the first of what became known as a Disney "package feature." Subsequent packages included *Melody Time,* with seven subjects; *Fun and Fancy Free* (1947) and *The Adventures of Ichabod and Mr. Toad* (1949), with two subjects each; and *Music Land,* with nine (recycling sequences from both *Make Mine Music* and *Melody Time*). When the ten-reel, seventy-five-minute *Make Mine Music* feature premiered in New York on April 20, 1946, the results were certainly uneven, but not entirely devoid of Disney magic or musical highlights.

After the opening credits, which appear on the outside of a movie theatre, the film opens with a hillbilly story of two feuding families, from which the "rustic ballad" "The Martins and the Coys" (written by Al Cameron and former bandleader Ted Weems) takes its name. It is followed by a "tone poem" using the music of "Blue Bayou," sung by the Ken Darby Chorus (Darby was an associate musical director of the film) as two white cranes fly through a quiet bayou. This replaced "Clair de Lune," recorded by the Philadelphia Orchestra under Leopold Stokowski, that had been dropped from *Fantasia* and had been provisionally slated for inclusion in its sequel. Then came one of the film's high points, "A Jazz Interlude" with the Benny Goodman big band, one of two segments that survived the *Swing Street* concept. It was followed by "a ballad in blue," the song "Without You," sung by Andy Russell, with on-screen rain and shadowy scenery reflecting the blue mood of the song. The fifth number, a "musical recitation," is a baseball sketch based on the poem "Casey at the Bat" by Ernest Lawrence Thayer, and features the song "Casey (The Pride of Them All)," sung by Jerry Colonna. A ballet scene follows, incorporating "Two Silhouettes," sung by Dinah Shore, and leads into Prokofiev's *Peter and the Wolf.* The animators added to the fairy tale "a mischievous duck and a feisty and temperamental cat as well as a highly eccentric wolf."[4] The eighth story is the other sequence from the *Swing Street* concept, again featuring Benny Goodman. The penultimate sequence has the Andrews Sisters singing "Johnny Fedora and Alice Bluebonnet," a Victorian tearjerker about two hats that fall in love. And the finale consists of an "opera pathetique" called "The Whale Who Wanted to Sing at the Met," featuring Nelson Eddy, who sang the soprano, tenor, baritone, and bass parts through overdubbing, and the Pied Pipers. It includes a brief version of "Shortnin' Bread," as well as excerpts from *The Barber of Seville, Lucia de Lammermoor, Tristan und Isolde, Faust,* and "May Heaven Grant You Pardon" from *Martha, oder Der Markt zu Richmond.* According to a press report from 1946,[5] Disney said his studio could not obtain the rights to use music from Leoncavallo's *I Pagliacci,* so Eddy wrote a piece intended to evoke "Vesti la Giubba," complete with sobs, causing some commentators to erroneously report that the aria had been included in the film.

Of these ten subjects, only four were considered by Disney as worthy of rerelease as shorts in their own right: *Peter and the Wolf, The Whale Who Wanted to Sing at the Met,* and the two Goodman items. The remainder he considered "execrable and [he] was tempted to sack the animators on the spot."[6] *The Whale Who Wanted to Sing at the Met* was rereleased as *Willie the Operatic Whale* in 1954.

Prokofiev, who had been greatly impressed by *Snow White and the Seven Dwarfs,* had met Disney in Hollywood in the spring of 1938, where they discussed future projects—possibly including the idea of *Fantasia.*[7] It is at this point that Prokofiev's *Peter and the Wolf* may have come to Disney's attention: the piece was given its U.S. premiere a week or two later by the Boston Symphony Orchestra conducted by Koussevitsky, with both Disney and Prokofiev in attendance. The film segment, animated by Ward Kimball, turned out to be Disney's favorite of *Make Mine Music,* and was reissued in 1955. When it was suggested he reissue *Fantasia,* Disney imposed the condition that *Peter and the Wolf* be included. (In the end, *Fantasia's* reissue did not include *Peter and the Wolf.*)

Yet if the *Peter and the Wolf* sequence was to Disney a glimpse of what might have been a new *Fantasia,* when the animators confronted the two jazz subjects provided by the Benny Goodman groups, they provided a resounding clue as to what *Swing Street* might have been, perfectly matching the music in mood and gesture in a way that was as appropriate to jazz as *Fantasia* was to classical music. If *Fantasia* inspires awe, then the jazz animations of *Make Mine Music* inspire simple delight. At the time of the film's release, the London *Times* noted that one segment, *All the Cats Join In,* was "a shrewd satire on the ways of the American teenage generation" that "had delightful ingenuity."[8] Goodman's two segments were subsequently rereleased as the short *Two for the Record,* and in 1955 they were added to *Johnny Fedora and Alice Bluebonnet* and *Casey at the Bat* by Jerry Colonna and combined with five selections from *Melody Time* for a new Disney "package feature" called *Music Land*.

♫

Given Disney's right-wing prejudices against blacks and Jews,[9] it is surprising that he not only chose to feature jazz, an African American art form, but also Goodman for the film. A photo in the Disney Archive at the British Library[10] shows Disney and Goodman at a dining table sharing drinks, suggesting their relationship at the time of making the film was also social. If today Goodman's cameos in *Make Mine Music* reawaken the old shibboleths that have always surrounded him—those of a white bandleader who came to exemplify jazz for millions of people during the Swing Era at the expense of the black originators of the music—it is also important to remember that Goodman was a jazz great in his own right, who presented black exemplars of the music by his side on stage and on film, and who was always unstinting in his praise for the contributions of his black band members and arrangers.[11]

Goodman had disbanded his regular orchestra on March 9, 1944, following a dispute with his booking office (MCA), and little was heard from him until May, when he made a couple of radio performances. In June he recruited an integrated orchestra in New York for his participation in *Make Mine Music,* including trumpeter Charlie Shavers, tenor saxophonist Don Byas, pianist Teddy Wilson, and drummer Cozy Cole. On June 12, he recorded two pieces for the animated feature: a big band version of "All the Cats Join In" (composed by Goodman's key arranger of the early 1940s, Eddie Sauter, with lyrics added by Alec Wilder and Ray Gilbert, and arranged by Goodman's staff arranger at the time, Johnny Thompson, who had also arranged several pieces for Goodman's appearance in the film *Sweet and Low-down* in February) and a quartet version of "After You've Gone," recorded with Wilson, bassist Sid Weiss, and Cole.

Although Goodman had used vocalist Evelyn White for "All the Cats Join In," the vocal in the film was by June Hutton and the Ken Darby singers, sung a capella, recorded in Hollywood, and overdubbed onto the big band sound track.[12] This performance, sans vocal, with Teddy Wilson's piano obbligato functioning as a solo—together with the quartet's version of "After You've Gone"—would appear on the Capitol label some years later, originally on a seven-inch extended play disc called *Two for the Record*. (They are not to be confused with a Capitol ten-inch 78-rpm disc released around the time of the film of "All the Cats Join In" by the Charles Wolcott Orchestra coupled with "Two Silhouettes" by Peggy Lee, bearing the legend "From Walt Disney's *Make Mine Music*"—despite a good clarinet solo on the former.) Goodman also recorded a separate version of "All the Cats Join In" for Columbia with a vocal by Liza Morrow on February 6, 1946, again using the Johnny Thompson arrangement, to coincide with the release of *Make Mine Music*. He performed it on sustaining radio broadcasts from the 400 Restaurant in New York through May and June, and his last known performance of it is in a September "Benny Goodman Show" broadcast.

Yet it is the soundtrack version that captures our attention. As the motion picture soundtrack anthology of big band performances recorded for MGM musicals between 1939–1948, *Alive and Kickin',* revealed, the original studio recordings for film soundtracks used "multiple microphonic angles" that produced "multichannel masters" not possible using standard 78-rpm recording technology.[13] The resultant sound quality is of an exceptionally high standard for the period. On "All the Cats Join In," the balance between the horn sections and rhythm section is excellent; the saxophone section, impeccably led by Goodman veteran Hymie Schertzer, is perfectly balanced in tonal weight and vibrato; the trumpet section phrases as one man under the leadership of Billy Butterfield; and the rhythm section is crisp and poised, with a clear distinction between piano, guitar, bass, and drums. Yet everything unites to form a propulsive "swing." The soundtrack vocal by June Hutton follows the Swing Era custom of having a girl singer, variously called "the femme warbler," "the canary," or "the chirp" by the music press of the day, as an "added extra" to front the all-male institution of the big band. Hutton and her backing group evoke times past rather than the present, and add to the period effect—the Capitol instrumental version without a vocal sounds far more streamlined. The solos—by Goodman, Wilson, Vernon Brown on trombone, Butterfield, and Byas—are models of well-conceived logic, each filling the brief windows of opportunity afforded them to maximum effect within the overall orchestral scheme. Sauter's composition unfurls with increasing intensity, spurred by Cole's drumming, and the high quality of the recorded sound make the precision with which Johnny Thompson's uncomplicated arrangement is interpreted seem like the workings of a well-oiled Swiss timepiece.

♪

Disney's animators home in on key signifiers of the Swing Era: a jukebox, the "hep cat," and teenagers enthusiastically Lindy Hopping. Typical for Disney, what we see is white youth, with dance and jive becoming the exclusive province of white audiences in his hands. That was about to change—black servicemen returning from wartime combat would soon rightly question what sort of freedom and democracy they had risked their lives for, when many of the rights they had fought for abroad were pointedly denied them at home.

The animators literally take the motif of "all the cats joining in" by having an animator's pencil construct the series of scenes. The pencil pushes a button that starts the jukebox. A boy searches his pockets for a nickel to call his girlfriend, picks her up at her house in his "old jalop" of the song's lyrics, and skids to a halt in front of a malt shop, where other teenagers are headed. The lot of them dance up such a storm that the jukebox explodes. The minimalistic animation actually works well in this sequence, which remains a perfect illustration of the impact of recordings on youth culture, an impact which would grow throughout the rest of the twentieth century. But it would not be until the title credits of Blake Edwards's *Pink Panther* (1963), featuring animation by David H. DePatie and Friz Freleng, that big band jazz—in this case, by Henry Mancini (with a memorable tenor solo by Plas Johnson)—and animation would again comfortably coexist.

Goodman's second appearance (the eighth sequence of the feature) is with his quartet playing "After You've Gone," a number he first recorded as a nineteen-year-old on May 17, 1929 (for some reason, it was never released). His next recording of the song, two years later, was destined to become an early jazz classic: as a member of the Eddie Lang–Joe Venuti All Star New York Stompers, with Jack Teagarden on vocal and trombone, Goodman contributes a telling solo of his own. Goodman's first recording of the song under his own name was with his trio, which included Wilson, on July 13, 1935.

Goodman and Wilson knew "After You've Gone" intimately, and in the 1930s, when the Swing Era was at its height and the pianist a regular member of Goodman's trio, they had worked up the dazzling clarinet and piano interplay on the bandstand that we hear here. This interplay is matched by the animators, who portray the piece as a dizzying chase through a surreal landscape.

Disney's publicity department at the time called it a "musical interpretation of the spirit of jive. It is a theme of quick changes and pulsating rhythm. It is an artist's dream, a fantasy in the world of modern music." It is also one of the few animated sequences—other than *Peter and the Wolf* and *The Whale Who Wanted to Sing at the Met*—that shows evidence of any budget being brought to bear on its creation, and because of this it is closer to the spirit of *Fantasia* than any of the other sequences in its conscious evocation of a "fantasy."

Jazz performance does not readily take to television or the cinema: jazz musicians are usually less demonstrative and more static than rock

musicians, something unrelenting variations in camera angles cannot overcome. The Goodman pieces and their animation, especially "After You've Gone," suggested a way for jazz to reach beyond its normal constituency, one that has never been fully exploited. Indeed, the marriage of animation and music for "After You've Gone" leave one yearning for a Charlie Parker solo to be similarly animated.

♫

Although Goodman did not know it when he was recording these numbers for Disney in 1944, the musical hierarchy around him was about to change. Swing had all but run its course, and today his performances stand as an absorbing valedictory statement for an era that had opened with such optimism almost ten years earlier. These two Goodman performances are among the last from the era that embrace a *pure* "Swing" style. As the European writer Simon Korteweg, coeditor of the magazine *Jazzwereld,* noted, they are among "the best recordings Goodman made in the Forties."[14] However, the innocence of the Swing Era—captured at its zenith with Goodman's exuberant performances in Busby Berkeley's *Hollywood Hotel* (Warner Bros., 1937) with its call-and-response ensemble figures, ingenious polyphony, "hot" solos, and driving rhythms—had by the time of "All the Cats Join In" been reduced to formula. Now the "hot solo" represented a reduction of a performing style to create a product that could be packaged and sold. Even as Goodman was making these recordings, elsewhere in New York a new small group style called bebop was being developed in clubs and after-hours joints, partly as a reaction to the formulaic procedures adopted by the big band arrangers. Bebop, with its greater instrumental freedom for the improviser, was about to burst onto the world and become a focal point in the evolution of jazz.

The musicians bringing together the advanced harmonic and rhythmic ideas of bebop had themselves come of age performing in the big bands and were looking for a style of music that was not shaped by the demands of the (white) musical marketplace. Their new style, worked on and polished over the preceding five years, had moved from the essentially diatonic conventions of swing to chromatic harmonies, thereby enlarging the number of possible note choices available to the improviser. Rhythmically, bebop broke free from

Scene from *All the Cats Join In* in *Make Mine Music.* © Disney Enterprises, Inc.

the four- and eight-bar boxes within which pre-bop improvisers contained their solos. Bebop musicians used angular, fragmented phrases that frequently crossed bar lines and began and ended in unexpected places, underlined by cross accents from the drummer that broke up the almost mechanical relentlessness of Swing Era rhythm sections. Goodman, who had refined the Swing style to a kind of perfection (exemplified by his solos on "All the Cats Join In" and the dazzling virtuosity of his work on "After You've Gone") would, by the time *Make Mine Music* was released, find himself already bypassed by these latest developments in jazz. As James Lincoln Collier pointed out in *The Making of Jazz*, "Swing players, many of them at the height of their powers" were forced to surrender the main ground of jazz to the bop musicians. "For a man like Goodman, still in his thirties when the bop movement took over, this was a bitter pill."[15]

Swing had run its course. By 1944, there was little new to say in the idiom. Johnny Thompson's arrangement of "All the Cats Join In" could have been made at any point in the preceding five years of Goodman's career. As Hsio Wen Shih has stated, "It is customary to date the decline of the 'band business' after the end of World War II, but, artistically, swing had died earlier. By the early 1940s the gradual elimination of stylistic variation had killed big band jazz. It was death by entropy. . . . There is a terrifying record, an anthology called *The Great Swing Bands* . . . if played without consulting notes or label, it is impossible to distinguish one [band] from another."[16] The time was right for new ideas. Around the corner were new, bebop-influenced big band sounds poised to emerge at the hands of Woody Herman, Dizzy Gillespie, Stan Kenton, and Boyd Raeburn, sounds that would force Goodman himself—the one-time King of Swing—to form his own bebop-influenced big band in November 1948. Although bebop musicians would never enjoy the widespread popularity of Benny Goodman and the other major stars of the Swing Era, bebop would change jazz expressionism forever.

But for the moment, that was all in the future. With "All the Cats Join In" and "After You've Gone," Goodman was a performer in complete harmony with the majority musical culture around him. The result was two neglected gems amid a Disney feature consciously striving to recapture the studio's magic after being blown off course during wartime propaganda productions. It seems appropriate that Goodman, who opened the curtain on the Swing Era at the Palomar Ballroom in Los Angeles on August 21, 1935, should also bring the curtain down on the era in June 1944, with these two exemplary performances.

The author wishes to thank Lawrence Appelbaum of the Library of Congress and Andrew Simons of the National Sound Archive of the British Library for their assistance in preparing this piece.

------

[1] *The Times,* June 27, 1946, p. 6.

[2] Ibid.

[3] Leonard Mosley, *The Real Walt Disney* (London: Futura Publications, 1985), p. 200.

[4] Ibid., p. 202.

[5] *Hollywood Citizen-News,* March 23, 1946.

[6] Mosley, op. cit., p. 202.

[7] Thanks to Harlow Robinson and his book *Sergei Prokofiev* (New York: Viking Penguin, 1987) for sorting out the sequence of Prokofiev's involvement with Disney.

[8] *The Times,* June 27, 1946, p. 6.

[9] See Mosley, op. cit., and Marc Eliot, *Walt Disney: Hollywood's Dark Prince* (London: Andre Deutsch, 1993).

[10] Disney Archive photo 24–37, British Library.

[11] See, for example, *The Kingdom of Swing* by Benny Goodman and Irving Kolodin (New York: Frederick Ungar Publishing Co, 1961), originally published in 1939.

[12] The fact that one vocal could be substituted for another, and both omitted from the Capitol release of the song, shows how different the techniques were in recording film soundtracks from those for 78-rpm records.

[13] *Alive and Kickin': Big Band Sounds at MGM* (TCM/Rhino R2 72721).

[14] Liner notes, *Bebop Spoken Here: Benny Goodman, Charlie Barnet* (Capitol OU 2008).

[15] James Lincoln Collier, *The Making of Jazz* (New York: Granada, 1978), p. 408.

[16] Hsio Wen Shih, "The Spread of Jazz and the Big Bands," in *Jazz,* edited by Nat Hentoff and Albert J. McCarthy (London: The Jazz Book Club, 1962), p. 187.

Sublime Perversity

The Music of Carl Stalling

by WILL FRIEDWALD

"EITHER MR. STEINER is going up those stairs or I'm going up them," Bette Davis supposedly threatened, regarding the climactic scene in *Dark Victory*, "but we're *not* walking up them together!"

Certainly, that no-less-histrionic thespian Mr. Daffy "Dumas" Duck was no less capable of displaying such a despicable demonstration of temperament. However, far from feeling that the musical score would compete with his function as an actor, the little black duck realized mighty sportingly that there could be no such thing as "overkill" in a cartoon. Where the dahling Miss Davis had two hours to inspire the audience's tear ducts to swell to capacity before that payoff of an emotional dam burst, ducks and wabbits were allotted a mere seven minutes to move their viewers to hysterics—and therefore needed all the help they could get. Just as Bette Davis's melodrama (a term derived from *mellos,* Greek for *music*) rates as a broad caricature of drama that requires a relentlessly exaggerated score, the Warner Bros. cartoons demand the most outrageous possible music.

But it ain't the bodacious battiness of the Warner 'toon tunes that makes it worthwhile to isolate them as a purely aural (non-visual) experience. Nor is it the remarkable craftsmanship and productivity required to assemble as many as three completely different one-reel symphonettes per month for nearly twenty years. Perversely, it's Carl Stalling's subtlety that makes him a musical auteur (or, to use Chuck Jones's term, *otter*) of sheer, unadulterated genius. Stalling and his orchestrator, Milt Franklyn, employed Sinatra- or Jones-like attention to the tiniest of details and the most minuscule of nuances, so that the most minute dynamic fluctuation on a violin string or flutely flutter carries with it mountain-moving significance.

Today we marvel that lush "full" animation, fifty-piece orchestras, and unfettered creativity were once taken for granted by Hollywood cartoonists, who generally looked at these somebody-chasing-somebody opuses as mere potboilers. The production schedule itself—it isn't important that it's good so long as it's on time—ultimately proved to be Stalling's greatest creativity factor. Determined to come up with a perfectly appropriate score for each film, and required to do so in less time than it takes to write most songs, the necessity for shortcuts became Stalling's numero uno artistic boost.

First consider the unavoidable diegetic elements of character, action, and setting: Tweety not yet having seen (tawn) a puddy tat in an apartment sounds different than Bugs being chased by Yosemite Sam in the wild west. Cataloging the contents of Stalling's tooney toolbox takes a little longer: blending the leitmotif concept of specific musical phrases for characters and ideas (as definitively delineated in Wagner's *Gesamtkunstwerk*) with the expansions on those ideas in terms of jazz's new expressive possibilities—

A publicity photo of Carl Stalling at the piano at Warner Bros. in the 1950s.
© Warner Bros. Courtesy of Mike Barrier.

especially by way of using horns as voices and vice versa—as effectively explored in Duke Ellington's instrumental oratorios (most notably *Black, Brown, and Beige*). However, Stalling uses them merely as landmarks, for no one before or since has displayed such sublime perversity in subverting the mainstream into the avant-garde.

Not that there was anything commonplace about Stalling's selection of pop tunes as raw material (no less than, say, Thelonious Monk's); ex-colleagues reduce him to a mere Mickey Mouse musician when they claim his free-association method extended only as far as playing "A Cup of Coffee, a Sandwich, and You" behind tableaux of caloric intake. Stalling's strength was his specificity: he could very cagily distinguish a love theme underscoring the scopophilic encounter of a suddenly feminized Daffy Duck stripteasing and the barely-able-to-look Mr. Meek (based on "It Had to Be You"), from a more voracious but inescapably French (albeit one-sided) amorous affair for Pepé Le Pew ("Cherie, Je t'Aime").

The ability to identify these themes doesn't necessarily help, for Stalling relies on the collective unconscious which, after having followed enough of Bugs Bunny's episodic adventures, unknowingly makes the connection between the few bars of the motif Stalling sneaks by and the plot development or idea put across on screen. As Stalling's tenure stretched from years into decades, he increasingly depended on the ability of the audience to decode his musical hieroglyphics and shorthand, and would fragment these familiar leitmotifs into ever tinier and tinier pieces of the musical mosiac. Just as Tex Avery made a systematic study as to the ultimate minimum number of frames needed for an audience to comprehend a visual gag, Stalling could transmit a musical joke or idea with an ever-decreasing number of notes.

Indeed, no other music maker so creatively stretched the iconography of western music, codified by Bach and Mozart, all the while still pledging allegiance to its basic precepts. Stalling and Franklyn's stiff adherence to classicalism wasn't merely conceptual, but often textural—as both volumes of the two CDs devoted to Stalling's music (*The Carl Stalling Project,* volumes one and two) prove. Once the music is isolated from the dialogue and sound effects (read: screams and explosions) it could easily be, on a blindfold test, taken for any of the more durable contemporary classics.

Stalling ever more aggressively reduced the duration of themes, especially after they were established, to mirror the tension mounting in the narrative. However, he (with Franklyn's help) also expanded them, played them excruciatingly slowly on out-of-tune violins to underscore a frustrated Fudd's slow-burn torture, or transposed them to staccato 32nd notes at the high end of the piano to portray a perspicacious puddy tat prancing behind trees and mailboxes, out of his prey's line of vision; as molehills metamorphize into mountains, the theme gets reharmonized into a monstrous mess of unresolving dissonances conveying colossal c-c-cat-astrophe. It gets wilder when themes collide, Bugs's cucumber coolness contrasted with his foe's (take your pick—Elmer, Sam, or even the redoubtable Pete Puma) frantic finagling.

You couldn't say which aspect of Stalling and Franklyn's art rates as the more satisfying: the individual elements of the concoction or the way they put them together. As orchestrators arranging tunes for conventional listening or dancing purposes, they could have probably earned a better living. What swing bandleader or Tin Pan Alley publisher wouldn't want Carl Stalling on the payroll? Surely celebrity would have beckoned had he toured the country with sixty pieces (plus Treg Brown on half-trombone as a special added attraction) as "Carl Stalling and his Famous Orchestra."

Perhaps some wily band booker even made him such an offer, but Carl Stalling undoubtedly said, "It will never work." He knew full well that his destiny remained at Schlesinger's, forever shouting, "Pay no attention to that man behind the curtain" as he worked the musical alchemy that inspired laughter and tears, and forever makes us looney-tooney.

Originally appeared in slightly different form as liner notes to The Carl Stalling Project *(Warner Bros., 1990). © 1990 by Will Friedwald. Reprinted by permission.*

Carl Stalling, Improviser & Bill Lava, Acme Minimalist

by KEVIN WHITEHEAD

"I just imagined myself playing for a cartoon in the theater, improvising, and it came easier."

—Carl Stalling

LIKE ARCHITECTURE AND counterfeiting, animation discourages improvising. You can point a camera at any live action and make a movie on the spot, but every cartoon frame is the top layer of months of meticulous execution and editorial scrutiny. And yet the improvisational impulse is not easily defeated. Disney's Shamus Culhane has described a state he and other animators would enter into: working from storyboards and an outline, he'd quickly sketch out all the action in a cartoon sequence, in a sustained burst of creativity he could maintain for days—never looking back or revising, just plunging ahead, in the course of which unexpected details of action or character would emerge. There are ways to tap into that spontaneity even while collaborating: the studio story conference or "gag meeting" aims to harness the same free-flowing energy.

One reason the best Warner Bros. cartoons are landmarks of twentieth-century art is their improvised feel, as if Bugs Bunny were making up his best stuff on the fly as a camera passively tracked him—as if the film makers knew as little as we did about what off-screen prop he'd grab next. And Stalling is Bugs's musical counterpart, reaching outside the box for any apropos musical comment. Surreal action calls for surreal accompaniment.

The belated acknowledgment of Stalling as a great modernist composer (due in no small part to improviser John Zorn and record producer Hal Willner) is a tribute to the composer's genius for self-effacement. Stalling's champions helped us hear what was right before our ears. He's a chameleon in camouflage: his music mirrors the action so perfectly you barely notice it as a separate thing. The score draws your attention away from itself and toward foreground activity—which is why even Stalling freaks can start watching a cartoon for the music and quickly get lost in the story. Even many lifelong cartoon watchers had to hear his music on CD—Warner released two volumes of *The Carl Stalling Project* in the 1990s—to realize how truly modern it is, and how much the postmodern musical language Zorn and company developed in New York in the 1980s owes to his cutup esthetic. Whether closely studied or unknowingly absorbed, his stuff is part of the shared heritage of those modern American vernacular musicians who grew up around a TV. Zorn got it right when he called it "the music of our subconscious."

But cutting from one recognizable style to another for utilitarian purposes wasn't Stalling's innovation. Movies were barely up and running before theater keyboardists could buy anthologies of cues and backgrounds, unrelated signature motifs to trot out at the first sign of a sunrise, tender embrace, or Indian attack. Stock situations can make do with stock music. But that tradition had its own roots in the wide-ranging descriptive music nineteenth-century theater orchestras and comic-revue pianists had to come up with to accompany stage shows.

Enter that precursor to Stalling and so much that's good in American music, Charles Ives. At Yale in the 1890s, he recalled later, he'd written music for theater orchestra involving "old tunes, college songs, hymns, etc.," sometimes superimposed in different keys, sometimes played out of tune or out of time—"ear stretching" exercises often reflected in his mature music. Ives wasn't a moviegoer, but even in the 1890s he was anticipating elements of cinematic syntax. When he quotes from a patriotic song, he's apt to ease into it, as if it's emerging from soft focus. His evocative music is often more about memories of events than events themselves, but the pictorial element is strong in his aural crossfades and overexposures. At Yale and later, he composed pieces that graphically depicted a football game, a fire brigade, and various street rhythms: walking, cantering horses, rocking trolleys. Ives sometimes called such sketches "cartoons."

Ives began to attract a following in the late 1920s, when Stalling was starting out in Hollywood. Nothing I've read suggests he knew Ives's music directly, although the L.A. Philharmonic played some in 1932 and '33, and film composer Bernard Herrmann, who began scoring in the 1940s, was a longtime Ives booster. At the very least, the parallels confirm that at certain times, certain ideas permeate the air.

Ives and Stalling knew the Tin Pan Alley repertoire well, and likely found some inspiration for their many works that cite well-known tunes in an early twentieth-century fad for songs that quoted other songs, such as George M. Cohan's 1904 "Yankee Doodle Boy," which cops from "Yankee Doodle," "Dixie," "The Star Spangled Banner" and "The Girl I Left Behind Me": an early example of pop music sampling. Such patchwork songs also include Irving Berlin's 1911 "Alexander's Ragtime Band" quoting "Old Folks at Home" and 1917's "Back Home in Indiana" tapping "On the Banks of the Wabash." Many of these patchwork tunes (like Cohan's) employed patriotic melodies, and those songs and that tradition enjoyed a revival during World War I.

These were the kinds of ideas (and associative melodies) a real cartoon composer could use. At the time Stalling came to Hollywood, cinematic syntax was leaking into other music too. By 1929, jazz pianist Fats Waller, another former theater organist, had developed his own crossfades: he'd finish up a musical idea with one hand while initiating a new one with the other. There were more parallel developments. The close-up and the jazz solo were ways of isolating and spotlighting an ensemble member; cinematic crosscuts and the call-and-response between a jazz band's brass and reed sections both served to build tension through rhythm and contrast.

All that was part of the cultural climate when Stalling sat down to imagine himself in a theater, watching a cartoon and playing along. He gave his scores the illusion of off-the-cuff spontaneity at least in part by mimicking those old ad hoc accompaniments. Note, however, that Stalling didn't work from finished cartoons, but from exposure sheets that outlined and timed out the action frame by frame—mindful that, once the film was complete, he might have to add or lose an eighth-note or two or three here and there, to accommodate a reworked gag. (The payback was, sometimes the animators would bend the action to the music.) There was nothing superfluous or tacked-on about Stalling's music; it shaded the action at every turn. Like editor Treg Brown's dynamic sound effects, it's part of the foundation, not the facade.

And so Stalling sat, with his mental catalog of (inherited or invented) stock cues at the ready, as rigorously specific as the coded percussion cues for sunrise etc. in kabuki theater: xylophone for trotting up stairsteps, woozy trombone for drunks, subtone clarinet for quiet moonlit action, Hawaiian guitar glisses for boomerang physics, a quick vibraphone arpeggio hanging in the air after a stunning blow to the head. Scattered among those were the pet quotations: Bugs in drag gets "The Lady in Red"; giddy success, "We're in the Money"; nautical firepower, Ives's fave "Columbia, the Gem of the Ocean"; a looker, female dummy, or Bugs in another color dress, "Oh, You Beautiful Doll." Raymond Scott's "Powerhouse" went with dynamos and futurism, and other quaint or colorful Scott tunes came in handy, but the now-widely-held notion that Scott's music defines the Looney Tunes sound, as if Stalling relied on it unduly, is a publicist's myth. Scott occupies only one corner of Stalling's large palette.

Warners Bros. had publishing rights to a gazillion pop songs, but there were times when Stalling, or copyright strictures, or musical necessity could throw you a curve. In 1956's *Half-Fare Hare,* Bugs rides the Chattanooga choo-choo to the tune of "Carolina in the Morning," whose faster melodic rhythm and emphatic downbeats lends itself better to Stalling's method than the more obvious choice.

Think of the melodies cited just above, if you know them: his favorites often have a quick melodic rhythm compatible with fast action and conducive to minute last-minute adjustments. Stalling's tempos, like the action's, were always multiples of the ¼₄ second it takes a frame to pass through a projector, and he and the animators could and did sync music and visuals down to small fractions of a second. It's part of what gives music and action that uncanny mirror-image effect, just as the hectic narrative rhythm directly inspires Stalling's quick-change, polyglot signature style. But we would not esteem him so if the music didn't work divorced from the images. Even if Stalling tells the same joke often, he tells it well every time.

With Stalling, as with Ives, the borrowed melodies also work as pure music, for those who don't recognize them. Often, quotations are woven into the fabric of a score as a recurring theme, like the snatches of Brahms's Lullaby in *To Itch His Own* (1958) (on *The Carl Stalling Project* volume one). But Stalling, like Ives, achieves a special intimacy with the listener who can name a tune and get the thematic reference—get the joke. (That lullaby may have been an in-joke too: the cartoon was Stalling's last assignment.) His musical universe, like Ives's, is expansive: high and low culture, the abstract and concrete, are brought together as part of the shared experience of composer and listeners, who know both the *William Tell Overture* and "Take Me Out to the Ball Game."

Beyond the action painting and quotations lies Stalling's pure composing. The forward surge of his scores derives much of its force from the short lulls between the fireworks, the little transitions that underpin a gag's setup—the chin leaning toward the next punch or punchline. It may take the form of a rapidly gathering dust devil for strings, but more often it's a vignette for upwardly yearning woodwinds: the sonority transparent enough not to distract from the action or dialogue, the melody abstract and lyrical enough to counterbalance all the compulsive joking. Those connective bits alone make Stalling a real composer rather than a glorified sound effects man.

Perhaps the least acknowledged partners in this musical enterprise, similarly at home with high and low musical rhetoric, were the amazing members of the Warner Bros. studio orchestra, who could handle all the rapid changes of key, time signature, dynamics, articulation, style, and mood with precision and high spirits. You get a sense of their attitude from the studio chatter on the first volume of *The Carl Stalling Project*: ready for fun, attentive to nuance, and eager for the challenge. Voice on a Speedy Gonzales session: "You want this to be typical? Huh? Hey, you want this to be Mexican?"

♫

But for all the improvisational openness and narrative anarchy, at golden-age Warner Bros. there were always countervailing tendencies toward acknowledging that animation is (a handmade) art for an age of reproduction. Think of the job of the in-betweener, drawing and inking and painting series of drawings which change only minutely from frame to frame, filling the gaps that get Elmer from one striking pose to the next.

Warner Bros. cartoons are distinguished by their strong house style; for evidence, look at the more muted work a Warner Bros. animator like Tex Avery did at MGM. (Tom and Jerry have their fun, but Bugs or Daffy take things a lot further.) And any perceived style—Rembrandt's or John Coltrane's or Warner Bros.—is based on repeated elements or preoccupations: those familiar tics (like Stalling's fast cuts) that let you identify the source. But necessity and habit help shape a style, too. Because animation is time consuming and therefore expensive, economic realities favor cost-cutting repetitive action: a chase scene that keeps traversing the same background, or a looping assembly-line sequence where the same gag's repeated verbatim, or even series cartoons featuring recurring characters, who get easier to draw (and, in Bugs's case, better looking) the longer the artists work with them. Like improvisers, animators are creatures of habit: licks fall easily under the fingers with repetition, and come faster to the hand.

Warner Bros.' cartoon world may seem a place where anything can happen, but some things happen rather a lot. Those repetitions help create a hermetic universe, where arcane laws of nature apply—set your fingers to some complicated task, and they become so knotted, only a wedged-in foot can dislodge them. In this world, most of the males sound like Mel Blanc and most females like Bea Benaderet. (One of the stars of early TV, from *Burns and Allen* through to *Petticoat Junction*, and the original Betty Rubble, Benaderet lent her superb characterizations to dozens of Warner Bros. cartoons, but may be best remembered for one of her first: as an obnoxious out-of-tune bobby-soxer in 1944's *Little Red Riding Rabbit*. That aside, like Blanc, she was a good singer whose contribution to these scores is easy to overlook.)

Warner Bros. animators proceeded almost as if they were shooting low-budget live action on a backlot, using a few favored props—an illusion reinforced by Warner Bros. stars like Bogart doing occasional cartoon cameos, as if popping in from a nearby soundstage. Animated characters dropped into each other's series cartoons the way the stars of circa-1960 Warner Bros. detective and cowboy shows would visit their sister series.

As a mirror of the action, Stalling's music necessarily reinforces that hermetic feeling as well as the toons' looney anarchy. He ranges wide but orbits back toward a finite range of musical gestures. If he has a weakness for *boing!!!*ing steel guitar and single-string viola glissandi, it's because characters often trampoline off power lines, and window shades always rise to expose a sleeper's eyelids to streetlight.

The Warners Bros.' canon is chock full of such repeated jokes and situations. Tortoise beats hare. "Oh, yes you are"—"Oh, no I'm not." Big slow Steinbeck Lennies want to know which way did he go. "Of course you realize, this means war." Bugs awakens to find a construction project underway over his hole. Daffy tries to deflect a predator onto Bugs. Little Red Riding Hood. The Three Little Pigs. (Never mind that one of the studio's best versions of that tale, *Three Little Bops* [1957], had a rockabilly score by jazz trumpeter Shorty Rogers.)

A publicity photo of Milt Franklyn at the organ at Warner Bros.
© Warner Bros., Inc. Courtesy of Greg Ford.

The outlandish music somehow makes what happens in this Looniverse seem realistic. An action that always gets the same musical tag seems more consequential, more grounded in normal reality—spurious reasoning, to be sure, but strangely persuasive anyway.

Out of all these bits and pieces, Stalling had concocted a musical language so perfectly suited to the medium that other composers couldn't resist it. Scott Bradley's Tom and Jerry scores are to Stalling's what an MGM cartoon is to a Warner Bros.': tamer, softer around the edges. Stalling's main disciple was Milt Franklyn, who was orchestrating his scores by the late 1930s—bearing in mind that Stalling often earmarked lines for specific instruments, having already developed his coloristic palette. Franklyn took over for him when Stalling retired in 1958, but he'd already scored more than five dozen cartoons by then, including the high-profile *What's Opera, Doc?* (1957). He was Billy Strayhorn to Stalling's Duke Ellington: an arranger and composer so good at entering into the spirit of the other's work, it's not easy to tell who did what. Franklyn's scores frankly echo Stalling's; he loves a plaintive viola melody and aspiring woodwinds as much as the master. There are times when his harmony seems a bit lusher, as if he thought Stalling hadn't gone far enough in that direction, but the refinement is not always an improvement. That sounds like Strayhorn too. Some of his scores are Stalling in watercolor.

Milt Franklyn died suddenly in 1962. By then, the business was changing. Money to produce feature cartoons was drying up, and Warner Bros.' amazing company of film makers had exhausted multiple possibilities after working with the same characters for twenty years. Even Mel Blanc sounded tired. The studio orchestra had been scaled back, too. Franklyn's replacement was William (Bill) Lava, since 1937 a prolific contributor of scores, songs, and ghostwritten bits to umpteen features and shorts including *Dick Tracy Returns*, *Revenge of the Creature*, *Jesse James at Bay*, *Abbott and Costello Meet the Invisible Man*, *So You Want to Build a House*, *P.T. 109*—and *The Horn Blows at Midnight*, which Stalling had also worked on, apparently separately.

Lava's early scores are still fainter evocations of Stalling, often mixed low, in deference to the increasingly prominent sound effects. The cost cutting was by now audible: electric guitar might fake a ukulele part, an accordion might suggest an orchestral swell, and there was less coloristic percussion. Lava's own style emerged out of these straitened circumstances, and you can't blame him for trying to stake out his own sound, or modernize an esthetic that was a quarter century old. (Popular music had been through some changes since the 1930s, after all.) But it didn't quite work. Even at a murmur, the music called more attention to itself than ever, partly because the period colors Lava brought to the paintbox could be more strident; his scores are easily identified by a heavier reliance on brass and saxophones. Stalling and Ives were rooted in nineteenth-century theater orchestras; Lava sounded inspired by staccato big band arrangers such as Neal Hefti. And his climaxes were less precisely calibrated to the action, as if he was trying to whip up audience interest in tired situations. Stalling always knew just how hard you could lean on a gag.

On a more cheerful note, one could now make out the end zone of the hermetic territory the animators had been exploring for decades. As if to compensate for budget cuts, the cartoons had slowly moved off the soundstage and out to remote locations, specifically to a landscape first glimpsed, in far lusher form, by 1949. By now it was almost denuded of vegetation, dominated by gravity-defying mesas and fragile outcroppings above mile-deep canyons, an unpopulated desert where delivery vans nonetheless go, to deposit crates full of ill-designed Acme products, paid for who knows how. This monument valley's very topography lets you know that ordinary laws of physics don't apply here.

The Road Runners are easily the most hermetic of Warner Bros. series cartoons, despite all the wide-open spaces. They're also the most purely musical in construction: they have the rhythm of a slow drum solo. The narrative episodes themselves are like a string of solos on a jazz tune, loosely tethered to a theme, the action always returning to recognizable cadences, or variations on favorite licks: a heavy object pulled onto a lighter one by a long elastic cord, Acme gizmos malfunctioning in implausible and invariably disastrous ways, an overhead shot of a tiny impact cloud at a canyon's far bottom. Devoid of dialogue, and heavy on stock situations, reaction shots, baldly predatory relationships, and rigorously circumscribed codes of action (the Road Runner rarely leaves the road), the Road Runner 'toons returned to the world of silent film.

The end times were coming; everything old was coming back. In the 1960s, Warner Bros. was subcontracting cartoons to independents, as the studio had from Leon Schlesinger before absorbing his operation in the 1930s. In 1965, eleven Road Runners were farmed out to Format Films. For most of those, Lava recorded a set of cues for a tiny ensemble, to be inserted as needed—a return to the stock solutions that silent-movie accompanists had employed way back when. But those movable cues also paralleled some 1950s and '60s compositions—"mobiles"—by, among others, Earle Brown (who was directly inspired by Alexander Calder), in which fixed "events" can be played in variable order. Mobiles were one element in the musical mix that gave rise to 1960s minimalism.

There is something curiously like minimalist music in the exacting process of animation. The seeming repetitions mask gradual change, as in the nineteenth-century stop-action photographs of Eadweard Muybridge, who by no coincidence was studied by animators and celebrated by composer Philip Glass. Lava's late Road Runners hew to that other minimalist tendency, to make do with less material. Scoring on the cheap, he unwittingly found himself in step with one of the 1960s' hippest musical trends, one more idea in the air, and perfectly suited to the medium. Necessity had driven him to an inspired capitulation.

Raymond Scott: Accidental Music for Animated Mayhem

by IRWIN CHUSID

HIS MERRY MELODIES are genetically encoded in every earthling. Since 1943, they've been heard underscoring the antics of Bugs, Daffy, Porky, and Elmer. In the early 1990s, his eccentric recordings provided counterpoint to the body-fluid fetishism of Nickelodeon's *The Ren & Stimpy Show*. His musical themes echoed across national television during 1967 in a now-forgotten cartoon parody called *Batfink*, directed and produced by Hal Seeger (of *Popeye* fame). In addition, *The Simpsons, Animaniacs, Duckman,* and *The Oblongs* have joined the cavalcade of animated programs that adapted his riffs. And if any further link were necessary to cement this legacy, his composition "Powerhouse" has been deployed as a round-the-clock "audio logo" on Turner Broadcasting's Cartoon Network since May 1998.

Surprisingly, however, composer Raymond Scott never wrote a note of music for a cartoon in his life. According to his widow, Mitzi, he never even watched the Saturday morning offerings. Scott seemed oblivious to the fact that generations of video-glazed adolescents have been absentmindedly humming his themes, all immortalized in an art form which he cared little about—if at all.

Scott's programmatic late 1930s novelty jazz instrumentals included such titles as "New Year's Eve in a Haunted House," "War Dance for Wooden Indians," "Reckless Night on Board an Ocean Liner," "Celebration on the Planet Mars," and "Egyptian Barn Dance"—all of which evoke comic imagery. But Scott had more important things to do than concoct musical flavorings for the misadventures of a wascally wabbit, a crime-fighting bat, and a short-fused asthmatic Chihuahua.

Raymond Scott in 1937. Courtesy of the Raymond Scott Archives.

Raymond Scott was born Harry Warnow, on September 10, 1908, in Brooklyn. He was a piano prodigy with an instinctive flair for science. Over the course of his career, he led two lives: as a pianist/composer/bandleader, and as an engineer/inventor/electronic music pioneer. From 1937 to 1939, he led the quirky Raymond Scott Quintette (actually a sextet, but Scott avoided the latter designation, claiming he wanted audiences to keep their minds on the music). Sporting a lineup of clarinet, trumpet, tenor sax, drums, bass, and Scott on piano, the RSQ was immensely popular on radio and the concert stage and in film. It was difficult to categorize, drawing on jazz, pop, classical, ethnic, and musique concrète elements. Although the RSQ sold millions of 78-rpm records, it was not highly regarded by hot-music purists, one of whom dismissed its oeuvre as "screwy, kittenish pseudo-jazz." (These three-minute pop masterpieces were reissued by Columbia in 1992 on *The Music of Raymond Scott: Reckless Nights and Turkish Twilights*, a compilation produced by the author; in 1999 the collection was remastered for release on Sony Legacy.) Scott later led a renowned big band, scored a Broadway musical (*Lute Song*), composed for ballet and film, and led the studio orchestra on NBC's popular chart-countdown television show, *Your Hit Parade*, from 1950 to 1957.

Never a "people person," Scott was more at home with machines (his first wife, Pearl, recalled that Scott walked out of his own wedding reception to return to work in the studio). Many of his compositions reflected a preoccupation with technology: "Powerhouse," "Oil Gusher," "Girl at the Typewriter," and "Love Song to a Microphone." He rehearsed his sidemen relentlessly (said disgruntled trumpeter Charlie Shavers, "I think he just liked to hear the band"),

Scott in 1938. Courtesy of the Raymond Scott Archives.

demanding superhuman perfection. He was often derided as a bully or a taskmaster. "All he ever had was machines—only we had names," remarked his drummer, Johnny Williams. Singer Anita O'Day, who vocalized briefly with Scott's early 1940s big band, called him "a martinet" who "reduced [musicians] to something like windup toys."

Having risen to prominence during the Swing Era of the 1930s, Scott kept pace with subsequent developments in music technology. He invented electronic sound generators, and in the mid-1950s was one of the first musicians to compose and record all-electronic jingles for TV and radio commercials. He later invented an instantaneous composition-performance console called the Electronium. It was Beethoven-in-a-box, a monstrosity that composed using artificial intelligence. In 1969, Motown impresario Berry Gordy was sufficiently impressed to place an order for the device, and later hired Scott to head the label's division of electronic research and development. (Scott retired from the position in 1977.) He was composing on a home-rigged MIDI system as late as 1987. That year, he suffered the first of six strokes, which left him unable to work and severely damaged his speech. He lived out his remaining years in obscurity and near-destitution at his and Mitzi's home in Van Nuys, California. He died on February 8, 1994, at a nursing home in North Hills.

Scott's cartoon legacy began unwittingly (from Scott's standpoint) when he sold his music copyrights, vested in Circle Music Publications, to the Warner Bros.-owned Advanced Music Corporation, on February 15, 1943. This accorded Warner Bros. music director Carl Stalling carte blanche to sprinkle Scott's melodies—particularly those composed from 1936 to 1939—into the highly seasoned musical gumbo that underscored Bugs's and Daffy's high jinks. Scott's "Dinner Music for a Pack of Hungry Cannibals," originally recorded in 1937 by the Quintette, was quoted three times by Stalling in the Friz Freleng-directed *Greetings Bait*, released May 15, 1943. (The quotes were six, eighteen, and nine seconds in duration, respectively.) Eventually, about 120 Warner Bros. cartoons, including some late 1980s episodes directed by Greg Ford, employed Scott melodies (Ford's soundtracks recycled Stalling recordings, albeit in new settings). Scott's most recognizable title, "Powerhouse," was adapted in over forty features. (A complete index of cartoon series usages of Scott is posted at www.raymondscott.com.) New placements of Scott melodies in Warner Bros. cartoons ceased in the early 1960s, when Scott's domestic copyrights reverted to the composer. He subsequently sold this catalog to Music Sales Corporation.

(Historically, Stalling was not the first to cast a Scott theme in an animated setting. Two years before *Greetings Bait*, George Pal enlisted Scott's "The Toy Trumpet" as the soundtrack for *Rhythm in the Ranks*, part of his Puppetoons series, produced for Paramount. Puppetoons, however, were not cartoons—they were films consisting of single-frame photographs, or stop-motion animation, of wooden puppets.)

In licensing Scott works for cartoons, Warner Bros. companies, though operating under the same corporate umbrella, acted somewhat autonomously, albeit cooperatively. The Warner Bros. Pictures, Inc., division obtained synchronization licenses from—and paid fees to—Advanced Music Corporation for the animated adaptation of each Scott title on an incident-per-cartoon basis. The going rate in the mid-1940s was a twenty-five dollar flat fee per usage (each distinct "needle drop" within a feature), a rate that increased to fifty dollars by the end of the decade. Scott, as writer, would have received 50 percent of this one-time publishing revenue.

Scott's most familiar and oft-quoted tune was "Powerhouse," which contains two distinct, unrelated sections, often referred to as "Powerhouse A" and "Powerhouse B": the frantic "A" passage evokes a coyote-chasing-roadrunner melee; the slower, ominous "B" passage suggests a menacing assembly line-gone-haywire (most famously employed in the conveyor belt scenes in Bob Clampett's *Baby Bottleneck*, 1946). Other Scott titles quoted in Warner Bros. productions were "The Penguin," "Twilight in Turkey," "Huckleberry Duck," "The Toy Trumpet," "Siberian Sleigh Ride," "Reckless Night on Board an Ocean Liner," "Singing Down the Road," "War Dance for Wooden Indians," "Egyptian Barn Dance," "The Happy Farmer," "In an 18th Century Drawing Room," "Boy Scout in Switzerland," and "Dinner Music for a Pack of Hungry Cannibals." Some titles, such as "The Penguin" and "Dinner Music for a Pack of Hungry Cannibals," were used in over a dozen features, while others were used only once. "Egyptian Barn Dance" was employed only in the opening credits to Chuck Jones's 1953 outer-spacecapade, *Duck Dodgers in the 24½th Century.*

The amount of Scott material in any Warner Bros. cartoon is typically overstated. Since the Scott revival began in the early 1990s, many journalists have mistakenly attributed to Scott composer credit for *all* Warner Bros. cartoon scores, or for *the majority* of music heard underscoring *Looney Tunes* and *Merrie Melodies*. In fact, most of the music heard in Warner Bros. features was composed by Carl Stalling, who also drew on operatic motifs, classical warhorses, public domain folk tunes, and copyrighted Tin Pan Alley standards (the latter, to no one's surprise, were owned by Warner publishing interests). In the case of Scott titles, Stalling's orchestral settings of compositions, originally written for and performed by a six-piece ersatz-jazz ensemble, were Wagnerian in scope, greatly exceeding Scott's ambitions. The scores were precisely pegged to on-screen action, and it's difficult to envision the explosive impact of these classic cartoons without Stalling's musical underpinnings. Since animation in the 1940s and '50s was largely regarded as a juvenile entertainment medium, however, it's doubtful Scott felt pride in—if he even cared about—this use of his work. Mitzi Scott, his third wife, whom Raymond married in 1967, said that her husband rarely watched television, and "never, never" cartoons. There exists but one public acknowledgement by Scott of his cartoon "legacy"—it occurred in 1985, during his last recorded interview, and the composer seemed disinterested in the topic. No historic journalistic references to the Scott-Stalling link have surfaced. Stalling was interviewed once during his life, years after retirement, and did not mention Scott.

Yet, in retrospect, Scott's early ensemble embodied classic animation soundtrack fodder. Drummer Johnny Williams's .45-caliber rimshots were guaranteed to make Yosemite Sam dance; his artillery included cowbells, bouncy tom-toms, and wake-the-neighbors cymbal crashes. Muted horns imitated toy trumpets, howling spooks, and drunken seafarers. Scott's idiosyncratic compositions toodled along at Keystone Kop tempos, interrupted by hairpin-turn rhythmic shifts and over-the-cliff dynamic spirals. His catchy melodies evoked Turkish casbahs, alpine echoes, oil gushers, typewriters, moon rockets, and robots. Jennifer Harper of the *Washington Times* described it as "music for mice that get hit in the head with an ironing board."

Scott wasn't the only bandleader/composer in the 1930s and '40s known for wacky titles and picturesque "novelty jazz." Such contemporaries as Reginald Foresythe ("Serenade to a Wealthy Widow"), John Kirby ("Rehearsin' for a Nervous Breakdown"), Ambrose ("Dance of the Potted Puppet"), Claude Thornhill ("Portrait of a Guinea Farm"), and Alec Templeton ("Mendelssohn Mows 'Em Down") recorded music that, looking back, has many of the same humorous, retro-cartoonish qualities. Did Scott's catalog come to embody the Golden Age of animation because of a mere business transaction? If only we had Carl Stalling around to offer an opinion. It's true that Scott, despite his insistent "purity" of performance, was by critical consensus less of a jazz "purist" than many of his contemporaries. Perhaps his music was deemed less "sacred" and, hence, more suitable for adaptation to what many considered a frivolous medium. Scott was a workhorse and a classically trained music scholar, but he was not without a sense of the absurd and a penchant for mischief. Journalist Carleton Smith in 1941 referred to him as "the Gertrude Stein of Dada Jazz." It's possible that, given a choice, Scott might have prohibited such "bastardization" of his compositions. But by selling his publishing interests, he relinquished any such control. The historical outcome bespeaks a paradoxical co(s)mic justice: this immensely complex, demanding body of work—composed by a perfection-gripped drill sergeant who couldn't tolerate mistakes—was ultimately used to underscore mayhem, madness, and loss of control.

Scott's animation legacy was furthered in 1967—again, as in the Warner Bros. films, without his involvement, endorsement, or concern. The popular *Batman* TV series sparked a caped crusader craze, which inspired a color cartoon parody called *Batfink*. Batfink was a pointy-eared crime fighter, with wings of steel and supersonic sonar, who tackled ruthless criminals with the aid of his Japanese sidekick, Karate. One hundred five-minute installments were produced for Columbia/Screen Gems by Hal Seeger (a legendary animator who had worked for Max Fleischer, Paramount, and Famous Studios; he produced *Popeye, Out of the Inkwell, Milton the Monster,* and *Fearless Fly*). Forty-six episodes included quotes from five Scott tunes: "Powerhouse," "The Toy Trumpet," "Dinner Music for a Pack of Hungry Cannibals," "Minuet in Jazz," and "Tia Juana." The show's music director was a craftsman many consider second only to Stalling in the annals of tunes for 'toons: Winston Sharples. A longtime music director for Paramount, Sharples (who died in 1977) wrote themes and scores for *Casper the Friendly Ghost, Felix the Cat,* and *Little Lulu,* and composed soundtracks for *Superman* and *Popeye,* among others.

When the producers of *The Ren & Stimpy Show* licensed Scott's Columbia recordings for their series in August 1992, they were fully aware that Scott's screwball pop was embedded in the musical montages created by Stalling for the cartoons which had mesmerized them since childhood. "Nowadays, people think that all the music in Warner cartoons is Raymond Scott," noted John Kricfalusi, creator of *Ren & Stimpy.* "There isn't actually that much, but it's so powerful, that hearing eight bars in a seven-minute cartoon, it's what you walk away remembering." Henry Porch, music coordinator for Spümcø, the original producers of *Ren & Stimpy,* wrote in *Spin* magazine that Scott's music "*screamed* animation." Porch observed that "*Ren*

& Stimpy dealt with abruptly changing emotions and attitudes, and Scott's music easily kept up, shifting gears at breakneck pace." Bob Camp, the show's creative director, confessed, "I put it on a lot when I'm drawing to put me in the cartoon mood." Kricfalusi felt that "Raymond had a cartoon sensibility, and a great sense of humor. If you could say there's color in music, Scott's pieces have a wild sense of color, just like cartoons."

Scott music was employed in twelve *Ren & Stimpy* episodes. The usages were awkward, if well-intentioned. Because they were not custom-arranged to underscore specific action, they could not synchronize on a dime as did Stalling's. The mood match was generally appropriate, however, and the use of Scott's work lent a classic air to the brutish bedlam of *Ren & Stimpy*. Titles featured were "Manhattan Minuet," "Powerhouse," "In an 18th Century Drawing Room," "Twilight in Turkey," "War Dance for Wooden Indians," "The Toy Trumpet," "At an Arabian House Party," and "Huckleberry Duck." One additional episode, the unaired "Man's Best Friend," reportedly rejected by Nickelodeon because of violence deemed unsuitable for young viewers, used four Scott recordings ("In an 18th Century Drawing Room," "Moment Musical," "Twilight in Turkey," and "New Year's Eve in a Haunted House").

"Powerhouse" has been quoted in four other syndicated cartoon series: *The Simpsons* ("And Maggie Makes Three," 1995); *Duckman* ("Aged Heat 2: Women in Heat," 1996); *George Shrinks* (TVO, Canada, 2001); and *Animaniacs* ("Toy Shop Terror," 1993), the last a Warner Bros. property strictly for the tooth-fairy set. In fact, the entire four-minute "Toy Shop Terror" was animated around Richard Stone's brilliant, Spike Jones–inflected arrangement of the complete "Powerhouse" (a feat Stalling never attempted). "It's a strangely wonderful piece of music," Stone told a BBC interviewer in 1996. "It's like it was written on Mars." Conducting it was a heavenly experience for Stone. "I must tell you," he confessed, "the opportunity of standing in front of forty pieces and hearing them play 'Powerhouse' was better than sex. It was the greatest moment in my entire life."

Two additional animated usages of Scott material hit TV screens around the turn of the century. In 1998, *The Drew Carey Show* used a brief excerpt from "Powerhouse" in a short animated/live action segment intended to evoke a vintage Warner Bros. mood. And in 2001, *The Oblongs* used an excerpt of the Raymond Scott Quintette's recording of "The Penguin" in an episode entitled "Narcoleptic Scottie." The melody underscored a scene in which a comatose pooch sprang to life and scampered around the yard.

The Cartoon Network has made "Powerhouse" the melody most readily associated with TV animation. The network's countless variations of the composition's two distinct melodies air at least half a dozen times each hour, to promote such programs as *Popeye*, *The Jetsons*, *Tom and Jerry*, *The Flintstones*, *Alvin and the Chipmunks*, *The Huckleberry Hound Show*, *The Pink Panther*, *Scooby-Doo*, *Top Cat*, *Speed Racer*, *Underdog*, *Batman*, *Taz-Mania*, *Johnny Quest*, *Cow and Chicken*, *Dexter's Laboratory*, *Two Stupid Dogs*, *Johnny Bravo*, *Freakazoid!*, *Beetlejuice*, *The Addams Family*, and others. A 1999 Cartoon Network "greatest hits" CD, *Cartoon Medley* (Kid Rhino 75693), begins and ends with, respectively, short and long versions of "Powerhouse."

One is tempted to address the peculiar appeal of Scott's music to generations of youngsters. All these serenades in the service of—cel-propelled babysitting? It could be maintained that Scott's music appealed to children *because he was one.* Some of the greatest writers and artists of children's literature (including Dr. Seuss, Lewis Carroll, Maurice Sendak) did not have children of their own. They were the mischievous, weirdo uncles ("You have 'em, I'll amuse 'em," said the chain-smoking Dr. Seuss), inclined to incite tots into a frenzy, leaving parents to calm down their little Damiens. Scott, however, had four children (Carolyn and Stanley, by his first wife, Pearl, and Deborah and Elizabeth, by his second wife, singer Dorothy Collins). While not a "people-person," he was probably even less child-oriented. Speaking with his offspring, one gets the impression that Scott generally conceded child-rearing duties to his spouse. He unquestionably loved his children, but seemed to prefer the audio lab to the family playroom. Scott was, in some respects, an overgrown adolescent—self-absorbed, irresponsible, unwilling to cooperate. He likely suffered from what we now call Attention Deficit Disorder: he'd commence a dozen projects, finish one, and start a dozen more, most of which would be abandoned, ad infinitum. Work, to him, was a form of play, but it was not a diversion that involved real children. Hence, the isolation from his family, and his preference for spending time with other "big kids" who shared his technical obsessions. In the early 1960s, he recorded *Soothing Sounds for Baby*, a three-LP series of electronic lullabies (available on CD: Basta 309064 /-65 /-66) geared for infants during their first eighteen months of life. But one shouldn't assume from the existence of these records that Scott actually cared about babies; *Soothing Sounds* seems to have been yet another creative composing and recording challenge, this one commissioned by the Gesell Institute of Child Development. The liner notes refer to Scott as "one of America's most versatile composers," citing the Quintette, his electronic commercial soundtracks, *Lute Song*, and television scoring—all work for "adults." But the notes make no claim that Scott had any particular expertise in the field of child psychology—and they didn't mention cartoons.

Scott's animation legacy has extended to commercials, for Lucky Strike cigarettes ("Be Happy, Go Lucky," 1953); County Fair Bread (featuring an original electronic score, 1962); the Canadian music video channel Much Music ("Boy Scout in Switzerland," 1992); and Hasbro/Cartoon Network's "Great Crate!" ("Powerhouse," 1997). In addition, a 1966 animated (but non-cartoon) short by Jim Henson, entitled "Limbo," featured a musique concrète soundtrack by Scott, who collaborated on several other short-form, pre-*Sesame Street* projects with Henson. The County Fair Bread and Henson soundtracks can be heard on the 2-CD set *Manhattan Research, Inc.* (Basta 3090782).

Scott did not live long enough to see the revival of his music reach full flower. He would have been surprised to know that, despite his pioneering electronic achievements, novelty jazz repertoire, big band catalog, and theatrical and film credits, his modern reputation rests on providing musical counterpoint for someone handing a stick of dynamite to a duck. As John Corbett noted in the *Chicago Reader*, "Quirky, memorable [Scott] themes like 'Powerhouse' in Warner Bros. cartoons arguably helped shape the post-war musical aesthetic as much as anything Elvis or the Beatles did."

For more information on Scott's career and work, visit the Raymond Scott Archives at www.raymondscott.com.

Winston Sharples and the "Inner Casper"

(or Huey Has Two Mommies)

by WILL FRIEDWALD

THE FIRST THING we see is a disconcerting, amorphous white blob, and the first sound we hear is "ghostly," dissonant music. It's the same sort of nightmarish theme one would expect to encounter in a horror movie, and it's a perfect accompaniment to the formless, colorless mass in center screen, which, we soon realize, is actually an object, gradually coming into focus. Soon the nature of the entity becomes clear: at the exact instant in which we become aware that the apparition in the center, ghostly though he may be, has the smiling, happy face of a cute cartoon character, then the dissonant strains on the soundtrack "resolve" into the familiar theme song of *Casper, the Friendly Ghost*. It's the use of music, no less than the on-screen action, that transforms the supernatural into the friendly.

It's a brilliant but typical sample of the ways in which the music of Winston Sharples (1909–1978) empowered animators to more effectively tell a story. For over thirty years, Sharples orchestrated and conducted scores for hundreds of one-reel cartoon shorts. Along with his colleagues, Warner Bros.'s Carl Stalling and MGM's Scott Bradley, Sharples, who spent the bulk of his career at Famous Studios, ranks as one of the big three musical directors of the Hollywood cartoon (an ironic term, considering that Sharples spent his whole career on the East Coast) of the 1940s and '50s.

Like Stalling and Bradley, Sharples collated his scores like a patchwork quilt, gathering musical threads from two primary sources. The first was traditional or folk themes (like "Rockabye Baby" or "Listen to the Mockingbird"), whose meaning would automatically be recognized by audiences. The second source was the library of contemporary pop songs owned by Famous's Paramount parent. But one point distinguishes Sharples from Stalling and Bradley: neither MGM nor Warner Bros. had a built-in supply of *leitmotifs* to identify their most famous characters. There was no "Bugs Bunny Theme" or "Tom and Jerry Theme" the way that there was and is a "Porgy's Theme" in *Porgy and Bess*. To those unfamiliar with the term leitmotif, this is an idea codified by Richard

© Harvey Famous Cartoons. Courtesy of the Archive of Popular American Music, UCLA Music Library, Special Collections.

Wagner in the late romantic era (most famously in his *Ring* cycle) that a specific, short musical theme should accompany a recurring character or idea. Sharples didn't actually write all the themes that he employed in the Famous Studio cartoons, but it's the way that he used these motifs that makes him special.

But first, a bit of background is in order: Winston Sharples was born March 1, 1909, in Springfield, Massachusetts. A child prodigy, he was playing piano in vaudeville from the age of eight. While Carl Stalling had started his career by accompanying silent films, Sharples, like Columbia's Eddie Kilfeather and his Van Buren Studios predecessor, Gene Rodemich, made his initial reputation in the dance band business. By the early 1930s, Sharples was a fixture in Vincent Lopez's orchestra, playing piano, occasionally bass, and, most importantly, arranging for that widely popular dance and show ensemble.

As Sharples's son, Winston Jr., recalls, Sharples went into film writing through a series of coincidences: not long after the death of Gene Rodemich, Walter Winchell coincidentally ran an item in his column praising the Lopez band and Sharples in particular. Amadee Van Buren read the notice, decided this was the man he wanted, and anointed Sharples the main music man at the Van Buren organization until its demise in 1937. At that point, Sharples moved across the street to the Fleischer Brothers Studio, where the chief composer, Sammy Timberg, was an inspired songwriter but, Sharples Jr. points out, was in need of someone with more accomplished notational skills. Sharples worked on the Fleischers' music staff throughout their last great era, the late 1930s, a period that encompassed the studio's relocation to Miami and two feature-length animated efforts.

When Paramount Pictures took over the Fleischers' operation in 1942, Timberg left the studio and Sharples became the sole music man on the payroll of the new Famous Studio. He remained in that position for the entire history of the company, even into the 1960s when TV work, ground out by the pound and even the ton, became the main order of business. After the Famous-ites returned to New York, Sharples himself bought a house in Springfield, Massachusetts, where he raised his family and wrote his scores. For several decades, his routine would be to commute down to New York every two weeks for a recording date (usually held at the Manhattan Sound Studio on 57th Street), then head back to his piano in Massachusettes to write out the next film. This was a time-consuming task that would generally occupy him until the wee small hours of the night before a session. The use of a fairly stable roster of musicians (including flautist Carmine Coppola) allowed Sharples to complete these tasks quickly and efficiently.

In these years, Sharples, whose official title was musical director for all of Paramount's east coast projects, also supplied scores for the studio's live action short output. However, this was nearly always canned music, stock passages that were recycled from film to film. In contrast, Sharples went all out for the cartoons, scoring appropriate notes for seven minutes of screen action, planned down to the fraction of a second.

As alluded to above, Sharples had an immediate asset in that each of his characters could be identified via the "hook" quotes from their theme songs—Casper, the Friendly Ghost is immediately summoned to mind with the six notes of his theme, as is Little Audrey via the first bar of "Little Audrey Says." *By the Old Mill Scream* (1953), in fact, opens with The Friendly Ghost himself singing his own theme, via the premise of an all-spook "Amateur Fright" competition in which the emcee announces "and now, little Casper will sing a haunting refrain." Needless to say, Casper's aria, an excerpt that opens at the ninth bar of the chorus ("I couldn't be bad or mean"), meets with extreme disapproval from the more orthodox, scare-oriented spirits that comprise Casper's community. (From there, the film

becomes the tale of a beaver who is sadly deficient in the tail department—
what would Freud have made of that?)

Two science fiction efforts, *Dizzy Dishes* (1955) and the 3-D *Boo Moon*
(1955), dramatically illustrate Sharples's mixmaster technique: the Audrey

© Harvey Famous Cartoons. Courtesy of Will Ryan.

epic *Dizzy Dishes* opens with the little
lass pouring over an outer space adventure story, which Sharples accompanies
with futuristic, science-fictiony sounds.
When her mother brings her "back to
earth" to do the dishes, the musical
mood switches from space opera to the
familiar strains of the "Little Audrey
Says" theme. When Audrey applies her
ingenuity to a pedestrian chore—setting
up a Rube Goldberg–like assembly line
contraption to clean said dishes—
Sharples trots out his standard "business
as usual" theme, Sammy Timberg's "It's
A Hap-Hap-Happy Day" from *Gulliver's Travels* (1939).

Visual and literary overtones of that
Fleischer feature figure heavily in *Boo
Moon,* in which Casper visits the lunar
landscape and plays Gulliver in a city of looney Lilliputians. Throughout, the
first two bars of the "Casper" theme underscore the action: when our hero is
despondent over his initial failure to find a friend (a recurring theme of the
series in more ways than one) the six notes of "Casper, the Friendly Ghost"
are stated in a minor key. As the hero decides to undertake his interplanetary
journey, the six notes are heard very passively, first on muted trumpet, then
flute (possibly played by Coppola), as if to indicate that both the hero and
story are headed somewhere, but aren't there yet. When a tribe of vicious tree
people out of Tolkien or Frank Baum (or even *MacBeth*) attack the Luna-
putians, the friendly ghost saves the day. Casper, who was at first treated as a
monster by the midget moonmen, is ultimately knighted by "King Bombo"
as "Sir Friend Casper." Sharples appropriately contrasts the familiar "friendly"
theme with a more menacing motif for the moon monsters. (In the last shot,
even the 3-D moon itself winks at us, real friendly like.) In both *Dizzy Dishes*

and *Boo Moon*, Sharples tells the story so effectively just by playing one melody off of another, that you almost don't need either dialogue or visuals.

As we've seen, Scott Bradley never had the luxury of any such theme that could automatically summon to mind Tom, Jerry, or Droopy; even Carl Stalling never so insistently employed "What's Up, Doc" (composed comparatively late in Bugs Bunny's career) to introduce the wascally wabbit. But nearly all the Famous stars had their built-in *leitmotifs*. Even "Goodie the Gremlin," an unsuccessful Casper variation who never made it past his "pilot" appearance (*Good and Guilty,* 1962), enjoyed a theme song that was more memorable than the cartoon that followed. Supporting players, too, got a piece of the musical action, such as Brownie bear, a one-shot ursine actor whose theme is performed by no less a personage than his nibs, the friendliest ghost you'll know himself, in *Casper Comes to Clown* (1951).

The one major exception was Baby Huey—the leviathan lummox never received an original theme, and from the beginning had to make do with "Rockabye Baby" as his motif. That nursery rhyme underscores the baby duck's presence from even before his emergence from the egg in *Starting from Hatch* (1953). (For his premiere episode, the dumb duck is gulled into thinking a hungry fox is his mother, and it ends when Huey at last meets his real mom and summarily announces, "I'm the luckiest duck in the world, I've got two mommies!" No wonder all the little mice are feeling gay.) By the time of *Huey's Ducky Daddy* (1953), Huey's feathered mommy has attached lyrics to the lullaby ("My baby Huey / Such a sweet child . . ."), but there's still no official Huey theme. And this is even in a film where even Huey's Scottish and "fowl"-tempered (but nonetheless ducky) Daddy rates a bagpipey, *Brigadoon*-like motif of his own. Still, much of Huey's speech is in rhythm, and is generally set to the cadence of the archaic nursery chant, "You're a dirty robber!"

On a similar note, Buzzy the Crow, for all the distinctiveness of the Amos 'n' Andy–style voice (addressing Katnip as "boss" is perhaps intended to make him seem even more African American) bestowed

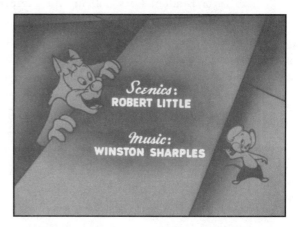

Scenics:
ROBERT LITTLE

Music:
WINSTON SHARPLES

© Harvey Famous Cartoons.

on him by Jackson Beck, never had his own theme. Whenever (as in *Cat-Choo*, 1951) the black crow would come up with a scheme to wrest himself from the clutches of Katnip (an early advocate of the self-help movement), Sharples would chime in with "Listen to the Mockingbird." However, Famous paralleled Warner Bros. in that their resident feline "heavy," i.e., Katnip, did double duty, a la Sylvester (of both Tweety and Speedy Gonzales fame). In his other series, Katnip enjoyed one of the most memorable theme songs in 'toondom.

As hard-core cat-and-mouse-o-philes know, the theme of Famous's eighteen Herman and Katnip episodes was "Skiddle-Diddle-Dee." Sharples's use of this theme proved especially rewarding when contrasted with his approximations of music from other cultures. *Cat Tamale* (1951) mixes Mexican melodies along with the skiddle-diddle, underscoring how Herman demolishes his feline foe bullfight-style as well as by dumping inflammatory south-of-the-border eats, like jumping beans and red hot tobasco sauce, into his opponent's pussy pallet. *Cat Carson Rides Again* (1952) skiddle-diddles in western themes, most notably Frank Loesser's "I Got Spurs that Jingle Jangle Jingle" as Katnip busts in on a saloon full of mice (now there's an appetizing sight). Both films are also unified visually by the brilliantly grotesque tortures the rodents inflict on Katnip's tongue—in the first it's flattened by a hot iron, in the second it's incinerated—leaving him nearly cat-atonic. (Make no mistake, Herman and Katnip are the real inspiration for "Itchy and Scratchy" on *The Simpsons*, not to mention National Lampoon's "Kit and Kaboodle" comic strip, even more than the considerably wittier efforts of Metro's *Tom and Jerry*.)

Sharples actually utilized contemporary pop songs far less extensively than Stalling or Bradley, Loesser being the exception. "I Got Spurs . . ." (introduced in Paramount's *The Forest Rangers*, 1942) turns up frequently in Famous westerns, and is the subject of a singalong in *Snooze Reel* (1951). "Heart and Soul" (Loesser's words, Hoagy Carmichael's music), most famous as a perennial four-handed amateur piano duet, often serves as a 'tooney love theme in Popeye the Sailor's romantic efforts. Likewise, "I Don't Want To Walk Without You" (Loesser's words, Jule Styne's music) is endearingly intoned by Olive Oyl in a provocative striptease for a *Klondike Casanova* (1946). Appropriately, Loesser and Hoagy Carmichael had been the only heavyweight Tin Pan Alley-ites ever to write directly for animation when they supplied the score to the Fleischers' second feature, *Mr. Bug Goes to Town* (1941). The Academy Award-winning writer of *Guys and Dolls, How to Suc-*

ceed in Business Without Really Trying, and many other classic shows has even deeper cartoon connections, having written a song for *Turkey Dinner,* a Walter Lantz cartoon from 1936.

Even though the hardly-lesser Loesser songs Sharples made use of derived from Hollywood films, their presence underscores the connection of the Famous-ites to Broadway and New York. Without so much as a title setting the scene in the Big Apple, *Boo Moon* opens with a mob of Manhattanites streaming and screaming out of a subway kiosk at the sight of Casper. Even in the wild west setting of *Cat Carson Rides Again,* the gay little mice have New York accents, and though *To Boo or Not to Boo* (1951) transpires in a rustic locale where square dances are not infrequent, the locals still address Casper as "bub" and sound like they stepped off the BMT bound for Brooklyn. (And that's in spite of how the big dance number, "Skip to My Lou," is obviously inspired by the arrangement of same from *Meet Me in St. Louis.*)

Casper, revealed to be an avid reader of Dale Carnegie, crashes a Halloween party a la *Victor/Victoria*—in other words, he's a ghost disguised as a non-ghost costumed as a ghost. Much as it pains me to disclose the ending to those who haven't yet experienced this haunting classic, it ends with Casper's newfound girlfriend also revealing herself to be a ghost. This turns out to be another case of turnaround: we've often seen girls dressed as ghosts, but rarely, one assumes, do ghosts go out disguised as girls.

Sharples juxtaposes a slew of rustic airs with Casper's theme, here, tellingly played out of kilter on a trombone when the ghost loses his balance and then his disguise. Perhaps Sharples, who scored hundreds of TV cartoons (some outside of Famous and Paramount) in the 1960s and then retired to Florida to spend his remaining few years playing golf and not worrying about having all his orchestrations ready for the next session, is trying to tell us something. Maybe it's that there's a little bit of a friendly ghost inside all of us, and that happiness is merely a matter of getting in touch with our inner Casper.

Originally appeared as "Winston Sharples: Cat and Mouse Melodies and Haunting Refrains," in The Harvey Cartoon History, *edited by Jerry Beck. New York: Harvey Comics, Inc., 1997. ©1997 by Will Friedwald. Reprinted by permission.*

An Interview with Hoyt Curtin

by BARRY HANSEN and EARL KRESS

Once the inevitable shift to television began in the late 1940s, the fate of Hollywood cartoons was sealed. Even though studio cartoon composers worked within tight schedules—Stalling produced a new, seven-minute score for Warner Bros. every ten days, on average—the new approach to creating animation for television meant a completely novel approach to scoring said shows. A single "episode" (whether divided among characters, as in *The Huckleberry Hound Show*, or comprising a single storyline, like in *The Flintstones*) demanded as much as twenty-two minutes of music from a composer—a considerable amount of underscore music to produce on a weekly basis by any standard. And just as every show had a new set of characters and adventures, so too would they need a catchy new theme song to grab the kids' attention Saturday mornings.

The man known for having almost single-handedly written more cartoon melodies than anyone began life in Downey, California, on September 9, 1922. He began playing piano at age five, and won a singing contest in a movie theatre when he was about twelve years old. Curtin went to school for music at USC; after serving in the Navy during World War II, he came back to Hollywood, where he got into TV music by writing commercial jingles—which possibly explains his affinity for catchy tunes. Curtin wrote several scores for the UPA animation studio, including the score for Academy Award winner *When Magoo Flew* (1955). He first met up with William Hanna and Joseph Barbera when he scored a Schlitz ad that they were producing; once he joined their studio in 1957, he began writing both themes and underscore music for their numerous television series. With Hanna-Barbera's variety of shows, Curtin had the chance to score comedies (*The Flintstones*), adventure shows (*Jonny Quest*), and everything in between, including *The Cattanooga Cats* and *The Smurfs*.

Curtin became known, after more than thirty years in the animation music business, for his economy of expression; he created memorable themes for dozens upon dozens of series, as well as original underscore music that could be used in any number of situations. When animation composers no longer had the resources of a Warner Bros. or MGM studio orchestra, Curtin ably devised a completely new means of creating meaningful music for cartoons. In this brief interview, he recalls some of the highlights of his life as a composer. He passed away on December 3, 2000.

HOYT CURTIN BEGAN playing piano with big bands while in college, but his real passion was writing music. He got his first professional break scoring industrial films, where he also learned the craft of cutting film. Hoyt picks up the story in this interview with Barry Hansen and Earl Kress from November 1994.

Q: You started at Hanna-Barbera in the very beginning with *Ruff and Reddy*?

A: I did. I was doing a TV commercial at MGM . . . for Leo Burnett. It was an animated beer commercial, Schlitz Beer, and that's where I met Bill and Joe. It was not long after that they got me on the phone. They called me and had this lyric. "Could you write us a theme song using this lyric?" [Hanna] said, "Get back to us and tell us if you can do that or not." So, like in five minutes, you know, I called them back. I sang the thing. It was silence. I thought, "Uh-oh, I bombed out." But they said, "Could you get that recorded?" So I said, "Why, sure." I already had the entire structure for producing music, especially for TV commercials. I used most of the same guys because they were the best players. So that's how I got started with them, just over the phone. I can remember Bill giving me *Yogi Bear* over the phone and *Quick Draw McGraw.*

Q: He'd give you the lyrics, and then you'd write the music?

A: That's right. We established a rapport right away, and every time they would get a show, they would call me, and sometimes I would go in. Like on *The Flintstones* I went in to talk to them about it because it was going to be a nighttime show. But it was just still Bill, Joe, and I because the networks weren't involved at that time. It wasn't formalized like it is now with big huge meetings, people around tables. God, that's awful.

Q: Did you write the music and also direct the recording sessions?

A: Arranged it and hired the band, conducted it and the whole bit. I always had a great arranger who I just found by accident. I couldn't do it [myself] even after I started doing *Quick Draw McGraw,* that soon into the business. I just couldn't keep up. I had an arranger to help me. I would sketch everything, and he would arrange it. His name was Jack Stern. He [was] the best in the business.

Q: In other cartoons, the music is scored very closely to the picture. Most of the Hanna-Barbera music was used over and over again, yet some of the cues sound scored, like something that you wouldn't make up out of thin air.

A: We would score these episodes to the picture because each picture has a rhythm of cutting and many had the same kind of gags in them so they could reuse them.

Q: Tell us about *The Flintstones* theme.

A: The first *Flintstones* recording was not the theme you hear now. It was called "Rise and Shine." It was just a booming thing where [Fred] is running home and gets the tablet from the kid on the corner and goes in and the garage door comes down. That was the first year. Then they thought, let's change it.

Q: The new theme, "Meet the Flintstones," that everyone remembers was actually used in underscore pieces before you used it as a theme.

A: I wrote some cues that were sad [with] a clarinet solo. Then I got to thinking about that, and that's the one I used. It was decided that we would do a jazz thing with singers and put a lyric on it. I have the original sketch in pencil, the first time I ever wrote that thing down.

Q: Let's talk a little about the underscore. The first underscore that was written for the studio was for the *Loopy de Loop* theatrical shorts.

A: That's right. I loved that show. He was funny.

Q: How many players were there?

A: Sometimes we would use four or five. *Loopy de Loop* was a cute little thing, and we didn't need [more than that].

Q: How many players are we talking about for *The Flintstones?*

A: Unless it was something really unusual, twelve guys could play the underscoring fine. I always wanted three woodwinds. I always wanted bass clarinet so the guy could play slap-tongue clarinet. A good tuba player, gotta have that. And then a drummer and a bass and a guitar and sometimes a keyboard, although I didn't always use keyboard, and a percussion guy from hell (usually Chet Ricord) because they help you out with the sound effects part.

Q: Now when we get to *Top Cat*, which was the next show, you had strings in that.

A: Yes, here's what happened on that. They needed it real fast, and I wanted a kind of downtown feel, and what I would do, I would have a microphone that I could talk into and a pickup on the piano, and I would play the [different parts the] orchestra was going to play. They could simply hear what I did on the piano and write that down for the horn player [for instance]. This saved us a lot of time. That particular underscoring job was not timed to people falling down and things like that. The music was supposed to provide a feel. It's a happy feel—it's got the right instruments—it's got the right tempo.

Q: Who did the "Judy Jetson" trumpet solo in *The Jetsons* theme?

A: Pete Condoli. When you hear that *Jetsons* piece, this is a difficult thing to play, very difficult. My fiddle guy who got all the fiddle players, I would warn him that you gotta get some fingerbusters coming, and so he would bring the right people to do it. We usually used six violins and four cellos. We couldn't afford violas. Violas were a luxury. We had a way of milking the violins so the six sounded real full.

Q: Did you actually compose all the underscore yourself?

A: I would sketch out. I didn't have time to orchestrate everything. The sketch tells them what instruments you're going to use, what the tempos are going to be, and a description of what the music should sound like, and then maybe I might write a cue or two, a few bars, so that they could see what I was talking about. That's all they needed.

Originally appeared in Hanna-Barbera's Pic-A-Nic Basket of Cartoon Classics *(Rhino R2-72290, 1996). © 1996 by Barry Hansen and Earl Kress. Reprinted by permission.*

Rock 'n' Roll Cartoons

by JAKE AUSTEN

OF COURSE BUGS BUNNY is Johnny Rotten and Woody Woodpecker is Little Richard. From a twenty-first-century perspective, it makes perfect sense that the subversive, rebellious tricksters that populated animation cels of the 1930s, '40s, and '50s laid the groundwork for the rock 'n' roll-ification of American popular culture. But certainly parents of yore giving their precious kids a nickel for the show had no idea that race mixing, fornication, and cultural revolution were being gestated on the silver screen ("Isn't that cute, son, Daffy Duck is a violent anarchist!"). Though tricksters and violence had always been a part of children's stories (from fables to the funny pages), sound movies added a volatile element with the potential to stir the savage beasts within viewers of all ages. Unfortunately, however, when children's cartoons and rock 'n' roll meet, concessions and compromises cause the anarchy and danger that mark both artforms' finest moments to disappear.

While musical scores for children's animation have a complex, amazing history, the history of diegetic songs contained in cartoons (music that one actually sees the characters singing or playing, as opposed to background music) is a little less complicated. Not long after the rock 'n' roll era took hold of American culture, the record buying tastes of the kids—from the British Invasion to MTV to hip-hop—influenced the musical content of kid's cartoons. During the early days of rock 'n' roll, television began its assault on movies and radio as America's prime entertainment source. To some, the transient nature of Top 40 rock 'n' roll styles may have seemed inappropriate to the elaborate, expensive full-animation cartoons that screened theatrically in the days before television. More logical was the marriage between cheaper, limited-animation cartoons made specifically for television and that "low" musical form that the kids digged.

In pre-TV cartoons, diegetic music tried to teach culture to the kiddies (Bugs, Daffy, or Tom picking up the conductor's baton to lead an orchestra or Disney's *Fantasia*, for example), or was limited to innocuous nursery-rhyme melodies or floral Hollywood harmonies. With a few exceptions (notably Disney's *Fantasia* sequel, *Make Mine Music*), when popular music of the day appeared in cartoons it would either be a nod to the adults in the theater (Sinatra and Bing references in Warner Bros. cartoons) or, in the case of Cab Calloway's occult *Betty Boop* appearance or the minstrel crows in *Dumbo*, a signifier of decadence. Basing a cartoon's entire premise on the exploits of pop musicians is another matter. Certainly the misadventures of traveling minstrels is a theme older than *The Canterbury Tales*, but the idea of presenting it as appropriate material for the wee ones was something that would involve baby boomer influence, TV's hypnotizing capabilities, and the (somewhat) unstoppable power of rock 'n' roll.

Elvis in Your Living Room

Television began to saturate living rooms during boomer adolescence, and in the early 1950s, despite the fact that its programming was heavy on violence (professional wrestling and westerns), TV was considered relatively safe fare for the young 'uns. Parents believed that TV, like the cartoon-heavy Saturday matinees that preceded it, was an innocuous, vanilla babysitter, and that it didn't invoke issues like sex, race mixing, and delinquency.

The same couldn't be said about the other emerging passion of the kids: rock 'n' roll. The massive power of the new generation was demonstrated when Elvis Presley mania trumped the Rudy Valee/Bing Crosby/Frank Sinatra swoonings of previous teen scenes. Not only was this frenzy bigger, it was blacker. For children to embrace, and the media to accept, a performer who overtly referenced the rawness and sexuality of black popular music represented a remarkable flexing of financial muscle. This generation would prove to be so massive in size and influence that its allowance money would force the hands of record, TV, and movie execs to ignore protesting church groups and give the public the Pelvis they demanded. Yet "the Man" was not ready to submit quite yet. Between 1956 and 1960, Elvis appeared on TV numerous times, and rarely was he allowed to be Elvis on his own terms. On Steve Allen's show, he had to wear a tux and sing to a basset hound. He was infamously shot from the waist up on Ed Sullivan's show (Ed at one point banned Elvis from the show, until public demand made him reconsider). When Elvis was released from the army, Frank Sinatra welcomed him home on TV, where Elvis appeared in uniform to make it clear to America that the U.S. Army had tamed him. It was during this same period that the classic theatrical cartoons of the 1940s began making their way onto the small screen, with Woody Woodpecker and Bugs Bunny getting their own shows in 1957 and 1960, respectively. But the reintroduction of the hooligans of the past likely did little to compensate youth culture for the loss of savage Elvis.

In an atmosphere where even the most popular performer in the world is handcuffed to protect the teenagers, imagine what protections had to be implemented for the preteens. Earlier in the 1950s, comic books had been successfully neutered by Dr. Frederick Wertham's congressional hearings. But comics were produced by obscure, creepy, small publishers that needed to be kept in check. For many parents, television's contents were controlled by accountable cultural authorities, so they felt little need to worry that the rock 'n' roll ills Elvis might unleash would get at their well-guarded tots. The fact that the bizarre *Andy's Gang* (1955–1960), which featured a clearly drunk Andy Devine and the near-satanic Froggy the Gremlin, and the sly *Soupy Sales Show* (1955, 1959–1962) were not considered subversive is a testament to the faith parents had in Kiddie TV. Not surprisingly, the first cartoon to reach the airwaves that dealt with the career of a young band in the rock 'n' roll era clearly had no intention of featuring any rock 'n' roll at all. However, it did manage to sneak in some genuine subversion.

Bucktoothed Trailblazers

Ross Bagdasarian, an Armenian American novelty song writer/bit actor, turned tape speed manipulation into gold when he had his first big hit with "Witch Doctor" in 1958. He recorded as the "witch doctor" at a slow speed while articulating clearly, then played the tape back at regular speed, producing the pygmy medicine man's comic, high-pitched voice. He followed "Witch Doctor" up with a Christmas single ("The Chipmunk Song") introducing the Chipmunks, three performing rodent siblings with an ambiguous relationship to their Svengali father figure, David Seville (Bagdasarian's non-ethnic alter-ego). How this human came to adopt (or father) three chipmunks was unclear, but what was clear as soon as the record was released, and sold faster than any single in history, was that Simon, Theodore, and especially the mischievous Alvin, were here to stay. For the next decade, the Chipmunks enjoyed success on novelty records, on live TV (as puppets on *The Ed Sullivan Show*), in comic books, as dolls, and as an animated television show. The success of the Chipmunks is due in large part to the care taken with their cartoon. Originally pictured on record sleeves as inhuman little rodents, when the cartoon was conceived the production house exerted great efforts to come up with a more suitable design for the kids.

There were high hopes for *The Alvin Show* (Format Films, 1961–65). Like *The Flintstones* before them and *The Simpsons* after them, The Chips were believed to appeal to adults and kids alike, and thus their cartoon debuted as a prime time show. It was hilarious, featuring excellent Bagdasarian songs (he also did the voices) and funny, expressive designs that capitalized on low-budget animation techniques by making the herky-jerky movements part of the humor. Bagdasarian's exquisitely constructed recordings proved perfect for animation, and since the characters were a musical group, it made sense for them to be performing songs (and viewers performed along as they followed the bouncing ball across the song lyrics, a segment of the show revived from the Fleischer brothers' late 1920s and early '30s Song Car-Tune shorts). One of the strengths of the show was that Bagdasarian represented the generation gap without fully submitting to it. Unlike Sammy Davis, Jr., wearing hot pants to "fit in with the kids," Bagdasarian knew he didn't grasp rock 'n' roll (a pop devotee, he cowrote the Rosemary Clooney hit "Come On-a My House") and he didn't fake it. When the Chipmunks usurp Seville's recording sessions with "rock 'n' roll," it's a charming fantasy version featuring clean sounding, professional swinging horns and the rodents chanting "cha cha cha." But despite avoiding rock 'n' roll rebel music, Alvin proved to be as antiauthoritarian as his cartoon predecessors and punk rock followers. He never suffered as a result of his nastiness, certainly leading many impressionable children down a delightfully wicked path.

© Ross Bagdasarian. Courtesy of Jake Austen.

The show proved to be not particularly appealing to adults, and was rerouted to Saturday morning in its second season, where it appeared in reruns until 1965. By that time, actual rock 'n' roll had enjoyed its breakthrough into the wholesome mainstream.

Moptops for Tiny Tots

The Beatles' film *A Hard Day's Night* (1964), with its absurd chase scenes and comical bantering, is often cited as the first instance of the cartoon-like anarchy that made them natural heirs (hares?) to Bugs Bunny's trickster throne. However, the moment America was truly invaded was months earlier, during the Beatles' press conference at Idlewild Airport after landing on U.S. soil. The deadpan American press was surprised and delighted by the quick-witted, goofy, comedic schtick that Ringo and company delivered in lieu of regular answers.

Actually, this was nothing new. Elvis Presley's interviews and stage banter were filled with borscht belt one-liners and bad puns. But at the height of Elvis mania, this aspect of his personality was ignored; the unleashed sexuality, the foreboding danger, and the juvenile delinquency he symbolized were all that scared fogeys and awestruck teens allowed themselves to acknowledge. Fans and foes alike refused to see the Shecky Greene side of the King. Though some kiddie ephemera was produced (bubble gum cards, toy guitars), something like an Elvis cartoon was unthinkable. Parents may have begrudgingly acknowledged that their thirteen-year-olds were lost, but the idea of willingly giving up the six-year-olds to devil music was unthinkable. Adults still believed they were in charge, and decided what was appropriate for their kids. They believed they were the gatekeepers of popular culture, and as the 1960s dawned, America still thought that the Rat Pack in tuxedos was running the show. Even the twist craze, where adults went to posh nightclubs and took lessons to learn the top teen dance, was in essence an exoticizing of the baby boom cultural revolution. By treating rock 'n' roll culture as some romantic novelty, like the Tango or a Tiki bar, they were taming and compartmentalizing it.

But by 1965, the inevitable was underway, and the old guard was primed for a fall. The road to Rolling Stones credit cards, Ramones songs being played over the P.A. at baseball games, and casual Friday was being paved. The Beatles got their own cartoon.

In addition to the Beatles' British charm and wit, a far more American reason ultimately hastened the decision that rock 'n' roll was appropriate for tiny tykes. There was a lot of money to be made by marketing the Beatles to tots as well as teens, and toymaker A. C. Gilmer understood that. Financing the show with the understanding that the merchandising of the cartoon images of the Beatles would make him a fortune, Gilmer worked with King Features and a British animation design house to make *The Beatles* (King Features 1965–1969) the first real rock 'n' roll cartoon, creating the mold for all rock 'n' roll cartoons to come. Although they borrowed the "follow the bouncing ball" sing-a-long aspect from Alvin, they innovated a frantic style of incorporating the songs into the story that would later become known as "MTV style." Of course, this was riffing off similar non-animated segments from *A Hard Day's Night*, which would be perfected in 1967 by *The Monkees* TV show. The other aspect *The Beatles* introduced that would become a constant in rock 'n' roll cartoons was shoddy animation. The Beatles' cartoon alter egos were charmingly designed, and the cartoon was funny, but unlike *The Alvin Show*, it did not make the most of the limited animation. Also, although the cartoon boasted that it featured the voices of the Beatles, it did so only in the songs. The spoken voices were performed by actors, including the great Paul Frees, an Elvis crony known for the voice of Boris Badenov on the cartoon *Rocky and His Friends*. One area in which the show didn't skimp was the inclusion of virtually the entire Beatles musical catalog up to 1965, including the German-language "Komm, Gib Mir Deine Hand."

Gilmer's calculations proved accurate. The show was a huge success, and the stellar early ratings were unprecedented in daytime TV. Apparently, the limitations of cheap animation and half-hearted Beatles impersonators were not a problem for the little kids. Despite sporting long hair, the Beatles (who were perpetually in their 1964 mode on the cartoon) were portrayed as clean-cut kids. Girls chasing them never led to sex, and Ringo's goofiness was never a result of drugs. When the smoke (never from cigarettes) cleared, marketing black-influenced music to toddlers had put a lot of loot in businessmen's pockets, and seemed to have left American civilization intact.

In the immediate wake of the Beatles show, a number of cartoon rock 'n' roll bands emerged, but, like the Chipmunks before them, their producers had little grasp of rock 'n' roll and were simply making fun of it or exploiting it half-heartedly (as bubblegum music later demonstrated, in rock 'n' roll, only wholehearted, unambiguous exploitation is smiled upon). Songs were rarely played, and the baggage of the rock 'n' roll lifestyle (gear, rehearsals, gigging, vans) were rarely seen. Cartoon bands included the Impossibles, a goofy superhero trio whose alter egos were a rock band (they appeared on *Frankenstein, Jr., and the Impossibles*, Hanna-Barbera, 1966). *The Super Six* (Depatie-Freleng, 1966–1969) featured Super Bwoing, a rock superhero with a flying guitar. *The Beagles* (Total Television, 1966–1968) were a duo of dogs who played music (their relationship to the Beatles ended at the pun name). The Beagles did release an LP, but it was mostly upbeat kiddie folk music.

Despite the moderate success of these post–Beatles cartoon bands, it wouldn't be until the decade's end that the cartoon rock revolution would begin. This would be accomplished by the convergence of two factors: the raising of bubblegum music to an artform and Hanna-Barbera's lowering of TV cartoon standards to a dubious anti-artform.

Bubblegum and Breakfast Cereal

Although the Beatles liberated rock 'n' roll for the pre-teens by making it safe for Saturday mornings in the early 1960s, the phenomenal success of their *Sergeant Pepper's Lonely Hearts Club Band* LP in 1967 essentially liberated (or enslaved) the adults by changing *rock 'n' roll* to *rock*, a "serious" art form deserving of its own *New York Times* critics and academic conferences. When the mature incarnation of the Beatles returned to animated form it was in a work of art, not a tool of toy store commerce. The sophisticated, psychedelic *Yellow Submarine* feature film (Apple, 1968) was a far cry from the chintzy, goofy TV cartoon (though, surprisingly, it was animated by the same production houses). By introducing the idea that rock musicians were serious artists who couldn't possibly be making music that the milk-and-cookies set could understand, however, it left a gaping hole of opportunity ready to be filled by some joyously crass impresarios.

In 1966, the Monkees shone a light on the limitless possibilities of pre-fab gold by going head to head with the Beatles on the charts, despite the fact that they were a fictional band who had most of their songs written, produced, and performed (except for the singing) by slick studio hotshots. If they could be successful, why not market records by studio musicians as groups who didn't even exist? If the songs get popular, *then* worry about who's in the band! Who needs a real-life band at all?

Bubblegum music does not avoid the kiddies of cartoons-and-Cocoa Puffs age; it ignores everyone else. It combines the finest pop craftsmen (on a mission to make a hit, not a piece of art), the slickest studio musicians, and the sweetest sounding vocalists (ideally, with voices that somehow combine total innocence with almost creepy seductiveness). It gives these people a mandate to make a song so catchy it is almost a jingle, and to make the subject matter about things little kids dig: candy! games! roller skates! But the writer also must, somehow, make candy, games, and roller skates overt, yet ambiguous, metaphors for sex. (Whether this was done to tap into preteen sexuality, to make the songs seem naughtier and more authentic to the kids, or as injokes by sleazy songwriters are points debated by bubblegum scholars.) Most important, the process can't be about glory or immortality or individual achievement; it has to be about brutally honest commerce (give the kids *exactly* what they want, and they'll pay), so no performer's egos are allowed. The architects of bubblegum, Buddah records owner Neil Bogart and the Super-K production team of Kasenetz-Katz, knew when they started in 1967 that bands like the 1910 Fruitgum Company and the Ohio Express

© Archie Comic Publications, Inc.
Courtesy of Jake Austen.

didn't really have to exist to have hits. If someone in the studio could come up with a winner, it didn't matter what band name was slapped on the label. But despite their prowess, the ultimate bubblegum achievement wasn't made by Bogart or Super-K. It was made by a little Jewish man who set the wheels of cartoon rock 'n' roll in fast motion.

The Archies had the only bubblegum superhit, "Sugar Sugar" (it hit number one on Billboard's chart in 1969), an amazing eleven-year tenure on TV, and one of the most interesting stories in rock 'n' roll history. The *Archie* comic, featuring the adventures of the wacky teenagers of Riverdale, was launched in 1942 by John Goldwater, but the Archies, the band, owe their creation to a different patriarch, Don Kirschner. In 1968, Kirschner was ousted by the Monkees despite almost single-handedly overseeing the production of the remarkable music that would make them the Beatles' only rivals at the time. His problems with the group stemmed from the fact that the Monkees wanted to play their own instruments on the records. Though a compromise certainly could have been made, Kirschner wasn't interested in submitting to these ungracious louts, and he vowed to show them all. In exile, he came up with the perfect band, one that would do his bidding, play the songs how they were supposed to be played, and never rebel. How could they be difficult . . . *if they're only cartoons?*

Working with Phil Spector songwriter Jeff Barry, hitmaking songwriter/artist Andy Kim, pop singer extraordinare Ron Dante, and sexy vocalist Toni Wine (as both Betty and Veronica), Kirschner crafted a bevy of surefire pop winners to be performed by the "band" on the new *Archie Show* (Filmation, 1968–1978). Every episode would end with the animated Archies playing a song, and if you dug the tune, it would be available on vinyl at your local record shop. Their first single, "Bang-Shang-a-Lang," just missed the top twenty. But when "Sugar Sugar" hit the top of the charts the following year, it made the Archies the *ultimate* cartoon rock 'n' roll band. Their huge hit allowed them to record five LPs of absurd, joyous, undeniable pop, including such naughty album cuts as "Hot Dog," which is either about penis worship or bestiality, and "Jingle Jangle," which equates an erection with Pinocchio's nose. Their contagious music was a perfect bubblegum balance of nice and naughty, and the program proved to be the perfect marriage of music and cartoons. Despite Filmation's limited animation style, the songs looked good being sung by the band, and fit into the show's structure well. The tunes kept the cartoon popular, and the cartoon (in the days before MTV) kept the songs on the tube and in the kids' heads. As cartoon rock 'n' roll reached its pinnacle of success, it became clear that, though TV cartoon characters were making no attempt to capture the dangerous, contrarian spirit of their cinematic ancestors, the absurd, fun music was closer in spirit to the simple, sexy tunes of early rock 'n' roll than the mature post-*Pepper* music that was being played on FM radio.

Filmation's attempts to replicate their Archie success proved fruitless. *The Hardy Boys* (1969–1971) featured a rock 'n' roll version of the famous mystery-solving brothers, who now moonlighted in a rock band. This production was meant to take the Archies model one step further. To coincide with the cartoon's debut, they cast a band that looked like the cartoon characters (a fat one, a black one, etc.) to record and tour. They released two LPs of moderate quality, with no commercial success. *Groovie Goolies* (1970–1973) was ostensibly an Archies spinoff, as these monster musicians were cousins of Archie's classmate, Sabrina the Teenage Witch. They released a decent bubblegum LP, but it, too, didn't catch on with the public. *The Brady Kids* was a parentless version of the live action show, with an emphasis on the kids' musical career. However, any success their recordings enjoyed could be attributed to the songs also being performed on the real *Brady Bunch* program. *Mission Magic* (1972) featured then-teenage Rick Springfield as an enchanted rock star, but the cartoon, and his debut U.S. LP that coincided with it, tanked, leaving Springfield in obscurity until the 1980s.

Also entering the cartoon rock fray was the Rankin/Bass production house, which attempted to recreate the success of the 1965 Beatles cartoon. Using that same model, they licensed the likenesses and music of two bubblegum-era acts whose genuine talent made them rise above the transient nature of the genre: the Jackson 5ive and the Osmonds. Running back to back for most of their time on the air, *The Jackson 5ive* (Rankin/Bass, 1971–1973) and *The Osmonds* (Rankin/Bass 1972–1974) both mimicked the Beatles cartoon by having adventures built around cartoon videos of their currently popular hits. These programs better the Beatles show (and the cookie-cutter Filmation and Hanna-Barbera shows), however, because of Rankin/Bass's whimsical, confident signature style (courtesy of *Mad* magazine's Paul Coker) that would also be featured in their popular holiday cartoons and stop-action animations (*Frosty the Snowman*, *Rudolph the Red-Nosed Reindeer*, etc.). Also, since rock 'n' roll was a more established part of the cultural landscape, these cartoons could include references to the lifestyle that *The Beatles* left out. Berry Gordy appeared in the Jacksons' cartoon, and some of the mechanics of the record industry were demonstrated, while the Osmonds (the show featured the boys touring the world to promote goodwill) took the "screaming fans" aspect to a new level by featuring a recurring character who was Donny's personal obsessed stalker.

Hanna-Barbera—Cartoon Rock Royalty

While Rankin/Bass was getting into the groove and Filmation was striking gold with the Archies, Hanna and Barbera, the cartoon kings, were ready to dive in deeper than Tito's and Jughead's bosses could imagine. Hanna-Barbera Studios was started in 1957, after Bill Hanna and Joe Barbera had spent nearly two decades directing high-end theatrical cartoons for MGM, winning an armful of Oscars for their work on the Tom & Jerry series. Hanna-Barbera studios had a mandate to exploit television's potential as a home for original animation, as opposed to a place where old theatrical cartoons were repackaged. By 1960, they had established a foothold on Saturday morning TV and had introduced *The Flintstones*, a show that trumped Alvin and his Chipmunk crew by becoming the first successful prime time cartoon. They also perfected cost-cutting techniques that, they accurately calculated, wouldn't adversely affect the appeal to crumbsnatchers (who by the 1960s and '70s rarely, if ever, saw full animation on the big screen).

Hanna-Barbera's "planned animation" consisted of a series of techniques to cut down on labor. If a character ran or walked one time, why animate it again? Just use the same footage every time! If the only thing moving in a scene is an arm or mouth, why not paint the rest of the body as background and just animate the moving part? So what if the colors of the moving sleeve and the still shirt don't quite match? On the musical side, the frugality involved "needle drops" (the audio equivalent of stock footage) and developing an innovative, but limited, library of sound effects to be used in every cartoon. While the theme songs for many of the programs were excellent, catchy compositions, the real sound of Hanna-Barbera is the eerily familiar musical cues that go along with a character shaking its head in disbelief or falling on its ass.

But by the late 1960s, new sounds were appearing on competitors' cartoons, specifically *The Archies*, and Hanna-Barbera wanted a piece of the rock 'n' roll pie. Unfortunately, by this time the Hanna-Barbera machine was so well oiled that the sparks of innovation that made the *The Flintstones*, *The Jetsons*, and *Top Cat* special were long burned out. The phenomenal success of their 1969 *Scooby-Doo* cartoon established what was essentially their last model, and for the next decade the idea of kids and a companion creature solving mysteries and getting into adventures was the cornerstone of the studio's assembly line production. What *The Archies*' success added to the mix was that now these kids would also be a band! Though Hanna-Barbera had dabbled in cartoon rock before (most successfully with rock 'n' roll episodes of *The Flintstones* and *The Jetsons* that featured musical characters like the Way-Outs, the Beau Brummelstones, and Jet Screamer), they suddenly threw themselves into it. They made efforts to work with bubblegum impresarios, and even started their own label, Hanna-Barbera Records. But on the animation front, little risk would be taken. The shows that resulted took "planned animation" to an extreme. Since each program would now feature a musical number or two, Hanna-Barbera would simply animate the band playing one time and then run the identical sequence weekly, with only the song changing. A second musical number would involve a song being played during a chase (à la *The Monkees*), and this would also rely on a series of sequences and actions that became very familiar very quickly.

The shows that came off this assembly line included *Pebbles and Bam Bam* (1971), featuring the rock 'n' roll adventures of the teenage progeny of Fred, Wilma, Barney, and Betty; *The Amazing Chan and the Chan Clan* (1972–1974), in which Charlie Chan's huge brood of children play pop music and solve crime; *Partridge Family: 2200 A.D.* (1974), featuring the family rock band in the future; *Butch Cassidy and the Sundance Kids* (1973–1974), featuring the voices of former Monkee Micky Dolenz and future Charlie's Angel Cheryl Ladd as rock 'n' roll secret agents; and *Jabberjaw* (1976–1978), about a giant shark who drums for the aquatic rock band, the Neptunes. Rock bands also hosted two Hanna-Barbera cartoon anthology shows, the pop art–influenced *Cattanooga Cats* (1969–1971) and *The Banana Splits* (1968–1970), who were live-action puppets (they were recently reborn as animated Web based cartoons). Also notable is the series *The New Scooby Doo Comedy Movies* (1972), which featured animated versions of guest stars from real life, including such musicians as Davy Jones, Mama Cass Elliot, Sonny and Cher, and Jerry Reed.

Though Hanna-Barbera was interested in Archies-style pop chart crossover success, they only produced three solid bubblegum bands from the entire brood, and none of them hit it big. It seems they all suffered from the unlikely malady of Too Much Soul. The Banana Splits' LP featured some catchy bubble-soul (including some session work by Barry White), and managed to slip a single into the top 100 (sales may have been negatively affected by their best songs being available free as flexi-discs on cereal boxes). *Josie and the Pussycats* (Hanna-Barbera, 1970–1974) became one of their most popular cartoons, and was a coup for Hanna-Barbera, as it was a license from the Archie Comics Group, who owned the rights to Filmation's competing cartoon rock 'n' roll juggernaut, the *Archies*. Attempting to replicate the soul music variation of bubblegum that the Jackson 5ive scored with, the producers hired a black singer (note that Val of the Pussycats, voiced by Patrice Holl-

© The Cartoon Network.

away, was one of the first black Hanna-Barbera characters) and stocked the studio with top soul session men. It was initially fruitless, as the songs never charted, but the theme song eventually proved memorable enough to keep the Pussycats in the collective consumer consciousness, meriting a live-action movie revival in 2001. Not yet aware that the formula combining bubblegum/soul and Hanna-Barbera was a bust, Josie's contemporaries, *The Harlem Globetrotters* (Hanna-Barbera 1970–76, 1978), went all out. Produced by Monkees and Archies don Don Kirschner, the album that accompanied the bizarre cartoon—in which the Globetrotters traveled the world playing ball, solving mysteries, and playing music (they were very talented)— should have reached the heights of the Billboard charts, or at least the *Jet* top twenty. Unfortunately, it never found an audience. In addition to Meadowlark Lemon, the leader of the 'trotters at the time, the LP features an all-star voice cast of R&B/doo wop legends, including members of the Coasters, the Drifters, the Platters, and the Cadillacs. Although the record is now beloved by collectors and connoisseurs, at the time it was too much for the target audience.

With the few noted exceptions, the music featured in Hanna-Barbera cartoons is weak, and one reason for this is that they fail to fully exploit the naughty double-entendre nature of classic bubblegum, instead featuring didactic songs designed to teach the kiddies lessons. This tactic failed to generate memorable music; even toddlers could recognize the insincerity and two-dimensionality of the planned-animation/needle-drop company's concern for their welfare. In 1969, *Sesame Street* had debuted on PBS, and with its sister show, *The Electric Company*, it presented educational pop music of a quality and genuineness that few questioned. Hanna-Barbera shared no mandates with the Children's Television Workshop, and consequently, their efforts to educate through song seem about as genuine as the food coloring in the sugary breakfast cereal advertised during their programs.

Saturday Morning Soul

The only bubblegum-era cartoon rock 'n' roll band that convincingly made "message music" (in this arena that means "don't smoke" and "avoid peer pressure" rather than "stop the war in Viet Nam") was *Fat Albert and the Cosby Kids* (Filmation 1972–1984). On the long-running program, comedian Bill Cosby brought the characters of his youth (who had been central to his standup comedy since the mid-1960s) to cartoon life, and the motley group of urban African American youth would meet up in the afternoons at the junkyard and bang out tunes on musical instruments made out of garbage (an accordion made from a hot water bottle and a radiator, a harp made out of a bedspring). Their songs, which ended every show in the early seasons (a TV in the clubhouse playing the Brown Hornet serial usurped band practice in the 1980s), would reiterate the lessons learned in this week's narrative. While the music wouldn't make the Jackson 5ive nervous, Fat Albert's smooth baritone was memorable, and the songs were catchy. Most important, their intentions seemed sincere, possibly stemming from the idea that Cosby (a successful actor and comic) didn't need to do a cartoon, but was genuinely interested in making a quality product for young people, particularly black kids with little representation on Saturday morning. Though Cosby opted against a pop crossover Cosby Kids LP (Fat Albert records were made for the kids' market), in recent days the black clothing manufacturer FUBU (and a host of bootleggers) have made Fat Albert and his friends a ubiquitous part of contemporary black fashion, and there is a live action movie being developed. Could a hip-hop Fat Albert CD be in the cards?

Speaking of which, one would expect the hip-hop generation to produce some genuine cartoon superstars. The combination of comical rap names (Flavor Flav, Yo Yo, Ice Cube), the exaggerated personalities (Busta Rhymes, Biz Markie, Redman), the Dr. Seuss–like rhyme schemes (especially in early rap), and the nursery-rhyme melodies that frequent the hooks of hip-hop hits would suggest that a successful kiddie show with a rapping protagonist was a natural. When you factor in budget-minded Hanna-Barbera logic (low-budget rap music can be produced less expensively than rock), you'd think a slew of touring, crime-solving rap acts was an inevitability. Perhaps the failure of the Globetrotters record had the big boys hesitant to explore black music. Also, rap's interest in authenticity is possibly recognized by even the youngest fans, who can rap along obliviously to adult-themed radio hits while still digging Elmo and Barney (both, incidentally, performed by black men) on their TV screens.

Despite no success stories emerging, there were some attempts at hip-hop animation, including two short-lived series. Kid 'n' Play were a marginal teenybopper rap act when the Hudlin Brothers saw them mention in an interview that they were interested in expanding into movies. Casting them as the leads in their successful *House Party* films launched the duo into a series of multimedia projects, despite

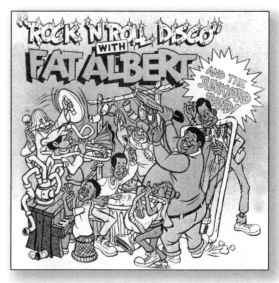

© Filmation Associates. Courtesy of Jake Austen.

the fact that their recording career remained lackluster. The cartoon *Kid 'n' Play* (Motown/Saban/Marvel 1990–1991) only lasted thirteen episodes. Kid 'n' Play were a teenage performing act on the show, looking for their big break, but the ultra-cheap Japanese animation and dull rap sequences didn't really capitalize on anything unique about hip-hop. It is notable that the voice cast featured black actors and actresses from prime time TV and feature films including Tommy Davidson, Dorian Harewood, Cree Summer, Dawnn Lewis, and Martin Lawrence (who also appeared in the *House Party* films).

Artistically more successful, but doomed by the "Where Are They Now" nature of pop music, was *Hammerman* (Bustin' Productions/DIC 1991–92 ABC). M. C. Hammer's show used Fat Albert as a model of an urban kiddie cartoon, and the humorously didactic stories dealt with juvenile delinquency and peer pressure. Whenever trouble brewed in Oaktown (Hammer is from Oakland), Stanley (Hammer's real name), a normal Joe who worked at an Oakland rec center, would don magical dancing shoes (that talked) and become Hammerman, a superheroic extension of Hammer's stage persona. The show was entertaining, convincingly urban, and every episode (like Cosby's show) had a musical number. But the quality of the program wasn't really an issue, because by 1992 M. C. Hammer was a punchline. Renewal for a second season wasn't a remote possibility.

Video Didn't Kill the Cartoon Rock Star

Outside of hip-hop, the music video era has produced a few interesting blips for cartoon bands. Less interesting are animated music videos by real acts (Madonna, A-Ha, Master P). More fascinating is the attempt to create Archies-like animated bands to compete with real acts. The new medium of music video made it possible to have such an act without the commitment of a TV network's time slot. This has been much more successful in England, where pop music traditions make the landscape for cartoon stars more inviting. *Top of the Pops*, the English equivalent of *American Bandstand*, is bizarrely populist; if a record sells, the artists will appear on the show, be they pop, punk, gay disco, or even nonexistent. When the Smurfs had a kiddie record on the charts, *Top of the Pops* managed to get the Smurfs to perform on the show. In the wake of success stories like that of the Wombles (a British furry puppet band that began producing hit records in 1974 and charted as recently as 1998), it was little surprise that the MTV era would produce new cartoon superstars in England. The first big success story was Jive Bunny, who in 1989 proved that the shoddiest animation imaginable and a goofy "mastermix" of oldies songs was enough to impress the Brits. Over the years the JB has sold over three million records, proving once again that the critics and the public come from different planets. Everyone agrees, however, on Gorillaz, a collaboration between cartoonist

Jamie Hewlett (of *Tank Girl* comics fame), Blur frontman Damon Albarn, rapper Del Tha Funky Homosapien, and various hipster all stars. The odd looking cartoon band "play" punk-dub-hip-hop pastiche music with a bored, jaded patina that matches the deadpan looks of the characters. The fact that the human participants make their presence known instead of totally pretending the cartoon characters are real, however, seems like too radical (and unendearingly ironic) a departure from the Archies model. At this writing, the band is planning to embark on its first world tour, and how that plays out will determine the cartoon rock authenticity of this act.

In America, the best we've done is come up with MC Skat Kat, who rapped a duet with Paula Abdul ("Opposites Attract," which hit number one on *Billboard*'s chart in 1990) and followed it up with a flop album by his band the Stray Mob. On a more traditional, though not particularly more successful, note, Dick Clark's production company tried to integrate music videos and Saturday morning cartoons. *Kidd Video* (DIC/Saban, 1984–1987) told the tale of a live-action teenage rock band who gets sucked into a cartoon dimension, where they become animated, and must fight the corporate rock villain Master Blaster, who plans to steal their rock 'n' roll magic. Clips of top 40 music videos were woven into the plot. A slight variation on this theme was *Wolf Rock* (DIC, 1984), in which a cartoon version of Wolfman Jack hosted the hits.

Other MTV-era cartoon rock series include *California Raisins* (Murakami-Wolf-Swenson 1989–1990), a cheapo animated version of the minstrel claymation creatures that sang Motown on raisin commercials; *Bill and Ted's Excellent Adventures* (Hanna-Barbera, 1990); and *Jem and the Holograms* (Sunbow, 1986–1987), a series based on an MTV-era Barbie doll ripoff. Although Mattel had created its own musical line of Barbie dolls (called Barbie and the Rockers), the hipper Jem dolls proved popular enough to warrant a series featuring an all-female group of new wave, orphan-saving rock stars who battle an evil rival band, the Misfits (a punky all girl band, not Glenn Danzig's New Jersey-based horror-rock band of the same name). The show featured video-styled music numbers, and Jem cassettes could be bought, not at the record shop, but at the toy store alongside the dolls.

Return of the Rodents

Fittingly, the most successful, enduring cartoon to emerge during this era was a revival of the first great cartoon rock band, the Chipmunks. The original series ran in Saturday morning reruns until 1965, around the time the Chipmunks' record sales were petering out as well. Though Bagdasarian would make low-profile Chipmunk LPs until 1969, he had obviously lost interest after the Beatles' success. Rock 'n' roll held less musical interest for him than novelty-tinged pop, and when it became necessary to make records where the Chips sang real rock songs (starting with a Beatles cover LP in 1964), he was just going through the motions. Bagdasarian retired to his vineyard and died a relatively young man in 1972. However, the Chipmunks story was far from over.

In the late 1970s Bagdasarian's son, Ross Jr., became interested in reviving the act. NBC began running reruns of the old *The Alvin Show* in 1979, inspiring morning disc jockeys around the country to do comedy segments where they would speed up recordings and pretend the Chipmunks were making a comeback recording Cheap Trick and punk rock songs. This led to Ross, Jr., doing the voices on an album called *Chipmunk Punk* in 1980, which became a minor hit. That resulted in a full-blown revival that, while never reaching the frenzy of the first Chipmunks singles, would burn longer and more steadily for the better part of the next two decades. After a sentimental animated Christmas special in 1981, Bagdasarian Productions plunged into a weekly cartoon, *Alvin and the Chipmunks* (Bagadasarian/Ruby-Spears, 1983–1990). The animation was less stylized and more "rad" for the 1980s, the gang was cuter, more "Smurf-ified," and they now had female equivalents, a rival rock band, The Chipettes (Brittany, Jeanette, and Eleanor). Although the new show was more squarely aimed at kids (the humor was less sophisticated, and there were more lessons learned), it proved to be more durable and merchandisable than the original. Musically, it was not comparable to the classic show, since the new Chipmunks made simple, cute cover versions or mild parodies of contemporary songs. But by aiming the music toward kids only, and not the *Billboard* charts, they were able to release more recordings over a longer period of time than the original Chipmunks. Although the show has been off the air for a decade, videotapes, some with new material, are still being released and are exceedingly popular with kids. Ultimately, the first cartoon rock 'n' roll band is the last one standing.

In the 1990s and the new century, cable TV, the Internet, cheap computer animation, and kids-only music outlets like Radio Disney have carpet-bombed pop culture with rock 'n' roll/cartoon hybrids. Postmodern references to Hanna-Barbera's bubblegum heyday not only pepper parodies (*Saturday Night*

Live's cartoon *X-Presidents* always ends with a dead-on Hanna-Barbera song sequence takeoff) but also genuine kiddie fare (*The Powerpuff Girls* and their Cartoon Network colleagues are virtually pastiches of past cartoon references). Just as Duran Duran and *NSYNC ultimately failed to live up to their labeling as the next Beatles, however, it's likely we'll never again see cartoons with the charm of the Chipmunks, the bubblegum synergy of the Archies, or the shamelessly unchecked mediocrity of Hanna-Barbera's 1970s cartoon rock renaissance. But with luck, we will someday see something far different and greater. While *The Simpsons* (on which three-fourths of the Beatles made animated returns) and *South Park* certainly have taken up the antiauthoritarian mantle of Bugs, Alvin, and company, we've yet to see the seemingly inevitable marriage of true, rebellious rock 'n' roll and amazing children's cartoons. Perhaps some young mind, contaminated by hours of animated adventures of music makers (no matter how crappily done), will one day create the ultimate cartoon rock 'n' roll band.

"Put One Note in Front of the Other"

The Music of Maury Laws

by GREG EHRBAR

RANKIN/BASS PRODUCTIONS was never a cartoon "studio" in the traditional sense. It was, and still remains today, a small New York-based production company with a core staff, contracting most of its creative team from project to project. Nevertheless, this plucky little organization produced a number of popular animated TV series, as well as a handful of feature films and TV movies, holding its own against such industry giants as Hanna-Barbera and Filmation in their heydays.

Rankin/Bass had its greatest success with TV specials, producing the greatest number of perennial animated TV films of any company. Virtually all of them are still enjoyed on broadcast TV and home video. Their enduring appeal to generation after generation is perhaps due the unique "blueprint" established by their first stop-motion special, *Rudolph the Red-Nosed Reindeer* (1964). A format never truly imitated by rival companies, it combined scripts steeped in their own self-contained myth, production design by highly distinctive illustrators, and, especially, musical scores incorporating the structures of both musical theater and feature animation of the first "golden age."

Maury Laws in Chicago, April 2002.
© Rick Goldschmidt. Courtesy of www.rankinbass.com.

From the early 1960s until the mid-1980s, Maury Laws was the musical director for nearly all Rankin/Bass films, including *Rudolph, Frosty the Snowman* (1969), *Santa Claus is Comin' to Town* (1970), *The Year Without a Santa Claus* (1974), and *The Hobbit* (1977). With Jules Bass (coproducer as well as lyricist), tunes such as "The Heat Miser/Snow Miser Song," "Put One Foot in Front of the Other," and "The Greatest Adventure (The Ballad of the Hobbit)" became a rich part of the animation landscape. Even when he was arranging and conducting the music of other composers (like Johnny Marks for *Rudolph*), the results bear the distinctive Laws stamp of sweeping strings, boisterous brass, and rhythmic phrasing.

A native of North Carolina, Laws started his career at the age of twelve, playing guitar and singing country music, graduating to featured vocalist in groups appearing throughout the United States and Canada. A stint in the Army during World War II allowed him to hone his skills. "Great musicians from every major band gave their talents to the war effort, and then there was me. I learned a lot from all of them, and when I was out of the service, I studied music formally," Laws told me.

Struggling in New York, Laws appeared with vocal groups during television's infancy, most notably on Ed Sullivan's, Arthur Godfrey's, Perry Como's, and Milton Berle's shows. In an era when it was common practice for small record companies to produce and market lower-priced "soundalike" records of popular hits, Laws found himself recording as many as six "soundalike" songs a day. The painstaking process of repeated listening to the originals, in order to properly re-create them, added to his knowledge of musical structure. Like many young music hopefuls, Laws even ghosted for famous arrangers too busy to handle their workload for hits like Brian Hyland's novelty number, "Itsy Bitsy Teeny Weeny Yellow Polka Dot Bikini."

Whether he realized it or not at the time, perhaps the projects that most foreshadowed Laws's work for Rankin/Bass were numerous children's records, particularly those for Pickwick's Cricket label from 1953 to 1954. In his simple arrangements for records such as "The Little White Duck," "Tubby the Tuba," and, most notably, "Peter Cottontail and the Search for Flopsy's Tail," there were unmistakable Laws touches that would later be heard in scores for such shows as *'Twas the Night Before Christmas* (1974) and *Here Comes Peter Cottontail* (1971). Among other early works that suggest future Rankin/Bass score accents are show tune records Laws arranged and conducted for Time Records. "Albums like *Percussion on Stage* were part of the current stereo craze, so all of us were arranging music that would pop back and forth from speaker to speaker," Laws recalls.

"I first met Jules Bass in 1962 when I was writing for TV commercials," he says. "He was a writer for a New York advertising agency and I was doing a lot of things for companies like General Electric. Arthur Rankin was an art director at ABC before he and Jules started the company."

After writing orchestrations for their first TV special, *Return to Oz* (1964), Laws was given his first shot as musical director for *Rudolph the Red-Nosed Reindeer*, with full responsibility for the entire score.

The music for *Rudolph* was produced in London. "We recorded in London or New York, most of the time, but the vocals might have been done in L.A., Nashville, Las Vegas, or wherever the actor might be."

Rudolph was a major breakthrough for Rankin/Bass and for Maury Laws. Considered the most-watched holiday special ever, the show has aired every year since 1964, yet it was intended to be shown only twice. It put Rankin/Bass (then known as Videocraft International Ltd.) on the TV animation map and set the course for numerous specials and series that kept Laws constantly busy throughout the 1960s. "I was never on staff at Rankin/Bass," he recalls, "but they gave me so much contract work that I was never available for anything else."

The first original score Laws and Bass wrote was for *The Daydreamer*, a 1966 theatrical feature combining live action and stop-motion. Anticipation was high for the feature, with Robert Goulet premiering the title song on *The Ed Sullivan Show*. At the last minute, executive producer Joseph E. Levine pulled it from wide release. "He was disappointed with the movie," Laws recalls. "He wanted another *Mary Poppins.*" The film's budget was nowhere near that of *Mary Poppins*, but the feature did receive some positive reviews and is frequently run on cable TV.

There is a tactile, textured feeling to all the music that Maury Laws arranged, conducted, and composed to accompany the distinctive, hand-crafted look of the "Animagic" stop-motion or stylized cel animation it accompanies. "I like to use various kinds of percussion to get that effect," Laws explained. "It creates a spark, a kind of bright feeling."

The musical scores are the crown jewels of the Rankin/Bass creative construct. From *Rudolph* on, the song pattern for each special (particularly the hour-long ones) reconfigured the form said to have flowered in Rodgers and Hammerstein musicals. There is a cold open, in which we are thrust into the story immediately, without titles. This usually creates a cliffhanger, building into an overture with titles. A "yearning" song is sung by a main character or his or her friend. One song is sung twice, often by a hero and a villain. And, as in *Oklahoma!,* the title song is not sung in its entirety until the end portion of the show.

Classic Disney scores of the 1930s and '40s also contain elements that the Laws–Rankin/Bass blueprint revives. Characters are assigned songs that play instrumentally when they are central to the action. Sometimes a character who does not sing, such as the Abominable Snow Monster in *Rudolph,* Papa Andersen in *The Daydreamer,* and Jack Frost in *Frosty's Winter Wonderland* (1976), has a theme nevertheless. Ironically, when Walt Disney all but abandoned traditional musical narrative format in the 1960s (films like *101 Dalmatians* and *The Sword in the Stone* relegated songs to incidental moments), Rankin/Bass became the only company to consistently turn out original musical scores for animation. When Disney animation entered its second "golden age" in the mid-1980s, the Broadway-style narrative initiated by *The Little Mermaid* was deservedly hailed as a monumental advance. It should be recognized, however, that Laws, Rankin, and Bass had been doing roughly the same thing, albeit on a more modest scale, all the years in between.

The formula for almost any given Rankin/Bass special was achieved through a specific production system. Laws says the process was exacting and consistent from show to show. "First they would record the dialogue and the basic song tracks. Then they would add some sound effects, which would change a little when the work was sent to Japan for animation.

"One of the things Jules and I always did was to make the celebrities comfortable with the material. We wrote the songs just for them. Performers like Fred Astaire and Danny Thomas could sing, of course, but we would be aware of their limitations and never give them vocal gymnastics. I think, for that reason, the stars always liked what we created for them. We never had anyone come back to us later and say they didn't like a song."

Some stars were so taken with their own custom-written songs, they took extra steps to maximize their performances. Phyllis Diller's enthusiasm for the Laws/Bass song "You're Different" from the feature *Mad Monster Party* (1967) inspired her to order a piano for her hotel room in order to practice it.

Agents for major stars often recommended roles in Rankin/Bass specials for their clients, Laws said. "Some celebrities can be a bit insecure. It's as if they're not really sure about what the public sees in them, and they don't want you to mess it up for them. So if they get an inkling that you don't know what you're doing, they can become a problem. But we always did our homework and were fully prepared." This confidence gave Rankin/Bass a star roster of such legends as Jimmy Durante, John Huston, Danny Kaye, Red Skelton, Otto Preminger, Angela Lansbury, Cyril Ritchard, and James Cagney, who was urged to perform a voice in *The Legend of Smokey the Bear* (1966) by President Lyndon Johnson.

Laws was especially pleased with Mickey Rooney's work for *Santa Claus Is Comin' to Town,* which he counts among his personal favorite specials. "He had just the right quality for what we needed. Keenan Wynn was very good too. I think, with that special, we hit everything just right."

Other personal favorites include *The Year Without a Santa Claus,* which introduced the Heat Miser and Snow Miser characters, and *The Hobbit,* perhaps the most lauded of the Rankin/Bass films, winning the Peabody Award and the Christopher Medal.

"For *The Hobbit,* Jules adapted the actual verse that Tolkien created in his books," Laws said. "I set it to music. The show turned out well, very nicely paced."

The rhythmic pace Laws finds so appealing in the best Rankin/Bass specials may be another key to their lasting appeal. "Jules always worked very hard to achieve a rhythmic pace in the shows. He would work out exposure sheets for every section that I would later fill in. We created virtually the entire soundtrack before the animation was done.

"When I sat down to compose for them, I'd think about the animated character that we're going to be seeing: who they are, what they are doing, and how they express themselves in the lyrics of their songs. I avoided that sort of cartoon scoring they used to call 'mickey mousing,' where the music apes every action the character is doing. Sometimes it happens, but not often."

Laws never set out to be an animation musical director. "I wasn't a big cartoon buff when I was young," he recalled. "At the movie theater, I was more excited to see a live-action adventure like *Bad Day at Black Rock.* But I always wanted to compose for film. With film scores, you have a wider range of opportunities. Records are based more on the popular style of the day. I never went for the 'flavor of the day' in my background scores. Maybe that's why people still enjoy them."

Laws is delighted with the resurgence of interest in Rankin/Bass specials. "When we did them, I was circulating in a crowd of fellow music people and my work didn't seem like a very big deal. Certainly we were pleased with what we were doing, but we weren't setting out to create classics. We even used to joke among ourselves about the standard Rankin/Bass endings in nearly every show. As I recall, there were only two or three: that Santa would come just in time to save the day, or that the villain would have a change of heart and turn good."

From the tree-trimming Abominable Snow Monster in *Rudolph* to the choo-choo cherishing Winter Warlock in *Santa Claus Is Comin' to Town,* the redemption of villains in so many Rankin/Bass specials was a concession to industry pressure to reduce TV violence. "Arthur Rankin and Jules often made visits to Washington to testify about the violence in TV shows. Romeo Muller [who scripted nearly every Rankin/Bass special] used to say, 'we're the Dickens of our time.' Dickens created a reformed villain in Scrooge."

Today's concerns about the effects of TV on children may be among the reasons parents want their kids to share the Rankin/Bass specials they grew up with. Almost every film has its own unique following. Filmmakers from Tim Burton to Pixar's John Lasseter credit Rankin/Bass as a creative influence. The demand for a soundtrack album to *Mad Monster Party* was heard over two decades after its release, finally resulting in a CD from Percepto Records. *Rudolph* toys abound at holiday time, and the show is spoofed often by comedy shows. There's a Web site devoted to the Miser Brothers of *The Year Without a Santa Claus.*

One of the Miser Brothers songs, "The Snow Miser Song," appeared in the recent feature film *Batman Forever,* in which Arnold Schwarzenegger, as Mr. Freeze, shows a clip from the special to his henchmen. On a *South Park* Christmas show, the characters inexplicably launch into the complete "Even a Miracle Needs a Hand" from *'Twas the Night Before Christmas.*

The Laws family enjoys the occasional feeling of celebrity, pointing at TV screens and saying, "My dad did the music for that" to friends who had watched the shows since childhood. In the mid-1960s, a young NBC tour guide who regaled her visitors with the creation of the *Rudolph* special, showing the animation figures that were then on display, later became Mrs. Karen Laws. They have been married for over thirty years.

Laws is amazed by the recent recognition of his years of hard work. "When so many of them first came out on video, I thought that would be the end of their playability on TV, but they still run and run. Last year, I was in the hospital and every night, the Family Channel would show two or three Rankin/Bass specials. It was the first time I had sat and watched them in a long time. We live in a small town, so the hospital staff made a fuss over me. People write letters about how much this or that song or show meant to them. I've even had people come to my front door and say, 'Are you Maury Laws, the guy who wrote "The Snow Miser Song?"' It's remarkable."

At the age of seventy-eight, Maury Laws has no intention of retiring completely from music. He arranges and conducts music for a number of prominent symphony orchestras, vocalists, and jazz artists. In recent years, he's even added a Rankin/Bass suite to his holiday concerts, playing to packed concert halls. He says he never really thought about how much of an impact the shows had on audiences, particularly children, until now. "I can't believe how much people really want to hear this music. We had no idea what it was to become when we first created it. Of everything I've ever done in my life, this has become the biggest thing to people, and I couldn't be more delighted and gratified."

Mr. Ehrbar thanks Rick Goldschmidt, Peter Bakalian, Arthur Rankin, Jr., and, of course, Maury Laws for helping to make this piece possible.

♫

PART II

Cartoon Music Today

Merrie Melodies

Cartoon Music's Contemporary Resurgence

by ELISABETH VINCENTELLI

WHEN CBS PULLED the plug on *Pee-wee's Playhouse* in 1991, they killed the show that had single-handedly brought oddball music back to "kids' programs." The Del Rubio Triplets, a trio of sixtysomething, platinum-blonde sisters doing wacked-out covers of "These Boots Are Made for Walking" and "Light My Fire," were repeat guests, for God's sake! And let's not forget Mark Mothersbaugh's theme music, in which the Devo member rehabilitated Martin Denny's exotica sounds long before "lounge" came back. Though it wasn't animation per se, *Pee-wee's Playhouse* breathed life into a tradition once embodied by Carl Stalling's Bugs Bunny soundtracks, a tradition thought to be dead. The show marked the moment when it became fun to listen to cartoons again.

Cartoon music has always been a haven for fans of left-of-center sounds. At Warner Bros. in the 1930s and '40s, Stalling basically reinvented the relationship between images and sounds, reinforcing and tweaking the visual narrative with borrowings from popular song, opera, and folk, as well as a constant set of other spoofs and allusions. Although his technique suited the cartoon form, Stalling worked within a particularly American tradition of abrupt interplay between high and low culture, and of orchestrated collisions between musical styles and techniques. (The orchestras in nineteenth- and early twentieth-century variety and vaudeville shows had to back up everything from knife throwing acts to parodies of operettas, and turned a dizzying mix of highbrow and low into an art itself. In 1899, for instance, a show titled *By the Sad Sea Waves* was set in a lunatic asylum and featured inmates and staff performing excerpts from *The Mikado* along with popular "coon songs," while a violin solo was followed by ragtime selections.) This same "anything goes" approach is now thriving in many scores for TV cartoons, after barely surviving an eclipse spanning close to three decades.

It's no coincidence that Stalling retired in 1958, just as television started replacing movie theaters as the prime outlet for cartoons, and animation took a nosedive. Suddenly, cartoons were perceived as being exclusively for kids—and kids aren't supposed to know the difference between elaborate animation and cheap shortcuts. Hanna-Barbera, which came to dominate American animation through the 1970s, relied on "limited animation" for its made-for-television cartoons, meaning that the studio used fewer drawings per frame than were used in theatrical animation. And impoverished visuals also meant impoverished scores. While music director Hoyt Curtin focused his efforts on the shows' themes with memorable results (think *The Flintstones'* "Meet the Flintstones"), the studio relied on "needle drop" scores (borrowing ready-made cues from music libraries) for the actual background music. Curtin's fans can get their fill with the four-CD box set *Hanna-Barbera's Pic-A-Nic Basket of Cartoon Classics* (Rhino, 1996). Things got even worse in the 1970s and early 1980s, when cheesy synthesizers ruled. It was only when *Pee-wee* led to *The Simpsons,* and animation started targeting adults again, that producers resumed spending time and money on music.

For more than ten years, *The Simpsons* have featured the most varied assortment of musical styles to be heard on TV—or anywhere else for that matter. Under the helm of music director Alf Clausen, the show fully explores the vaudevillian polymorphous cultural perversity that's inherent in the best animation. *Songs in the Key of Springfield* (Rhino, 1997) and *Go Simpsonic with The Simpsons* (Rhino, 1999) offer a dizzying tour through decades of American popular music that's unparalleled in our drab, boundary-ruled audio lives. Clausen covers the complete musical spectrum from operetta to punk via jazz, blues, disco, and Kraftwerk, while guests have included Sonic Youth, who re-arranged the theme song for the "Homerpalooza" episode; Tito Puente, who performed "Señor Burns" in the "Who Shot Mr. Burns, Part Two" episode; and Shawn Colvin, in the recurring role of Christian singer and Ned Flanders paramour Rachel Jordan. Even the show's numerous tributes to musicals are usually better in their concision and wit than what's currently on Broadway. Where else can you hear "Capital City," a tribute to "New York, New York," sung by Tony Bennett, next to *Oh, Streetcar!,* a musical version of *A Streetcar Named Desire,* in which Marge rousingly appeals to "the kindness of strangers" while Ned Flanders wails "Stella!/Can't you hear me yell-a/You put me through hell-a/Stellaaaaa!"? The spirit of vaudeville truly is alive and well a century after its golden age, except it's not at the Variety Theater anymore: it's on Fox.

Musical mayhem is even more pointed in *Animaniacs,* a show that includes lots of pastiches ("Feelin' Groovy" becomes "Make a Gookie"); but the show is at its best when the references are less direct. The song "I'm Mad," for instance, is set on a road trip during which the Warner siblings, Yakko, Wakko, and Dot, drive Dr. Scratchansniff crazy. Written by Randy Rogel, "I'm Mad" is positively Sondheimian at times, especially when Wakko provides a plaintive counterpoint to Yakko's and Dot's sung-through argument. And when the car gets to its destination, an amusement park, Rogel drops Nino Rota allusions that must have delighted, oh, a good dozen adults. Like Clausen, the musicians working on *Animaniacs* have a full orchestra at the ready—composer Richard Stone once said, "We're very fortunate that the word *synthesizer* doesn't exist in the Warner Bros. vocabulary." (*Animaniacs* CDs include *A Hip-Hopera Christmas, Yakko's World,* and *The Animaniacs Faboo! Collection,* all on Rhino.) With its periodic episodes of random violence and its pileup of music and visuals, the show harks back not only to old Warner Bros. shorts—the recording sessions even take place in the very studio where Stalling used to work—but to tried-and-true traditions of rigorously timed anarchy. Buster Keaton's memoir recounts a stage brawl he executed during his days as a vaudeville performer: "In the middle of this fight the orchestra leader . . . got to his feet, tapped his baton, and had the orchestra playing 'The Anvil Chorus,' to which we kept time by hitting one another." Keaton might as well have been describing an *Animaniacs* episode.

While someone like Alf Clausen is a veteran who got his start twenty years ago as music director on the *Donny and Marie* show, upstart brats who would have formed a band a decade ago now work for cable and hire alt-musicians to score their animated shenanigans. How else can we explain an entire episode of *Space Ghost Coast to Coast* with music by Sonny Sharrock (who also did the theme) and Sonic Youth's Thurston Moore as a guest? Or Primus doing *South Park*'s theme? Danny Elfman got his second wind in movies and television after first making a name as Oingo Boingo's leader; another Boingo alum and Elfman's longtime arranger, Steve Bartek, provided evocative scores for the wonderfully dark *Nightmare Ned.* Mark Mothersbaugh heads Mutato Muzika, his own studio/production company in West Hollywood, has re-scored dozens of *Popeye* cartoons for Turner Broadcasting Systems, Inc., and composes music ranging from trippy to hip-hop–flavored for Nickelodeon's enormously popular *Rugrats*. (The show once delivered a cover of the Go-Gos' hit song "Vacation" that can only be described as fairly psychotic.) Cartoons are among the few places apart from Broadway where it's still perfectly acceptable to break into song at the slightest provocation, which is probably why the *South Park* bad boys' feature debut basically was an old-fashioned musical.

In the mid- to late 1990s, one composer who truly bridged musical genres and generations was Pat Irwin, who kept the vaudeville/Stalling tradition of pastiche and interpolation alive while at the same time staying connected to current avant garde and pop music when he scored Nickelodeon's *Rocko's Modern Life*. A veteran of many bands, including the New York–based instrumental group the Raybeats and, a side gig, the B-52's, Irwin spent five years as musical director on *Rocko,* cranking out astonishing musical cues that hold up with the best Raymond Scott. Leading a six-piece combo, Irwin brought together musicians whose paths would never have crossed without Viacom—trombonist Art Baron used to play with Duke Ellington, while drummer Kevin Norton spent time in the Microscopic Septet and Anthony Braxton's band. Like the orchestras playing behind various vaudeville acts, Irwin's band could turn on a dime and swiftly suggest moods and action. Animation is such a healthy field for composers that, after ending his run on *Rocko,* Irwin was hired to flex different muscles on ABC's *Pepper Ann*: "We record *Pepper Ann* in Los Angeles with a unionized band, so the musicians are very different from the ones I used to play with in New York," Irwin said. "In L.A. I have a guy who played with the Beach Boys, another who is in the Philharmonic!" (Sadly, no one has bothered to release Irwin's compositions on CD.)

Culture survives in odd ways and in odd places. Cartoon music is an exciting field these days; it has a scope and quality that's hard to find in other TV shows, in movies, or even on the radio. And isn't it satisfying to know that by laughing uproariously when the *South Park* boys induce an audience to begin killing one another by performing Philip Glass (an entirely reasonable response), we partake in a proud tradition that once made sure one of the geniuses of American film was hit on the head to the tune of "The Anvil Chorus"?

Originally appeared in the Village Voice, *March 3, 1998; updated November 2001. © 2001 by Elisabeth Vincentelli. Reprinted with permission.*

An Interview with Mark Mothersbaugh

by DANIEL GOLDMARK

Mark Mothersbaugh may well be known forever as one of the founding members of Devo. Yet his career as a composer for film and television has proved more enduring than his image as a guy wearing a yellow jumpsuit and horn-rimmed glasses. His interest in electronic music—or, rather, music that is produced electronically—quickly became his trademark. At a time when digital music was exploding throughout the industry, Mothersbaugh's long-standing interest in electronic instruments (he now owns Raymond Scott's Electronium, a composing machine created decades before digital technology) has allowed him to make a name for himself in a wide variety of different musical venues.

Mark Mothersbaugh among his instrument collection at his recording studio, Mutato Muzika, in Los Angeles, CA in 2002.
© Daniel Goldmark.

Mothersbaugh has worked as the supervising composer on a variety of children's animated series, including *Rugrats* and *Beakman's World*, as well as on the groundbreaking series *Pee-wee's Playhouse*. He has also become known as a film composer in his own right, working on a wide variety of projects, including all three features (*Bottle Rocket, Rushmore, The Royal Tenenbaums*) directed by Wes Anderson to date. Where Hoyt Curtin's themes brought about a new economy of melodic writing to cartoons, Mothersbaugh's music expands such cartoon tunes with his original melodies, yet at the same time uses an even more rarified instrumental palette to create an altogether new timbre for animation. His may not have been the first rock group to play for cartoons (see Jake Austen's essay), but his idiosyncratic sound led a revolution in cartoon scoring, showing that synthesized scores can still create as much a sense of movement and vitality in cartoons as a "live" orchestra.

When we spoke on January 28, 2002, our discussion included his early influences as a composer, his first experiences with animation and children's television, and, naturally, his synthesizers.

Daniel Goldmark: How did you get into doing *Pee-wee's Playhouse?* I mean, there's *Rugrats* and all the other things you do, but even though *Pee-wee* was mostly live action, it's still far more animated than most of the cartoons that are being produced nowadays; it seems like that's where you really came to be associated with that sound.

Mark Mothersbaugh: The ironic thing is that I actually did animation for music before I did music for animation. There was a Devo video called "Today My Baby Gave Me a Surprise"—it was a Devo song but in it, I animated . . . well, I had written the music too, so I guess I did do the music first. Anyway, I did animation of two potato men—a hippo swims up a river really fast, and he opens his mouth and two potato men are inside and they're playing the teeth of the hippo like they were marimbas, to the [singing] "da-dah-da," to the synth part that's like a marimba part at the end of the song. I actually *was* animating before I did music.

The first music I wrote was probably for a Hawaiian Punch commercial that was animated. It was robots dancing to a piece of music that I'd scored, and kids then dancing to the robots. It was kind of similar to what we'd done on tour with Devo the year before, where we had robots dancing behind us on a video screen and we were in front of them. Every time one of them got out of step I'd turn around and shoot him with an imaginary raygun and he'd explode.

DG: So the Hawaiian Punch commercial was done in the midst of Devo?

MM: Right; it was 1982, I think.

DG: How much exposure to cartoons had you had at the time? Were you really a big animation fan?

MM: Oh, yeah, since I was a kid. In America, you know, you grow up getting to watch cartoons on TV—it was readily available. My favorite cartoons were Max Fleischer's. *The Sorcerer's Apprentice* [from *Fantasia*, 1940]—Mickey and the brooms—was the animation that scared me the most. My father had a little 8mm projector at home. He mostly shot home movies—a lot of birthday cakes, stuff like that. But he bought a couple of things; there was one Max Fleischer cartoon of dogs breaking into a butcher shop and stealing all the meat and then running down the road, waving a stream of sausages and different things. That was the first animation I really remember. And that was silent, it didn't have music yet; or if it did, it didn't have music on the form that my father had, on 8mm.

DG: A lot of those commercial [home-use] film prints were silents—that may very well have had sound. But that's funny that the first cartoons that you can remember didn't have music at all. Did you get turned on to any of the composers—Stalling, Bradley—before you really became involved in music?

MM: Yeah, when I was a kid my favorite cartoon music was Bugs Bunny music, the Cab Calloway Fleischer music. That's what you got exposed to. The Disney music was something I was a little less interested in. But the Looney Tunes stuff was amazing because it had musical sound effects; Carl Stalling, and Ray Scott by association, since he wrote a lot of that music, they were kind of the Beatles of that genre, of cartoon music. They did it first and did it best, and got to explore all that territory when it was unexplored.

DG: When you first started doing film scoring, not just for cartoons, were people asking you to do things like what you were doing in Devo, "We really want you to do stuff like that," or were they saying, "Do whatever comes to mind"?

MM: Well, what happened . . . things happened really kind of all at the same time. I think it was 1982 when that commercial happened, and it won a bunch of awards. So I got a lot of people calling me because they'd seen that Hawaiian Punch commercial and it really didn't have much to do with Devo. It was good timing for me because I had a Fairlight [synthesizer]. I'd been using a lot of sound effects; before that it was mostly analogue sound effects in Devo songs. Once I had a Fairlight . . . it was a sampler, and I was sampling a lot of things. I was taking ratchet sounds and pneumatic drills and things and turning them into percussion and instruments that you could use. The music in that commercial had a lot of room for that because it was robots.

Through the years, it's much less so now than it was, people will say, "Hey, I was a fan." You get hired by people that were fans a lot; these would be the people who gave me my first chance, who thought, "Hey, he could be good." It was based on something they'd already seen, it wasn't just picking my name out of the phone book or something. Devo had an influence and people kind of expected something. My career as a composer beyond Devo has been greatly affected by being in Devo.

DG: Was it the same kind of connection that got you the job doing *Pee-wee's Playhouse*?

MM: Paul Reubens was in Groundlings. When he was first creating *Pee-wee's Playhouse*, he was creating it at this comedy workshop, the Groundlings Theatre. My girlfriend at the time was Laraine Newman, and she had helped found this theatre. So they were friends and he was a Devo fan. When he did the Roxy show, which was the first thing he did outside of the Groundlings Theatre as Pee-wee, he asked me to score it. It was 1980, I think. Devo was still pretty active then, so I didn't have a chance to consider it. I'd scored some projects other than Devo before; the year before that I'd scored an Ionesco play off-Broadway that Russ Tamblyn and Dean Stockwell put on—they had hired me to do that. And then that same year Neil Young asked Devo to be in a movie . . .

DG: Oh, *Human Highway*. . .

AC: Right, *Human Highway*. And Dean Stockwell was the director, and he ended up taking the music I'd written for his play and he put it in the movie as an underscore. So I passively was one of the composers for that movie.

Paul knew Laraine, and he'd asked me to do [his Roxy show], and I couldn't do it. We were going on tour again, this was 1980, '81, and he had someone named Jay Cotton score that for him—a Texan who he knew through the visual artist Gary Panter, who worked on the first *Pee-wee's Play-*

house and was responsible for a lot of the way the visuals looked. Then it came around time to do a movie, and I don't know where I was, but Danny Elfman was available and so *Pee-wee's Big Adventure* happened. I went and saw it and thought, "Wow—that's pretty great!" I never was a big Oingo Boingo fan, and I didn't like it that they got compared to Devo, because I thought what we were about was really, really different. I had to say, that was the best thing he'd ever done; I liked the film he'd done with his brother, *Forbidden Zone*, I thought that was really good. But *Pee-wee's Big Adventure*—that was amazing.

Anyhow, so it came around time to do the TV show. Devo was off tour, we'd signed a bad record deal with another company . . . [Paul Reubens] asked me if I wanted to score *Pee-wee's Playhouse*, and I said, "Well, I don't know if I can do it every week, because I'm going to be touring." And he said, "What if you do half of them?" And I said OK. So the first season I did the first few episodes, and after that I did every other episode for a while, and by doing the first couple I got to write the theme song and come up with themes for the characters. I didn't have the advantage of using a big orchestra. The budget was very small and it was a turnaround where I'd get a tape on Monday and it had to be back in New York on Thursday, because they would lay it to picture on Friday and go through the censors at NBC on Friday, and on Saturday morning it would be on TV. That was the first TV show I ever did. I didn't know anything about locking to film. MIDI still hadn't been invented yet, I think. I'd write most of *Pee-wee's Playhouse* on a 16-track, 2-inch tape and I'd record a lot of it in the Fairlight; then we'd just hit the "go" button for every cue when it started up. Because of the technology I had it really affected the way the score sounded and what was written. I think it made it a lot more, in one sense, kind of psychotic—if you look back at the episodes, the cues kind of blurt out from cue to cue. Especially in the ones I did.

There were other composers. Every other week he'd have a guest composer. Danny [Elfman] did a couple episodes; he had a couple of the really choice ones and he did a nice job on them. My favorite was maybe Todd Rundgren's—it was a fashion show. He had one piece of music that was my favorite piece of music of all the Pee-wee shows.

DG: You mentioned the budget on *Pee-wee's* being minimal. That sort of leads to an important question for me, that being your almost exclusive use of keyboard, to the exclusion of almost anything else . . .

MM: Well, on *Pee-wee* we put guitar, and percussion, especially on the *Pee-wee* stuff, because Devo still hadn't taken a break yet. We were still writing music around the *Pee-wee* schedule. The Devo guys all played on Pee-wee's stuff . . . it wasn't totally to the exclusion—yet. It took a few more years when technology got about two steps better.

DG: That's actually what I wanted to lead you to. How did it happen that you came to focus so much on the keyboard?

MM: It was the advent of MIDI. It changed things. It made it so instruments could talk together and you weren't putting down one track at a time in the recording studio. It meant that I could record twenty-four or thirty-two tracks or more of snyths and samplers and drum machines without an engineer or somebody else there. I could be doing a lot of work on my own, where normally you couldn't. I'd be waiting for an engineer to show up so I could play the things down to tape, one at a time. It started with the Fairlight, which was pre-MIDI. There were eight channels in it, so I could write music that had up to eight different parts in it with that, but I'd have to augment other things to it. It wasn't MIDI yet, so if you had a drum kit, it was one channel dedicated to a snare, one to a high-hat, one to a cowbell; your eight channels of the Fairlight were pretty much eaten up by your percussion setup.

Once the MIDI thing happened, there were some sequencers—the ones I went with were Rolands, they were these dedicated sequencers, pre-computer sequencing. Roland had these little keyboards and they also had a computer sequencer that came with it—that's how I got into MIDI. And MIDI ended up making it easy to sit up all night and write a whole episode of music, and then, the next day, you could write music for two different commercials, and you could do music for two or three different TV shows in the same day. Before that time, that was kind of unheard of. The MIDI thing allowed it, so I could take one keyboard up to the living room in my house, set up a VHS machine and a screen. If you wrote a piece of music to the film, you could run the tape back, and the music would play at the exact same place it played the time before, and I was thinking, "Hot damn!"

Devo at that time was kind of shriveling, and we had this bad record deal, so we were riding that out. Commercial and TV shows were coming in left and right. Cable was hitting its own stride, Nickelodeon was fairly new. The guys who were head of Nickelodeon at the time were Devo fans. When I met them,

© Nickelodeon.

they said, "Yeah, when we were in college, we used to go to Devo concerts, yeah I remember. . . ." They had those kinds of stories. But the best thing about it was that somehow, I got hired to do *Rugrats* then. I think it was Gabor Csupo, of Klasky Csupo, he was one of the creators of the show. He collected avant-garde music. One of the last things I had done on the Fairlight was kind of

Muzaky—I called it *Musik for Insomniaks*. It was kind of inspired by tapes of Esquivel and Bob Thompson that made me want to write this album of music, because I just wanted stuff to listen to around the house that was melodic and in some ways the antithesis of Devo. But not really, because in some ways it was the same; the best thing about the Fairlight was that it was eight-bit, very low tech. You could sample a guitar, but none of the instruments really sounded like they should have. The saxes didn't really sound like saxes, and the trumpets didn't really sound like trumpets. I always thought they sounded like acoustic instruments as much as Formica wood paneling looked like real wood. It was better, but not as good—it was very limited, but for a certain aesthetic, it was better, in a way. I was really into pop art at the time. When I went to school, it was as a visual artist. If they hadn't shot the kids at Kent State, Devo might not have actually formed. They closed down the school, and Gerry [Casale] and I stayed home and wrote music together and that's kind of how we got started on doing a band. . . . Where were we?

DG: Let's see . . . did the folks at Klasky Csupo give you any indication of the kind of direction they wanted?

MM: Right—anyhow, this *Musik for Insomniaks*? I released it. Gabor Csupo collected avant-garde music and found this tape [of *Musik for Insomniaks*, which had been released in Japan on the Tokyo Radical Artists label] and called me up and said, "Would you let me use some of this for this show I'm creating? I like your music because it's simple and childish. Well, childlike . . . it's very simple. . . ."

DG: Did he actually say childish the first time?

MM: Yeah—that was funny. So I said, "I've scored other TV shows before. Why don't we talk about this? Maybe I can write you something new." I still had the Fairlight at the time. Most of the instruments were played on the Fairlight. What I did was sample a lot of voices to make up percussion and bass and different instruments. I went to the mall, went to Hammacher Schlemmer and bought a toy piano, and sampled it and then returned it. That became the musical universe for *Rugrats*. The theme song was the first thing that I wrote for the show.

DG: You've actually been working with the same musical template ever since you started? I'm sure it's expanded. . . .

MM: Yes and no. Of course it has expanded. Other people have come on the show—there were other composers that worked with me. At the time I started, I was doing four or five TV shows a week. I was doing a show for Disney, a child's show called *Adventures in Wonderland*. On that show, we needed a number of composers because the schedule of the production was so fast—two new underscores and eight songs per week. I'd say, "I can't write eight songs a week." And they said, "Well, you must have some friends that you would trust to work with you." So I got the other Devo guys; my brother Bob and Bob Casale both came on board and started working with me on the show. We ended up with twenty composers writing songs, including Bill Mumy, you know, "Will Robinson" [from *Lost in Space*]. The show was a lot of fun, and it changed my thinking about scoring from being a guy sitting in his bedroom with one keyboard.

My studio took over the house. There were two studios in the house, and then I got the house next door and put in a studio there. We were churning out science-fiction TV shows, and a lot of kid's shows, and MTV's *Liquid Television*, and *Beakman's World*, things like that. There were a couple of composers working on *Rugrats*. My name was always on there because of the theme song, but people's names got added to the billing for whoever did that episode. My brother's been scoring the show for the last seven or eight years. I've come in and done a few episodes here and there. He's brought his own style to it—he uses the same basic palettes. Characters have themes that have stayed pretty consistent through the years. We still use a lot of those old Fairlight sounds, not only in every episode, but when there was a Broadway show and for both of the features that have been done, we still use those little eight-bit Fairlight samples.

DG: One of the criticisms I've heard of cartoon music is that, for productions that don't have much time, they slap things on at the end and use minimal instrumentation. What you've done is unusual in that you have someone with a lot of experience writing music like this, coming from a different background than typical composers, and so the music is much more compelling that it normally would be. Do you feel that what you've done has had an influence on other composers for animation? Do you hear your style come up in other things?

MM: In other areas—*Rugrats*, not particularly—but in other areas. . . . *Rugrats*, yes, of course. You always hear things that you can tell—the temp music was probably episodes that I recognize. In commercials that's even more prevalent. You know that it was something that you had written; you hear it, and enough notes are changed so that they don't have a problem with copyright.

DG: It seems to be a big issue nowadays, where a director will put on a temp track [for the composer] and say "I want something very similar to that," and what ends up being created is derivative of the temp track. It seems that you're trying to avoid that; for *Rugrats* you wanted to create something new as opposed to taking stuff off an album that already existed. Would that be your tendency most of the time?

MM: Of course. In some cases you can prove it works better. Wes Anderson, for instance—I've done three movies with him now, and while he was writing the script for *The Royal Tenenbaums* (2001), he was sending me drafts. I would sketch music, which I would send back to him, so that while he was on the set, shooting this movie, he had music to listen to that he ended up temping into the first cut of the film. Instead of going somewhere else and temping it with something—John Williams, somebody else's music—he ended up temping in music I'd written for the movie. By the time we did the final recording for the film—with his films we don't use one track of synth, we don't even use samples, it's all real instruments, he's really adamant about that—most of the themes had been written by the time he'd done the first cut.

DG: I listened to the soundtrack you gave me [Mothersbaugh's score for the live-action/animation feature *The Adventures of Rocky & Bullwinkle* (2000)] and really liked it. It really struck me how much influence someone like Carl Stalling might have had on you because the music is *that* indicative of movement, more so than what traditional feature film underscoring might sound like. This music was really underscoring movement and action and was meant to have that feeling.

MM: You know, after that film, I felt like I could score anything. Honestly, I had a confidence after doing that movie that I didn't have before. I was always a little bit intimidated by the fact that I hadn't gone to school for music. When I did all the orchestrations out of MIDI, I felt safe. That was a territory where I felt I could deal with everything and keep it under control. Once it became orchestral, especially with the first Rugrats movie [*The Rugrats Movie* (1998)], I was nervous going into it. The head of the music department at Paramount had wanted someone else to score that movie. I was lucky that the creators of that film—Gabor Csupo and Arlene Klasky—that they defended me and supported me. If they hadn't done that, I wouldn't have gotten a chance to score for a big orchestra. I'd still be doing films that are easy to do for me, where it's thirty players or less, but I wouldn't be getting the chance to do orchestral scores. And now, because of them, I've done a number of big orchestral scores.

Robots, Romance, and Ronin

Music in Japanese Anime

by MILO MILES

JAPANESE ANIMATION, known as anime, has slipped into the fabric of American entertainment media. Almost everyone, especially parents, has seen swatches of anime on video—if not *Pokémon,* then *Sailor Moon* or *Macross.* Those who explore beyond the most popular titles for children will find anime that looks so exotic, bright, dynamic, and confident that American watchers might assume that almost everything in the form is hip, futuristic, and experimental. As someone who devours a wide range of music, I've listened to soundtracks from a host of flashy anime videos with high expectations, but found most of them surprisingly formulaic, old-fashioned, soppy, and stiff when played at home without the visuals. Still, a few vigorous, gleaming anime soundtracks match the imagination and action of the drawings on screen. This guide will touch on some of the finest.

Understanding anime matters, because it has a particularly immediate aura of cool nowadays, both in its homeland and in America. Trendy Japanese gallery artists like Takashi Murakami draw heavily on cartoon images for the so-called "superflat" style. Pace-setting U.S. animation, like Genndy Tartakovsky's *Samurai Jack,* could be called "Amer-Anime." Anime zealots (known as "anime otaku") have plenty of media resources. Boutique shops, glossy fanzines, and zesty Web sites keep the faithful informed up to the minute. But there's very little help for discriminating listeners who want to grab an anime CD that will stand up to listening on its own.

A serious problem is that there's no satisfactory anthology introduction to anime music. The only easily available domestic item, *The Best of Anime* (Rhino), falls short for fanatics and newcomers alike. The tinker-toy themes of historic shows such as *Gigantor* put off latter-day devotees, and those who are not in the know about recent insider hits like *Oh My Goddess!* and *Macross Plus* will be left unmoved by the themes, which are no more than pleasant souvenirs. There's little help for those who simply want to enjoy anime sound-tracks as songs that belong in an eclectic music fan's collection.

If one wants to hear the roots of the best modern anime soundtracks, the early solo work of Ryuichi Sakamoto is ideal. (Sakamoto is best known in the West for his elegant, restrained movie soundtracks such as that of *Merry Christmas, Mr. Lawrence* [1983].) On *Esperanto* (1986), *Musical Encyclopedia* (1986), and even the more muscular *Neo Geo* (1987), Sakamoto pioneered pop electronica that set a miniature scene in every track with what sounded like cavorting, spinning, or resting characters, set to springy percussion and aptly high-pitched chorus chants. (Although superficially similar at times, these tunes have none of the oily languor of the recently revived "lounge" music.) Sakamoto's work could be adapted to anime in the same way that Carl Stalling set Raymond Scott's wacky and winsome jazz to animation. The Sakamoto numbers are self-contained, never intended to work as a soundtrack. The potential of the wacky and winsome mode in anime was confirmed, however, by the antic, unique *Cynical Hysterie Hour* (1990) by John Zorn, which was written for Kiriko Kubo's cartoon shorts of the same name, but has so far not been synchronized with them.

Now available on Zorn's own Tzadik label, *Cynical Hysterie Hour* involves players including guitarists Marc Ribot, Robert Quine, Bill Frisell, and Arto Lindsay, as well as drummer Bobby Previte and percussionist Cyro Baptista, so the twenty-three tiny tunes (almost all less than two minutes long each) have outsized vitality and precision. Darting from ruminative country and blues interludes to clattering bursts of punk thumps and sunny samba breaks, *Cynical Hysterie Hour* blends a child's energy with an adult's shrewdness. Kubo's drawings use the blunt, hyper-simplified and blatantly cartoony style that often signals an experimental, faux-innocent attitude in anime. Several established Japanese performers write more tranquil, equally toy-like songs and instrumentals that could fit with more mainstream anime figuration and plotting. These include Pizzicato Five (ripe for an upscale spy or fashion-world adventure), Fantastic Plastic Machine (romance and comedy built in already), Takako Minekawa (clouds drift by, rain falls, lonely girls look out windows), and Yoshinori Siunahara (the world as a sterile but cheery airport disco).

Anime music does not have to directly mirror the action on screen, or sound "cartoonish" itself. The blandly polite and tasteful music of the later Disney full-length features shaped the background music for many early anime productions. Among the more sophisticated recent incarnations of this style is Joe Hisaishi's work for *Princess Mononoke* (1999), which dwindles to a thin stream indeed without the sumptuous visual foreground. Perhaps pastoral settings are not conducive to radical thoughts about music. The angst of a future metropolis had already broken through in every way with Katshuhiro Otomo's *Akira* (1988), where Disney sub-classical lulling finally gave way to avant-ambient.

The *Akira* soundtrack, constructed by Shoji Yamashira and performed by the group Geinoh Yamashirogumi, slides through musical cultures and knits them together with the easy grace of Toru Takemitsu. But the disturbing results seem to twirl through unknown psychic space not far removed from Teiji Ito's soundtrack for Maya Deren's *Meshes of the Afternoon*. Yamashira combines synthesizer washes and pulses with echoes of Javanese gamelan, Tibetan Buddhist chanting, and Japanese taiko drummers. But this simply sounds like the combination of styles that happened to evolve in the

© 1988 Kodansha

future Neo-Tokyo of *Akira*. This is a sequence of music with an internal logic unlike any other and the single most mesmerizing anime soundtrack.

Those looking for anime on audio CD are particularly in luck with *Akira,* because the soundtrack appears at this time in two complementary packages, each worthwhile in its way. The "original soundtrack" version (Demon DSCD 6, British import) plays like a regular album of music and belongs in the collection of every fan of adventurous sounds, not just anime buffs. Japanamation specialists, however, must also pick up the "original Japanese soundtrack" version (Demon DSCD 7, British import), because it includes the sounds of the movie running along with the music. These two strains interact in a relentless, sometimes violent ballet that recalls the thrilling eye-and-ear coordination of master exploratory animators John and Faith Hubley and Norman McLaren. The voices, noises, and music click like a seasoned trio of collaborators.

Nothing comes close to matching *Akira*, but of course, there are imitators, or simply soundtracks operating in the same orbit. The slyest is the *Ghost in the Shell* album (1998), a standout effort from the prolific Kenji Kawai. This is a "conceptual" sequence of tracks—spare, stately, dominated by electronic and natural percussion and ritualistic chants. Two starkly melodic musical themes, one for the cyborg heroine and the other for her elusive, beloved Puppet Master, slide closer over the course of the album and finally merge over the closing credits. (Be sure to seek out the original Japanese version of the movie; this very satisfying musical conclusion was ditched in favor of an amiable but misguided rock number for the English-speaking edition.)

There are numerous anime scores that fall between traditional elegant sounds and avant-ambient, some worthy to go to the head of the New Age class. A fine example is *Patlabor 2 the Movie: Original Soundtrack "P2"* (Demon DSCD 15, British import, 1996). Kenji Kawai is again in charge. This time he boosts conventional verse-chorus pop-song structure for a few numbers, avoids the acerbic choir chants that make *Akira* and *Ghost* jittery, and adds swatches of synthesizer space rock that are far more introspective than the anime norm. Particularly intriguing cuts, like "IXTL," evoke the airy side of 1970s rock-jazz fusion.

The final type of progressive anime soundtrack either directly involves current techno or hip-hop performers, or simply reflects a vigorous fan's interest in contemporary pop and funk. These soundtracks actually match the form's casual image of being bright, dynamic, hip, and futuristic—call them "wild style" anime. Recently, this has become very marketable in the United

States through the success of domestic cartoon series like *Powerpuff Girls* (surely the American *Pokémon*) with their lite drum 'n' bass theme tune, and *Samurai Jack,* which borrows numerous techniques and appearances from anime, but fast-paced music ideas from recent Hollywood youth flicks. Leiji Matsumoto, a veteran master of sci-fi anime, recently did a series of videos for the très cool French techno artists Daft Punk. Likewise, the brainy hip-hop collective Gorillaz aided their hit single "Clint Eastwood" by recreating themselves as an anime-style martial-arts gang in video clips. The group even performs on stage behind a scrim on which an animated film fills in for their real bodies—they have become today's multimedia equivalent of the old cartoon Archies.

Some sturdy earlier soundtracks were forerunners of the current wild-stylers. One example is the first volume of *Key the Metal Idol* (Viz, 1997; movie released in 1994). This appealing, if disorienting, album alternates cuts with wiry electric guitar solos and lean, leaping arrangements with big tormented ballads that suggest classy versions of standard Japanese pop-schmaltz (more soulful accordions, fewer dripping string sections, and soaring synthesizers). It sounds as if it were created by committee, not a band, but it is not an embarrassment when compared to contemporary youth-action-movie soundtracks from the West. *Key the Metal Idol*'s plot, about a female star singer with mental instability and many secrets, came to fruition with the Hitchcockian *Perfect Blue* (1997), which sadly gave the heroine only glossy pap to sing.

Drenched in music awareness, *Cowboy Bebop* is the prime anime series that goes all the way into wild style and promises to become an enduring favorite equal to *Akira*. A number of episodes are named after Rolling Stones songs or albums, some thoroughly obscure (as Monty Python would say, "Nobody expects 'Jamming with Edward'!"). Yoko Kanno and the group Seat Belts drive many of the songs and instrumentals, but while Kanno contented herself with high-quality syrup and stratosphere synths for spectacular-effects titles like *Macross Plus*, here she jumps from genre to mode to form with abandon, as blithely as the series' spaceships vault from one corner of the solar system to the other. The repeated theme, "Tank," suggests a reenergized James Bond ditty, but the constant, intelligent references to blues, country, and especially jazz are nourishing fare. When the Seat Belts are flapping free, and their horns are under control, they wing it with the sharpest Japanese acid-jazz combos, like United Future Organization.

Even better, the voluminous *Cowboy Bebop* material—pop tunes, torchy numbers, electronica and rave-up rock—hits equally hard as part of the visuals or as CDs (almost: some overwrought ballads wither without image distraction). The richest music selections are available on *Cowboy Bebop Volume One* and *Cowboy Bebop Volume Three: Blue* (both RCA Victor, Japanese import). These soundtracks, a success by word of mouth as much as the series they accompany, can show the way for anime. These already look like the cartoons of tomorrow. For the music to keep up, anime composers will have to understand that fun does not mean froth, poised does not mean stiff, and no matter how fast you go, hold the groove.

A footnote on useful websites for those who want to find out more about anime and listen to samples of the music: *http://store.yahoo.com/animenation* is the mother of all anime sites on the web; and *http://animemusic.com* is a clearly organized website that sells many available anime soundtracks.

An Interview with Richard Stone, Steve Bernstein, and Julie Bernstein

by DANIEL GOLDMARK

The revival of interest in Carl Stalling's music serendipitously occurred at the same time that an overall renaissance began in the world of television animation. Within a period of a few years, the children's network Nickelodeon began to commission new animated shows, leading to the creation of *The Ren & Stimpy Show*, *Rugrats*, *Doug*, and numerous others. At the same time, Warner Bros. revived interest in its most valuable commodities—its trademarked animation characters—with the creation of the new generations of Looney Tunes characters, better known as *Tiny Toon Adventures*, followed by *Animaniacs*, *Pinky and the Brain*, *The Sylvester & Tweety Mysteries*, and *Taz-Mania*, to name a few.

Richard Stone (born in Philadelphia in 1953) worked as a music editor throughout the 1980s on such films as *Platoon, Witness,* and *Pretty in Pink.* He got into the Warner Bros. animation world by working for supervising composer Bruce Broughton on *Tiny Toon Adventures*; he would later become the supervising composer on *Animaniacs, Histeria!, Freakazoid!,* and several other Warner Bros. series. His longtime interest in the music of Carl Stalling made him the perfect composer for such a job. Because the *Animaniacs* series' intent was to bring back the Warner Bros. animation aesthetic—zany characters, illogical actions, sharply-written wordplay—Stone was free to develop his own comic musical language. Stone's approach to scoring was thus largely influenced by Carl Stalling's; he incorporated or referred to many of the same old chestnuts that Stalling was fond of, as well as dozens upon dozens of more recent songs—everything from Debussy's "Clair de Lune" to parodies of Broadway musicals. He was also fortunate enough to be able to work with two of his closest companions, Steve and Julie Bernstein.

Steve worked primarily as a composer and conductor with Stone, while Julie started as an orchestrator and eventually worked as a songwriter and composer of original underscores.[1] In this interview from June 2, 2000, they spoke of working together on scores, how to make a small ensemble sound full, and the interplay between comedy and music when writing for animated cartoons.

Richard Stone, Julie Bernstein, and Steve Bernstein at the 1999 Daytime Emmy Awards.
© Julie Bernstein. Coutesy of Julie Berstein.

RICHARD STONE: Some time around 1994 or 1995, the studio had a project of releasing a lot of cartoons overseas. They needed M&E [music and effects] tracks to sell overseas. A lot of the old cartoons did not have M&E tracks—they just didn't make it. So their idea was to take those cartoons and track them with a library made up of the session tapes of Carl Stalling and Milt Franklyn. So they had DATs [digital audio tapes] of everything and they hired a few of us to sit in our houses and actually build a database, cue by cue, describing each cue and where it went . . . [2]

JULIE BERNSTEIN: In non-musical terms.

RS: . . . so that music editors could look up the word "spooky" and find sixteen cues with the word "spooky" as the description.

DANIEL GOLDMARK   And these were music editors overseas, not here?

RS: No, here, because they were tracked here. Effects would be laid in, and then they'd have their M&E and they could sell it overseas.

JB: We had to take every segment . . . well, first of all, we had to distinguish between one segment and the next one, and then we had to describe it in nonmusical terms. It took a long time and was very, very difficult.

Steve Bernstein: Especially with Milt's stuff. It seemed to be more difficult; it was less cohesive, not more descriptive of the action.

JB: Ultimately, we came up with a little language. We knew what type of music we'd start to hear; we'd call it "this." It became easier, but it was very tough at first.

RS: The nicest thing for me was, there was one cartoon where they asked me to go into a studio and rerecord the scene. And that was Daffy's "Figaro" in . . . name that cartoon . . . with Schlesinger and Porky . . .

DG: Oh, *You Ought to Be in Pictures* [1940].

RS: Yeah! For some reason, they wanted it instrumental only, so that the foreign singer could sing over it. So I made a really complicated click track out of it and went in and took it all down by ear. It was so exciting to record that; you know, at Warner Bros., in that room, and at those fast tempos and everything.

JB: You started acting very strange then . . .

RS: Yeah, I started acting like Milt. You know, "PART NINE!"[3]

DG: Was it before or after Greg [Ford] and Hal Willner had dug this stuff up [for *The Carl Stalling Project*] that you did this? They'd already had their way with it and the studio asked you to catalog it?

RS: It was long after that. I first heard what was then this underground tape that was floating around town, before the first *Carl Stalling Project* CD came out. It was about the time that *Tiny Toons* was starting.[4] So this was maybe five years after that. The nice thing was that I had this nice set of DATs of all the material, a lot of material. A lot of cool stuff; it was wonderful to hear the outtakes. You could hear the musicians talking at the beginnings and ends of cues. Certain voices always come out better than others, and they're talking about the events of the day, their wife's cooking, going fishing—the really nice thing is that nothing has changed. These people are just the same. They sound a lot like our tapes.

DG: The process really hasn't changed much at all.

RS: Until now . . .

DG: How did you come to work together? Or, even before that, who was there first?

SB: Rich was there first. Well, it's complicated, it goes back before that. When I came into this . . . well, you [Rich] were working on *Tiny Toons*, and I was orchestrating for several other composers on *Tiny Toons* and writing and ghosting many cues. Fred Steiner, Art Kempel. And Mark Waters was working with Rich on *Taz-Mania*; he had an opportunity at Disney, and by leaving made a vacancy. And Mark had recommended me to Rich . . .

RS: Mark's recommendation was so high that I took him on the spot.

SB: Without hearing a note, which is, I think, unprecedented.

JB: Well, Rich, you were also desperate. [everyone laughs]

RS: This was during a period when I was responsible for *Taz-Mania*, and I was still doing some *Tiny Toons*, and *Animaniacs* was just starting up. There were a lot of things going on—I was quite crazed. Sometimes you just have to trust people, and Steve turned out to be so incredibly brilliant that now, nine years later . . .

JB: I thought *Animaniacs* was just a germ at the time . . .

RS: Oh yeah, it was a germ . . .

JB: It was a germ, but there wasn't anything going on yet . . .

RS: I was being called into meetings a lot. That's really how it happened. Steve stayed on for maybe six months to a year of *Taz-Mania* . . . ?

SB: Yeah, I did quite a few, actually.

RS: And then he came over to *Animaniacs,* where he was sorely needed. I sort of kept other people on *Taz-Mania* where they were sorely needed, because they did quite well for that ensemble, which was one of the first ensembles of its kind in town; since then it's [been] used a lot. It's a synthesizer setup: piano, live drums, two doubling woodwind players, a trumpet, and a trombone and an occasional violin. We might have a violin solo in one session and not another; the violin would double all the string parts, making the sound fuller.

JB: So it would sound almost like an orchestra.

RS: Basically all of the tutti sections would be doubled by whatever live instrument was there, and if we had a solo, then they played the solo. We kind of worked this language out that . . .

JB: . . . the live trumpet would play the top notes, the live trombone would play the bottom notes, so you wouldn't know that . . .

DG: . . . you wouldn't know the difference [that the rest was synthesized].

SB: You'd know the difference, but it wouldn't be as obvious. It sounded a lot better.

DG: People who knew to listen for it would notice it, but kids certainly aren't going to be paying attention to that.

JB: So it sounded like an orchestra, and there were actually seven live people, and the cost was a lot cheaper.

RS: And within a year, Mark Waters was using that exact ensemble on *Goof Troop* at Disney. And since then, any person with a budget bigger than a home synth budget—that's the ensemble they use, it works very well. In fact, if I'm not mistaken, we used it on the second and third *Animaniacs* albums.

DG: What was the budgetary difference for the composing and the performing of the scores between *Animaniacs* and *Taz-Mania* and any of the other shows? *Animaniacs*, I imagine, had the largest budget. Judging by the buildup that it had, and the press hype, and how much money they were investing in it image-wise, it would make sense for them to try to meet that with the actual product.

RS: When *Tiny Toons* was running, Bruce Broughton would tell all of us, "Twenty-seven bodies, you may not have more than twenty-seven bodies on the stage." Okay. I once brought in a twenty-eighth body and was spoken to about it; you know, does this person really have to be there? When I did *Animaniacs*, it became twenty-nine or thirty, and occasionally if we were doing an opera parody or something like that, I would bring in French horns. I don't think we ever had more than thirty-two, though. It was usually the same string section.

JB: And a harp.

RS: Sometimes a harp for a Christmas special or something like that. But it was always kept pretty much under wraps. Our overtime was always limited. But I must say, they gave us a lot more leeway on *Animaniacs* and *Histeria!* than they did on *Tiny Toons*, which was a little bit more tight with the money.

DG: Was there a reason they were like that with *Tiny Toons*, other than the fact that it was the first show like this and maybe they weren't sure . . .

RS: I think that that was the case, and I think that, by the time *Animaniacs* came along, *Tiny Toons* was such a success they felt like, "so what if we spend another $1000 on a half hour that's already cost a million?"

It was nice to pick and choose and once in a while use a harp or use French horns, or bring in a particular takeoff, like the scene in *Close Encounters of the Third Kind* where the mothership talks with a tuba. And we brought in Tommy Johnson, who played the original tuba part in the movie and he's there playing our version of it. The funny part of our story is where he's competing against Pavarotti, who's on the ground singing.

JB: Actually, it was "Take Me Out to the Ball Game."

RS: Oh, right, "Take Me Out to the Ball Game."

JB: You know, it was "daah-da-da." And then "daah-da-da-da." And then it went into this tune . . .

RS: . . . Pavarotti exploded at the end.

SB: Didn't we have harmonica?

RS: Right—we brought in Tommy Morgan to play harmonica if we'd do a Western. There are all these wonderful old players, some of whom were around when Milt Franklyn was around.

DG: I've looked at the recording logs for the Tom and Jerry cartoons, and [Scott Bradley] usually had nineteen pieces. He talks about only having nineteen pieces, you didn't need to have more than nineteen—"why do you need a big orchestra?" But there was one score where he [added] six saxes. Did you ever do something like that, where either the writers wanted it that way or you just wanted to shake things up and completely screw with the orchestration?

RS: We wouldn't dare do that, first of all, because we were under very tight reins from above. Occasionally, if there was a big band, jazz kind of sound that they wanted, we could bring in extra saxes.

SB: *Freakazoid!* would have that frequently.

JB: But all of our wind players played sax—they all doubled. So we would have every single woodwind player playing a saxophone. We would have a big band.

RS: There were enough brass players so there *was* a big band. And we had the best drummer in town; he used to play with Frank Zappa. Needless to say, we had the best musicians in town in every genre.

SB: They really needed to be, because the music would change every bar and a half, and the tempos too, literally; they needed to be the best, otherwise it couldn't be played in the time that we had to rehearse and record.

RS: Which is the frustrating thing now, when we're all out looking for jobs. People will say, "Can you do John Williams adventure music?" Well, of course we can. "Can you do jazz?" Well, of course we can. We've been writing in so many of these genres for so many years in these very tight-knit, hard-to-write little cues. People don't hear it that way because it's animation.

DG: Within *Animaniacs*, each segment seemed to have a particular style. "Goodfeathers" obviously went off of Scorsese's style, but also the Italian/Nino Rota/Carmine Coppola/*Godfather* sound. The core *Animaniacs* segments would be [inspired by] the early Warner Bros. cartoons, even by *Tiny Toons* itself. How did you devise the breakdown for how each segment was going to sound?

RS: Well, very early on, we were having meetings. I got to meet with [executive producer] Steven Spielberg on three occasions in this conference room. He wanted to hear themes for all the different characters. Yakko, Wakko, and Dot had a theme, Pinky and the Brain, who were, at that time, on the show—they didn't have their own show yet—they had their own theme. Mindy and Buttons had a theme, the Goodfeathers had a theme . . .

JB: Rita and Runt had a theme . . .

DG: Slappy [Squirrel] had her own theme. She was directly out of the old school.

RS: [Her theme was Dvorak's] "Humoresque"—and that was actually [senior producer] Tom Ruegger's idea. So those were the themes. Then when you get into the actual musical environment that all of these universes were in, each had their own basis of that kind of flavor. In the first couple of "Goodfeathers," I used a mandolin and tried to make it [in that vein]; it went away after a while—simply because they, then, here put in situations where they were put in the middle of satirizing musicals. Steve did "West Side Pigeons," and there was "Pigeon on the Roof."

DG: I don't think I ever saw that! I definitely saw "West Side Pigeons," though. My favorite "Goodfeathers" was when Squit gets hiccups. When they finally go away . . . what was the music, *Swan Lake*? He flies in the air, and we get the [singing] "ba-daaa-daa," you know, because suddenly he's so happy, and even in that brief second, it really works.

RS: Well, that was a very Warner-y cartoon. It had a single subject, there was a lot of visual gag action, it had that story arc and a very simple ending, and "The End—That's All, Folks!" It was a very satisfying cartoon.

JB: I think "Pigeon on the Roof" was where they satirized everyone and everything. It mentioned as many outside references as it could.

DG: It seemed like *everything* in *Animaniacs* was like that, though—that's why I enjoyed it so much. I was always on the lookout for, "where's the next inside gag"? Like the *Apocalypse Now* spoof—who was it that twisted the Doors' "The End" around just enough so that nobody would get in trouble?

RS: I did that. I did ninety percent of the songs up to a certain point, and then Julie did one hundred percent of them. And that point was fairly early on.
  The other thing to say about all the different characters having their own music is that like any show, it kept evolving as we did more of it. The Pinky and Brain universe was a much darker place; the sort of walking around, talking, under-dialogue music was always minor instead of major because that worked better. Brain was always saying, "Well, Pinky, we're going to attach the modulator to the so-and-so." "Oh, really, Brain?" And minor just worked better. Of all the characters, they could never be cute. Cute was something I fought against all the time.

SB: I liked living in the Pinky and the Brain universe . . .

RS: Oh, yeah! You could be as dark and dramatic as you wanted.

DG: It seemed very sci-fi oriented.

RS: Yes. We used a theremin sound a lot. It was sort of this retro, sci-fi feel.

DG: Yeah, and appropriately so. You could say that Brain is modeled on Orson Welles, and that [Bernard] Herrmann used a theremin in *The Day the Earth Stood Still*—there's a nice bit of reasoning there.

RS: And the Brain was always building these machines and had blueprints of machines that had a very retro look to them. And the background was very dark and a lot of it takes place at night . . .

DG: Having it in minor makes a lot of sense because so much of what the Brain was doing was very diabolical and so it's very easy to go into a minor sting, or a sting after he would say, "We're going to take over the world!!!"[5]

SB: It makes the comedy work, too.

RS: Yeah—I was going to say that it set off the jokes. The formula of Pinky and the Brain was that Brain would go into these descriptions of how he was going to take over the world, which were all outrageous, and then Pinky would say, "Gee Brain, is there anything that gum won't stick to?" or something really stupid. So you'd go through this diabolical music and then *stop* and give Pinky just a little thread to talk over, and then Brain would make a face and say something, and then move on to the next scene. The serious stuff really helped to set the comedy off.

DG: Well, everything Pinky says is a one-liner. "I think so, Brain, but isn't Regis Philbin already married?" All of those . . .

RS: Which brings up a technical point of something that we were forced to do over the years and I sorted of minded it, but now I realize that it really helped things. When regular "walk and talk" dialogue was going on, we were forced to sort of stay out of the way and play very, very neutral music—just a little "boom-chick, boom-chick," or angular woodwind solos or something. Under a punchline, we were told to just stay out of the way, using only one or two notes, very lightly. Then there'd be a reaction shot, of somebody reacting to the punchline, making a face to which we'd put a trombone "wah" or something. This really underscores the comedy—it underlines it: "This is the punchline, don't forget it." If you don't do that, if you do "boom-chick, boom-chick" through the dialogue and then through the punchline and then through the reaction, it takes so much away.

SB: The structure, especially of that show, was the comedy—it was character and it was comedy, and our job was to underline it the best we could.

RS: Yeah—and when I see other studios' products, and composers who actually do *not* do that, I think it takes away from whatever comedy, however dismal, was there.

DG: That was always the Warner Bros. style—especially Carl Stalling's style—was to, not necessarily put the jokes into neon, but develop a sound that we would come to associate with, "this is the gag." So, every time something happens to the Coyote, we get a certain kind of sound; every time Daffy, in *Rabbit Seasoning* or *Duck! Rabbit! Duck!*, says, "Shoot me now!" "No, shoot me later!"—all of those gags, they always end with the same kind of music, so we're coming to *expect* the same kind of music.

RS: Stalling would actually *stop* for a couple of bars and have nothing. If you look in his scores, he'll have four bars where he'd just write in the words "sound effects." The Coyote loading his rifle and something explodes—he leaves that blank. We were forced to write explosion music—like a big, sharp-nine chord under an explosion—which, of course, we could never hear after they put the sound effects in. Our producer would often see our scores [with the animation] before the sound effects were laid in; so, to please him . . . He wanted these big brassy chords all the time. I thought they'd have been better off not there, but he insisted on it.

SB: The tornado episode of "Mindy and Buttons" could have just not been written at all because it was all wind effects through the entire thing. But I wrote probably more notes in that episode than I've written since or before. It was just covered by winds!

RS: We knew it was going to be that way, but we did it anyway.

DG: What did Spielberg think of the themes?

RS: He liked them very much. He wasn't overly effusive—he just said, "Oh, they're very good. I like them!" He was fine. It was a very unemotional experience for him—but you can imagine how I felt.

DG: Some cartoon themes persist and some have faded over time. Tom and Jerry had themes originally—they were gone quickly, certainly within a few years. Some of the characters are directly associated with the theme; the character I'm thinking of is Chicken Boo, where the segment is so short anyhow, you get the intro theme, you have the gag—which is only two minutes—and then you get the out music, which winds it up.

RS: Same with Katie Kaboom.

DG: The thing I loved about Chicken Boo, of course, was working the "Chicken Reel" into his theme. You don't really get it until the end—you get to the end of the singing, and it turns into the "Chicken Reel."

RS: That's the thing about the structure of those cartoons. He'd be posing as this person or that person, and you'd play it that way. Then the rubber nose and glasses come off, and then you play the "Chicken Reel." That was the fun of it.

DG: Were you getting the stories episode by episode; were you actually getting two "Chicken Boos" or two "Goodfeathers" episodes at a time? Because it's an anthology show . . .

RS: Yeah, we just got what came in. When you had spotting sessions, Tom [Ruegger] would have these huge, huge stacks of tapes. And whatever would come back and be ready, he'd want to get done. He'd ask, "How many minutes *maximum* can you do?" And I'd say, "Twenty-two minutes." And his secretaries would work out a total of twenty-two minutes [of scoring] that he would want to get done at that time, either to get in certain shows, or he really wanted to see how it was going to turn out, or whatever. It was up to him.

DG: So it was possible that you could be doing all *Animaniacs* one day, or all "Goodfeathers," or all "Mindy and Buttons," or all bumpers . . .

RS: Oh, yeah! You know at the end of the show, after the end titles are over, when the shield [on the Warner Bros. water tower, where Yakko, Wakko, and Dot live] opens up and they have some little punchline?

JB: That was a fun day . . .

RS: We did all of those, and there were over forty-five of them, forty-five to fifty of those, and they were all individually scored. And we did one after another. Some of them were one second long, and others were thirteen seconds.

JB: That was a very hard day, because the musicians don't get to get into this role of playing; they just have to keep starting and stopping.

RS: Yeah, for two hours.

JB: It's very boring and tedious.

RS: So there were days like that, and then there were days like the half-hour Christmas special, and it would all be within one show. In the middle [of those long sessions] we would even combine sessions for different series. We would do some cues from *Pinky and the Brain*, some cues from *Freakazoid!*, some cues from *Animaniacs*. It would make the billing a big problem, but I said, "We'll do what we can do, and you guys can figure it out." Fortunately every segment, no matter how small, had its own production number; it was their job to figure it out. We just went in and did the scoring—twenty-two minutes of music, and that's it.

---

[1] Besides being close friends, Stone and the Bernsteins were also neighbors, living only a few houses down from one another in West Hills, California. This made my interviewing the three of them easy to arrange. Sadly, this may have been one of the last interviews Richard Stone ever conducted; he was already undergoing treatment for cancer when we gathered at his house, and he passed away less than a year later, on March 9, 2001.

[2] Stone is referring to the audio tracks for the Warner Bros. animated cartoons, which would have been recorded and mixed together on separate reels of film—literally, the "soundtrack" for an animated cartoon. In some cases, new music and sound effects tracks are created if the originals are damaged or are in otherwise bad shape, or missing altogether.

[3] This is a reference to the voice of Milt Franklyn, who can be heard on the tapes mentioned above, calling out the numbers for the various cues in the recording sessions with Carl Stalling, and later on his own. His voice can also be heard on several tracks of the two *The Carl Stalling Project* CDs.

[4] *Tiny Toon Adventures* premiered in 1990.

[5] In film music parlance, a "sting" is a musical chord that appears suddenly on the soundtrack, usually to musically punctuate something that has happened on screen, such as the discovery of a corpse or the [unexpected] appearance of a character.

An Interview with
Alf Clausen

by DANIEL GOLDMARK

Defying the expectations of fans and critics alike, *The Simpsons* continues, after more than a decade, to provide show after show of original, biting comedy; it long ago surpassed *The Flintstones* to become the longest-running animated prime time series ever. Music has always had an important role on the show—in the first prime-time episode of the series (not including the Christmas episode, "Simpsons Roasting on an Open Fire," 1989), Marge takes the family to the opera (*Carmen*—in Russian, no less) when she thinks Bart, a supposed wunderkind, needs encouraging ("Bart the Genius," 1990). Since that time, numerous musicals, operas, and ballets have visited Springfield; Lisa has had several elementary school band traumas; Homer has sung his share of Broadway-inspired soliloquies; dozens of rock, folk, country, jazz, and punk musicians have passed through town; and countless films, commercials, and television shows have been spoofed.

Alf Clausen has scored practically all of this music, beginning with the third episode of the second season, "Treehouse of Horror" (the first Halloween special, in 1990). Probably one of the busiest men in cartoon music today, Clausen worked as a bandleader on *Donny and Marie*, as well as composer for a variety of television series, including *Moonlighting* and *ALF*, before he was tapped as the composer for *The Simpsons*. When the show is in season, he composes the music for a twenty-two minute episode every week, which includes conducting a full orchestra in a weekly recording session. Every episode places new demands on Clausen: he might face a Disney satire one week, a simple love story the next, and a Sondheim-esque creation the week after that. Through all of this, Clausen must write music that does not step on the dialogue, yet at the same time is interesting and evocative enough to underscore montage sequences, scene transitions, and full-blown production numbers. In this interview from July 7, 1997, we discussed both his influences as a composer and the challenges he faces on the show, especially with its parodies of well-known musical styles and genres.

© 20th Century Fox Film Corp.

DANIEL GOLDMARK: What was your upbringing in cartoon music? What was your exposure—or did you have any?

ALF CLAUSEN: I did. I hadn't thought a lot about it for many, many years until someone asked me the question, "If you were stranded on a desert island, what animated features or animated shows would you like to have with you?" [laughs] My comment, first of all, was after composing the music for well over 150 episodes of *The Simpsons* and well over 4500 music cues, an animated movie was the last thing I'd want with me on a desert island. Once I get past that, I'd like to have the entire *Rocky and His Friends* series, because that was my all-time favorite—that's what I grew up on. I remember watching that over and over and over again. The humor was absolutely amazing on that series—I just loved it. So that's really what I remember more than anything. I think very early on as a child, I would go to the Saturday matinees at my local movie theatre. They'd always have Westerns as the matinees—either Roy Rogers or Gene Autry or Tim Holt, who was a big cowboy guy in the Midwest. And they almost always had a short before the Western feature, and more often than not it would be a cartoon, a Merrie Melodies or something like that—a lot of the Warner Bros. stuff. I kind of grew up on that—from an early age.

DG: Were you a fan of those at all?

AC: Oh, yeah, I loved it, but I didn't love it from an obsessive viewpoint, I loved it as a viewer. I don't think I became really obsessive until *Rocky and His Friends*. That's the one that made me really stop and think.

DG: Because the Looney Tunes and Merrie Melodies would use pop tunes, classics, jazz, folk tunes, and things like that, do you recall that you were picking up tunes from cartoons at all?

AC: I'm sure there was a lot of that present. I don't remember consciously doing it, because at the same time I was starting my early musical training. My first instruments were French horn and voice. Being a French horn player you're exposed to all those classic pieces in the first place. I'm sure that there were many times when I heard them in the movies and shorts and thought, "Oh yeah, I really like that piece; I played it last week," or something would stick with me and then three months down the line I'd be introduced to it in concert band. So it kind of worked hand in hand.

DG: What did you think about Disney? Were you a fan of the films?

AC: Oh, yeah. The shorts and the features too. That was a big part of Midwestern upbringing, the wholesomeness of Disney. I remember seeing *Fantasia* and just being knocked out. It was an amazing experience. And once again, it never really stuck with me from an obsessive viewpoint. I'm almost embarrassed to say that sometimes, because there are some composers who work in animation, who've been in animation as long as they can remember; they have an unbelievable background and a wealth of source material floating around in their heads that they remember from very early ages. *The Simpsons* is the first animated show I ever worked on—I was a drama guy. I certainly had the background, no question about it, but I know that, like my partner in crime, my compadre, Rich Stone, you know, has an amazing wealth of the Carl Stalling influence; I'm kind of in awe of someone who is that steeped in that tradition from an animation perspective.

DG: At the same time, not being as sunk into that [tradition] as you are, I think would be a definite advantage, because it lets you create your own ways of looking at things as opposed to using what someone else has established.

AC: Oh, sure.

DG: I'd be the last one to say anything bad about Stalling, because he was a brilliant composer, but his forte was making parodies or making comments on the scene at hand with the music he was using—making visual jokes, orchestrating the music in some sort of funny way so that it would correspond with what's going on. That's very much a part of the Looney Tunes vocabulary. I think that it's created what most people think of as cartoon music—the sound he worked with for years. But at the same time, because *The Simpsons* is *not* Looney Tunes, and in a way it's much closer to real life than the Warner Bros. cartoons or any of those, the music can therefore be less in the Looney Tunes vein and work equally with the . . .

AC: I agree with you. I think that, because of the fact that we draw from all influences, we're not hemmed in stylistically by expectations so to speak, and that's kind of the way the entire series has been too. I think that it was either Matt Groening or Dave Silverman who made the observation in some interview that, from the very beginning, there were no expectations for the series, and that's why it allowed everybody to fly and do their absolutely best creative work, because nobody was trying to put a fence around everyone and say, "We want you to create within this little pasture here. . . ."

DG: . . . and that was coming right off of it being on *The Tracy Ullman Show* . . .

AC: Right. And they've been very good to me that way over there as well. They have given me—within the confines of reason, obviously—a lot of latitude to do all sorts of different kinds of things. That's why it's been so much fun.

DG: Have you ever wanted to put something in musically that they just said, I don't think so, whether it be a gag or a sting or something that you thought would work and they had other ideas for?

AC: Once in a while. As creative as the team is, I have noticed something very interesting about writers in general, and that is that many of them don't have a music face and they go for the obvious each time when selecting music.

DG: There do seem to be one or two characters that have music that returns. Besides the obvious—Itchy and Scratchy have a theme, Krusty has his theme—the one I'm thinking of is the "Cape Feare" episode (1993), because after that it seems like Sideshow Bob gets that motif. I saw the episode with the blimp and the atomic bomb ["Sideshow Bob's Last Gleaming," 1995] that was just on, and then I watched the "Cape Feare" episode again last night, I realized that they both use that theme. I didn't have a chance to watch the recent episode with David Hyde Pierce ["Brother from Another Series," 1997] . . .

AC: It's there again, yes.

DG: So that has become something . . . was that your decision, or was it mutual with the producers?

AC: Well, it was mutual, but it was my suggestion. I brought it up a number of times, and I said, at this particular point, with his whole mindset going on, it really serves us well to bring that thing back and remind people where he came from.

DG: Is there anyone else you've done that with?

AC: Mr. Burns. There's a Burns theme that keeps coming back. Whenever he goes into his very evil mode, "I think I'm going to kill this person . . . ,"— whenever that happens we start to creep in with the same scary theme for him.

And there's also a theme for Kang and Kodos from the Halloween episodes with the theremin.

DG: Right! They're always pulling back, showing Kang and Kodos on their ship, passing their judgment on the silly humans.

AC: Right. And they've got this theremin theme that comes back.

DG: And that's from the first Halloween episode ["Treehouse of Horror"]?

AC: Right. 7F04. [laughs]

DG: That's very good—you don't know all of them, do you?

AC: The reason I know that one is that it's the very first episode I did. It was my audition episode, and I wrote the little theme for Kang and Kodos for that.

DG: How do you keep the music from disappearing? I mean, you have music, and then [sound] effects, and then dialogue. I realize that in a show like this, dialogue comes first and there's no question about that. In the time that you have in the open, how can you really make yourself heard?

AC: It was a hard lesson for me to learn. I took a while to get into that groove. I grabbed onto it pretty quickly and realized that if I was going to survive musically, it was going to have to be the same; it's almost sound-effects driven in many ways. Unfortunately, in many series, including this one, the pecking order is dialogue first, sound effects next, and music third. I suffer some big hits at times. I get very frustrated by it. I've raised the issue many times. It fixes itself for an episode or two and tends to sink back to the same order again. It's really difficult for me and my music editors, because we try to convince the producers that the only way that music can be effective for them is if it's on an equal playing field, not necessarily blowing everybody out, but at least equal. If it's not at least equal, it tends to sound like a mistake. In defense of the system, there is so little dubbing time available and there are so many things to focus on that if the music works, they leave it alone, not realizing that maybe it could be raised one or two or three decibels and it would work much better. As long as it works, they're fine with it, and they move on and concentrate on dialogue and sound effects. It's a common complaint of all composers, and it's a common thread that you'll find in any interview you conduct. And yet I'm very realistic about it. I know that I take third place on this ladder, but third place nevertheless to me has to be relatively equal in existence and it's not always . . . it comes with the territory.

DG: Have you ever put anything in [musically] just for the hell of it, just for your own satisfaction?

AC: Oh, I know I have. I can't pull one right out of the air now, but Chris Ledesma, my music editor, and I have chuckled about it every once in a while and we'll say, this is going to be our joke this time. The interesting thing about the whole concept of the series is that, overall, the producers don't want the music to make a statement—no musical jokes. The dialogue has got to be what's driving it, and it's got to be funny, and the visuals have to be what's funny, but the line is drawn at the music. Music doesn't make it funny—I made that comment in the interview [in *Film Score Monthly*] about an old friend of mine who said "You can't vaudeville vaudeville." That is the focus that I've used through this whole thing. I really think it does work best overall with comedy and music too; you play the music straight, and you play the sincerity of the moment, and the absurdity of the actions are what make the scene funny.

DG: It contributes to the mood, and it would seem empty without it. But it can't actively drive the comedy, on an obvious level, at least. But somebody who just tuned in will clearly hear the stinger chords that you put in.

AC: I think when we've had a choice of which direction to move we try to "smart it up" as opposed to "dumb it down," and thinking it's better if ten people get the joke—because those ten people have gotten it and the joke's there, as opposed to not going with the joke because we were afraid somebody's not going to get it.

DG: There are several sequences in which I know I'm not getting the joke, and it may be because I haven't seen enough movies. . . .

AC: Me too, still! Because some of those [references] are very esoteric, very oblique. Sometimes it's really interesting, doing music spotting with these guys; usually we have one of the production staff sitting in the music spotting with a script. As we do music spotting, they'll be going through the script to see if there are any notes that have been written by the scriptwriters as to musical references. Sometimes they are very outside and left-handed; if that person doesn't happen to be there that day and we don't have someone paging through the script, sometimes we ourselves can miss them. I know that there have been cases where some of the scenes have been direct parodies from movies, animation-wise, and I say, "Thank God this person was there with the script to read the notes during the music spotting session, because there was a movie that I haven't seen!" But it's very much intentional that the scene is lifted right out of the movie.

DG: The "See My Vest" parody ["Two Dozen and One Greyhounds," 1995] comes so close to *Beauty and the Beast*; I mean, you really need to be paying attention to hear the differences. The point is it's making a jibe at something that's considered a classic—that's what Warner Bros. was famous for doing, taking the Disney reverence for classical music with *Fantasia* and turning it on its ear with *What's Opera, Doc?* and all those other cartoons, saying, "Here's what I think of classical music." Is that what you were doing with that?

AC: It's really tricky with me. Obviously, I have to be very, very careful. And I don't know how I ended up in this position; it's kind of scary sometimes that they ask me to do these things. It's an interesting skill to develop. Sometimes the references that I'm thrown are very, very specific, and other times the references are more generic and they say "we'd like it in the spirit of a Disney movie," and they'll leave it wide open as to what I think that should be, which makes it a lot easier and a lot safer for me, because it can be something that's totally original.

The other part of it is really tricky and it's a fine line to walk. I always take the approach that we're paying homage to these things, that we're trying to do so in a, how should I say it. . . . We like to show them that we honor that music, and that it's a tribute to it rather than trying to totally poke fun at it.

DG: How about when Homer is chasing Bart around the house and it's a parody of the Road Runner and Coyote; did you go and watch a couple of Road Runner cartoons to get some musical ideas or did you already know what you wanted?

AC: Because of the fact that this stuff comes so fast and furious, and there are so many cues to deal with on a weekly basis, so many different styles—if I have any question at all, I'll have one of the production assistants go out and rent a tape or CD. They assemble a tape of clips of stuff for me and I can sit here when I'm in the composition process and look at something very quickly without having to figure out where, on an hour-long tape, this thing is . . . they assemble all that stuff for me for reference.

The interesting observation that I make about the whole focus [of parody] is . . . I go through this a lot with the producers, especially when we get into "temp-itis," temp track love, temp love,[1] and I always try to bring up the issue [that] somewhere in the past this piece of music was written as an original piece of music, it wasn't meant to duplicate something else, it will always be an original piece of music. Therefore, why do we lean on something that already exists; we have somebody here to create an original piece of music to suit your purposes to a "T". Sometimes I win the battle, sometimes I lose the battle. Once again we come back to the identification syndrome. They say, well, "Everyone remembers what it was like sitting in the back of their '67 Chevy necking with their first girlfriend to *this* piece of music." And I say, "But everybody *doesn't* remember that. Everybody was not in the same place at the same time; they didn't have the same experience." But they have their own memories to bring that can't be erased. But, you do what you do.

DG: *Stop the Planet of the Apes, I Want to Get Off* [from "A Fish Called Selma," 1996]. Was there a particular composer you were trying to emulate or that inspired you?

AC: No, no. That was simply Troy McClure at his best.

DG: I can think of several other musical-type numbers, like the bordello episode ["Bart After Dark," 1996] with "We Put the Spring in Springfield," and the Stonecutters song, of course [in "Homer the Great," 1995]. You've clearly had many opportunities to do musical theatre.

AC: It's great—I've always loved musical theatre. I had my first opportunities in college to participate in musical theatre, because the college I went to in North Dakota put on a revue every spring and I played in the pit band for a couple of years. Then they decided they were going to put on regular Broadway musicals. They did them very well; by the time I was a senior in college, I ended up conducting the pit orchestra for my first Broadway musical—I believe it was *The Pajama Game*. They were very serious about it and did a great job. It was really fun for me, and that was my first exposure to the entire scope of a Broadway musical. When I finished my sophomore year in college I got the opportunity to go to New York City, and I lived in Manhattan for six weeks one summer and I stayed with my cousin who was a professional musician, a choir director, and a concert pianist and opera coach. He and his wife showed me Manhattan for six weeks, including musical theater. In that amount of time I saw the original *West Side Story* with Carol Lawrence and Larry Kert, and the original *The Music Man* with Robert Preston, the original *My Fair Lady* with Rex Harrison and Julie Andrews, and the original *How to Succeed in Business Without Really Trying* with Robert Morse. It was amazing, just amazing; something really clicked for me—whew! what an existence this is! I didn't know much about it, but I thought it would be really fun to participate in eventually in some way, shape, or form. And even though I'm not writing musical theater, all of sudden, ba-doom, I get a chance to write musical theater on this show. It's really fun.

DG: Is that something you like to do in your spare time?

AC: Oh, yeah. I've written a couple of works already. I've done an oratorio for soloists, choir, studio orchestra, and narrator. It's two hours and fifteen minutes long.

DG: The subject?

AC: The Book of Jeremiah. It's *When Jeremiah Sang the Blues*. The subtext of it is Watergate. We've had seven performances of it already—the public's reaction has been incredible. I've been waiting for some time to launch it again. . . .

DG: Let's talk about the "Mr. Sparkle" commercial ["In Marge We Trust," 1997]. They hit on every stereotypical image and idea that you see in Japanese advertising. How did you do the music for that?

AC: We looked at a lot of Japanese commercials, first of all. I don't know where they got them . . . then one of the production assistants went shopping at record stores, looking for whatever they could find. Eventually they found this record store in Koreatown, bought a number of CDs, and let the producers listen to all of them. And they said, "nope, nope, nope, nope, hmmmm, that's kind of interesting, nope, nope, nope," and finally came up with two or three things and narrowed it down into a, you know, "this kind of works, let's see if we can come up with something in this general feel."

DG: Regarding "The Simpsons Spin-off Showcase" [1997]; usually "real" spin-offs always have something missing; the writers played on that by having the Simpsons appear in all the spin-offs in that episode. I think the spin-offs were meant to show how weak these characters would be on their own. The take-off on *The Sonny & Cher Show*, *The Simpson Family Smile-Time Variety Hour*—it was a combination of *Sonny & Cher* and *Laugh-In*. But the music for that—"The Peppermint Twist"? How did that come up?

AC: Well, the song was actually submitted as part of the script, once again. The writers put that together. They wanted to come up with a medley of things that were reminiscent of those old-time variety shows and at one point they said, "Hey, Alf, you want to come watch some of these?" And I said, "No, I don't have to, I lived it. I was the musical director for the *Donny and Marie* show. I've been through this and I know exactly what you want. You tell me what songs you want and I'll make them work for you." And I had to write this theme at the beginning that was very reminiscent of the way the variety show themes were done, the wakka-wakka guitar and what not.

DG: I was a huge fan of *Donny and Marie.* . . .

AC: Yes, it was a very successful show. I was fortunate enough to do it during its best year; I did the third season as musical director. They really spent the money on it and were at the height of their ratings, before they moved it up to Utah. It was a great experience—we had wonderful guests on the show and I had a wonderful band. We had a thirteen-piece band on that show—it was known as the best band on television at the time. A lot of the guys in that band still work for me today and were on the tracks of *The Simpson Family Smile-Time Variety Hour*. It was really wild—I came up with the idea but I never pursued it; it was an interesting publicity aside, that it was something like the twenty-year reunion of the *Donny and Marie* band.

"The Love-Matic Grandpa" was designed to be one of those sickeningly-sweet sitcom themes from that era.

DG: That one was really . . . gross. I remember thinking, "this is so good," it makes you think of all those shows. And the "Chief Wiggum, P.I." [theme] was a play on *Magnum P.I.* . . . .

AC: *Magnum* and *Miami Vice* and *Quincy* thrown in . . .

DG: Do you keep all of your scores?

AC: I have copies of every episode I've done in numerical order and every score in numerical order, because I use them for reference all the time. Once in a while I'll have to go back in; they'll say, "we really love this cue from such-and-such an episode, five years ago." We research it, we find it, and I've got everything right there.

DG: Do you start with a piano score or do you go right for the big guns?

AC: Early on, if I was going to orchestrate a cue, maybe I'd sketch for myself a four- or six-line sketch on paper. I found that, as time went on, I got frustrated at how it would slow me down to write a lot of the same information on each score page—bar numbers, timings, time signatures, stuff like that. I just thought to myself, "I'm really duplicating my efforts here for naught." So what I do now is I actually write directly to the score page. If it gets to be a complex kind of a cue I'll sketch, really lightly, maybe on two or three blank lines of the score page, just to keep my place and know where I am, but then I can put all of the information down as a final—the timings, the time signatures, and all that stuff. I'll just go back and erase my sketch marks when I'm done. If someone else orchestrates for me, when it's really under the gun, then I'll write nine-line sketches. They're very thorough.

DG: I'm sure you must give the orchestrator ample indication of "brass here," "strings here," . . .

AC: Oh, yeah, they're very thorough. Most people don't go to that kind of detail, but I've always been a control freak. I can crank out nine-line sketches pretty quickly.

DG: You're so under the gun that you don't have time to fool around; you can't say, later on, this is what I want. You have to lay it down and get it out.

AC: Right, right.

DG: How often is it that you can't orchestrate yourself, that you're *that* under the gun?

AC: I would say maybe sixty to seventy-five percent of the time I do my own orchestration.

DG: That's great.

AC: As the years go by, it doesn't become any easier, I find.

DG: It would seem to me that the more you know about orchestration and the more you become familiar with it after twenty or thirty years of doing this kind of stuff, it just makes it that much more difficult because you have so many things to draw on. You know, "Well, I can do this, I can do this," you can make those decisions.

AC: Yes, I have a lot of choices.

DG: The more you know, the more choices you get to make. It gives you a broader palette. . . .

AC: But there's no time to think of it that way. It's really amazing; I never really imagined what it would be like composing under this type of pressure for this long a period of time and how unbelievably emotion-driven it can be. I think, in the early days, I let my head drive my choices; it was always an intellectual process. But when you do it on a week-to-week-to-week-to-week basis and you get really tired, your head starts to close up and then it becomes emotionally driven. That's both good and bad, but I think overall it's good because you tend to react to a scene, for the most part, the correct way first. If you can connect the emotional content of that along with intellectual process and have enough of a backlog of craft to go with all of that, then that's what makes the whole process a success on a week-to-week basis.

---

[1] Temp tracking is the practice of using preexisting music to help the editor piece together a cartoon before the final "original" music is written. "Temp-itis" refers to directors or writers who fall in love with the temp track so much that they don't want new music (e.g., the music for Kubrick's *2001: A Space Odyssey*).

I Kid Because I Love

The Music of The Simpsons

by WILL FRIEDWALD

"I kid because I love."
—Krusty the Klown, "Brother from
Another Series" (1997)

IT'S LONG BEEN a trend in the musical arts that revivals and rehash have become more popular than original works—the hottest tickets on Broadway in the 1990s, with a few exceptions, were classic shows of the 1940s, '50s and '60s. The latest development at the millennium would seem to be that concept parodies have become more popular than the original icons that they're parodying. The show of the year—and most likely the decade—on the Great White Way right now is *The Producers*. No one is about to claim it's a great show that will live forever, along with the best of Lerner and Loewe or Rodgers and Hammerstein, but it's a wonderfully crafted entertainment that artfully serves its purpose, which is, if not to parody specific other musical comedies, to make fun of the entire Broadway establishment.

The same thing could be said for the music on *The Simpsons*—almost all of which, except Danny Elfman's opening title theme, is composed by the brilliant Alf Clausen. It doesn't come out of the tradition of cartoon music à la Carl Stalling or Scott Bradley. Unlike those cartoons scored by Hoyt Curtin (all those Hanna-Barbera TV toons) or Win Sharples, most of the characters don't have *motifs*—i.e., there's not a Bart Simpson theme that you'll hear week after week whenever America's bad boy makes his appearance. Rather, in some ways like *The Producers,* the major musical inspiration for *The Simpsons* would seem to be the old *Mad* magazine of the 1960s, in which every week seemed to be a story set to the score of either *My Fair Lady* or *The Sound of Music*.

For whatever reason, more people want to see *The Producers* than any other musical comedy in many years. Still, at least on Broadway there are other options, particularly such offbeat but original entries as *Urinetown* and *Bat Boy* (which closed the day this is being written), not to mention those very tuneful revivals of such traditional fare as *Kiss Me, Kate* and *The Music Man*. The viewer searching for music on television, however, has few other options. Not surprisingly, there's not another sitcom, or indeed, any kind of "com," that features so much music: gone are the days when Ricky Ricardo used to sing "Babalu" every other week at the Club Tropicana, or when Tony Bennett was likely to drop in on *Make Room for Daddy*. And since there hasn't been a new musical variety show on the air almost since the 1970s, the glory years of the kind of shows that our favorite family savaged on *The Simpsons Smile-Time Variety Hour* (in "The Simpsons Spin-Off Showcase," 1997), it's not going too far to say that the only good music on TV in the last thirty years has been either Ken Burns's *Jazz* or *The Simpsons*. (With the exception of *South Park*, none of the other entries in the recent cycle of "postmodern" cartoons—i.e., *The Ren & Stimpy Show* or *The Simpsons'* companion show, *Futurama*— makes much use of original music.)

Pauline Kael, in her review of *Blazing Saddles* all those years ago, made a distinction between films which exist on their own and those, like *Blazing Saddles*, which can't be enjoyed unless the viewer is familiar with other movies. You don't have to have seen *High Noon* to appreciate *Blazing Saddles*, but you have to be at least conversant with the basic clichés of the Western movie genre. *The Producers* and *The Simpsons* are a bit of both—not direct parodies of specific genres, but new stories and characters in which the parody element, while not essential, serves as a great framework for the writers to savage any piece of pop culture that strikes their fancy.

Obviously, my own point of view on this subject is somewhat skewed— a rock 'n' roll guy could come along and make the point that the show's basic musical stock in trade is rock 'n' roll legends, from the Beatles to 1990s grunge acts. (To be honest, I never even heard Iron Butterfly's "In a Gadda Da Vida" until I witnessed Reverend Lovejoy leading his congregation through that so-called "hymn" in "Bart Sells His Soul," 1995.) Other kinds of music turn up on the show too, from country-western to reggae and contemporary Christian pop. However, it seems to me that the essential vocabulary of the show is Broadway-style showtunes and classic pop, not to mention a sampling of jazz now and then.

The span of musical references is amazingly wide—something as (deliberately) annoyingly *contempo* as Poochie's rap (in "The Itchy and Scatchy and Poochie Show," 1997) combines hip-hop, rock, pop, and even an early soul hit by Bobby "Blue" Bland called "I Pity the Fool." The episode "A Fish Called Selma" (1996) culminates in a Broadway musical treatment of *Planet of the Apes*. This production is titled *Stop the Planet of the Apes, I Want to Get Off*, a play on the title of the hit British show *Stop the World, I Want to Get Off*, which opened on Broadway in 1962. Yet the first extended song we hear is "Dr. Zaius," which was the name of the character played (in monkey makeup) in the original *Planet of the Apes* movie in 1968 and is set, as I eventually figured out, to the 1986 disco-y hit "Rock Me Amadeus" by somebody or something named Falco. It's hard to imagine a viewer who would be equally well versed in the works of both the Leslie Bricusse–Anthony Newley team, the creators of *Stop the World*, and Falco, whatever that is.

Incidentally, Newley and Bricusse may be the writers most often singled out by Clausen and *The Simpsons* writing staff—in addition to *Stop the World*, the show has also taken a hack at "The Candyman" (from *Willie Wonka and the Chocolate Factory*), which Homer revives as "The Garbageman" in "Trash of the Titans" (1998), with spectacular choreography that makes him into the Gower Champion of garbage, the Tommy Tune of trash, the Bojangles Robinson of rubbish. The lyricists even use the term "arse" to give the text a suitably British feeling. "You Only Move Twice" (1996) goes after Bricusse and Newley's theme for James Bond's archnemesis, *Goldfinger* (from the Bond picture of that title), reworked into *Scorpio*, a supervillain who's unusually preoccupied with providing proper benefits for his employees.

One trademark of Broadway writers is their ability to make their music fit the setting and subject matter of the stories they're trying to tell. Frederick Loewe wrote what sounds like traditional Scottish music for *Brigadoon*, but for his next show, *Paint Your Wagon* (stay tuned, *Simpsons* fans) four years later, wrote what anybody would automatically assume were authentic American frontier folk songs. Then he went to George Bernard Shaw's England with *My Fair Lady*, Colette's Paris in *Gigi*, and medieval music for King Arthur's Court in *Camelot*. Likewise, Clausen doesn't just write "Broadway" music as if that were only one generic style. Clausen is much more specific than that; on top of which, like most satirists, he's never funnier than when he's attacking the mediocre. In "The City of New York vs. Homer Simpson" (1997), Marge and the kids attend a show described as a "musical salute to the Betty Ford Clinic." The resultant song, "You're Checkin' In," is psyche-delic-era pop Broadway, more ludicrous than Galt MacDermot or Stephen Schwartz at their pop-iest.

The Simpons writer Jeff Martin seems to have delighted in writing "excerpts" from a full Broadway score in a more traditional vein for *Oh, Street-car!*, the musical version of *A Streetcar Named Desire* (in the episode "A Street-car Named Marge," 1992). He responded to the challenge by coming up with what might be the most hysterically mediocre musical of all time (not count-ing *Carrie*). This adaption of Tennessee Williams's great American drama never fails to reduce the playwright's great lines and characters to the most unctuous of clichés—the ending number, in fact, is a cockeyedly optimistic salute to "the kindness of strangers" concept (ending with the bromide, "A stranger's just a friend you haven't met!"). It's hard to imagine an adaption of any work that could so thoroughly and hysterically misread its source mate-rial. I haven't seen André Previn's operatic treatment of *A Streetcar Named Desire*, but I doubt that it offers anywhere near as much in the way of toe-tappin' fun as this mini-adaption.

Other musical parodies resonate with affection for their source mate-rial—as Krusty the Klown says, they kid because they love. I can't think of many cartoons that parody Leonard Bernstein, yet "Boy Scoutz in the Hood" (1993) goes after the great conductor's most famous show tune, "New York, New York" (from *On the Town,* 1944) which is heard here as "Springfield, Springfield"; where the original Comden-Green lyrics pointed out the mag-nificence of New York in a humorous way, this homage to the Simpson fam-ily's hometown only seems to underscore the humdrumness of this particular 'burb (one of the most exciting things Bart and Milhouse find to sing about is "The stray dogs go to the animal pound").

"Marge vs. the Monorail" (1993) utilizes Meredith Willson's *The Music Man* as a starting point. This time, a Harold Hill-like huckster (the late Phil Hartman as Lyle Lanley, a name as close to Harold Hill as they could get) bilks the Springfieldites into erecting a monorail with the same zeal, and practically the same song ("Ya Got Trouble" becomes "The Monorail Song"), as Robert Preston did in both the stage and the Warner Bros. productions of *The Music Man*. Other times, individual songs, are sent up, like "Send in the Clowns," ("those soulful, doleful, schmaltz-by-the-bowlful clowns"), with lyrics that, I imagine, would send Stephen Sondheim into hysterics, and "It Was a Very Good Year" ("a very good beer"), that I know for a fact amused composer

Ervin Drake to no end. The recent episode "Behind the Laughter" (2000) includes a brief glance at the Broadway hit *Rent*.

In at least one episode, Clausen and the writers send up an entire musical tradition without so much as writing word number one of a new parody lyric. The 1993 episode "Cape Feare," which took its cue from the 1991 *Cape Fear* with Robert DeNiro (which itself was a remake of the 1962 *Cape Fear* with Gregory Peck and Robert Mitchum, based on a novel by John D. MacDonald), finds serial killer Sideshow Bob (Kelsey Grammer) stalking the Simpson family, particularly Bart. At the climax, he corners the kid on a boat and is about to brutally slaughter our favorite ten-year-old when Bart chimes in with a request. At this point, my mind flashed back to an old episode of the Peter Sellers–Spike Milligan *Goon Show,* in which cops threaten a cornered killer:

Policeman:	"Come out with your hands up, or else I'll sing the third act of *Tosca*."
Killer:	"And then what?"
Policeman:	"Then I'll sing the fourth act!"
Killer:	"But there is no fourth act in *Tosca*."
Policeman:	"Aha! You have less time than you think."

The *Simpson* variation on this bit is to have Bart request that he get to hear Bob sing all of both acts of Gilbert and Sullivan's *H.M.S. Pinafore* before he dies. Naturally, by the time he gets through the entire operetta, the boat they're on has sailed into police custody. But in the meantime, we get a delicious three-minute capsulization of Gilbert and Sullivan's first great *opera buffo.* Even the soundtrack (included on the Rhino CD *Go Simpsonic with The Simpsons*), sans visuals, is a laugh and a half, starting with the opening number—"We Sail the Ocean Blue"—a choral number—done by Grammer solo and a capella, bereft of the chorus and of the orchestra. On other numbers, Bart joins in as the chorus, supplying the choral responses ("hardly ever") in "I Am the Captain of the Pinafore." What makes it so funny is that Clausen and Grammer take it absolutely straight, even when doing "Poor Little Buttercup"; the only silly moment is when Grammer stumbles into an ungainly falsetto note on the line "he remains an Engl*ish*man."

The major musical property most viciously and lovingly savaged by Clausen is easily the Disney blockbuster *Mary Poppins*. Disney references (particularly during "Itchy and Scratchy," the ultraviolent cartoon within a cartoon that suggests Tom and Jerry as directed by John Carpenter) abound in the show. In fact, a page of *The Simpsons* Archive Web site (www.snpp.com) is devoted to tracking the number of times Uncle Walt's classics turn up in some form or another. There's an especially choice send-up of *The Little Mermaid* in the 1994 episode "Homer: Bad Man"; when our hero gets hit with sexual harassment charges, he announces his intention to move his family under the sea, which leads to a fantasy sequence in which Homer is shown frolicking with, and speedily consuming, dancing shellfish ("no accusations . . . only happy crustaceans"). The reference to *The Little Mermaid* underscores another point concerning the pre-*Producers* 1990s—namely that between the domination of the big Disney musicals (*The Little Mermaid, The Lion King, Beauty and the Beast, Aladdin,* etc.) at the box office and the Oscars and *The Simpsons* on TV, it would seem that animation was the only cinematic medium in that decade that was even bothering to use music at all.

Goofing on *Mary Poppins* affords an opportunity to go after Disneyana and the musical comedy genre at the same time. Whereas the mermaid joke is just a one-minute bit, the *Mary Poppins* parody goes all out. When the Mary Poppins-esque figure arrives, she gives her name as "Shary Bobbins," and insists that she's a "completely original character, like Ricky Rouse or Monald Muck." The parody includes swipes at most of the classic Sherman brothers songs: "The Perfect Nanny" ("Minimum Wage Nanny," in which Bart slides in his catchphrase, "eat my shorts" and Homer does the same with "no fat chicks"), "A Spoonful of Sugar" (Bobbins exhorts the kiddies to make the chores go faster: "do a half-assed job"), and most memorably, "Feed the Birds." Instead of feeding pigeons, this song, titled "A Boozehound Named Barney," advocates the buying of drinks for Barney Gumble, Springfield's resident alcoholic and champion belcher. The words and minor key melody are ace, but what caps it is the vocal by Barney himself, sung by Dan Castellaneta (better known as the voice of Homer) in a high tenor that manages to be completely pathetic yet perfectly in tune at the same time. This not-at-all-cautionary tale so effectively advocates the life of a boozehound that Bart wants to become one himself. "Not 'til you're fifteen," his father advises.

The writers of *The Simpsons* have worked in all manner of rock stars over the years, such as the Who, the Ramones, Spinal Tap, and the Be Sharps (in a witty episode that comes in second only to the original *This Is Spinal Tap* feature as a mock-Rockumentary), and one of the show's most gloriously mundane moments occurs with Clausen's approximation of a soft rock ballad. When I first heard "Can I Borrow a Feeling" in "A Milhouse Divided" (1996), I thought it was too accurate to be a parody, but just lousy enough to actually be a hit. It strikes precisely the right note between misled sincerity and overt mawkishness; the song is so cheesy that even Paul Williams himself couldn't have written it when he was drunk, and so touchy-feely-wimpy that even Karen Carpenter wouldn't sing it if she were alive. (Incidentally, the breakup of Milhouse's parents is alluded to in a deleted chorus from "The Garbageman," not heard in the final recording but in a demo version included on the *Go Simpsonic* CD.)

Just the same, I like to think that Clausen's own heart resides in Broadway-style material and classic pop singers like Tony Bennett. Bennett is said, in fact, to be the first celebrity to do a guest appearance on the show; conversely, Bennett himself remembers that *The Simpsons* was the first show he did when he began trying to capture the youth market at the end of the 1980s, and, as such, it helped lead to his subsequent triumphs on *The Late Show with David Letterman* and MTV. His song, "Capital City," is a clever spin on the Sinatra hit "New York, New York," and, like most Sinatra parodies of that vintage, uses words like "nutty" and "cuckoo" ("it makes a king feel like some kind of nutty, cuckoo super-king"). Tony's office (RPM Productions, on West 57th Street) has a cel from this episode framed and hanging on its walls. (Incidentally, Bennett only supplied the singing; an unidentified actor spoke the singer's one line of dialogue.)

Sinatra himself never actually appeared on *The Simpsons*—in fact, Bennett may be the only performer of that generation to show up—but he remains a strong presence on the show. In "Krusty Gets Busted" (1990), the first episode built around Bart's hero (thereby contributing to the surreal time-shifting nature of the show's continuity—Bart grows up watching a live TV kid show in which a clown host throws pies and introduces violent cat-and-mouse cartoons—if this isn't the 1950s masquerading as the 1990s I don't know what is), the Klown is described as coming from Tupelo, Mississippi. Clearly this is an Elvis Presley reference, or perhaps a wiseass comment on the nature of stardom, i.e., all superstars come from Tupelo. However, this was very early in the series; as time went on, it was more frequently inferred that Krusty's showbiz sensibilities lay more with Sinatra and the rat pack.

When, in a send-up of *The Jazz Singer*, the Klown is estranged from his rabbi father, Lisa reconciles the two with a quote from the world's most famous Jew, Sammy Davis, Jr. In another reconciliation, Krusty and his former sidekick-turned-criminal-mastermind Sideshow Bob are reunited by Sinatra "himself" on a telethon, just as the real-life Sinatra did for Dean Martin and Jerry Lewis. When Krusty does a comeback TV special, he comes back singing "Send in the Clowns," one of the same songs that Sinatra performed on his *Ol' Blue Eyes Is Back,* his 1973 post-retirement TV spectacular. When Krusty offers to take the kids of Kamp Krusty to "the happiest place in the world—Tijuana!" we hear a Sinatra imitator (one Gene Merlino) re-creating the Chairman's 1953 single, "South of the Border," complete with every Billy May–style nuance of the original arrangement. And that's only listing a few of the Krusty-specific Sinatra-isms.

Sinatra may be a recurring presence on *The Simpsons*, but saxophonist Bleeding Gums Murphy is an actual musical character on the show, appearing at the center of two episodes, "Moaning Lisa" in the first season (1990) and "Round Springfield" in the sixth (1995). (Both of those episode titles are plays on song titles, incidentally, the first associated with Nat King Cole, the second by Thelonious Monk.) In the first, Lisa (this has to be the only series in which one of the main characters is actually a musician) meets Bleeding Gums—"a terrific horn player with tones of soul"—for the first time. She's feeling depressed, and Bleeding Gums (the name is presumably a goof on such jazz and blues nicknames as Howlin' Wolf and Cleanhead) shows her how to elevate her mood by playing the blues. In one of the greatest lines in the history of television, Lisa asks if playing the blues is supposed to make her feel better, and Bleeding Gums answers, "The blues isn't about feeling better, it's about making other people feel worse."

Murphy returns in "Round Springfield," only to die early in the episode. Lisa spends the rest of the half hour trying to honor his memory by getting the local radio station to play BGM's only album, a collector's item rarity entitled *Sax on the Beach*. In the finale, she jams with Murphy from beyond the grave, and he appears in the sky, looking rather like the ghost of Hamlet's father, only holding a saxophone. I'm somewhat disappointed that they then play Carole King's "Jazzman" rather than something by Duke Ellington, but the show's heart is clearly in the right place—especially when Murphy ends the posthumous jam session in the sky to go off on "a date with Billie Holiday."

Further evidence that Clausen's heart lies in jazz and show tunes can be found in the show's all-musical episode, "All Singing, All Dancing" (1998)—in this compendium of the show's musical moments, all the highlights are in the adult pop and Broadway traditions. (Granted, another clip show could be pasted together and called "The Simpsons Rocks," consisting entirely of rock and contempop material—none of which is more memorable than Barry White rendering the "snake-whacking day song" in a voice considerably lower than Lisa's baritone saxophone.) Near the end of "All Singing, All Dancing," the Simpsons themselves dismiss this particular episode as "a cheesy clip show." Actually, it's a brilliant clip show, a veritable *That's Entertainment Parts One, Two,* and *Three* of Clausen's and the cast's best work.

The piece opens with Homer about to enjoy what he presumes is a shoot 'em up Western starring Clint Eastwood and Lee Marvin. What he gets instead is *Paint Your Wagon,* Joshua Logan's strangely lifeless 1969 film of Lerner and Loewe's 1951 Western-style Broadway musical. Yes, it features Clint Eastwood and Lee Marvin singing—and that's not even the main problem of the film. In any event, Homer is looking forward to some typically violent antics (perhaps with Lee and Clint as a humanoid Itchy and Scratchy) and instead gets Clint and Lee, both expertly voiced by Dan Castellaneta, doing a lot of what Homer summarily dismisses as "fruity singing." It also shows Clausen's smarts in that he realizes that of all the songs in both productions of *Paint Your Wagon* (including several that were written by Lerner and André Previn for the movie version, since Loewe had already retired by then), there was not one title song for either production, a song actually titled "Paint Your Wagon." As with *Oh, Streetcar,* Clausen contrives a new song with this title that positively revels in its own mediocrity: "I'm gonna paint this wagon / Gonna paint it fine. / Gonna use oil-based paint, / Because this wood is pine." This turns out to be merely the wraparound material for a show that repackages the show's musical highlights. In an idea borrowed from the rhyming dialogue of Rodgers and Hart's 1933 *Hallelujah, I'm a Bum!,* the whole episode is done entirely in verse.

Like Marge says, it's toe-tappin' fun. Before closing, I should mention that nearly all the highlights mentioned above are included on the two Rhino compilation CDs, *Songs in the Key of Springfield* and *Go Simpsonic with The Simpsons.* Enough musical moments remain in the now thirteen-year (and still counting) run of the series to fill many more discs. In fact, there are nearly enough shows-within-shows, all with their own theme songs, to comprise a disc of their own. "Everyone Loves Ned Flanders," "Cletus, the Slack-Jawed Yokel," "The Love-Matic Grampa," "The Simpsons Smile-Time Variety Hour," "Skinner and the Superintendent," "Apu in 'The Jolly Bengali' "—all are prime samples of what *The Simpsons* may, in the end, do best, which is to make fun of the entire medium of television itself. As with their parodies of rock, jazz, Broadway and the classics, to quote Krusty one more time, the Simpsons—and their creators—kid because they love.

An Interview with John Zorn

by PHILIP BROPHY

In the liner notes to the first volume of *The Carl Stalling Project*, John Zorn states that "All genres of music are *equal*—no *one* is inherently better than the other—and with Stalling, all are embraced, chewed up and spit out . . ." While he was describing Stalling's approach to music, Zorn could have easily been referring to his own—showing just how much the work of Carl Stalling and Scott Bradley has, undoubtedly, influenced the way music has been written for other kinds of music than that for cartoons, whether you use the label serious, art, avant-garde, contemporary, or experimental.

John Zorn is most often identified as a jazz musician, yet his vast output as a composer in every possible style and format defies this label. A wide variety of creative elements mediate his work: his varied compositional techniques (indeterminacy; structured improvisation or "game theory"); his work with other modern musicians/groups and composers (Bill Frisell, The Golden Palominos, Guy Klucesvek, Naked City); his exploration of Jewish heritage (his record label, Tzadik, has released more than sixty albums in the Radical Jewish Culture series, including several by Zorn himself); and most importantly here, his experiments with the styles of other composers—Ennio Morricone, Ornette Coleman, and Carl Stalling, among others. Zorn's manner of creating pieces in many ways follows Stalling's, in that both take pieces from every imaginable genre and style—including sound effects and, in Zorn's case, dialogue tracks and musique concrète—and string them together to create a coherent musical narrative. As Zorn points out in this interview with Philip Brophy, Stalling influenced both his compositional style and the way he came to appreciate the fundamental structure of music—showing that cartoon music isn't just for kids.

PHILIP BROPHY: What sort of pleasure do you get from Carl Stalling's music?

JOHN ZORN: The way it's all chopped up: that's what I respond to right away, have since I was young. There's an insatiable love for music. Anything gets thrown into the mix without any fear whatsoever of being a colonialist or a thief. He just takes and makes, that's what great composers do, what Igor Stravinsky did. "The great composer steals, the lesser composer borrows" is one of his great quotes. Stalling is a perfect example of someone able to use different quotes, different elements, sound effects, other peoples' music: Raymond Scott's, which was available in the Warner Bros. catalog at the time and was free.

Carl Stalling was a very different composer from Raymond Scott. Although he used elements and melodies from Scott, it's not unlike the way Charles Ives used American folk themes. Stalling's sense of time, his sense of narrative, completely revolutionized the idea of musical development. This was before the post-modern experiments. He created something completely new, and he did it in part in collaboration with people at Warner Bros. Studios, such as Milt Franklyn, who did the orchestration, and Treg Brown, who did sound effects; I assume that the directors of the cartoons had some input. Stalling is an interesting composer because he was a nine-to-fiver, he just did his job, he wasn't trying to make the great avant-garde music of the 1940s. He probably didn't even think of himself as a composer. From a young age he was playing for silent movies. That helped create his weird sense of musical logic. His music was always connected with a visual counterpart, and that guided the music to non-musical development, more a filmic sense of development. Themes never appear again: they happen once, then are thrown away when the gag is done. He's truly a visionary, even though he was self-deprecating. Directors thought the great thing Stalling did was to arrange Tchaikovsky. Not at all. What was great was his "mickey mousing," which functioned as the meat of the composition. This is still shockingly original.

PB: It's interesting you mentioned Treg Brown, because I've never been able to figure out the relationship between him and Stalling. It's hard to distinguish between the sound effects and the music score, almost like Satie's *Parade*. Violent percussive sounds become musicalized. Sometimes with Stalling's music you hear this "daroom boom" and wonder: what was the actual orchestration?

JZ: There are many different examples. I've seen Stalling's scores, and he had a very particular ear for sound and for orchestration. I know that Milt

Franklyn did a lot of the work. Quincy Jones didn't do his orchestration, and even Jerry Goldsmith, who is one of the great geniuses of film music, had Arthur Morton to do all his orchestration. They all worked very closely with an orchestrator. You do your job and then pass it onto someone else.

PB: You said something once that has always stuck in my mind. You were talking about the ear "growing tired of tape splices." When I read that, I thought of Varèse saying the opposite. It's a contradiction but linked; when he said the tape recorder was the thing that he was always waiting for . . .

JZ: We're talking about something different. Varèse was waiting for the tape recorder whether he liked tape splices or not. We're unsure if he would have been able to create works without using any tape splices. We don't know, maybe Stockhausen loved tape splices: this is speculation.

PB: The point I was making is that Stalling has got that organic tape splice effect in his music. . . .

JZ: Absolutely. He used tape splices, because the music was too complex to be able to perform it all the way through. The way he worked is like the way I work in the studio, doing sections at a time. But I have a multi-track at my disposal, and can keep it on one piece of tape without splicing. He would do sections at a time and then splice them together, pick the best takes and use a click track, which was one of his great inventions. The one luxury Stalling had, that I do not, was that he could do many takes and keep them all. . . . I can't keep them. I have to wait for the right take and then move on. I've got to make a decision. Keep it and move on, it's a trade-off. For me it works.

PB: In a way *Torture Garden* [1989] reminds me of Carl Stalling, because of the violence but also because of the bizarre comic sense.

JZ: I'm not going to lose that no matter how old I get. There's always going to be a weird sense of humor. Rather than violence, I'd say *extreme*. . . . There's something very extreme about *Torture Garden*. It's like taking the aesthetic of Carl Stalling to an even greater extreme. It's one of my most popular records; it's been used for Sega TV commercials, video games, for the past couple of years.

PB: Have you found with your music that it is dealing with a "cartoony" sensibility? By that I don't mean a kitsch, campy, nostalgic sensibility, but the actual structure and density and form of cartoons.

JZ: This is another interesting point—the difference between appreciating kitsch and appreciating art. I'm very serious about my approach to cartoon music, about my own music. But it doesn't mean that I can't put humor into it. It is very difficult to communicate with people. Humor is even more oblique, because it's not a word, it's a kind of a flavor. Humor goes right to the heart of the matter, it's very personal, and people get very upset. I can only be who I am, and do what I do. It's strange to be so serious about something like cartoons.

PB: Obviously you don't even consider that you are being serious about them.

JZ: I'm digging them! I'm digging them! But I'm digging them on another level than other people. It is a personal vision of another kind of music that never existed before, has never existed again and could never exist again. In the 1950s, Les Baxter experimented with all kinds of world instruments, strange time signatures, "wall paper." This man was a genius, as original as Igor Stravinsky or Anton Webern. I'm not anti-European-music—Berg is one of my absolute favorites. But there is an American sensibility, a maverick tradition of living in this crazy country and forging a vision out of rock. People who survive the tribulations a person with an original idea has to go through in this country are heroes. Stalling and Les Baxter are completely unknown. It's our duty to do something about that.

PB: Can you talk about your working relationship with the Kronos Quartet?

JZ: The piece I want to speak about is "Cat o' Nine Tails" [1993] which is subtitled "Tex Avery, Director, meets the Marquis de Sade." They really loved playing it. It was difficult for them because Stalling created many different mood and genre shifts, but kept the same tempo for most of the piece. Then he goes through these crazy shifts with "Cat o' Nine Tails" every few bars. For a small group, this is very difficult and it was a challenge to them. But they took it on very seriously and performed the piece wonderfully. They are really good at playing American music. Maybe it's part of the humor. They understand there's a wit there, there's something not European, not weighted down with centuries of history. Maybe I'll be criticized, but I can answer to my own conscience, and talk with my peers.

PB: Have you actually done any film scores. . . ?

JZ: They are very obscure little films. I have done some major ones too. I did *The Golden Boat* [1990], which is a Raoul Ruiz film. I did the original score for a film Walter Hill directed. It was interesting the way they pillaged what I had done for them. It was very inspiring in a certain way.

PB: Did you do anything for the Japanese films?

JZ: Yes, I did some Japanese cartoons. There's a cartoonist named Kiriko Kubo, who does *Cynical Hysterie Hour*. It's a hysterical play on American words and it's weird. She always had a dream of making a cartoon series in the Warner Bros. tradition, on that artistic level. She made a lot of money and decided that she would finance herself to do four seven-minute cartoons for shorts in movie theaters. It was a great project. I orchestrated four cartoons with slightly different groups. It was a nice opportunity. All my records come out on Japanese labels now, because I spent ten years there and I've developed a very good working relationship with three record companies there.

PB: John, is there an extensive musicography of what you have done?

JZ: It's funny you should mention that. There are these guys on the Internet . . . there's a Zorn thing on the Internet, they're maniacs. Those are the recent discographies . . .

Originally appeared in Kaboom!: Explosive Animation from America and Japan. *Sydney, Australia: Museum of Contemporary Art, 1994. © 1994 by Philip Brophy. Reprinted with permission.*

Rhapsody in Spew

Romantic Underscores in The Ren & Stimpy Show

by JOSEPH LANZA

LIKE A RAY of hope beaming through a forest of fur balls, the specter of romance haunts the gritty kitty world of Ren and Stimpy. Romance in this case takes the form of incongruously pretty music engineered to subvert an otherwise predictable regimen of slapstick sadism, relentless verbal assaults, and pukeworthy jokes about bodily functions.

Take, for example, a brief but poignant moment in the rarely seen episode, "Man's Best Friend" (1992). An obese, wild-eyed, "All-American" lout (the notorious George Liquor) purchases Ren and Stimpy from a pet store. Before using them as guinea pigs for bondage and discipline experiments, he gives his first lesson in tough love by cramming them into a goldfish bowl. The sight of these masochistic mammals squirming in their cramped quarters is all the more dreamlike with the added stimulus of lushly plucked strings, an acoustical pillow associated less with animal cruelty and more with images of 1950s-era honeymooners on a shopping spree.

There is a similar moment of backhanded beauty in "Rubber Nipple Salesmen" (1992). As he and Ren try to market their stock of synthetic teats, Stimpy looks up to a smiling sun and suddenly launches into an "I Have a Dream" speech, declaring that "one day everyone, everywhere will know the wonders of my nipples!" The ethereal soundtrack accessorizing this revelation offers another kind of epiphany—a confluence of violins and voices that connotes a soft-focus vignette of lovers prancing hand in hand through Elysian Fields.

Such all-too-brief interludes of sweetness and light show up quite frequently in the Ren and Stimpy oeuvre. On the surface, they are just further examples of "postmodern" irony—fashionable gags made at the expense of (what is at least perceived as) middle-class "kitsch." After repeated viewings (and listenings), however, such fragrant sound bytes offer that proverbial key to another dimension—an obverse twilight zone where everyday feelings of alienation and doom give way to glimpses of emotional utopia. This blend of nihilism and innocence raises nagging questions: Where does this music come from? And why do we have to swim through rivers of ironic snot to experience its splendor?

Musical hygiene has taken such a 180-degree turn in the past couple of decades that these silky contours—once the sound marks of hypernormal life—violate present-day canons of "modern" and "serious" music. In an age when most folks cannot stomach anything sweet without expecting the safe haven of a sour center, such creamy-on-the-melody alternatives are taboo. These sounds are unabashedly sentimental, have no jazz base, and, in some respects, truly do issue from another place and time. Almost all of the selections were recorded in the 1950s and early '60s and are the exclusive domain of production music libraries. Such libraries are storehouses of ready-made melodies (known in the business as "cues") that have enhanced the emotional palettes of feature films, television shows, radio and television commercials, and those "enlightening" industrial films made for grammar school kids during the Cold War's glory days.

Production music continues to be an under-explored cultural treasure. It represents a vast repertoire of emotions and sensations morphed into audio codes, all of them properly cataloged under numbers and titles and leased out to filmmakers and other image brokers wishing to avoid, or at least minimize, legal copyright hassles or exorbitant musicians' union fees. Here, some of the best background music comes from composers whose names do not ring an immediate bell and from distributors who usually make it their policy not to sell directly to the general listening public.

These "mood music" libraries carry styles to suit everything from thrillers to scholarly documentaries, but they are most fascinating for their more dulcet offerings—textures ranging from cascading strings and pizzicato flurries to pastoral woodwinds and burnished brass. This is music for the tender hours, and is not the customary zany-to-violent fare.

The term "mickey mousing" (filmmaking parlance for synchronizing music to action) indicates the degree to which animators have inspired directors to manipulate actors and props to the beat of brash and novel sound effects. (The slashing of the knife and the rhythm of the screeching fiddle in *Psycho* come to mind.) But *The Ren & Stimpy Show* was among the very first of today's smart cartoons to reverse this technique. Pairing Ren and Stimpy's frenetic activities with a romantic orchestra can best be described as "gale-storming"—a term this author invented in homage to the 1950s television star Gale Storm, yesteryear's doyenne of wholesome feminine fluff.

While mickey mousing makes people seem to move like cartoons, the art of gale-storming adds extra layers of subtext and human pathos to Ren and Stimpy's two-dimensional flatland. Even when Ren subjects George Liquor's face to a slo-mo pummel or Stimpy probes Ren's throat with a giant ladleful of "All-Purpose Icky Tasting Medicine," the buttery melodies are never far behind to tempt viewers with vague thoughts of a parallel world free from acrimony or foul odors.

Romantic movie music is, of course, the ideal criterion for stirring the emotions of both sexes to girly heights. Jazz has often been deployed to signal the presence of a whore or the spasms of a withdrawing junkie, but lushly orchestral cues have almost always proven crucial whenever the narrative gets "mushy," helping viewers to control their overworked smirk reflexes and to suspend disbelief. While great film composers like Max Steiner and Henry Mancini made screen history with such grand backdrops, production music libraries have offered similar fare by relatively anonymous orchestras and sold it according to time increments or "needle-drops."

In 1989, Ren and Stimpy's creator John Kricfalusi (or John K.) joined with Jim Smith, Lynne Naylor, Bob Camp, and other rebel animators to form Spümcø. Their purpose was to "make cartoons for *people* instead of *morons,*" and they relished the addition of honey-spun underscores for extra complexity. From the 1991 pilot episode "Big House Blues" onward, they got these cues from two prime sources: APM (Associated Production Music) and CPM (Capitol Production Music).

In recent years, APM has served as the American arm of Great Britain's KPM—the Xanadu of production music libraries. KPM (an acronym derived from the surnames of the company's main innovators, Robert Keith, William Prowse, and Peter Maurice) started a long time ago as a ticket selling firm, but it got into the background music trade in the mid-1950s. With selections arranged and composed by maestros including Laurie Johnson, King Palmer, and Jack Beaver, KPM was essentially the prime orchestrator of baby-boomer memories in both Great Britain and North America. In recent years, the same tunes have reemerged to entertain boomer babies on such campier-than-thou venues as Nick at Nite and *Late Night with Conan O'Brien*. Directors like the

Coen Brothers and Oliver Stone have also managed to include KPM treasures that many viewers also encountered (perhaps for the first time) during Ren and Stimpy's exploits.

There is, for example, "Happy-Go-Lively," an audio delight executed with a "let's go shopping" zeal that rouses thoughts of bejeweled dowagers beelining for a white sale. (The tune has also appeared on a TV ad for a Martha Stewart program.) It was a savvy choice for accenting the sprightly steps of Stimpy and Muddy Mudskipper as they ape the lo-tech style of running more suited to Hanna-Barbera characters. (The composer, Laurie Johnson, became best known for his background music to the 1960s television series *The Avengers* and for Stanley Kubrick's *Dr. Strangelove*.)

The contrast between action and underscore is quite vivid in gems like "The Boy Who Cried Rat" (1991), where the jolly jaunt tempo of King Palmer's "Holiday Playtime" accompanies Ren as he dons rodent drag and incites Stimpy into a Tom and Jerry chase. Later on, the dinnertime delight of Andrew Fenner's "Folli the Foal" sweetens the spectacle of Stimpy attempting to swallow Ren whole.

When helping to choose many of these KPM cues, John K. (a native Canadian) exercised the kind of frosty irony common to humorists of the more northerly persuasion. He was especially incisive when picking the right themes for Mr. and Mrs. Pipe, the missing-from-the-neck-up husband and wife suburbanites that occasionally creep into Ren and Stimpy's lives to alternately patronize and punish them. They invariably sound like "eeediots" as they banter about in the hollow lingo of couplese, leaving it to the bright and glamorous panache of Cyril Watters's "Crêpe Suzette" or Clive Richardson's "Gay Activity" to highlight their connubial follies.

Another prominent KPM selection is an elegant waltz tune by G. French (KPM often initialized the composers' Christian names in its catalogs) entitled "Fully Fashioned." Once tailored to evoke ballroom grandeur, it adds extra sumptuousness to a scene in "Nurse Stimpy" (1991) as Stimpy treats Ren's Pepto-Bismol-pink bottom to a "bubbly sponge bath." This same triple-layer treat in three-fourths time also ends up as an *anal*gesic in "Jiminy Lummox" (1992), a Spümcø story adapted by the company's successor, Games Animation, when Stimpy stretches his pajama bottoms over a rump laden with dangling crawfish.

The Games Animation episodes (which began around the fall of 1992) continued with the same "retro" sounds. The music of romance, forthrightly created to dignify human intimacy, becomes a backdrop for other inter-primate gross-outs in "Monkey See, Monkey Don't" (1992). The lilting strains of Peter Yorke's "Hollywood Romance" counterpoint Ren's descent into dementia as he pulls a chigger out from a macaque's back, stuffs it into his mouth, and barfs along to the dramatic crescendo.

Capitol Production Music, the second major source for *The Ren & Stimpy Show*'s underscores, started around 1951, when independent packagers convinced Capitol Records to represent such musical libraries as Mutel and Langlois. Capitol then assembled its own library in 1955 and commissioned its own bevy of composers. When Nelson Riddle initially turned down the offer to write and arrange some of these new cues, Capitol went to versatile composer William Loose who, with his collaborator John Seely, pounded out hundreds of tunes for Hi-"Q," one of the first Capitol libraries.

By 1957, Loose and Seely had their music on no less than twenty-four shows per week. They also collaborated with Sam Fox, Cadkin-Bluestone, Zephyr, and other production libraries that Capitol represented. These were the sources for much of the skip-happy backgrounds so familiar to fans of the original *Gumby Show*, as well as behind the antics of Huckleberry Hound, Quick Draw McGraw, and Yogi Bear. Ren and Stimpy watchers may also encounter a comfort blanket of violins from Loose's "On the Plaza."

As the Spümcø motto—"The Danes Call It Quality"—indicates, the ghosts of Denmark haunt Ren and Stimpy lore. A leading contender in Hamlet's gene pool is Danish composer, arranger, and entrepreneur Ole Georg. The company was formally known as Capitol Production Music by the time Ole Georg became the library's overseer in 1964. Since then, his name has appeared on the closing credits to many films for music that is now available from OGM (Ole Georg Music), the principal supplier of music to CPM for many years. He has spent his entire adult life in studios, perfecting the science of meticulously timed cues that have also appeared on animation favorites such as *Dilbert* and *Who Framed Roger Rabbit?*

"I come from a country where they invented Lego blocks," Ole Georg explains. "For me, music goes by the same principle. You build a score through small pieces and you have to equalize the sound. This was important when we worked in distant recording studios. We'd record in compatible keys so that we could edit from one studio to another."

Ole Georg also understands the vital need to retain a gentler, more romantic sound: "We live in such insecure times. We all tend to think about our childhood or early years when it was kind of safe and nice to be a human being. People associate this music with *The Adventures of Ozzie and Harriet*, security, home life, and family institutions. That's the reason we've made a point of cultivating this vintage catalog. No production library can be successful without one."

Ole Georg's OGM catalog has also embellished Ren and Stimpy with romantic themes of a more "classical" pedigree. There are snippets from Strauss's *Die Fledermaus* in "Big House Blues" (1991), Brahms's Lullaby in "Haunted House" (1992), and Debussy's "Prelude to the Afternoon of a Faun" in "Powdered Toast Man" (1992). And no Ren and Stimpy aficionado could forget the visual poetry in the "Yak Shaving Day" short (1991), when a hoary beast squirms out from a bathtub drain and proceeds to slide a razor across his face to the toe-tapping splendor of Tchaikovsky's "Dance of the Sugar Plum Fairy."

The time-tested selections from both KPM and CPM have one prime selling point: they were recorded with three-dimensional analog orchestras and full string sections. This is a rare luxury today, a situation due more to economic than aesthetic considerations. There was a time when hyper-electronic audio was touted as the music of the "future." But today, many are languishing in a cheaply digitized new world order full of synthesized strings that often sound more like reloading toilet tanks. "If you want to be authentic, you cannot do stuff like that," Ole Georg observes with concern. "The moment you go to synthesizers, the soul of the music is often down the drain. For *The Ren & Stimpy Show*, you have to have the music as it was recorded at that time: live, with all of the small, charming mistakes."

As of late, the same snooty art critics who once thumbed their noses at Norman Rockwell now find his work suitable for framing at the Guggenheim. Perhaps such changes of heart may set a precedent, to encourage more music critics to lend an appreciative ear to Ren and Stimpy's "happy happy, joy joy"—even if it means gulping spoonfuls of "shaving scum" to help the sugar go down.

Mr. Lanza would like to extend special thanks to John Mortarotti for his assistance and depth of knowledge in the production music field. Thanks also to The Spümcø Ren & Stimpy Archive: http://victorian.fortunecity.com/russell/105/spumrs.htm

JOHN KRICFALUSI

© John Kricfalusi

End Title

A Very Visual Kind of Music

The Cartoon Soundtrack Beyond the Screen

by JOHN CORBETT

"All great deeds and all great thoughts have a ridiculous beginning."
—Albert Camus

SOME OF THE broadest implications of cartoon music have nothing at all to do with animated images, but are the result of what happens when the visual content is removed altogether and the listener is left to grapple with the sounds on their own terms. This has been a latent aspect of cartoon soundtracks since their inception and standardization—something potentially evident to anyone who has turned away from the screen, even momentarily, but kept their ears tuned—but it has been brought more directly to the surface as a set of historical, artistic, and commercial music projects originating in the late 1970s. In these newer contexts, we can discern something independent from the functional category of music made to accompany cartoons, something perhaps best described as a cartoon music aesthetic.

In his 1942 essay "The Myth of Sisyphus," Albert Camus fixes on a peculiar image of human gesticulation in search of a definition of that keystone concept of existentialism, the absurd. "At certain moments of lucidity, the mechanical aspect of their gestures, their meaningless pantomime makes silly everything that surrounds them," he writes. "A man is talking on the telephone behind a glass partition; you cannot hear him, but you see his incomprehensible dumb show: you wonder why he is alive."[1]

What makes this imaginary man's movement absurd? His muteness, of course, the simple fact that the glass suppresses any sounds that might justify or explain his idiotic-seeming movements. The absurd is revealed through a disarticulation of the sound/image relationship: we can't hear the man's voice, which makes his motions seem haphazard and silly; furthermore, we can't hear the voice on the other end of the line, which presumably prompts him. His motions are arbitrary, they lack sufficient motivation, and seem over-the-top, wooden, and stilted because they have no explanatory sounds—or to be more precise, because while they do appear to have some auditory source of motivation, this source remains concealed. And through the obfuscation of motivation, the man's motions reveal their inherent artificiality. Here we find one of the primary texts of modern philosophy expressing one of its central concepts in terms of the denaturalization of audio and image connectedness. A silent, Merce Cunningham–like choreography of everyday gestures calculated to evoke the alienating feeling of seeing without hearing. The telephonist dancing behind the glass: a sound movie with no soundtrack.

The converse of this is also possible. Take a set of sounds that are motivated by a specific sequence of images, sounds designed to follow the contours of those images very precisely, and then remove the images: presto, instant alienation effect. In film soundtracks, a synaesthetic logic was long ago established that automatically links simultaneous images and sounds. This is a special relationship that film-sound theorist and electroacoustic composer Michel Chion dubbed "synchresis" (a combination of "synchronism" and "synthesis"), in which sounds and images are perceived as having an immediate and intractable connection, even when there is tenuous evidence to confirm such a relationship.[2] When sounds and images occur at the same time, they are perceived as having deep ontological kinship, and when that bond is broken, the separate component parts automatically seem foreign, strange, arbitrary, unnatural. Hence, the disarticulation of sound and image leads, in the audio register, to a sense of absurdity that is potentially as profound and disorienting as Camus's animated telephoner.

Seeds for the creation of a cartoon music aesthetic are sewn in this disarticulation, this fundamental disruption of the naturalized relationship between animation and the music that accompanies it. In many cartoon soundtracks, as in much narrative Hollywood cinema, music is not meant to draw attention to itself, but instead functions to enhance the visuals, to explain them or give them depth, shape, definition, to reinforce the appropriate mood or emotion. Except in special cases in which the music itself is made thematic (as in *What's Opera, Doc?*), the cartoon soundtrack exists as an adjunct to the images, as what Claudia Gorbman describes as "unheard melodies." The music is audible but not consciously attended to specifically because it inconspicuously conspires with the images to advance the narrative. If the music calls too much attention to itself, its artifice begins to show. It risks growing absurd (in Camus's sense of the word).

Gorbman writes: "To judge film music as one judges 'pure' music is to ignore its status as part of the collaboration that is the film. Ultimately it is the narrative context, the interrelations between music and the rest of the film's system, that determines the effectiveness of film music."[3] This is surely true if one's aim is an analysis of the film music *in situ*. However, film music has often existed outside of its "natural" habitat. Image-less film music is, in fact, the basis of an entire sub-market of the music industry: the soundtrack.[4] Soundtracks are sold independent of their images, but what we are interested in here is another kind of productive misreading or misappropriation, one in which music that has been created expressly to be experienced in tandem with an image track is separated and treated as a discrete aesthetic object. The chain can stop there, in the form of an alienated set of sounds, or this misreading and misappropriation can inspire the creation of new works based on the revealed logic of a soundtrack with absent images.

One of the things that differentiates the cartoon soundtrack from many other forms of narrative film music is the way it deals with the cut. Film music is most often designed to help disavow or "soften" cuts, to create a sense of seamlessness and continuity through what is essentially a violent and disruptive act of leaping from one time-space representation to another. Hence, many of the key film music conventions are meant to bridge gaps— between shots, scenes, segments—and create an overall sense of unity.[5] Cartoon soundtrack codes are largely based on film soundtrack codes, and they map these practices onto a medium in which the "cut" is actually a fiction created to simulate filmic cuts.[6] But in cartoons, some of the norms of music editing are also notably different; soundtracks tend to move at a very different pace—much faster—and are more sudden, drastic, and are very often cued directly to "cuts" in the image track. If you watch a Warner Bros. cartoon from the 1940s or '50s, most of the changes in the soundtrack occur in hard sync with visual edits. The practice of "mickey mousing," or creating audio isomorphs for visual events, further suggests the intimacy of sound/image links in classic cartoons.

If you do an experiment and view a conventional film segment—try, for instance, the first shark-attack scene in *Jaws*—with the sound turned off, one

of the first things that happens is that the film edit points become more evident. This makes sense, because it shows that the soundtrack is doing its job
of smoothing over discontinuities, setting mood, and making the action seem
all part of a whole. In the case of *Jaws*, the absence of a soundtrack makes the
sequence in fact almost illegible as narrative; it certainly removes the sense of
foreboding, the situation's logic and the terror of the intercuts between placid
beach and hostile ocean. Now, if you do the converse with a cartoon soundtrack and turn the screen off, you get a similar effect in another medium—
the sound edit points become much more prominent, often disconcertingly
so. In this case, the image provides a rationale for the manic shifting of sounds.

The most significant revelation in the development of a cartoon music
aesthetic is the realization that cuts are made invisible (better yet, inaudible,
or at least unrecognizable) through their synchronous relationship with the
image action. By eliminating the image, the quick edits float to the surface;
shifts in music (style, arrangement, orchestration, density, texture, dynamic,
tempo) become monstrous, impossible, dizzying, disorienting. In the absence
of a visual anchor or motivation, the rapid-fire changes in sound begin to do
something else: they take on a quality at a distance from the narrative (though
arguably still related to it) and acquire more than a little sense of the absurd.
Rick Altman has postulated that a "sound hermeneutic" exists in film soundtrack in which sounds tend to ask questions that are answered by images.[7] If
this is true, then a soundtrack with no images ends up posing a lot of unan-
swered questions. At the fast clip typical of cartoons, with music and sound
effects changing drastically all the time, it's more like a firing line.

To demonstrate the rapidity of changes in a typical cartoon soundtrack,
consider this verbal description of the major shifts in the first minute of Carl
Stalling's soundtrack for the Warner Bros. cartoon *Stage Fright* (1940). Begin:
frantic theme (three seconds); bang, followed by solo trombone with plunger
(six seconds); rapid upward orchestral arpeggio followed by single vibraphone
chord (three seconds); Russian march motif led by bassoon (four seconds);
out-of-tempo B-section of theme, with same instrumentation, punctuated
after four seconds by crash sound effect, then reiteration of A-section of theme
(eleven seconds); rapid upward orchestral arpeggio (half-a-second); solo violin with rustling sounds (one second); orchestral flourishes ending in upward
arpeggio (four seconds); solo viola, mournful and microtonal (three seconds);
hillbilly-like theme (four seconds); strings alone decelerating (four seconds);
woodwinds alone (four seconds); different hillbilly theme with pizzicato

strings (three seconds); interruption of theme by sinister one-note oboe and tympani, joined by strings (five seconds).

This shows how quickly the soundtrack changes character in this cartoon. But speed is a raw measurement, without regard for content. By adding narrative to the equation, we arrive at a more precise formulation for the cartoon aesthetic: suddenness. What is particular to this, then, is not simply the idea that edits happen every few seconds, but that music and sounds are constantly interrupting one another, interrupting themselves, cutting off flows, and breaking continuity. For our purposes, we can define the sudden as an abrupt change in consequence, a feeling that the narrative implies one direction but then denies or revokes that implication and starts off down another path. Often, in cartoons, this is accomplished thorough drastic contrasts, emphatic changes in things like timbre, type of sound (instrumental/sound effects), and especially dynamic. Sudden shifts from piano to fortissimo are part of what gets the blood racing while listening to a cartoon. Any resting point is provisional, and calm moments are always waiting to be perturbed. All these changes represent breaks in expectation, quick-time punctuated equilibrium.

Intertextuality is undoubtably part of the cartoon music aesthetic—shifting between styles or specific motifs, from sound effects to melodies and back. Cartoon soundtracks have in fact been productively analyzed in terms of their stylistic heterogeneity (as pastiche or collage), but they can also be assessed in relation to what they suggest formally and structurally (in terms of incongruity, discontinuity, atomization, and lack of an overarching dramatic logic). Since changes in a cartoon soundtrack are so often cued by changes in the image track, when the images are removed so is most of the motivation for those changes. Thus the changes sound arbitrary, like hyperactive jump-cuts. A jump-cut represents two shots that are too distant in space or time, or both, to be seamlessly edited together. In cartoon music aesthetics, soundtrack edit points are often likewise left showing, and the reason for cutting from one sound to another—the now-missing change in image—is rendered obscure, arbitrary. To link this to Camus's image of the absurd phone conversation, the observer is once again in a situation of disarticulation: the direct visual cue for any cartoon sound is missing (like the sound of the man on the phone) and the narrative rationale for that sound is also gone (like the person at the other end of the line).

This is not unlike Karlheinz Stockhausen's notion of "moment form" composition, in which the instant of an event is never meant to imply a subsequent one. The effect is one of atomization, intensification of the immediateness of each event, a lack of encompassing compositional framework, forward direction, and motivation, and hence a lack of any sense of a cumulative linear time line. When cartoon soundtracks are separated from their images, a similar effect is produced.[8] This cluster of concepts—suddenness, lack of motivation, absence of justifying master narratives, immediateness, jump-cutting, and, especially, intertextuality—has been central to many disparate musical developments over the last four decades. Eclecticism, postmodernism, and the cartoon music aesthetic have grown up together. In jazz, one need only mention the Art Ensemble of Chicago, Willem Breuker, and Carla Bley to conjure ideas of stylistic hybridity; in rock and pop, recent work by Boredoms and Beck, as well as vintage tracks by Brazil's Os Mutantes, Caetano Veloso, Tom Ze, and other tropicalia mainstays suggest a parallel development. And a great deal of the vitality of hip-hop comes from its sensitivity to intertextuality—like dub reggae, it's essentially a studio music. No surprise, perhaps, to find Schoolly D's hip-hop classic "Saturday Night" (1987) quoting the animated version of *The Three Little Pigs,* making a cartoon quotation into another intertext.

The kind of high-level alienation available in the cartoon music aesthetic attracted the attention of a number of experimental and improvising musicians in the 1970s, most notably among them John Zorn and Eugene Chadbourne. American free improvisors and composers with long and varied discographies, they performed together extensively during the late 1970s, and, according to fellow traveler Henry Kaiser, at that time they openly exchanged ideas and information about compositional strategies.[9] Guitarist Chadbourne's *There'll Be No Tears Tonight* (Parachute, 1980) is a set of classic country songs performed in a way that that he described as "free improvised country & western bebop." His treatment of a medley of Johnny Paycheck numbers delves into the cartoon aesthetic without direct reference; in places that would normally feature guitar breaks, the solos often take a sudden and incongruous leap away from the song, speeding up to a frenetic pace or diving away from the tonality of the tune into noises or textures, then abruptly rejoining the song where it might have been before it was so rudely interrupted.

Zorn played on other tracks on *There'll Be No Tears Tonight*. In his own early solo reed music, he used rapid changes and a pervasive sense of suddenness. This was faciliated by a vast collection of bird calls with which he augmented his alto saxophone and clarinet (often broken down into parts).

With these tools, Zorn was prepared to make very fast shifts between different timbres, textures, and qualities of sound, as is clearly evident on *The Classic Guide to Strategy*, issued as two volumes in 1983 and 1985, and later reissued as a single CD (Tzadik TZ 7305, 1996). The second side of the first volume was subtitled "Cartoon Music," and Zorn's game calls often sounded like direct quotations of specific cartoon characters, especially (for obvious reasons) Donald Duck. Zorn's solo guitar oeuvre *The Book of Heads*, originally written for and dedicated to Chadbourne in 1978 (later recorded by Marc Ribot), features equally manic shifts and use of cartoonish sound effects; one of the suite's etudes (dedicated to Dutch percussionist Han Bennink) includes the telling direction: "From one to the next as fast as possible."[10] Zorn's composition "Road Runner," written for accordionist Guy Klucevsek, sports images from a Road Runner cartoon collaged into the score.[11] Clearly, in these settings Zorn was thinking about the cartoon aesthetic in terms of its use of suddenness, the artistic qualities of narrative interruption.

> Sometimes I literally have a narrative going on in my head, because I'm thinking of a particular cartoon segment, or I'll follow the walking up the stairs and falling off a cliff, and the 'BAM!' And sometimes I specifically think like that, and I'm sure it must come through like that to some people. And other parts in which I'm not thinking like that at all, I'm sure they've got their own narratives working. It's a very visual kind of music.[12]

In the mid-80s, Zorn's music changed dramatically; where up to that point he had been using fragmented noises, he increasingly began to use fragmented stylistic references. For him, this meant throwing away the bird calls. As he explained in 1987:

> I'm not using calls anymore. I used them because I had this very fast music in my head; it moved very quickly and I was working with noises. Now I want to use genre as an equally valid material. Before, I was very proud of going through a whole concert without playing one note that was written. Now I feel like I want to include all kinds of genres.[13]

The projects that grew out of this turn to genre pastiche are some of Zorn's best-known, and they include the excellent transitional record *Locus Solus* (on which he's still using the game calls, but also flirting with rock and hip-hop genres), his extensive work with the band Naked City, his two out-standing studio collages using his "file card" system, *Godard* and *Spillane*, and the string quartet "Cat O' Nine Tails," perhaps his most directly cartoon-inspired piece.[14]

Another outgrowth of the emergent cartoon music aesthetic, fueled in part by Zorn's popular successes in this period, was the production and commercial release of some of Carl Stalling's work in two volumes of compiled tracks released on Warner Bros. in 1990 and 1995. The first of these two historical projects—both of which were coproduced by Greg Ford and Hal Willner—employed Zorn as a production consultant and included a short testimonial in liner notes written by him. Where Chadbourne and Zorn had taken inspiration and ideas from the cartoons, using intertextuality and discontinuity as improvisational and compositional devices, these cartoon music collections allowed listeners direct access to Stalling's work, without the images.

Thus the idea—unthinkable in the era(s) when the animations were created—of attending to cartoon music as a discrete, stand-alone aesthetic entity has been granted a sort of retroactive official legitimacy through commercial production. In his notes, Zorn praises Stalling's extremeness, compares him to Copland, Cage, Partch, Ellington, Parker, Gillespie, and Varèse, and describes his as "the music of our subconscious." Zorn's claim is true, however, because Stalling's music had previously operated at a subconscious level, without being brought to the foreground. The music's merrie melodies were unheard, their impact felt but left unrecognized, efficacious but not noteworthy. It doesn't detract from Stalling's creative genius—after all, there were plenty of uninteresting and less effective cartoon composers—to admit that what we now hear as his music's extremeness is, at least in part, an artifact of its being extracted from its original relationship with images and narrative.

As an interesting coda to this developing cartoon music aesthetic, in 1994 Bill Frisell, guitarist in Zorn's Naked City, composed music to accompany *Tales from the Far Side*, a TV version of Gary Larson's *The Far Side* comic strip. We've come full circle from the separation of sounds from moving images to the creation of music designed to help animate images that started life as still cartoons. Ironically, Frisell's dreamy, ambient music retreats to the background, emphasizing continuity, setting context and mood, and changing slowly and deliberately. His is more like a classical Hollywood movie soundtrack, suggesting cows, sheep and misbegotten people floating in a cloud of eerie Americana. The music is rarely cued directly to visual events. Only the sound effects are sudden. Frisell's *Far Side* is music for cartoons without the cartoon music aesthetic.

---

1 Albert Camus, *The Myth of Sisyphus and Other Essays*, trans. Justin O'Brien (New York: Vintage International, 1991 [1942]), pp. 14–15.

2 Some experimental filmmakers have attempted to make films in which simultaneous sounds and images are perceived as having no relationship. See, for instance, Michael Snow's *New York Eye & Ear*. The point is that it is quite difficult to produce the impression of material independence for sounds and images when they occur at the same time.

3 Claudia Gorbman, *Unheard Melodies: Narrative Film Music* (Bloomington: Indiana University Press, 1987), p. 12.

4 See, for example, the collection *Soundtrack Available: Essays on Film and Popular Music*, eds. Pamela Robertson Wojcik and Arthur Knight (Durham, NC: Duke University Press, 2001).

5 Gorbman, pp. 89–90.

6 This is simply to say that, for example, the structure of a shot/reverse shot in a cartoon is not necessitated by the medium the way it is in film, but is instead modeled directly on the already extant filmic convention. Thus, codes of continuity editing, which are obviously stretched in playful ways in cartoons, are nevertheless still taken as the starting point for the creation of a consistent time-space continuum in any given cartoon.

7 Rick Altman, "Moving Lips: Cinema as Ventriloquism," *Yale French Studies*, No. 60, Vol. 1 (1980), p. 74.

8 Soundtracks have created conditions for certain composers who are not prone to use unusual structures to take very interesting chances, working with form in unconventional ways; hear, for instance, Howard Rumsey's Lighthouse All-Stars playing Bob Cooper's score for the film *A Building Is Many Buildings* and Stan Getz's score for *Mickey One*.

9 Henry Kaiser, personal interview, 1993. Kaiser told me that Chadbourne initiated Zorn into multistylistic composition, something that he had initially resisted; the veracity of this statement is difficult to test.

10 Reprinted on the back of the liner booklet to *The Book of Heads*, Tzadik Records TZ 7009, 1995.

11 Reproduced in *John Zorn*, eds. Walter Rovere and Carla Chitti (Corso, Italy: Materiali Sonori Edizioni Musicali, 1998), plates xxiv and xxv.

12 John Zorn, in Rovere and Carla Chitti, p. 114.

13 Zorn, interview by Josef Woodard, "Zornography," in *Option*, July/August 1987, p. 36.

14 Zorn's own film music can be attended to as a discrete aesthetic object, too, since it has been exhaustively documented in a series of seven volumes on Tzadik; the final volume includes *Cynical Hysterie Hour*, his soundtrack for a Japanese cartoon.

Cartoon Music:

A Select Discography

BY GREG EHRBAR

THE LISTINGS BELOW are intended to complement the material in this volume and are by no means definitive, but should provide an overview of the recorded works by animation composers. All of the titles were commercially available at one time in the United States.

Carl Stalling

Mickey Mouse and His Friends *Disneyland* LPs DQ-1231 (1968)
This is the first LP to include Stalling's "Minnie's Yoo Hoo!" from *Mickey's Follies,* which was rerecorded in 1968 for the *Mickey Mouse Fortieth Anniversary TV Show.*
The Carl Stalling Project Warner Bros. LP 9 26027-2 (1990)
The Carl Stalling Project 2 Warner Bros. LP 9 45430-2 (1995)
That's All Folks!—Cartoon Songs from Merrie Melodies & Looney Tunes Rhino 2-CD Set R2-74271 (2001)

Sammy Timberg

Betty Boop Mark 56 LP (1974)
Betty Boop: Scandals of 1974 Mark 56 LP (1974)
Betty Boop: Boop-Boop-Be-Doop Pro-Arte CD CDD-440 (1989)

Walt Disney

Disney soundtracks were the first to appear on records, but they were reissued so many times we have included only selected releases and omitted non-soundtrack recordings. Some soundtracks were not commercially available until decades after the film premiere, so some titles are listed by album release rather than film release. For the most part, background score composers are listed. For more details, consult *The Golden Age of Walt Disney Records, 1933–1988* by R. Michael Murray (Krause Publications, 1997).

Snow White and the Seven Dwarfs (Churchill/Harline) RCA Victor 78 rpm J-8 (1937), Y-17 (1949); Disneyland LP WDL-4005 (1956), DQ-1201 (1959, 1963, 1968, 1987); Disney CD 60850-7 (1993)

Pinocchio (Smith/Harline) RCA Victor 78 rpm P-18 (1940), Y-349 (1947); Disneyland LP WDL-4002 (1956), DQ-1202 (1959, 1963, 1978); Disney CD 60845-2 (1992)

Who Killed Cock Robin? (Churchill) RCA Victor 78 rpm BK-5 (1940)

Lullaby Land (Harline/Churchill) RCA Victor 78 rpm BK-7 (1940)

The Pied Piper (Harline) RCA Victor 78 rpm BK-5 (1940)

Mickey's Grand Opera (Harline) / **The Orphan's Benefit** (Churchill) RCA Victor 78 rpm BK-8 (1940)

The Grasshopper and the Ants (Harline) / **Mickey's Moving Day** (Harline/Malotte) RCA Victor 78 rpm BK-5 (1940)

Three Little Wolves (Churchill) / **Three Little Pigs** (Churchill) RCA Victor 78 rpm BK-5 (1940)

Dumbo (Churchill/Wallace) RCA Victor 78 rpm Y-350 (1941); Disneyland LP WDL-4013 (1957), DQ-1204 (1959); Disney CD 60949-7(1997)

Three Little Pigs/Orphan's Benefit Victor 78 rpm Y-1 (1944), Y-32 (1949)

Bambi (Churchill/Wallace/Plumb) RCA Victor 78 rpm Y-391 (with dialogue, 1949); Disneyland LP WDL-4010 (1957), DQ-1203 (1959, 1963, 1978, 1987); Disney CD 60880-7(1996)

Lady and the Tramp (Wallace) Studio & Soundtrack Songs: Decca 10" LP DL-5557 (1955), 12" LP DL-8462 (1957), Disney Picture Disc 3103 (1980); Full Soundtrack: Disney CD 60951-7 (1997)

Song of the South (Uncle Remus) (Amfitheatrof/Smith) Disneyland LP WDL-4001 (1956), DQ-1205 (1959, 1963)

Los Tres Caballeros (Spanish only) Disneylandia PA-ST-3000 (c.1956), WDL-1039 (1958), 1239M (1978)

Fantasia Disneyland LP WDX-101 (1957), STER-101 (1961, 1982); Disney CD 600072 (1990)

Cinderella (Wallace/Smith) Disneyland LP DQ-1207 (1959, 1963, 1987); Disney CD 60879-7 (1996)

Peter Pan (Wallace) Disneyland LP DQ-1206 (1959, 1963, 1976); Disney CD 60958-7 (1997)

Sleeping Beauty (Bruns) Disneyland LP WDL/STER-4018 (1959), Buena Vista STER-4036 (1970); Disney CD 60881-7 (1996)

Mary Poppins (Sherman/Sherman/Kostal) Buena Vista LP STER-4026, RCA Victor COP/CSO-111 (1964), 5005 (1973); Disney CD 016 (1989)

The Jungle Book (Bruns) Buena Vista LP BV/STER-4041 (1967), Disneyland ST/STER-3948; Disney CD 606122 (1990)

Alice in Wonderland (Wallace) Disney CD 60960-7 (1997)

101 Dalmatians (Bruns) Disney CD 60654-7 (1998)

The following is not the original soundtrack, which no longer exists, but is a later recording of the same music:

Four Alice Comedies (Dessau) RCA Victor Red Seal (Germany) CD 09026-68144 2 (1996)

Notable Disney Compilations

Walt Disney's Music Cavalcade Includes excerpts from *Steamboat Willie* (P.D./Jackson), *The Old Mill* (Harline), *The Skeleton Dance* (Stalling), and *The Band Concert* (Harline/P.D.) Disneyland LP WDL/STER-4021 (1959)

The Magical Music of Walt Disney Includes excerpts from the shorts *Mickey's Follies* (Stalling), *Delivery Boy, Blue Rhythm, The Whoopie Party* (Churchill), *Mickey's Gala Premiere* (Churchill), *Mickey's Grand Opera* (Harline), *Symphony Hour* (Wolcott), *Building a Building* (Churchill), and snippets from the features *The Reluctant Dragon, Saludos Amigos, The Three Caballeros, Make Mine Music, Melody Time,* and *Fun and Fancy Free,* plus previously unreleased material from other features, all from direct soundtracks with assorted titles, dialogue, and sound effects. Ovation LP OV-5000 (1978)

The Disney Collection, Vols. 1 & 2 The first commercial release of soundtrack songs from *So Dear to My Heart, Saludos Amigos* (complete title song), and *The Mickey Mouse Club* animated titles (Dodd). Disney CD-002, 003 (1987)

Scott Bradley

Tex Avery Cartoons Milan CD 73138 35635-2 (1993)
Complete soundtracks of the MGM classics *Cell Bound, Little Johnny Jet, TV of Tomorrow, Three Little Pups, Deputy Droopy*, and *Dragalong Droopy.*

Winston Sharples

The Harvey Comics Collectibles Box Set EDEL America CD Set 037142EDL (1997)
An impressive set that comprises comic book reprints; a booklet by Jerry Beck, Andrew Lederer, and Will Friedwald; and two enhanced CDs, which contain (not nearly enough) theme music from Harvey/Famous cartoons.

Darrell Calker / Gordon Zahler

Woody Woodpecker's Family Album Decca LP DL-8659 (c.1950s)
Woody Woodpecker and His Friends Peter Pan LP1120 (1981)
Woody Woodpecker Golden LP-112 (1962); Drive CD GD-47112 (1998)

Phil Scheib

TV Terrytoons Cartoon Time RCA Bluebird LBY-1031 (1959)
Deputy Dawg RCA Camden LP CAL-1048 (c. 1960)
The Hector Heathcote Show RCA Camden CAL/CAS-1053 (1964)
The Adventures of Mighty Mouse Peter Pan LP 8200 (1977)
The New Adventures of Mighty Mouse Peter Pan LP 1118 (1980)

Hoyt Curtin

Here Comes Huckleberry Hound Colpix LP CP-207 (c. 1960)
Mr. Jinks, Pixie, and Dixie Colpix LP CP-208 (c. 1960)
The Flintstones Colpix LP CP-302 (1960)
The Jetsons Colpix LP CP-213 (1962)
Top Cat Colpix LP CP-212 (1963)

The above five albums contained two or more soundtracks from Hanna-Barbera shows, using the existing background scores or reedited with Curtin/Hanna-Barbera stock music.

Quarry Stone Rock/A Night in Bedrock Forest B-H 45 rpm BH-61-001 (c. 1960)

Songs of the Flintstones Golden LP-61 (1961)

"Meet the Flintstones" originated on this LP before it became the series theme. Includes the immortal "Car Hop Song." Most of the music on this album became TV background music sans the vocals.

Super Snooper and Blabbermouse: Monster Shindig Hanna-Barbera LP HLP-2020 (1965)

The Flintstones: Flip Fables Hanna-Barbera LP HLP-2021 (1965)

Huckleberry Hound: Stories of Uncle Remus Hanna-Barbera LP HLP-2022 (1965)

Yogi Bear and Boo-Boo: Little Red Riding Hood / Jack and the Beanstalk Hanna-Barbera LP HLP-2023 (1965)

Magilla Gorilla: Alice in Wonderland Hanna-Barbera LP HLP-2024 (1965)

Pixie and Dixie with Mr. Jinks: Cinderella Hanna-Barbera LP HLP-2025 (1965)

Snagglepuss: The Wizard of Oz Hanna-Barbera LP HLP-2026 (1965)

Wilma Flintstone: Bambi Hanna-Barbera LP HLP-2027 (1965)

Doggie Daddy and Augie Doggie: Pinocchio Hanna-Barbera LP HLP-2028 (1965)

Touché Turtle and Dum-Dum: The Reluctant Dragon Hanna-Barbera LP HLP-2029 (1965)

Jonny Quest: 20,000 Leagues Under the Sea Hanna-Barbera LP HLP-2030 (1965)

Top Cat: Robin Hood Hanna-Barbera LP HLP-2031 (1965)

Gemini IV: Walk in Space/Gemini V: Eight Days in Space Hanna-Barbera LP HLP-2034 (1965)

The Flintstones: Songs from Mary Poppins Hanna-Barbera LP HLP-2035 (1965)

Super Snooper and Blabbermouse: James BOMB Hanna-Barbera LP HLP-2036 (1965)

The Jetsons: First Family on the Moon Hanna-Barbera LP HLP-2037 (1965)

The Flintstones: Hansel and Gretel Hanna-Barbera LP HLP-2038 (1965)

Sinbad, Jr.: Treasure Island Hanna-Barbera LP HLP-2039 (1965)

Atom Ant: Muscle Magic Hanna-Barbera LP HLP-2041 (1965)

Winsome Witch: It's Magic Hanna-Barbera LP HLP-2042 (1965)

The Hillbilly Bears: Hillbilly Shindig Hanna-Barbera LP HLP-2044 (1965)

Precious Pupp and Granny Sweet: Hot Rod Granny Hanna-Barbera LP HLP-2045 (1965)

Secret Squirrel and Morocco Mole: Super Spy Hanna-Barbera LP HLP-2046 (1965)

The Flintstones: S.A.S.F.A.T.P.O.B.S.Q.A.L.T. Hanna-Barbera LP HLP-2047 (1966)

Yogi Bear and the Three Stooges: The Mad, Mad Dr. No-No Hanna-Barbera LP HLP-2050 (1966)

The New Alice in Wonderland, or What's A Nice Kid Like You Doing in a Place Like This? Hanna-Barbera LP HLP-2051 (1966)

The Flintstones and José Jiminez: The Time Machine Hanna-Barbera LP HLP-2052 (1966)

William Castle: The Tell-Tale Heart Hanna-Barbera LP HLP-2056 (1966)

G. I. Joe: The Green Berets Hanna-Barbera LP HLP-2057 (1966)

The above Hanna-Barbera Cartoon Series LPs generally followed a format of original story material, some pop-style songs, and existing Hanna-Barbera stock music by Hoyt Curtin and Ted Nichols.

Hear/See/Do Hanna-Barbera Record of Safety Pickwick / Baker-Rhodes Marketing LP (1973)

An oddball, with voice actor legends performing their signature characters plus those usually done by others, with Curtin/Hanna-Barbera library music.

Heidi's Song K-Tel NU-5310, K-Tel Picture Disc NU-5320 (1982)

Hanna-Barbera's Christmas Sing-a-Long Kid Rhino CD R2-70450 (1991)

The second half of this recording consists of latter-day Curtin/Hanna-Barbera compositions from various holiday TV specials and made-for-TV movies.

The Flintstones: Modern Stone-Age Melodies Rhino R2-71649 (1994)

The Flintstones Story Kid Rhino Cassette R4-71627 (1994)

Hanna-Barbera Classics Rhino R2-71886 (1995)

Hanna-Barbera's Pic-A-Nic Basket of Cartoon Classics Rhino R2-72290 (1996)

Cartoon Classics and Wacky Sounds by Hanna-Barbera Rhino Special Products 3-CD Set R2-79808 (1994)
Battle of the Planets Super Tracks STCD-603 (2001)

Maury Laws

The New Adventures of Pinocchio FTP LP MLP-7002 (1961)
Rudolph, the Red-Nosed Reindeer Decca LP DL74815 (1964); MCA CD MCAD-22177
The Daydreamer Columbia LP OL/OS-2070 (1966)
Original TV Adventures of King Kong Epic LP BN/LN-24231 (1966)
Cricket on the Hearth RCA Victor LP (1967)
Santa Claus is Comin' to Town MGM LP SE-4732 (1970)
Frosty the Snowman MGM LP SE-4733 (1970)
'Twas the Night Before Christmas Disneyland LP 1367 (1976)
Frosty's Winter Wonderland Disneyland LP 1368 (1976)
The Hobbit Disneyland LP 3819 /Buena Vista LP Set 103 / LP 5007 (1977)
The Return of the King Disneyland LP 3822 (1980)
Rudolph, Frosty, and Friends' Favorite Christmas Songs Sony Wonder CD LK-67766 (1996)
Mad Monster Party Retrograde/Percepto CD FSM-80125-2 (1999)

Cartoon Pop Groups

Let's All Sing with the Chipmunks Liberty LP LST-7132 (1961)
Sing Again with the Chipmunks Liberty LP LST-7159 (1961)
Around the World with the Chipmunks Liberty LP LST-7170 (1961)
The Alvin Show Liberty LP LST-7209 (1961)
The Chipmunk Songbook Liberty LP LST-7229 (1962)
The Banana Splits Decca LP DL-75075 (1968); HB Premium Division 45 rpm 34578 & 34579 (1968)
The Beagles Harmony HS-14561 (1968)
The Archies Calendar LP KES-101 (1968)
Everything's Archie Kirshner LP KES-103 (1969); RKO CD RKO-1024 ("The Archies") (1999)

Jingle Jangle Kirshner LP KES-105 (1969); RKO CD RKO-1029 ("Archie's Party") (1999)

Here Come the Hardy Boys RCA Victor LP LSP-4217 (1969)

The Hardy Boys: Wheels RCA Victor LP LSP-4315 (1969)

Cattanooga Cats Forward LP ST-F-1018 (1969)

Hot Wheels Forward LP ST-F-1023 (1969)

Sunshine Kirshner LP KES-107 (1970)

Globetrotters Kirshner KES 108 (1970)

The Archies Greatest Hits Kirshner LP KES-109 (1970)

This Is Love Kirshner LP KES-110 (1970)

Josie and the Pussycats Capitol LP ST-665 (1970)

Doctor Dolittle Presents the Grasshoppers Carousel/Bell LP CAR-3504 (1970)

Groovie Goolies RCA LSP-4420 (1971)

Presenting the Sugar Bears Big Tree LP BTS-2009 (1971)

Fat Albert and the Cosby Kids Paramount (1973)

Mission Magic (Rick Springfield) Wizard Records (1974, Australia release only)

Rock 'n' Roll Disco with Fat Albert and the Junkyard Band Kid Stuff 094 (1980)

Fat Albert & the Cosby Kids: Halloween Kid Stuff KS-029 (1980)

Creativity Starring Fat Albert and the Cosby Kids Kid Stuff KS-021 (1980)

The Chipmunks: Songs from Our TV Shows IJE LP-3300 (1984)

Josie and the Pussycats: Stop Look and Listen—The Capitol Recordings Rhino Handmade CD RHM2-7783 (2001)

Contemporary Composers

Richard Stone

Tiny Toon Adventures Warner Bros. Cassette (1992)

Animaniacs Kid Rhino CD R2-71570 (1993)

Animaniacs: Yakko's World Kid Rhino CD R2-71763 (1994)

Animaniacs: Variety Pack Kid Rhino CD R2-72181 (1995)

Animaniacs: A Hip-Opera Christmas Kid Rhino R2-72647 (1997)

Alf Clausen

Songs in the Key of Springfield Rhino CD R2-72775 (1997)
Go Simpsonic with The Simpsons Rhino CD R2-75480 (1999)

Mark Mothersbaugh

Musik for Insomniaks, Volume 1 Enigma 73365 (1988)
Musik for Insomniaks, Volume 2 Enigma 73366 (1988)
Rugrats the Movie Casual Tonalities CD XOCD-9943 (1998)

John Zorn

Manhattan Cascade (Guy Klucesvek) Composers 626 (1991, "Roadrun-
    ner")
Short Stories (Kronos Quartet) Nonesuch 79310 (1993, "Cat O' Nine
    Tails")
The Book of Heads Tzadik 7009 (1995)
The Classic Guide to Strategy Tzadik 7305 (1996)
Film Works, Vol. 7: Cynical Hysterie Hour Tzadik 7315 (1997)
Grand Guignol Avant 2 (1998, "Torture Garden")
Cartoons / S & M Tzadik CD 7330 (2000)

Other Cartoons

Ren & Stimpy: You Eediot! Sony CD LK-57400 (1991)
Ren & Stimpy: Radio Days Sony CD LK-66510 (1995)
Pinky and the Brain: Bubba Bo Bob Brain (Craig Bartock) Kid Rhino CD
    R2-72636 (1997)

Compilations

Cartoon Classics: Classical Favorites from Classic Cartoons RCA Victor
    60738 (1992)
Mad About Cartoons: Over 70 Minutes of Digital Madness Deutsche Gram-
    mophon 39515 (1993)

Greatest Hits: Cartoons Sony Classics 62368 (1996)

Three collections of classical works most frequently featured in cartoons. These are *not* soundtrack recordings from the cartoons, but rather standard repertoire recordings.

Tunes from the Toons Pro-Arte CD CDD-3400 (1991)

Billboard **Presents Family Christmas Classics** Kid Rhino CD R2-72171 (1995)

Nick at Nite Presents a Classic Cartoon Christmas Sony CD BK-67764 (1996)

Toon Tunes R-Kive/Kid Rhino/Razor & Tie CD R2-72528 (1996)

Toon Tunes Kid Rhino CD R2-72752 (1997)

Nick at Nite Presents A Classic Cartoon Christmas, Too Sony CD CD BK-63448 (1997)

Tunes from the Toons: The Best of Hanna-Barbera Empire Music (UK) (1999)

Toon Tunes: Funny Bone Favorites Kid Rhino CD R2-74336 (2001)

Toon Tunes: Action-Packed Anthems Kid Rhino CD R2-74337 (2001)

Bibliography

Books or articles on cartoon music or cartoon composers

Barrier, Michael, Milton Gray, and Bill Spicer. "An Interview With Carl Stalling." *Funnyworld* 13 (Spring 1971), 21–29.

Bond, Jeff. "Tiny Tune Titans." *Film Score Monthly* Volume 4, Number 7 (August 1999), 22–28.

———. "Yabba Dabba Crew: Working with Hoyt Curtin at Hanna-Barbera." *Film Score Monthly* Volume 6, Number 4 (April/May 2001), 20–23.

Bradley, Scott. "Cartoon Music of the Future." *Pacific Coast Musician* (June 21, 1941), 28.

———. "Evoluzione della musica nei disegni animati." In *Music e film*, edited by S. G. Biamonte. Rome: Edizioni dell'Ateneo, 1959.

———. " 'Music in Cartoons,' Excerpts from a talk given at The Music Forum October 28, 1944." *Film Music Notes* IV:III (Dec. 1944), np.

———. "Open Forum." *Hollywood Reporter* (28 October, 1946), 10.

———. "Personality on the Sound Track: A Glimpse Behind the Scenes and Sequences in Filmland." *Music Educators Journal* XXXIII:3 (January 1947), 28–30.

Brophy, Philip. "The Animation of Sound." In *The Illusion of Life: Essays on Animation,* edited by Alan Cholodenko. Sydney: Power Publications, 1991.

Care, Ross B. "The Film Music of Leigh Harline," *Film Music Notebook* 3:2 (1977), 32–48.

———. "Symphonists for the Sillies: The Composers for Disney's Shorts." *Funnyworld* 18 (Summer 1978), 38–48.

———. "Threads of Melody: The Evolution of a Major Film Score—Walt Disney's *Bambi*." In *Wonderful Inventions: Motion Pictures, Broadcasting, and Recorded Sound at the Library of Congress*, edited by Iris Newsom. Washington: Library of Congress, 1985.

Carroll, Joe. "Sound Strategies." *Animatrix* 7 (1993), 31–36.

Chusid, Irwin. "Carl Stalling: Music to Toon By." *Animation Magazine* 31 (October/November 1994), 74–75.

Curtis, Scott. "The Sound of the Early Warner Bros. Cartoons." In *Sound Theory, Sound Practice,* edited by Rick Altman. New York: Routledge, 1992.

Dahl, Ingolf. "Notes on Cartoon Music." *Film Music Notes* 8:5 (May–June 1949), 3–13.

Danly, Linda. "Buddy Baker: An Appreciation." *The Cue Sheet* 13 (Jan 1997), 4–23.

Ford, Greg. Brochure notes for Carl Stalling, *The Carl Stalling Project: Music From Warner Bros. Cartoons 1936–1958* (Warner Bros. Records 26027), 1990.

Friedwald, Will. "Winston Sharples: Cat and Mouse Melodies and Haunting Refrains." In *The Harvey Cartoon History*, edited by Jerry Beck. New York: Harvey Comics, Inc., 1997.

Goldmark, Daniel. "Carl Stalling and Humor in Cartoons." *Animation World Magazine* 2:1 (April 1997), np.

———. ". . . And That's Not All Folks!" Brochure notes for *Warner Bros. 75 Years of Film Music* (Rhino Records 75287), 1998.

———. *Happy Harmonies: Music and the Hollywood Animated Cartoon.* Ann Arbor: UMI Dissertation Services, 2001.

Grant, Barry Keith. " 'Jungle Nights in Harlem': Jazz, Ideology, and the Animated Cartoon." *University of Hartford Studies in Literature* 21:3 (1989), 3–12.

Guernsey, Otis L., Jr. "The Movie Cartoon is Coming of Age." *Film Music Notes* 13:2 (Nov–Dec 1953), 21–22.

Jones, Chuck. "Music and the Animated Cartoon." *Hollywood Quarterly* 1:4 (July 1946), 363–370.

Kaufman, J. B. " Who's Afraid of ASCAP?: Popular Songs in the Silly Symphonies." *Animation World Magazine* 2:1 (April 1997), np.

Kennicott, Philip. What's Opera Doc?: Bugs Bunny Meets the Musical Masters." *Classical* 3:1 (January 1991), 18–24.

Kremenliev, Boris. "The Tell-Tale Heart." *Film Music* XIII:IV (March–April 1954), 11–15.

Malotte, Albert Hay. "Film Cartoon Music." In *Music and Dance in California*, edited by José Rodriguez. Hollywood: Bureau of Musical Research, 1940.

Martin, Donald. "Two Outstanding Films with Music." *The Etude* LVIII:12 (December 1940), 805, 846.

McLaren, Norman. "Notes on Animated Sound." *The Quarterly Journal of Film, Radio, and Television* VII:3 (Spring 1953), 223–229.

Mellot, Albert. "*The Two Mouseketeers* with Score Excerpts." *Film Music Notes* XI:V (May–June 1952), 9–11.

Morton, Lawrence. "Film Music Profile—Leigh Harline." *Film Music Notes* IX:IV (March–April 1950), 13–14.

Newsom, Jon. "'A Sound Idea': Music for Animated Films." *The Quarterly Journal of the Library of Congress* 37:3–4 (Summer–Fall 1980), 279–309.

Patten, Frederick. "All Those Japanese Animation Soundtracks." *Cinema Score* 15 (Winter 1986–Summer 1987), 135–139.

Redewill, Helena Munn. "Laugh and the World Laughs (An Interview)." *The Triangle* (February 1932), 91–94.

Sanjek, David. "No More Mickey-Mousing Around." In *Kaboom!: Explosive Animation from America and Japan.* Sydney: Power Publications, 1994.

Sartin, Hank. "From Vaudeville to Hollywood, from Silence to Sound: Warner Bros. Cartoons of the Early Sound Era." In *Reading the Rabbit: Explorations in Warner Bros. Animation,* Kevin Sandler, editor. New Brunswick, New Jersey: Rutgers University Press, 1998.

Smith, Paul J. "The Music of the Walt Disney Cartoons: A Conference with Paul J. Smith." *The Etude* LVIII:7 (July 1940), 438, 494.

Steele, R. Vernon. "Scoring for Cartoons: An Interview with Scott Bradley." *Pacific Coast Musician* (May 15, 1937), 12–13.

Sternfeld, Frederick W. "Kubik's McBoing Score." *Film Music Notes* X:II (Nov–Dec 1950), 8–16.

Strauss, Neil. "Animated Rhythms: Tunes for Toons." *Ear Magazine* 3 (July–August 1989), 14–15.

Tebbel, John R. "Looney Tunester." *Film Comment* 28:5 (Sept–Oct 1992), 64–66.

Tietyen, David. *The Musical World of Walt Disney.* Milwaukee: Hal Leonard Publishing Corporation, 1990.

"Tubby the Tuba," *Film Music Notes* VII:I (Sept–Oct 1947).

Vincentelli, Elisabeth. "Merrie Melodies: Cartoon Music's Contemporary Resurgence." *The Village Voice* (March 3, 1998), 59.

Winge, John H. "Cartoons and Modern Music." *Sight and Sound* 17:67 (Autumn 1948), 136–137.

Books or articles on animation that mention music

Adamson, Joe. *Bugs Bunny: Fifty Years and Only One Grey Hare.* New York: Henry Holt and Company, 1991.

Allan, Robin. *Walt Disney and Europe: European Influences on the Animated Feature Films of Walt Disney.* Bloomington and Indianapolis: Indiana University Press, 1999.

Barbera, Joe. *My Life in 'Toons.* Atlanta: Turner Publishing, Inc., 1994.

Barrier, Michael. *Hollywood Cartoons: American Animation in Its Golden Age.* New York: Oxford University Press, 1999.

Bashe, Philip, and Mel Blanc. *That's Not All Folks!* New York: Warner Books, 1988.

Beck, Jerry, and Will Friedwald. *Looney Tunes and Merrie Melodies: A Complete Illustrated Guide to the Warner Bros. Cartoons.* New York: Henry Holt and Company, 1989.

Brion, Patrick. *Tom and Jerry.* New York: Harmony Books, 1990.

Burke, Timothy, and Kevin Burke. *Saturday Morning Fever: Growing Up with Cartoon Culture.* New York: St. Martin's Griffin, 1999.

Cabarga, Leslie. *The Fleischer Story,* 2nd edition. New York: Da Capo Press, 1988.

Canemaker, John. *Felix: The Twisted Tale of the World's Most Famous Cat.* New York: Pantheon Books, 1991.

———. *Tex Avery.* Atlanta: Turner Publishing, Inc., 1996.

Culhane, John. *Walt Disney's* Fantasia. New York: H. N. Abrams, 1983.

———. Fantasia 2000: *Visions of Hope.* New York: Disney Editions, 1999.

Freleng, Friz, and David Weber. *Animation: The Art of Friz Freleng.* Newport Beach, CA: Donovan Publishing, 1994.

Friedwald, Will, and Jerry Beck. *The Warner Brothers Cartoons.* Metuchen & London: Scarecrow Press, 1981.

Furniss, Maureen. *Art in Motion: Animation Aesthetics.* London: John Libbey & Co., 1998.

Gimple, Scott M., editor. *The Simpsons Forever! A Complete Guide to Our Favorite Family . . . Continued.* New York: HarperPerennial, 1999.

Heraldson, Donald. *Creators of Life: A History of Animation.* New York: Drake Publishers, Inc., 1975.

Jones, Chuck. *Chuck Amuck.* New York: Avon Books, 1989.

———. *Chuck Reducks: Drawing from the Fun Side of Life.* New York: Warner Books, 1996.

———. "What's Up, Down Under? Chuck Jones Talks at *The Illusion of Life* Conference." In *The Illusion of Life: Essays on Animation*, edited by Alan Cholodenko. Sydney: Power Publications, 1991.

Leskosky, Richard J. "The Reforming Fantasy: Recurrent Theme and Structure in American Studio Cartoons." *The Velvet Light Trap* 24 (Fall 1989), 53–66.

Lutz, E. G. *Animated Cartoons: How They Are Made, Their Origin, and Development.* Bedford, Massachusetts: Applewood Books, 1920, rep. 1998.

Maltin, Leonard. *Of Mice and Magic: A History of American Animated Cartoons.* New York: Plume Books, 1987.

Merritt, Russell, and J. B. Kaufman. *Walt in Wonderland: The Silent Films of Walt Disney.* Perdenone, Italy: Le Giornate del Cinema Muto, 1992.

Richmond, Ray, and Antonia Coffman, editors. *The Simpsons: A Complete Guide to Our Favorite Family.* New York: HarperPerennial, 1997.

Russett, Robert, and Cecile Starr. *Experimental Animation: An Illustrated Anthology.* New York: Van Nostrand Reinhold Co., 1976.

Sampson, Henry T. *That's Enough, Folks: Black Images in Animated Cartoons, 1900–1960.* Lanham, Maryland: The Scarecrow Press, Inc., 1998.

Sandler, Kevin, editor. *Reading the Rabbit: Explorations in Warner Bros. Animation.* New Brunswick, New Jersey: Rutgers University Press, 1998.

Sartin, Hank. *Drawing on Hollywood: Warner Bros. Cartoons and Hollywood, 1930–1960.* Ann Arbor: UMI Dissertation Services, 1998.

Schneider, Steve. *That's All Folks!: The Art of Warner Bros. Animation.* New York: Henry Holt and Company, 1988.

Stephenson, Ralph. *The Animated Film.* San Diego, New York: A. S. Barnes and Co., 1973.

———. *Animation in the Cinema.* New York: A. S. Barnes and Co., 1967.

Taylor, Deems. *Walt Disney's Fantasia.* New York: Simon and Schuster, 1940.

Wells, Paul. *Understanding Animation.* New York: Routledge, 1998.

Books or articles on film music that mention animation

Anderson, Gillian B. *Music for Silent Films 1894–1929*. Washington, Library of Congress, 1988.

Berg, Charles Merrell. "Cinema Sings the Blues." *Cinema Journal* 17:2 (1978), 1–12.

Burlingame, Jon. *TV's Biggest Hits: The Story of Television Themes from Dragnet to Friends*. New York: Schirmer Books, 1996.

Evans, Mark. *Soundtrack: The Music of the Movies*. New York: Da Capo Press, 1979.

Feisst, Sabine M. "Arnold Schoenberg and the Cinematic Art." *The Musical Quarterly* 83:1 (Spring 1999), 93–113.

Gabbard, Krin. *Jammin' at the Margins: Jazz and the American Cinema*. Chicago: University of Chicago Press, 1996.

Gorbman, Claudia. *Unheard Melodies: Narrative Film Music*. Bloomington: Indiana University Press, 1987.

Lang, Edith, and George West. *Musical Accompaniment of Moving Pictures*. Boston: Boston Music Co., 1920; reprint New York: Arno Press & The New York Times, 1970.

London, Kurt. *Film Music*. London: Faber & Faber Ltd., 1936; reprint New York: Arno Press & The New York Times, 1970.

Lowan, Lester, editor. *Recording Sound for Motion Pictures*. New York & London: McGraw-Hill Book Company, Inc., 1931.

Manvell, Roger, and John Huntley. *The Technique of Film Music*. New York: Hastings House, 1975.

McCarty, Clifford. *Film Composers in America: A Filmography 1911–1970*, Second Edition. New York: Oxford University Press, 2000.

Murray, R. Michael. *The Golden Age of Walt Disney Records 1933–1988*. Antique Trader Books, 1997.

Prendergast, Roy M. *Film Music: A Neglected Art*. New York: W.W. Norton & Company, 1977.

Rapée, Erno. *Encyclopedia of Music for Motion Pictures*. New York: Belwin, 1925; rep. New York: Arno Press & The New York Times, 1970.

———. *Motion Picture Moods for Pianists and Organists*. New York: Schirmer, 1924; rep. New York: Arno Press & The New York Times, 1974.

Sabaneev, Leonid. *Music for the Films.* New York: Arno Press, 1978.

Shilkret, Nathaniel. "Condensed from 'Some Predictions For the Future of Film Music' in *Music Publishers' Journal* Jan., Feb. 1946." *Film Music Notes* V:VIII (Apr. 1946), 14.

Wojcik, Pamela Robertson, and Arthur Knight, editors. *Soundtrack Available: Essays on Film and Popular Music.* Durham and London: Duke University Press, 2001.

Tootell, George. *How to Play the Cinema Organ: A Practical Book By a Practical Player.* London: W. Paxton & Co., Ltd., 1927.

Books or articles on other music that mention animation

Chusid, Irwin. Brochure notes for Raymond Scott, *Reckless Nights and Turkish Twilights: The Music of Raymond Scott.* The Raymond Scott Qunitette. Sony 53028, 1992.

————. "50 Years of Musical Mayhem." *Animation Magazine* 24 (Summer 1993), 43–47.

Cook, Nicholas. *Analysing Musical Multimedia.* Oxford: Clarendon Press, 1998.

Cooper, Kim, and David Smay, editors. *Bubblegum Music Is the Naked Truth: The Dark History of Prepubescent Pop, from the Banana Splits to Britney Spears.* Los Angeles: Feral House, 2001.

Short, Marion. *Covers of Gold: Collectible Sheet Music—Sports, Fashion, Illustration, & the Dance.* Atglen, PA: Schiffer Publishing Ltd., 1998.

About the Contributors

Jake Austen edits *Roctober*, the journal of popular music's dynamic obscurities, and produces the cable access children's dance show *Chic-A-Go-Go*. His work has appeared in *Nickelodeon* magazine, *Playboy*, *Spice Capades: The Spice Girl Comic Book*, and *Bubblegum Music Is the Naked Truth*.

Michael Barrier founded and edited *Funnyworld: The World of Animated Films and Comic Art,* the first serious magazine devoted to those subjects. He is the author of *Hollywood Cartoons: American Animation in Its Golden Age*.

Philip Brophy is director of the CINESONIC International Conference on Film Scores and Sound Design, as well as a sound designer and film composer. He has published widely on the subject, including in *The Wire, Real Time*, and *Film Comment*.

Ross Care's score for a west coast revival of Tennessee Williams's *The Glass Menagerie* was recently called "enormously effective" by the *Los Angeles Times.* As a critic Care also writes on film and film music for the genre magazine *Scarlet Street* and the Library of Congress.

Irwin Chusid is director of the Raymond Scott Archives, and author of *Songs in the Key of Z: The Curious Universe of Outsider Music*. He has been a radio personality on WFMU since 1975.

John Corbett is a writer and producer based in Chicago. He is the author of *Extended Play: Sounding Off from John Cage to Dr. Funkenstein* and *Microgroove: Further Forays into Other Music,* and his "Vinyl Freak" column appears monthly in *Down Beat* magazine. Corbett is adjunct associate professor at the School of the Art Institute and was appointed Artistic Director of the 2002 Berlin JazzFest.

Greg Ehrbar, a twice Grammy-nominated writer/producer, compiled the Toon Tunes and *Billboard* Family Classics series for Rhino records. A Disney veteran, he has written network TV specials; numerous film adaptations for books and audio; and award-winning ads for TV, print, and radio. He has also edited a popular magazine and helped bring vintage Golden Records to CD.

Will Friedwald is the author of seven books: four on popular music and jazz, including *Jazz Singing, Sinatra! The Song is You, The Good Life* (with Tony Bennett) and *Star Dust Melodies: The Biography of 12 of America's Most Popular Songs*, and three on animated film, including *The Warner Bros. Cartoons* and *Looney Tunes and Merrie Melodies.* He is also the morning host of Standard Time on Sirius Satellite Radio (www.siriusradio.com).

Daniel Goldmark is an assistant professor of musicology at the University of Alabama in Tuscaloosa, Alabama. His *Tunes for 'Tunes: Music and the Hollywood Animated Cartoon* will be published by the University of California Press. Daniel also worked as an editor and producer for Rhino Entertainment in Los Angeles, where he produced cartoon music–related collections like *Crash! Bang! Boom! The Best of Warner Bros. Sound FX* and *That's All Folks! Cartoon Songs From Merrie Melodies and Looney Tunes*, and as an archivist and music coordinator for Spümcø Animation.

Charles L. (Chuck) **Granata** is a record producer, music historian, and author of the award-winning book *Sessions With Sinatra: Frank Sinatra and the Art of Recording.*

Barry Hansen, writer, musicologist, and music maven, is better known as Dr. Demento, host to radio's weekly two-hour festival of "mad music and crazy comedy," heard on nearly one hundred stations coast-to-coast since 1970.

Earl Kress has written for many television series including *Steven Spielberg Presents Tiny Toon Adventures, Back to the Future, The Addams Family, Steven Spielberg Presents Animaniacs,* and *Steven Spielberg Presents Pinky and the Brain.* He was a contributing writer on the feature-length Animaniacs movie, *Wakko's Wish,* and is currently writing for the preschool show *Baby Looney Tunes*, the internet cartoon *The Kellys*, as well as *Looney Tunes, Scooby Doo!, Bart Simpson* comic books, and an *Animaniacs* video game.

John Kricfalusi is the creator of *The Ren & Stimpy Show*.

Joseph Lanza is the author of *Elevator Music: A Surreal History of Muzak, Easy-Listening and Other Moodsong*. He was also executive producer for a two-disc collection entitled *Music for TV Dinners* that includes several of the tracks discussed in his essay. His next book is about the legendary crooner Russ Columbo.

Leonard Maltin first wrote about Walt Disney in a special issue of his magazine *Film Fan Monthly* in 1967, which he later expanded into the first edition of his book *The Disney Films* (1973, revised in 2000). He is also the author of *Of Mice and Magic: A History of American Animated Cartoons*, but is perhaps best known for his annual paperback reference, *Leonard Maltin's Movie & Video Guide*, which he has edited since 1969. Since 1982 he has been a commentator and interviewer on television's *Entertainment Tonight*, and now co-hosts the weekend movie panel show *Hot Ticket*. He has appeared in animated form on episodes of *South Park* and *Freakazoid*.

Milo Miles has worked as a music journalist and editor for many years. He is a regular contributor to the *New York Times, Rolling Stone,* the *Village Voice* and National Public Radio's *Fresh Air*.

Stuart Nicholson is the author of several books on jazz, including highly acclaimed biographies of Ella Fitzgerald, Duke Ellington, and Billie Holiday. He has written extensively on jazz for newspapers and magazines in both the United States and Europe.

Neil Strauss is a pop music critic and cultural correspondent at the *New York Times*. He also writes regularly for *Rolling Stone*. He cowrote the *New York Times* bestsellers *The Long Hard Road Out of Hell* with Marilyn Manson and *The Dirt* with Motley Crue, and he edited a book of radio-related writings called *Radiotext(e)*. If he could switch places with any prominent figure in the whole world, Neil Strauss would choose Bugs Bunny.

Yuval Taylor has also edited *The Future of Jazz* and *I Was Born a Slave: An Anthology of Classic Slave Narratives*. He has worked as an editor at Da Capo Press, A Cappella Books, and Lawrence Hill Books.

Elisabeth Vincentelli is music editor at *Time Out New York*. Born and raised in France, she now lives in Brooklyn.

Chris Ware was born in 1967 in Omaha, Nebraska, and is the author of *Jimmy Corrigan, the Smartest Kid on Earth* (Pantheon) and The ACME Novelty Library series of booklets and pamphlets (1993–present), and is erstwhile editor of the music journal *The Rag Time Ephemeralist*. He lives in Chicago with his wife Marnie; they have not reproduced.

Kevin Whitehead is the author of *New Dutch Swing* (Billboard Books), about improvised music in Amsterdam, and is jazz critic for NPR's *Fresh Air*. He writes for the *Chicago Reader* and cohosts a weekly show on WNUR-FM.

David Wondrich writes about music and alcohol for publications such as *Esquire,* the *New York Times,* the *Village Voice, Williams-Sonoma Taste,* and *Gotham*. He lives in Brooklyn, New York.

Index

Abbott and Costello Meet the Invisible Man, 148
Abdul, Paula, 189
Academy Awards
  Dumbo, 26
  Hanna-Barbera Studios, 110, 183
  Pinocchio, 28
  When Magoo Flew, 169
Acme, Marvin, 105
Advanced Music Corporation, 154, 155
"Adventures in a Perambulator," 126
Adventures in Wonderland, 215
Adventures of Ichabod and Mister Toad, The, 26, 31, 32, 127
Adventures of Rocky and Bullwinkle, The, 216
Adventures of the Galaxy Rangers, The, 11
Aesop's Fables Studio, 46
aesthetics, 279
  of animation, 225
  of cartoon music, 279–285
"After You've Gone," 129, 131, 133
Akira, 221, 222
Albarn, Damon, 189
"Alexander's Ragtime Band," 143
Algar, Jim, 83
Alice in Cartoonland, 21
Alice in Wonderland, 31, 33, 34
Alive and Kickin', 130
Allen, Gracie, 117
All the Cats Join In, 128, *132*, *133*
"All the Cats Join In," 129–131, *132*–134
Alvin and the Chipmunks, 190

Alvin Show, The, 176, 177, 184, 190
Amazing Chan and the Chan Clan, The, 184
Amfitheatrof, Daniele, 33
Anderson, Wes, 216
Andrews Sisters, 126, 127
Animaniacs, 205, 230, 232
  and music of Raymond Scott, 151, 158
  and music of Richard Stone, 225, 228, 229
animation
  aesthetics of, 225
  art of, 101
  and improvisation, 141
  limited, 177, 178, 204
  planned, 183, 184
  stop-action, 182, 195
anime, 219–224
"Anvil Chorus, The," 205, 206
APM (Associated Production Music), 271
Apocalypse Now, 233
Archies, The, 180, 183, 223
Archie Show, 181
Armstrong, Louis, 62, 64, 65
Ashman, Howard, 35
Astaire, Fred, 196
Audrey, Little, 163–164
Avery, Tex, 52, 146

Babes in Arms, 107
Baby Bottleneck, 155
Baby Huey, 165
"Baby Mine," 26, 31
Bach, Johann Sebastian, 7, 23
  Toccata and Fugue in D Minor, 94, 126
Back Alley Oproar, 106
"Back Home in Indiana," 143
Badenov, Boris, 178

Baer, Manny, 62
Bagdasarian, Ross, 175, 176, 190
Bagdasarian, Ross, Jr., 190
"Baggage Coach Up Ahead, The," 69
"Baia," 32
Baker, Buddy, 35
Bakshi, Ralph, 11
"Ballad of Davy Crockett," 34
Bambi, 22, 30, 32
Banana Splits, The, 184
Band Concert, The, 67
Band Master, The, 112
"Bang-Shang-a-Lang," 181
Baptista, Cyro, 220
Barbera, Joseph, 169, 182–183
Barber of Seville, 106
Barn Dance, The, 44
Barnyard Concert, The, 107
Baron, Art, 206
Barry, Jeff, 181
Barry, John, 36
Bars & Stripes, 104
Bartek, Steve, 205
Bass, Jules, 194
Batfink, 151, 157
Batman, 157
Baton Bunny, 93, 112
Baxter, Les, 266
Beagles, The, 179
Beakman's World, 207, 215
Bear Raid Warden, 117
Beatles, The, 160, 178
  Hard Day's Night, A, 177
  Sergeant Pepper's Lonely Hearts Club Band, 179
  Yellow Submarine, 179
Beatles, The, 178, 179
Beauty and the Beast, 35
Beaver, Jack, 271
Beck, Jackson, 166

Beethoven, Ludwig von, 7, 121
   Pastoral Symphony, 85
Benaderet, Bea, 146
Bennett, Tony, 204, 259
Bergen, Edgar, 29
Berkeley, Busby, 133
Berlin, Irving, 143
Bernstein, Elmer, 36
Bernstein, Julie, 225–237, *226*
Bernstein, Leonard, 256
Bernstein, Steve, 225–237, *226*
Best of Anime, The, 219
Betty Boop, 63
Big Broadcast of 1937, The, 81
*Bill and Ted's Excellent
   Adventures*, 189
Black, Brown, and Beige, 139
"Blame It on the Samba," 33
Blanc, Mel, 104, 146
Bland, Bobby "Blue," 259
"Blue Bayou," 127
"Blue Danube, The," 108
Bogart, Neil, 180
Boo Moon, 164–166
Boop, Betty, 62, 64, 65, 66
"Boozehound Named Barney,
   A," 258
Boswell, Peyton, 86
bouncing ball, 178. *See also*
   "Song Car-Tune"
"Boy Scout in Switzerland,"
   155
Bradley, Scott, 9, *115*, 231, 253
   biography, 119
   Carl Stalling and, 115
   select discography, 292
   Winston Sharples and, 161
Brady Kids, The, 182
Brahms, Johannes, 274
   Hungarian Dances, 110, 111
   "Lullaby," 274
Braxton, Anthony, 206
"Brazil," 32
Bricusse, Leslie, 255
Bride of Frankenstein, The, 31
Broadway influences, 196,
   253–257
Broken Lance, 28
Broughton, Bruce, 225
Brown, Bernard, 7
Brown, Earle, 149

Brown, Treg, 9, 38, 53, 143,
   264
Brown, Vernon, 130
Brubeck, Dave, 26
Bruns, George, 34, 35
Buena Vista Sound, 89
Bugs Bunny, 52, 108–110, 141,
   144
Burke, Sonny, 34
Burns, Mr., 243
Burton, Tim, 198
*Butch Cassidy and the
   Sundance Kids*, 184
Butterfield, Billy, 130
Butterfly, 113n
Buzzy the Crow, 165
Byas, Don, 129, 130
By the Old Mill Scream, 163

Cahn, Sammy, 34
California Raisins, 189
Calker, Darrell, 10
   select discography, 292
Calloway, Cab, 62, 63, 64
Cameron, Al, 127
Camp, Bob, 157
Camping Out, 25
Camus, Albert, 279
"Can I Borrow a Feeling," 259
"Capital City," 204
Capital Production Music, 273
Carl Stalling Project, 139, 142,
   227, 286
Carmen, 113
Carmichael, Hoagy, 166
"Carolina in the Morning," 144
Carpenter, John Alden, 126
Carson, Jack, 104
*Cartoon Classics: Classical
   Favorites from Classic
   Cartoons*, 104
"Cartoonia," 119
Cartoon Medley, 159
Cartoon Network, 159, 191
car tune. *See* "Song Car-Tune"
Casale, Bob, 215
"Casey (The Pride of Them
   All)," 127
Caspar Comes to Clown, 165
Caspar the Friendly Ghost, 157,
   161–164, 167

Castellaneta, Dan, 258
Cat Carson Rides Again, 166,
   167
Catch As Cats Can, 53
Cat-Choo, 166
Cat Concerto, The, 9, 104, 110
"Cat o' Nine Tails," 266, 286
Cat Tamale, 166
Cattanooga Cats, 169, 184
"Celebration on the Planet
   Mars," 151
Chadbourne, Eugene, 284
Charles Wolcott Orchestra, 130
Charlie Brown, 11
"Cherie, Je t'Aime," 139
"Chicago," 54
Chicken Boo, 236
"Chicken Reel," 236
Children's Television Workshop,
   186
Chili Con Carmen, 107
Chion, Michael, 280
Chipmunk Punk, 190
Chipmunks, The, 189, 190
"Chipmunk Song, The," 175
Chip 'n' Dale's Rescue Rangers,
   11
Churchill, Frank, 10, 24–28,
   30–32, 126, 272
Cinderella, 33
Cinephone Studios, 7
Circle Music Publications, 154
Clampett, Bob, 52, 58n, 59n,
   108, 155
Clark, Dick, 189
Classic Guide to Strategy, The,
   285
Clausen, Alf, 204, 205,
   239–252, *240*
   select discography, 297
   and *The Simpsons*, 253–262
click track, 7, 117, 227
"Clint Eastwood," 223
Cohan, George M., 143
Coker, Paul, 182
Cole, Cozy, 129, 130
Cole, Nat King, 10
Collins, Phil, 36
Colonna, Jerry, 127, 128
"Columbia, the Gem of the
   Ocean," 144

Columbia/Screen Gems, 157
Colvin, Shawn, 204
Concert Feature, The, 76
"Concerto for the Index
	Finger," 117
Condoli, Pete, 172
Confrey, Zez, 8
"Confusion Among a Fleet of
	Taxicabs Upon Meeting with
	a Fare," 9
Convict Concerto, The, 104
Coppola, Carmine, 163
copyright, 7, 39, 49, 54, 144
Corny Concerto, A, 108
Cosby, Bill, 186
Cotton, Jay, 210
Courage of Lassie, 121, 122
Cowboy BeBop, 223, 224
"Cow Cow Boogie," 32
CPM (Capitol Production
	Music), 271, 273, 274
"Crêpe Suzette," 272
"Cruella de Vil," 34
Csupo, Gabor, 213, 214, 217
cues, 211, 250, 270, 273
	average, 8
	database of, 226–227
	movable, 149
Culhane, John, 81
Culhane, Shamus, 141
"Cup of Coffee, a Sandwich,
	and You, A," 139
Curtin, Hoyt, 5, 10–12, 169,
	204
	select discography, 292–295
cuts in cartoon editing,
	281–282
Cynical Hysterie Hour, 220,
	267

Daffy Duck,105, 137, 235
"Daffy Duck's Rhapsody," 104
Dance of the Weed, 116, 119
Dante, Ron, 181
Darby, Ken, 33, 127, 129
Daum, Glen, 11, 12
David, Mack, 33
Davis, Bette, 137
Davis, Miles, 26
Day, Doris, 104
Daydreamer, The, 195

Death and Transfigurations, 95
Debussy, Claude, 8, 274
	"Afternoon of a Faun," 119
	"Clair de Lune," 126, 127
	"Prelude to the Afternoon of
	a Faun," 274
de Forest, Lee, 6, 62
Del Rubio Triplets, 203
Del Tha Funky Homosapien,
	189
De Nat, Joe, 10
Denny, Martin, 32, 203
de Pachman, Vladimir, 10
DePatie, David H., 131
DePaul, Gene, 32
Deren, Maya, 221
Dessau, Paul, 113n
detail sheets, 117
Dick Tracy Returns, 148
Diller, Phyllis, 196
"Dinner Music for a Pack of
	Hungry Cannibals," 9,
	154, 155
Dinner Time, 6
Dipsy Gypsy, 104
Discontented Canary, The, 115
Disney, Roy, 46, 47, 126
Disney, Walt, 6, 7, *25*, 73–90
	and *The Band Concert*,
	67–72
	and Disney Studios, 21–36
	and *Make Mine Music*,
	125–130
	and music, 23–25, 28–29,
	246
	select discography, 289–291
Disney Studios, 21–36, 82, 85
	second golden age, 34–36,
	196
"Dixie," 22, 70
Dizzy Dishes, 164
Dodd, Jimmie, 35
Dolenz, Mickey, 184
Donald Duck, 30, 31, 68, 71,
	105
Donald's Apple Core, 35
Donizetti, 106
	Lucia de Lammermoor, 106,
	128
Don Juan, 6
Dot, 205, 232

Dot and the Line, The, 93
Doug, 225
Drew Cary Show, The, 158
Dr. Jekyll and Mr. Mouse, 123
Dr. Seuss, 9
*Dr. Seuss's How the Grinch
	Stole Christmas*, 93
Dubin, Al, 35
Dubin, Joseph S., 35
Duck Amuck, 93
*Duck Dodgers in the 24 1/2th
	Century*, 155
Duckman, 158
Duck Pimples, 31
Duck! Rabbit! Duck!, 235
Dukas, Paul, 75
Dumbo, 24, 26, 31, 71

Eddy, Nelson, 123, 126, 127,
	128
Edouarde, Carl, 7
Edwards, Blake, 131
"Egyptian Barn Dance," 151,
	155
Electric Company, The, 186
Electronium, 154, 207
Elfman, Danny, 205, 210, 211,
	253
Ellington, Duke, 206
Emmett, Daniel Decatur, 70
"End, The," 233
Esperanto, 220

Fain, Sammy, 31, 33, 34
Fairlight (synthesizer), 211,
	212, 213, 215
Famous Studios, 157, 161–163,
	166
Fantasia, 73–90, 95, 107
	and *Make Mine Music*, 125,
	128
	mentioned, 7, 22, 27, 30
Fantasound, 74, 82–90
Fantastic Plastic Machine, 220
Fat Albert and the Cosby Kids,
	186
Faust, 128
Fearless Fly, 157
"Feelin' Groovy," 205
Felix at the Circus, 6, 113n
Felix the Cat, 17, 157

Filmation, 181, 193
Firehouse Five Plus Two Band, 36
Flanders, Ned, 205
Fleischer, Dave, 61
Fleischer, Lou, 62
Fleischer, Max, 6, 61, 66, 157
Fleischer Studios, 6, 61, 66, 162, 163
Flintstones, The, 10, 113, 169–171, 183
Flotow, Friedrich von. *Martha*, 106, 128
Flowers and Trees, 75
Forbstein, Leo, 54
Ford, Greg, 12, 154, 227, 286
Forest Rangers, The, 166
Format Films, 149
Frankenstein Jr., and The Impossibles, 179
Franklin, Dave, 8
Franklyn, Milt, 9, *147*, 148, 238n, 264
    Carl Stalling and, 50, 55, 137, 139–140
    session tapes, 226
Freakazoid!, 225, 231
Frees, Paul, 178
Freleng, Friz, 52, 108, 110, 131, 154
    Rhapsody in Rivets, 104–105
    Rhapsody Rabbit, 105
French, G., 272
Friend, Cliff 8
Frisell, Bill, 220, 286–287
Frosty the Snowman, 182
Fudd, Elmer, 108, 109, 140
"Fully Fashioned," 272
Fun and Fancy Free, 32, 33, 127
Funicello, Annette, 34
Funny Little Bunnies, 27

Gallopin' Gaucho, 23, 39, 44
Games Animation, 272
"Garbageman, The," 259
Garity, William, 82, 83
Garner, Marcellite, 59n
"Gay Activity," 272
Geisel, Ted, 9
Georg, Ole, 273, 274

George Shrinks, 158
Gerald McBoing Boing's Symphony, 10
Ghost in the Shell, 222
Gigantor, 219
Gilbert, Ray, 33, 129
Gillespie, Dizzy, 134
Gilmer, A. C., 178
Glass, Philip, 150, 206
Glass Harmonica, 113n
Glinka, Mikhail. *Russlan and Ludmilla*, 106
Goddess of Spring, The, 27
Goldsmith, Jerry, 36, 265
Goldwater, John, 180
Good and Guilty, 165
"Goodfeathers," 232, 233, 236
Goodie the Gremlin, 165
Goodman, Benny, 8, 125, 127–134
Goodwind, Doug, 11
Goof Troop, 229
Gordy, Berry, 154, 182
Gorillaz, 188, 223
Go Simpsonic with The Simpsons, 204
Goulet, Robert, 195
Grammer, Kelsey, 257
Gray, Milton, 38
"Greatest Adventure (The Ballad of the Hobbit)," 194
Greene, Walter, 11
Grieg, Edvard, 75
    Lyric Suite, 57n
    "March of the Dwarfs," 57n, 75
    Norwegian Dances, 97
    Peer Gynt Suite, 40
Groening, Matt, 242
Groovie Goolies, 182
Guaraldi, Vince, 11
Gulliver's Travels, 164
Gumble, Barney, 258

"Hail to the Chief," 22
Half-Fare Hare, 144
Hallelujah, I'm a Bum!, 261
Hammer, M. C., 188
Hammerman, 188
Hammerstein, Oscar, 195

Hanna, William, 169, 182–183
Hanna-Barbera Studios, 179, 182–186, 191, 193, 204
    Academy Awards, 111, 169
    and Hoyt Curtin, 10, 169–172
"Happy Farmer, The," 155
"Happy-Go-Lively," 272
Hardy Boys, The, 181, 182
Harlem Globetrotters, The, 185
Harline, Leigh, 10, *25*, 26–30, 32
    Music Land, 24
Harman, Hugh, 7, 58n, 107
Harris, Dave, 9
"Heart and Soul," 166
"Heat Miser/Snow Miser Song, The," 194
Hefti, Neil, 149
Heindorf, Ray, 54
Hench, John, 85
Henderson, Charles, 30
Henson, Jim, 160
Herbert, Victor, 38
Herman, 166
Herman, Woody, 134
Hérold, Louis-Joseph-Ferdinand, 68, 106
Herrmann, Bernard, 142
Hewlett, Jamie, 189
"Hi-De Hades," 27
Hilliard, Bob, 33
Hindemith, Paul, 6, 113n
Hisaishi, Joe, 221
Histeria!, 225, 230
Hobbit, The, 197
Hoffman, Al, 33
Hollaway, Patrice, 184
Hollywood Hotel, 132
"Hollywood Romance," 273
Homeless Flea, The, 119
Horn Blows At Midnight, 148
"Hot Dog," 181
How the Grinch Stole Christmas, 93
Hubley, Faith, 222
Hubley, John, 222
"Huckleberry Duck," 155
Huckleberry Hound Show, The, 169
Huermer, Dick, 83

Huey's Ducky Daddy, 165
humor in music, 17, 266
Hutton, June, 129, 130

"I Am the Captain of the
    Pinafore," 257
"I Don't Want To Walk
    Without You," 166
"I Got Spurs that Jingle Jangle
    Jingle," 166
*I'll Be Glad When You're Dead
    You Rascal You*, 65
I Love to Singa, 107
"I'm Forever Blowing Bubbles,"
    53
"I'm Mad," 205
improvisation, 5, 141, 284–285
"In an 18th Century Drawing
    Room," 155
"Invitation to the Waltz," 126
"I Pity The Fool," 259
Irwin, Pat, 206
Ising, Rudolf, 7, 58n, 107
Isle of the Dead, 28
"It Had To Be You," 139
Ito, Teiji, 221
"It's a Hap-Hap-Happy Day,"
    164
"It Was a Very Good Year," 256
Ives, Charles, 8, 142, 143, 145
Iwerks, Ub, 45, 47, 59n
Iwerks Studios, 7, 48
"IXTL," 222

Jabberjaw, 184
Jackson, Wilfred, 22, 28–30,
    45, 56–58nn
Jackson 5ive, 182
Japanese animation, 219. *See
    also* anime
"Jazz Interlude, A," 127
Jazz Singer, The, 82, 107, 260
Jem and the Holograms, 189
Jesse James at Bay, 148
Jetsons, The, 10, 172
"Jiminy Lummox," 272
"Jingle Jangle," 181
Jive Bunny, 188
Joel, Billy, 36
Johann Mouse, 110, 111
John, Elton, 35, 36

"Johnny Fedora and Alice
    Bluebonnet," 127, 128
Johnson, Laurie, 271, 272
Johnson, Plas, 131
Johnson, Tommy, 230
Jolson, Owl, 107
Jones, Chuck, 9, 52, 93, 155
    Baton Bunny, 112
    *Duck Dodgers in the 24 1/2
        th Century*, 155
    parody of classical music,
        108–110
    Road Runner, The, 53
Jones, Quincy, 265
Jones, Spike, 8
Jonny Quest, 11, 169
Josie and the Pussycats, 184,
    185
Jungle Book, The, 34, 35

Kanno, Yoko, 223
Karate, 157
Kastenetz-Katz, 180
Katie Kaboom, 236
Katnip, 165, 166
Kaufman, Louis, 119
Kawai, Kenji, 222
Keith, Robert, 271
Kempel, Art, 228
Kenton, Stan, 134
Key the Metal Idol, 223
Kiddie Koncert, 112
Kidd Video, 189
Kid 'n' Play, 187
Kilfeather, Eddie, 162
Kim, Andy, 181
Kimball, Ward, 128
Kirby, John, 8
Kirschner, Don, 181, 185
"Kiss in the Dark, A," 38
Klasky, Arlene, 217
Klasky Csupo, 213, 214
Klondike Casanova, 166
Koestelanetz, Andre, 104
Koko the Clown, 6
"Komm, Gib Mir Deine
    Hand," 178
Kostal, Irwin, 88
Koussevitsky, Serge, 128
KPM, 271, 274
Kricfalusi, John, 157, 271

Kronos Quartet, 266
Krusty the Klown, 256, 259,
    260
Kubik, Gail, 10
Kubo, Kinko, 220, 267

Ladd, Cheryl, 184
Lady and the Tramp, 34
"Lady in Red, The," 144
Lantz, Walter, 107, 112–113
Larson, Gary, 286
Lasseter, John, 198
Lava, William, 9, 11, 35, 148,
    149
Laws, Maury, *193*, 193–199
    select discography, 295
"Lazy Countryside," 33
Ledesma, Chris, 244
Lee, Peggy, 34, 130
leitmotifs. *See* theme music
Leoncavallo, Ruggiero. *I
    Pagliacci*, 128
Le Pew, Pepe, 139
Lerner, Sammy, 10, 62
Leven, Mel, 34
Lewis, Bert, 24
Lewis, Meade Lux, 10
Light Calvary, The, 106
"Light My Fire," 203
"Limbo," 160
Lindsay, Arto, 220
Lion King, The, 35, 36
"Lions on the Loose," 119
"Listen to the Mockingbird,"
    166
Liszt, Franz, 9, 104, 106, 110
    Second Hungarian Rhapsody,
        104, 106, 110, 113
Little Audrey, 163, 164
"Little Audrey says," 164
Little Lulu, 157
Little Mermaid, The, 35, 196,
    258
Little Red Riding Hood, 146
Little Whirlwind, The, 31
"Little White Duck, The," 194
Living Desert, The, 31
Livingston, Jerry, 33
"Llama Serenade," 32
Loesser, Frank, 166–167
Lone Ranger, 104, 107

Long-Haired Hare, 93, 106, 108
Looney Tunes, 7–8, 12, 58n, 144, 242
and music of Raymond Scott, 155
new generation of, 225
Loopy de Loop, 171
Loose, William, 273
Lopez, Vincent, 162
"Lord's Prayer, The," 30
Lovejoy, Reverend, 254
Lullaby Land, 27
Lundy, Dick, 112

Macdonald, Jim, 7, 59n
Macross, 219
Macross Plus, 220
Mad About Cartoons, 104
Mad Monster Party, 196, 198
Magical Maestro, 106
Magic Fluke, The, 104
"Make a Gookie," 205
Make Mine Music, 32–33, 90, 113n, 125–135
Malotte, Albert Hay, 30
Maltese, Mike, 109, 110
Mancini, Henry, 36, 131
Manhattan Research, Inc, 160
Manilow, Barry, 36
March of the Trolls, 75
Marsales, Frank, 7
"Martins and the Coys, The," 127
Mary Poppins, 34, 195, 257
Matsumoto, Leiji, 223
Maurice, Peter, 271
"May Heaven Grant You Pardon," 128
McClure, Troy, 247
McGraw, Quick Draw, 170
McLaren, Norman, 222
MC Skat Kat, 189
"Meet the Flintstones," 171
mellos, 137
Melody, 35
Melody Time, 32, 33, 126, 127
Mendelssohn, Felix, 75, 106
Fingal's Cave, 54
Hebrides, The, 106
Ruy Blas, 106

Menken, Alan, 35
Menuhin, Yehudi, 79
Mercer, Jack, 63
Merlino, Gene, 260
Merman, Ethel, 62
Merrie Melodies, 7, 8, 103, 155
"Merrily on Our Way," 26
"Merrily We Roll Along," 8, 51
"Merry-Go-Round Broke Down, The," 8
Meshes of the Afternoon, 221
MGM Studios, 9, 93, 110, 281
Mickey Mouse, 6, 7, 21, 67, 71
first voice of, 45
shorts, 24, 35
and *The Sorcerer's Apprentice*, 75
Mickey Mouse Club, 35
mickey mousing, 7, 95, 264, 270–271, 281. *See also* synchronization
Maury Laws on, 197
MIDI, 212
"Midnight/Wild Ride Home," 33
Mighty Mouse: The New Adventures, 11–12
Milky Waif, The, 123
Miller, Glenn, 8
Miller, Roger, 36
Milton the Monster, 157
Minekawa, Takako, 220
Minnie Mouse, 22, 59n
Minnie the Moocher, 63, 64
Mission Magic, 182
mobiles. *See* cues, movable
Monkees, The, 178, 179, 181
Monteux, Pierre, 119
Morgan, Tommy, 231
Morrow, Liza, 130
Morton, Arthur, 265
Mothersbaugh, Bob, 215
Mothersbaugh, Mark, 11, 203, 205–217, *207*
select discography, 297
motifs. *See* theme music
Moussorgsky. *Night on Bald Mountain*, 74, 126
Mr. Bug Goes to Town, 166
"Mr. Sparkle," 249

MTV style, 178
Muller, Romeo, 198
Mumy, Bill, 215
Murphy, Bleeding Gums, 260
Musical Encyclopedia, 220
Musical Miniatures, 112
Musical Moments from Chopin, 112
Music Land, 23–24, 27, 107, 127–128
Music Man, The, 256
Music of Raymond Scott: Reckless Nights and Turkish Twilights, 152
music room, 28, 41, 57n
Music Sales Corporation, 154
Musik for Insomniaks, 214
Mutato Muzika, 205
My Dream Is Yours, 104
"My Favorite Dream," 33
My Old Kentucky Home, 6

Nash, Clarence, 59n
needle drops, 183, 204, 271
Nelly's Folly, 93
Neo Geo, 220
Newley, Anthony, 255
Newman, Laraine, 210
New Scooby Doo Comedy Movies, The, 184
"New Year's Eve in a Haunted House," 151
"New York, New York," 204
Nickelodeon, 212, 225
Nightmare Ned, 205
Norton, Kevin, 206
Norvell, Red, 8
Notes to You, 106
Novachord, 31

Oblongs, The, 158
O'Connell, Charles, 79, 80
O'Day, Anita, 154
OGM (Ole Georg Music), 273
Oh, Mabel, 6
"Oh, You Beautiful Doll," 144
Oh My Goddess!, 220
"Oh Streetcar!," 204
"Old Dan Tucker," 70
"Old Folks at Home," 143

Old Man of the Mountain, 64
Old Mill, The, 27
Olive Oyl, 63, 166
Oliver and Company, 36
"Once Upon a Wintertime," 33
One Froggy Evening, 93
100 Men and a Girl, 81, 107
101 Dalmatians, 34
"One O'Clock Jump," 8
"On the Banks of the Wabash,"
    143
"On the Plaza," 273
"Opposites Attract," 189
Op'ry House, The, 45
Oscars. *See* Academy Awards
Osmonds, The, 182
Oswald the Lucky Rabbit, 21
Otomo, Katshuhiro, 221
Out of the Inkwell, 157
Overture to William Tell, 112
Oyl, Olive, 63, 166

package feature, 32, 127
Pagliacci, 128
Paint Your Wagon, 261
Pal, George, 104, 155
Palmer, King, 271
Panter, Gary, 210
Paramount Studios, 62, 157,
    162, 167
parody, 24, 108–109, 190,
    247, 254
Partridge Family:2200 A.D.,
    184
*Patlabor 2 the Movie: Original
    Soundtrack "P2,"* 222
Paul, Les, 90
Pavarotti, Luciano, 231
Pebbles and Bam Bam, 184
Pee-wee's Big Adventure, 211
Pee-wee's Playhouse, 203, 207,
    208, 210, 211
"Penguin, The," 155
Pepper Ann, 206
Perfect Blue, 223
"Peter Cottontail and the
    Search for Flopsy's Tail,"
    194
Peter Pan, 26, 31, 34
Phonofilm, 6
Pickup on South Street, 28

Pied Piper, The, 27
Pigeon on the Roof, 232, 233
Pigs in a Polka, 108, 109, 110
"Pink Elephants On Parade,"
    31
Pink Panther, 131
Pinky and the Brain, 225, 233,
    234
Pinocchio, 28, 30
Pixie Picnic, 112
Pizzicato Five, 220
Pizzicato Pussycat, 110, 111
Plane Crazy, 22, 23, 39, 44
Plumb, Edward, 28, 30, 32
Poddany, Eugene, 9, 50
Pokémon, 219, 223
Poochie, 254–255
"Poor Little Buttercup," 257
Popeye, 62, 63, 66, 157, 205
Porky the Pig, 108
Porter, Terry, 89
"Powerhouse," 8, 144, 151,
    153–155, 158–160
Powerpuff Girls, 191, 223
Presley, Elvis, 160, 174, 175
Previte, Bobby, 220
Primitivia, 32
Primus, 205
Princess Mononoke, 221
Prokofiev, Serge, 90, 113n
    Peter and the Wolf, 90, 113n,
    126, 127, 128
P.T. 109, 148
Puente, Tito, 204
Puma, Pete, 140
Puppetoons, 155
"Put One Foot in Front of the
    Other," 194

Questel, May, 63
Quimby, Fred, 119
Quine, Robert, 220

Ra, Sun, 5
Rabbit of Seville, The, 93, 108,
    109
Rabbit Seasoning, 235
Raeburn, Boyd, 134
Rankin/Bass Productions, 182,
    193, 196
Ravel, Maurice, 24, 30

Raye, Don, 32
Raymond Scott Quintette, 9,
    152
"Reckless Night on Board an
    Ocean Liner," 151, 155
Redman, Don, 62
Reluctant Dragon, The, 26
Ren & Stimpy Show, The, 151,
    225, 269–274
    and music of Raymond Scott,
    157, 158
Respighi, Ottorino. *Birds, The*,
    121
Reubens, Paul, 210
Revenge of the Creature, 148
Rhapsody in Rivets, 104–105,
    108, 110
Rhapsody Rabbit, 105, 106,
    108, 110, 111
Rhythm in the Ranks, 155
Ribot, Marc, 220
Richardson, Clive, 272
"Rise and Shine," 171
"Road Runner," 285
Road Runner, The, 149, 150,
    285
Robin Hood, 36
"Rockabye Baby," 165
"Rocked in the Cradle of the
    Deep," 46
Rocko's Modern Life, 206
Rocky and His Friends, 178,
    240
Rodemich, Gene, 10, 162
Rodgers, Richard, 195
Rogel, Randy, 205
Rogers, Shorty, 147
Rooney, Mickey, 197
Rossini, Gioachino
    Barber of Seville, The, 109,
    113, 128
    "Largo al Factotum," 106,
    109
    Semiramide, 106
    Thieving Magpies, The, 106
    William Tell Overture, 68,
    71, 104, 106, 107
Rotoscope, 61
Royal Samoans, The, 62
"Ruben, Ruben," 22
Rubinoff, David, 62

Rudolph the Red-Nosed Reindeer, 182, 193, 195
Ruegger, Tom, 232, 236
Ruff and Reddy, 170
Rugrats, 206, 207, 213, 215, 225
Rugrats Movie, The, 216
Rundgren, Todd, 211
Russell, Andy, 127

Sailor Moon, 219
Saint-Saëns, Camille
Carnival of the Animals, 121
Danse Macabre, 39
Sakamoto, Ryuichi, 220
Saludos Amigos, 32, 126
Samurai Jack, 219, 223
Santa Claus is Comin' to Town, 197, 198
Satie, Erik
Airs to Make One Run, 96
Dreamy Fish, The, 96
Parade, 264
"Saturday Night," 284
Sauter, Eddie, 129, 130
Sax on the Beach, 260
Scarlet Pumpernickel, The, 93
Scheib, Philip A., 6
select discography, 292
Schertzer, Hymie, 130
Schifrin, Lalo, 36
Schlagobers (Whipped Cream), 96
Schlesinger, Leon, 49, 149
Schnittke, Alfred, 113n
Schoenberg, Arnold, 118, 123
"School Days," 40
Schoolly D, 284
Schubert, Franz. *Ave Maria*, 77
Scooby-Doo, 183
Scott, Mitzi, 156
Scott, Raymond, 8, 12, 144, 151–160, 207
photograph, *152, 153*
Seeger, Hal, 151, 157
Seely, John, 273
"Send in the Clowns," 256, 260
Sesame Street, 186
Seven Faces of Doctor Lao, 28
Seville, David, 175

Sharp, Sid, 80, 83
Sharples, Winston, 10, 157, 161, 253
select discography, 292
Sharrock, Sonny, 205
Shavers, Charlie, 129, 153
Sherman, Richard, 32, 34, 35
Sherman, Robert, 32, 34, 35, 258
Shore, Dinah, 126, 127
"Shortenin' Bread," 123, 128
Shostakovich, Dimitri, 113n
Shostakovich: Film Music, 113n
"Siberian Sleigh Ride," 155
Sideshow Bob, 257
Silly Little Mouse, The, 113n
Silly Symphonies, 7, 23–24, 75, 103, 126
Harline, Leigh, 26–27
Stalling, Carl, 37, 39–41, 47, 57n, 58n–59n
Silverman, Dave, 242
Simple Things, The, 35
Simpson, Bart, 253, 257, 259
Simpson, Homer, 248, 255, 261
Simpson, Lisa, 260
Simpsons, The, 5, 113, 158, 204, 253–262
and Alf Clausen, 239–240, 246–250
Broadway influence, 254–257
Disney takeoffs, 258
Sinatra, Frank, 259, 260
"Singing Down the Road," 155
Siunahara, Yoshinori, 220
Skeleton Dance, The, 7, 22, 39–41, 44, 75
"Skiddle-Diddle-Dee," 166
Sleeping Beauty, 34, 35
Smetana, Bederich. *Bartered Bride, The*, 106
Smith, Paul, 27, 28, 30–33, 35
Smith, Pete, 119
Smurfs, The, 11, 169, 188
Snooze Reel, 166
Snow White, 64
Snow White and the Seven Dwarfs, 26, 27, 30, 81, 128

So Dear to My Heart, 33
"Someday My Prince Will Come," 26
"Song Car-Tune," 6, 62, 176.
See also bouncing ball
Song of the South, 33
Sonic Youth, 204
"Sooner or Later," 33
Soothing Sounds for Baby, 159–60
Sorcerer's Apprentice, The, 75, 76, 83
sound effects, 53, 183, 237n, 244, 264, 285
Sousa, John Philip, 68
"South of the Border," 260
South Park, 198, 205, 206
So You Want To Build A House, 148
Space Ghost Coast to Coast, 205
Spector, Phil, 181
Spencer, Norman, 7
Spicer, Bill, 38
Spielberg, Steven, 232, 235–236
Springfield, Rick, 182
Springtime, 41
Spümcø, 271
Stage Fright, 282
Stalling, Carl, 37–56, *47, 138*, 204, 253
as composer, 145, 263–265
at Disney Studios, 22–23
and improvisation, 141–150
John Zorn and, 286
list of Disney compositions, 58n–59n
music of, 137–140
Richard Stone and, 225–227, 242
Scott Bradley and, 115
select discography, 289
session tapes, 226
Stage Fright soundtrack, 282
style, 235
and Walt Disney, 6–7
at Warner Bros. Studios, 8, 155–156, 203
Winston Sharples and, 161–162
"Star Eyes," 32

Starting from Hatch, 165
"Steamboat Bill," 22, 56n
Steamboat Willie, 7, 22, 39, 56n, 70, 107
Steiner, Alexander, 30
Steiner, Fred, 11, 228
Steiner, Max, 36
Stern, Jack, 171
Sting, 36
sting, 238n
"St. James Infirmary," 64
Stockwell, Dean, 210
Stokowski, Leopold, 30, 73–90, 127
    Bugs Bunny as, 109
Stone, Richard, 158, 225, 242
    select discography, 296
Stop the Planet of the Apes I Want to Get Off, 247
Strauss, Johann, 112
    "Blue Danube, The," 108
    "Tale of the Vienna Woods, The," 108
Strauss, Richard, 96
    Die Fledermaus, 274
    Don Quixote, 121
Stravinsky, Igor, 30, 86
    Norwegian Moods, 97
    Rite of Spring, 87, 90, 126
"Sugar, Sugar," 180, 181
Superfriends, 11
Superman, 157
Super Six, The, 179
surrealism, 63, 141
surround sound. *See* Fantasound
Sweet and Lowdown, 129
Swing Street, 126–128
Sword in the Stone, The, 34
Sylvester & Tweety Mysteries, 225
synchresis, 280
synchronization, 42–45, 94–95, 117, 155, 158, 280. *See also* mickey mousing
    early, 7
synthesizer. *See* Fairlight (synthesizer)

"Take Me Out To The Ball Game," 145, 231

Takemitsu, Toru, 221
Tale of the Priest and His Servant Balda, 113n
Tale of the Vienna Woods, The, 107
Tales from the Far Side, 286
Talkatroons, 63
"Tank," 223
Tartakovsky, Genndy, 219
Taylor, Deems, 74, 107, 108
Taz-Mania, 225, 228, 229, 230
Tchaikovsky, 34, 35
    "Dance of the Sugar Plum Fairy," 274
    Nutcracker Suite, 95
    Swan Lake, 233
Tea for Two Hundred, 31
Teagarden, Jack, 131
temp track, 216, 247
Terry, Paul, 6
Terrytoons, 6
    theme music, 8, 138, 162, 165–166, 236
    in *The Simpsons*, 243–244, 253
There'll Be No Tears Tonight, 284
theremin, 233, 234, 244
"These Boots are Made for Walking," 203
Thieving Magpie, The, 106
Thomas, Danny, 196
Thomas, Frank, 36
Thompson, Johnny, 129, 130, 134
Three Caballeros, The, 32, 126
Three Little Bops, 147
Three Little Pigs, 25, 47, 284
tick system, 7, 42, 44, 45
Timberg, Sammy, 10, 62, 162, 163, 164
    select discography, 289
Tin Pan Alley, 8, 32
Tiny Toon Adventures, 225, 227–228, 230
To Boo or Not to Boo, 167
"Today My Baby Gave Me a Surprise," 208
To Itch His Own, 145
Tom and Jerry, 9, 123, 124, 183

Scott Bradley and, 111, 115, 118, 119, 231
    theme music, 236
Tom and Jerry in the Hollywood Bowl, 112
Toot, Whistle Plunk, and Boom, 35
Top Cat, 162, 172
Torture Garden, 265
Tot Watchers, 115
"Toy Trumpet, The," 155
"Trees," 33
Trick or Treat, 35
Tristan und Isolde, 128
"Tubby the Tuba," 194
Turkey Dinner, 166
"Turkey in the Straw," 22, 56n, 68, 70–72
20,000 Leagues Under the Sea, 31
"Twilight in Turkey," 155
Two for the Record, 128, 130
Two Girls and a Sailor, 120n
Two Mouseketeers, 112
"Two Silhouettes," 127, 130

Ub Iwerks Studios. *See* Iwerks Studios
underscoring
    dialogue, 34
    music, 272, 273
United Future Organization, 223
UPA (United Productions of America), 34, 169

"Vacation," 206
Vallee, Rudy, 62
Valiant, Eddie, 105
Van Beuren Studios, 10
Van Buren, Amadee, 162
von Suppe, Franz, 106
    Beautiful Galathea, 106
    Jolly Robbers, 106
    Morning, Noon, and Night in Vienna, 106
    Poet and the Peasant, The, 106, 112

Wagner, Richard, 27, 68, 113, 162

Der fliegende Holländer, 109
Die Walküre, 109, 113
Flying Dutchman, The, 106, 107
Gesamtkunstwerk, 138
Rienzi, 106, 109
Ring of the Nibelungen, The, 109
Siegfried, 109
Tannhäuser, 106, 109
Wakko, 205, 232
Wallace, Oliver, 10, 26, 31–34
Waller, Fats, 143
Walter Lantz Studios, 10, 112
"War Dance for Wooden Indians," 151, 155
Warner Bros. Pictures, Inc, 155
Warner Bros. Studio Orchestra, 8, 145, 146
Warner Bros. Studios, 7, 144, 149, 225
  Carl Stalling at, 37, 47, 49, 50
  cartoon style, 141, 146–147, 235, 246
  and classical music, 108
  copyright, 144
  improvisation, 141
  Jazz Singer, The, 22, 107
  music mellos, 137
  Raymond Scott and, 154, 155, 157
  Road Runner, The, 149, 150
  soundtracks, 38
  theme music, 162
Warner Bros. Symphony Orchestra, 8, 12, 59–60n

Washington, Ned, 28
Waters, Mark, 228, 230
Watters, Cyril, 272
Waxman, Franz, 31
Weber, Carl Maria von, 126
Weems, Ted, 127
Weiss, Syd, 129
"We Put the Spring in Springfield," 247
"We're in the Money," 144
"We Sail the Ocean Blue," 257
"West Side Pigeons," 232
Wetzler, Peter, 11
Whale Who Wanted to Sing at the Met, The, 106, 127, 128
What's Opera, Doc?, 93, 108, 109, 148, 280
"What's Up, Doc," 52, 165, 246
"When I See an Elephant Fly," 31
When Magoo Flew, 169
When the Cat's Away, 22, 45
"When You Wish Upon a Star," 28
White, Barry, 184
White, Evelyn, 129
Who Framed Roger Rabbit?, 105
Whoopee Party, The, 25
"Who's Afraid of the Big Bad Wolf," 25
Wilder, Alec, 129
Wild Waves, 45, 59n
Williams, John, 216
Williams, Johnny, 154, 156

William Tell Overture, 68, 94, 104, 106, 107
  mentioned, 67, 71, 113, 145
Willie The Operatic Whale, 128
Willner, Hal, 12, 141, 227, 286
Wilson, Teddy, 129, 130, 132
Wine, Toni, 181
"Witch Doctor," 175
"Without You," 127
Wolcott, Charles, 30, 32, 33
Wolf Rock, 189
Wrubel, Allie, 33
Wynn, Keenan, 197

Yakko, 205, 232
Yamashira, Shoji, 221
"Yankee Doodle," 22, 118
"Yankee Doodle Boy," 143
Year Without a Santa Claus, 197
Yellow Submarine, 179
Yogi Bear, 170
Yorke, Peter, 273
You Ought To Be In Pictures, 106, 227
"You're Different," 196

Zahler, Gordon, 292
Zampa, the Pirate, 68, 106
"Zip-A-Dee-Doo-Dah," 33
"Zip Coon," 70
Zorn, John, 5, 263–267, 284–286, 287n
  Carl Stalling Project, 142, 286
  select discography, 297